BUSINESS AGILITY AND INFORMATION TECHNOLOGY DIFFUSION

T0137475

IFIP – The International Federation for Information Processing

IFIP was founded in 1960 under the auspices of UNESCO, following the First World Computer Congress held in Paris the previous year. An umbrella organization for societies working in information processing, IFIP's aim is two-fold: to support information processing within its member countries and to encourage technology transfer to developing nations. As its mission statement clearly states,

> *IFIP's mission is to be the leading, truly international, apolitical organization which encourages and assists in the development, exploitation and application of information technology for the benefit of all people.*

IFIP is a non-profitmaking organization, run almost solely by 2500 volunteers. It operates through a number of technical committees, which organize events and publications. IFIP's events range from an international congress to local seminars, but the most important are:

• The IFIP World Computer Congress, held every second year;
• Open conferences;
• Working conferences.

The flagship event is the IFIP World Computer Congress, at which both invited and contributed papers are presented. Contributed papers are rigorously refereed and the rejection rate is high.

As with the Congress, participation in the open conferences is open to all and papers may be invited or submitted. Again, submitted papers are stringently refereed.

The working conferences are structured differently. They are usually run by a working group and attendance is small and by invitation only. Their purpose is to create an atmosphere conducive to innovation and development. Refereeing is less rigorous and papers are subjected to extensive group discussion.

Publications arising from IFIP events vary. The papers presented at the IFIP World Computer Congress and at open conferences are published as conference proceedings, while the results of the working conferences are often published as collections of selected and edited papers.

Any national society whose primary activity is in information may apply to become a full member of IFIP, although full membership is restricted to one society per country. Full members are entitled to vote at the annual General Assembly, National societies preferring a less committed involvement may apply for associate or corresponding membership. Associate members enjoy the same benefits as full members, but without voting rights. Corresponding members are not represented in IFIP bodies. Affiliated membership is open to non-national societies, and individual and honorary membership schemes are also offered.

BUSINESS AGILITY AND INFORMATION TECHNOLOGY DIFFUSION

IFIP TC8 WG 8.6 International Working Conference
May 8-11, 2005, Atlanta, Georgia, U.S.A.

Edited by

Richard L. Baskerville
Georgia State University
USA

Lars Mathiassen
Georgia State University
USA

Jan Pries-Heje
IT University of Copenhagen
Denmark

Janice I. DeGross
University of Minnesota
USA

 Springer

Library of Congress Cataloging-in-Publication Data

A C.I.P. Catalogue record for this book is available from the Library of Congress.

Business Agility and Information Technology Diffusion, Edited by Richard L. Baskerville, Lars Mathiassen, Jan Pries-Heje, and Janice I. DeGross

p.cm. (The International Federation for Information Processing)

Printed on acid-free paper.

ISBN 978-1-4419-3810-7   e-ISBN 978-0-387-25590-3

Printed in the United States of America.

9 8 7 6 5 4 3 2 1
springeronline.com

Contents

Part 6: Challenges Ahead

Part 7: Panels

Preface

This book developed as the collective product of the International Federation for Information Processing (IFIP) Working Group 8.6, a working group dedicated to the study of diffusion and adoption of information technology innovations. The book proceeds from the IFIP Working Conference on Business Agility and IT Diffusion held in Atlanta, Georgia, in May of 2005.

The conference employed a public call for papers and attracted a total of 42 submissions. These included 27 full research papers, and 15 other papers, case studies, practitioner experience reports, posters, and panels. The conference program committee refereed submissions in a double-blind review process. Selection of the papers for inclusion in this book (and appearance at the conference) was difficult, as the quality of these submissions led to an impressive number of positive reviews. Ultimately we selected 13 research papers, two case studies, and three experience reports, along with three panels. The papers submitted by the conference's three keynote speakers were editorially reviewed and also appear in this book.

Staging a conference and producing a book is never possible without the commitment and hard work of many individuals and organizations. We want to thank IFIP and the sponsors for promoting the conference and providing support and funding for its implementation. The sponsors are IFIP, Georgia State University, Robinson College of Business, Gartner, Microsoft, and Intel. Also the conference has been supported by the Computer Information Systems Department and Center for Process Innovation at Georgia State University.

The Program Committee has been active in shaping and promoting the conference and they have played a key role as reviewers and selectors of the contributions to the conference and this book. The Program Committee members are

- Ivan Aaen, Aalborg University, Denmark
- Pekka Abrahamsson, Technical Research Centre of Finland
- Ritu Agarwal, University of Maryland, U.S.A.
- Carole Brooke, University of Lincoln, UK
- Deborah Bunker, University of New South Wales, Australia
- Lisa Brownsword, Software Engineering Institute, Carnegie Mellon University, U.S.A.
- Alistair Cockburn, Humans & Technology, Salt Lake City, U.S.A.
- Jan Damsgaard, Copenhagen Business School, Denmark
- Tore Dybå, SINTEF, Trondheim, Norway

- Robert G. Fichman, Boston College, U.S.A.
- Brian Fitzgerald, University of Limerick, Ireland
- Robert L. Glass, Indiana, U.S.A.
- Helle Zinner Henriksen, Copenhagen Business School, Denmark
- Juhani Iivari, University of Oulu, Finland
- Karlheinz Kautz, Copenhagen Business School, Denmark
- Tor J. Larsen, Norwegian School of Management, Sandvika, Norway
- Linda Levine, Software Engineering Institute, Carnegie Mellon University, U.S.A.
- Gonzalo Leon, Technical University of Madrid, Spain
- Tom McMaster, University of Salford, UK
- Peter Axel Nielsen, Aalborg University, Denmark
- Bala Ramesh, Georgia State University, U.S.A.
- Frantz Rowe, Universite de Nantes, France
- V. Sambamurthy, Michigan State University, U.S.A.
- Rens Scheepers, The University of Melbourne, Victoria, Australia
- Carsten Sørensen, The London School of Economics, UK
- John Venable, Curtin University of Technology, Australia
- Richard Veryard, Veryard Projects, London, UK
- Richard Vidgen, University of Bath, UK
- Eleanor Wynn, Intel Corporation IT, U.S.A.
- Robert Zmud, University of Oklahoma, U.S.A.

The Organizing Committee has been responsible for the implementation of the program and for setting up an environment during the conference that facilitates inter-action and future collaboration amongst the participants. The Organizing Committee members are

- Richard Baskerville
- Lars Mathiassen
- Jan Pries-Heje
- Carol Patterson

- Mark Lewis
- Nannette Napier
- Alina Dulipovici
- JJ Po-An Hsieh

Finally, we want to thank the publisher, Springer, and in particular Janice DeGross without whose professional guidance, manuscript management, and copyediting, it would not have been possible to produce the book.

With a committed network of collaborators that at all times have demonstrated agile academic and practical capabilities it has been a pleasure to participate in designing and organizing the "Business Agility and IT Difusion"-2005 event.

Atlanta and Copenhagen
February 2005

Richard Baskerville
Lars Mathiassen
Jan Pries-Heje

Part 1

Why Agility Now?

1 AGILITY IN FOURS: IT Diffusion, IT Infrastructures, IT Development, and Business

Richard L. Baskerville
Georgia State University
Atlanta, GA U.S.A.

Lars Mathiassen
Georgia State University
Atlanta, GA U.S.A.

Jan Pries-Heje
IT University of Copenhagen
Copenhagen, Denmark

Business agility is a relatively new paradigm painted as a solution for maintaining competitive advantage during times of uncertainty and turbulence in the business environment (Sharifi and Zhang 2001). Agility is a concept that extends adaptability and flexibility to include speed and scalability. Agile organizations are not only capable of change, but they are nimble, capable of changing quickly and gracefully. The concept of agility arose first from flexible manufacturing (Kidd 1995), and has been quickly adopted by organizations producing software in the form of agile software development (Aoyama 1998; Cockburn 2001).

It seems patently obvious that organizational information technology plays a crucial role in shaping business agility. The ability to quickly change the type and flow of information within an organization must underlie a rapid and graceful reorganization. But there is a fundamental gap between the IT function and the rest of the organization. This gap, called the IT paradox, is a setting in which top management sees the value of an effective IT operation and infrastructure, but lacks a real understanding of how IT essentially contributes to business value (Morgan 2004).

This IT paradox has grown more critical in the wake of frenzied spending on IT driven by the Y2K and dot-com imperatives. The subsequent economic downturn drove a widespread, fundamental reexamination of organizational investments in information technology. During periods of economic growth, organizations may drive forward IT projects with some disregard for how these align with the rest of the organizational IT portfolio. In such a period the IT paradox was less of a problem. In the subsequent downturn, however, organizations reflect on the unbalanced IT infrastructure that emerges from the disregarded portfolio. During this latter period, the focus of many projects is on stabilizing the IT infrastructure rather than developing new competitive advantage. As a result, organizations are balancing their IT spending, seeking to become better positioned (i.e., more agile) in preparation for the next economic expansion (Leidner, Beatty, and Mackay 2003). Not surprisingly, the globalization of the IT workforce is one aspect of this economic and infrastructure repositioning (Hoffman 2003).

The purpose of this book is to improve our knowledge of how IT can enable business agility and thereby help close the gap of knowledge that defines the IT paradox. This is a timely purpose as organizations rebalance their IT infrastructure and portfolio of IT innovations in preparation for the next economic expansion.

The book is organized along the plan illustrated in Figure 1. We explore the issues, concepts, motives, factors, techniques, and challenges of developing business agility with IT in six major sections. First, we set the stage for exploring business agility and its relationship to IT diffusion by asking the question: Why agility now? Second, we approach the relationship by exploring its four most distinct parts: (1) agile IT diffusion, (2) IT infrastructures agility, (3) agile development, and, at the core, (4) business agility. Finally, we look at some of the challenges that confront us ahead.

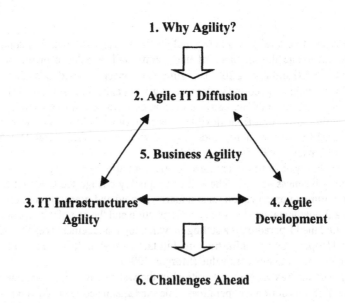

Figure 1. Plan For The Book

1 WHY AGILITY NOW?

Part 1 sets the stage. *Chapter 1* introduces the topic and provides an overview of the research contributions that are included in this book.

We ask, "Why agility now?" We believe there are at least three answers. First, it continues to become harder to survive and succeed in today's business environment. Being agile, and being capable of sensing and responding to both predictable and unpredictable events is a promising strategy in times of change and uncertainty. There is a lot of recent activity about agility, promoted in the form of agile software development, agile manufacturing, agile modeling, and agile iterations. Second, IT diffusion is known to be a process that takes time and effort. Numerous IT projects succeed in developing a product, but fail in changing the behavior of the target group. As a result, diffusion just doesn't happen! It is hardly surprising that agile IT diffusion has become desirable. Third, the importance of flexibility in developing IT solutions for rapidly changing business environments is well recognized, especially for Internet applications (Pries-Heje et al. 2004). In this arena, agility refers to the ability to quickly deliver solutions and nimbly adapt to changing requirements.

Chapter 2, by Kautz, Henriksen, Breer-Mortensen, and Poulsen provides an introspective for the group that has commissioned this book as the proceedings from a conference by the International Federation for Information Processing Working Group 8.6. This group focuses on the diffusion of IT innovations. Chapter 2 provides an overview of the essential concepts and background that this working group brings to our question. It includes a detailed analysis of all previous IFIP Working Group 8.6 conference proceedings, and concludes that the group has been successful thus far in focusing scholarly attention on the phenomenon within its scope, and marshaling intellectual progress toward its objectives.

Chapter 3 introduces agility concepts and their relationship with agile software methods. Conboy, Fitzgerald, and Golden provide an overview and synthesis of agility concepts, applying these insights to propose a framework for agile software methods. The framework distinguishes between required resources and resulting impact, presenting on that basis four different categories of agile practices: change creation, action, reaction, and learning.

The next four parts comprise the heart of the book, describing the factors and techniques that lead organizations to business agility. From the perspective of our working group, business agility depends on the intrinsic and dynamic relationships between IT diffusion, IT infrastructure, and IT development capabilities (see Figure 1). We start by reviewing each of these IT-related capabilities and finally develop the core theme of business agility.

2 AGILE IT DIFFUSION

Part 2 explores the complex relationship between IT diffusion and business agility. Diffusion of innovations, and in particular diffusion of new approaches to the development of IT or software, constantly reshapes organizational IT capabilities. This part explores two aspects of the creation of business agility through IT diffusion. First, chapters 4, 5, and 6 help explain why efforts to improve software practices succeed (or fail to succeed). Chapter 4 uncovers how collaborative practices are associated with process deployment. Chapter 5 connects software process improvement and business agility by showing how choke points in the social communication networks can inhibit software innovation and, as a consequence, business agility. In Chapter 6, we extend our exploration of these social networks into those supporting interorganizational adoption of software innovations, learning how these social networks enable the creation and sharing of the knowledge essential for adoption of new software innovations. Second, chapters 7 and 8 provide techniques for enabling the innovation diffusion on which business agility depends. The two chapters bring focus on the role of the change agent, how to time the enrollment of a change agent, and how the shortcomings of a change agent can be overcome socially, exemplified by personal humor.

Chapter 4 by Aaen, Böjesson, and Mathiassen analyzes 18 software process improvement projects according to characteristics like set up, process creation and diffusion, and navigability. Eleven of the less successful projects focus on defining a solution but not on deploying a process. Seven of the more successful projects focus on collaboration as a means of simultaneously defining and deploying practices.

Chapter 5 by Nielsen and Tjørnehøj demonstrates how social network mapping can reveal communication choke points that can inhibit both agile business responses and software process improvement initiatives.

In *Chapter 6*, Hovorka and Larsen discuss how knowledge flows affected the adoption of a large-scale software system in several counties within New York state. They find that an organization's agility is based on its ability to acquire, assimilate, transform, and exploit knowledge, and that this ability can be increased through strong and dense networks. They also examine how social communication networks can influence the agility of organizations. For example, they find that having strong and dense communication networks can facilitate knowledge flows and increase the chance of adoption.

Chapter 7 by Börjesson, Martinsson, and Timmerås describes an action research study of diffusion of innovation techniques as a means for implementing software process improvement. The paper provides a particularly rich explanation of how change agents can co-opt key opinion leaders at a critical juncture (the chasm) in order to achieve a precipitous diffusion of a process innovation.

Chapter 8 by McMaster, Wastell, and Henriksen examines the role of humor as an empowerment tool. The concept of humor in organizations is clearly an under-researched area. This paper compares the role of a jester with that of a change agent and finds that a jester has characteristics lacking in a change agent. They conclude that there is a cathartic role for a jester in agile IT diffusion.

3   IT INFRASTRUCTURES AGILITY

Part 3 explores the relationship between the agility in IT infrastructures and the agility in business. IT infrastructures can both enable and inhibit business agility, perhaps even simultaneously. We begin in Chapter 9, showing the dramatic impact that a change in infrastructure can have on organizational performance by enabling agile decision-making. Chapters 10 and 11 explain how the infrastructures involved in inter-organizational systems and supply chains are related to either business agility or business torpidity.

In *Chapter 9*, Vance reports the results of a lab experiment involving better and timelier information. Simulating supply chain decision-making, the experiment shows how remarkable improvements in financial performance can follow from agile business practices operating with better information technology, in this case simulating the addition of RFID as part of the information infrastructure.

In *Chapter 10*, Nagy applies the adoption position model to explain reasons for failure to adopt interorganizational systems in order to enable supply chain agility. Three cases are presented focusing on how the relative power between firms shapes adoption practices and outcomes.

Chapter 11 by Holmqvist and Pessi presents lessons from a Volvo initiative to innovate and improve a global supply chain. The lessons are based on several years of continuous development, integrating legacy systems and new IT-infrastructure elements. These efforts led to new relations and channels that enabled unprecedented levels of business agility.

4 AGILE DEVELOPMENT

Part 4 explores the relationship between IT or software development and business agility. In this part of the book, we explore the factors upon which development agility depends, along with techniques for building it. Chapter 12 illustrates the unrecognized benefits that can follow from the adoption of agile development methods. We follow this with Chapter 13, which explains how software agility arises from innovations in both processes and base technology. Chapters 14 and 15 explore the practical limits of agile development, highlighting problems in specific agile techniques. This part concludes with Chapter 16, which models the strategic connection between agile IT development projects and business agility.

In *Chapter 12*, Fitzgerald and Hartnet present a longitudinal study of the use of agile software methods within Intel. The study demonstrates how agile methods lead to systematic practices that require disciplined application of the involved techniques as well as careful customization of the method to each specific development context.

In *Chapter 13*, Lyytinen and Rose outline a theory of agile development. In their model, exploration, exploitation, and agility issues are included, and a sequential learning model developed. The value of the model is illustrated with findings from software development organizations. The study concludes that software agility is affected by the scope and depth of innovative activity in base technologies as well as in continued process innovations.

In *Chapter 14*, Abrahamsson presents the results from a series of case studies in which test-driven software development was adopted. While test-driven development has been argued to facilitate agility and dramatic quality gains, this study shows that adoption of test-driven development is difficult and the potential benefits are far from readily available.

Chapter 15 by Toleman, Darroch, and Ally describes experiences of developers in adopting eXtreme Programming in a low-budget setting. While the project was generally successful, insights suggest problems with system metaphors and pair programming.

In *Chapter 16*, Nickolaisen describes a model that has proved effective in guiding resource allocation decisions for IT projects. The model positions strategies on two dimensions: the degree to which activities are mission-critical, and the degree to which activities provide market differentiation. It provides one example of how improved business agility results from smart use of this model.

5   BUSINESS AGILITY

Part 5 explores business agility, the core theme of the book, and the part around which all other parts revolve. Chapters 17 and 18 explore the factors that are driving organizations to seek agility, and also why this agility is unfolding in some arenas, and is not unfolding in others. In Chapter 19, we develop a framework for characterizing the differences in business agility among firms. Chapter 20 concludes this part of the book by explaining the essence of business agility with directions for seeking it.

In *Chapter 17*, Donnellan and Kelly describe the forces that drive increasing needs for business agility. They analyze the IT that is being developed to enable this agility in the semiconductor industry and show how this IT has diffused across the industry.

Chapter 18 by van Oosterhout, Waarts, and van Hillegersberg defines a framework and surveys four industry sectors in the Netherlands. The authors find a number of interesting differences among sectors. But they also find that executives across sectors feel that they are forced to become agile, for example due to increasing unpredictability of government regulation. Furthermore the study reveals that today's businesses lack the agility required to quickly respond to largely unanticipated changes.

Chapter 19 by Overby, Bharadwaj, and Sambamurthy presents a framework for business agility and the enabling role of digital options. Based on a distinction between sense and response capabilities the paper identifies four different types of firms: agile, languid-lazy, lost-leaping, and limited.

In *Chapter 20*, Dove discusses the cornerstones of business agility: response ability, dynamic knowledge management, and value-based decision making. The paper offers on that basis the requirements to design and develop agile business practices and IT infrastructure support.

6   CHALLENGES AHEAD

Part 6 concludes the work by recognizing some of the challenges that confront us in the quest to enable business agility with IT. Two chapters offer prospects for the future, especially highlighting the need to explore innovation in very large systems and the need for new work in IT or software development.

In *Chapter 21*, Dittrich, Pries-Heje, and Hjort-Madsen describe a large IT infrastructure and development project that is daring in both scope and innovation. It crystallizes broad gaps in the knowledge that ought to inform a large Federated organization seeking to migrate onto an entirely new IT infrastructure. Such gaps include the role of an IT vision, the feasibility and coordination of dramatic change, and communication of vision and change.

In the final chapter, *Chapter 22*, Levine concludes our work by reflecting on the experiences and contributions from the software agility movement. This paper identifies on that background the key challenges and dilemmas involved in agile software practices and goes on to discuss how to further develop this software development paradigm.

After Chapter 22, we have completed the book by including the descriptions of three panels that were part of the IFIP working conference that drove the creation of this book. Although it was impossible to include full transcripts of the panel discussion, the insights into the discourse developed by the panelists are, at least partly, revealed.

The six parts of the book, and the 22 chapters collectively explore the motivation for a study of business agility and IT diffusion, the four major aspects of business agility, and the challenges before us. In a world in which change and uncertainty drive the needs for business agility, and digital information drives business, agility in IT is critical for business success. We believe it is important to understand how IT agility, and thereby business agility, is multifaceted: composed of agile IT diffusion, IT infrastructure agility, and agile IT development. In the 21 chapters that follow, you will learn how, these facets can together provide a concerted pathway to business agility.

REFERENCES

Aoyama, M. "Web-Based Agile Software Development," IEEE Software (15:6), 1998, pp. 55-65.
Cockburn, A. *Agile Software Development*, Reading, MA: Addison-Wesley, 2001.
Hoffman, T. "Outsourcing Debate Driven by Cost, Agility," Computerworld (37:9), 2003, p. 14.
Kidd, P. T. *Agile Manufacturing, Forging New Frontiers*, London: Addison-Wesley, 1995.
Leidner, D., Beatty, R., and Mackay, J. "How CIOs Manage IT During Economic Decline: Surviving And Thriving Amid Uncertainty," *MISQ Executive,* (2:1), 2003, pp. 1-14.
Morgan, R. E. "Business Agility and Internal Marketing," *European Business Review* (16:5), 2004, pp. 464-472.
Pries-Heje, J., Baskerville, R., Levine, L., and Ramesh, B. "The High Speed Balancing Game," *Scandinavian Journal of Information Systems* (16), 2004, pp. 1-46.
Sharifi, H., and Zhang, Z. "Agile Manufacturing in Practice: Application of a Methodology," *International Journal of Operations and Production Management* (21:5/6), 2001, pp. 772-794.

ABOUT THE AUTHORS

Richard L. Baskerville is professor and chairman of the Computer Information System Department at Georgia State University. His research and authored works regard security of information systems, methods of information systems design and development, and the interaction of information systems and organizations. Richard is the author of *Designing Information Systems Security* (J. Wiley) and more than 100 articles in scholarly journals, practitioner magazines, and edited books. He is an editor of *The European Journal of Information Systems,* and associated with the editorial boards of *The Information Systems Journal* and *The Journal of Database Management.* He is a Chartered Engineer, holds a B.S. *summa cum laude,* from The University of Maryland, and the M.Sc. and Ph.D. degrees from The London School of Economics. Richard can be reached at baskerville@acm.org.

Jan Pries-Heje is an associate professor at the IT University of Copenhagen, Denmark. Jan holds M.Sc. and Ph.D. degrees from Copenhagen Business School. He is a certified ISO 9000 auditor and Bootstrap assessor, and has been project manager for a number of multi-media and IT-related change projects. From 1997 through 2000, he worked as a consultant in IT quality and software process improvement. He is chairman of the Information Systems Research in Scandinavia (IRIS) Steering Committee, serves as the Danish National Representative to IFIP TC8 (since 1999), and is currently an associate editor for *MIS Quarterly, Information Systems Journal,* and *European Journal of Information Systems.* His research interests include information systems development, software engineering, and software process improvement. He focuses on organizational and managerial issues. Jan has published more than 100 papers in these areas in journals and conferences. He can be reached at jpr@itu.dk.

Lars Mathiassen is Georgia Research Alliance Eminent Scholar and Professor in Computer Information Systems at Georgia State University. His research interests focus on engineering and management of IT systems. In particular, he has worked with project management, object-orientation, organizational development, management of IT, and the philosophy of computing. Lars can be reached at lmathiassen@gsu.edu.

2   INFORMATION TECHNOLOGY DIFFUSION RESEARCH: An Interim Balance

Karlheinz Kautz
Helle Zinner Henriksen
Toke Breer-Mortensen
Helle Helweg Poulsen
Copenhagen Business School
Copenhagen, Denmark

Abstract   *In this article, we review the work of the IFIP TC8 WG 8.6 on Diffusion and Transfer of Information technology in the period 1993 through 2003. Starting with working group's aim and scope declaration, we analyze the 113 contributions that have been published in the seven conference proceedings of the group. While we can conclude that the group by and large works toward and within its own aim and scope declaration, we also find the group as of yet has no joint terminology and no shared theoretical basis. These are challenges which the group should take up in its future work.*

1   INTRODUCTION

The first work in information technology diffusion research can be found in the late 1970s (Perry and Kraemer 1978). New technological possibilities and the wide-spread use of IT in the 1980s then led to growing attention to the topic in various academic disciplines and commercial sectors. This is reflected in the foundation of three different interest groups in the field of IT diffusion. The IEEE Computer Society has a special interest group on Software Engineering Technology Transfer, which can be traced back to the early 1980s, while members of the Information Systems community in 1988 founded the Diffusion Interest Group in Information Technology (DIGIT). After a pilot conference in 1993, IFIP TC 8 approved their working group, 8.6, on Transfer and Diffusion of Information Technology in 1994 (referred to here as the working group or simply the group). The group tries to bridge the gap between the software engineering and the IS communities. It consists of about 30 regular members and its main joint activity is a working conference, held approximately every 18 months. The group has thus far had seven conferences which have been attended by about 420 delegates.

As an official IFIP organization, the group has an approved aim and scope document defining its objective: "To foster understanding and improve research in practice, methods, and techniques in the transfer and diffusion of information technology within systems that are developed and in the development process." The range of the group's work is further detailed in 10 statements covering its scope.

We take this declaration as our starting point and ask whether the group is relating its work to its declaration and whether it works toward achieving the formulated objectives. We are also interested whether there are any significant trends visible in the group's work across time. The objective of this paper is to analyze if the actual work undertaken in the group as reflected in the proceedings of the conferences corresponds to the IFIP WG 8.6 declaration. Other researchers (Fichman and Kemerer 1999; Prescott and Conger 1995; Wolfe 1994) have provided overviews of IT diffusion research in general. Wolfe (1994), in particular, has provided recommendations to researchers concerning the further development of the field. We are more interested in providing an overview of the work by the group than in outlining specific guidance as to what the community should do in future research. This search for an identity or even a paradigm within a research community resembles the debate that has taken place in the IS community as a whole as reflected in Volume 12 of *Communications of AIS* (articles 30 through 42). The contribution of this paper is, hence, a methodological voyage rather than a set of normative recommendations to how the group should act in the future.

The paper will proceed as follows. In the next section, we will explain the research method that will help us to answer the questions posed above. In section 3, we will present our results, which will be discussed in section 4, and we will end with a number of conclusions in section 5.

2   RESEARCH METHOD

The overall research method we apply is that of a literature study. In the seven previous working conferences (Levine 1994; Kautz and Pries-Heje 1995; McMaster et al. 1997; Larsen et al. 1998; Ardis and Marcolin 2001; Bunker et al. 2002; Damsgaard and Henriksen 2003), the group has published a total of 113 scientific contributions. These are analyzed with regard to the group's aim and scope declaration. However, instead of taking the aim preamble and all 10 scope statements into account, we concentrate on the two main statements defining the range of the group's work as dealing with "diffusion, transfer, and implementation of both mature and immature information technologies and systems in organizations and among organizations, sectors, and countries" and the "development of frameworks, models, and terminology for information technology transfer and diffusion." To operationalize the aim and scope declaration we use the following dimensions to code and analyze the articles: terminology used, types of technology, unit of analysis, and nature of exploration. To be able to further reflect on these dimensions, we decided to take a closer look at the research approach and the research methods used in the work in general and across some of the dimensions. These six dimensions are briefly introduced next.

2.1 Terminology Used

Terminology development is explicitly mentioned in the aim and scope document. Prescott and Conger (1995) point out a need to clarify concepts and terms that are used within IT diffusion research. With the starting point being their list of concepts used, we developed a classification including includes the terms that we found during our coding and analysis. The following classes were identified: (1) adoption, (2) diffusion, (3) implementation, (4) introduction, (5) transfer, (6) adaptation, (7) assimilation, (8) acceptance, (9) routinization, (10) institutionalization, and (11) others. The last category includes terms such as absorption, appropriation, deployment, penetration, transition, spreading, and uptake, which were less frequently mentioned. In our investigation, we look at which of these are used and which are defined before usage through the work of the group. For our analysis, it should be noted that an article can contain several of these terms.

2.2 Types of Technology

Information technology including information systems and information technologies in the development process are explicitly mentioned in the aim and scope and lie at the center of what defines IT research (Benbasat and Zmud 2003). Although both Swanson (1994) and Lyytinen and Rose (2003) provide a classification of IT innovation, we could not find a scheme that covers the way the group deals with the information technology concept, thus we followed the strategy of Barothy et al. (1995) and developed a typology during coding and analysis. It resulted in the following classes:

- Information and information systems technologies in general: these were works with a broad focus on IT/IS without a particular emphasis on a specific technology or system type

- Interorganizational IT such as interorganizational information systems in general, for example, EDI

- Networked technologies like Internet or Web technologies, e-commerce, e-government, or e-service technologies, CSCW or groupware systems, and IT infrastructur

- Diverse technologies, which focus on particular technologies beyond those mentioned already

- Software development technologies such as methods, techniques, CASE or other software tools, and approaches and methods for software process improvement

Finally, we identified articles that dealt with the concept of IT outsourcing as a technology concept and articles that did not deal with technology at all.

2.3 Unit of Analysis

The unit of analysis is explicitly mentioned in the aim and scope with a focus on "organizations and among organizations, sectors, and countries." We did not find any appropriate classification in the literature beyond Glasson (1994), which was part of the data material, thus we developed one during coding and analysis. Beyond the four units mentioned—organization, interorganizational, sector, and country—we found articles dealing with individuals, a particular region, the specific class of academia to practice diffusion, a class of others covering diffusion from producers to suppliers or to third world countries, and a final class of "not applicable," covering conceptual articles without a particular unit of analysis. Again, articles could have several units of analysis.

2.4 Nature of Exploration

The nature of exploration is mentioned in the aim and scope declaration as development of frameworks and models. We were inspired by Saunders et al. (2002), who use the term in their study on power and information technology and distinguish between framework development, propositions developed, hypothesis testing, and research question explored. During coding and analysis we found (1) model and theory development, (2) model and theory evaluation, (3) hypothesis testing without aiming at developing or testing an explicitly described model or theory, (4) investigation of a specific research question without explicitly aiming at building or evaluating a model or theory, and (5) self-reflective explorations, which reflect over the work of the group or the nature of the IT diffusion research field.

A special case of theory and model development and evaluation is the utilization of Rogers' theory of diffusion of innovations first published in 1962 and since then refined in five editions of his seminal book. It has been claimed that he is one of the most important researchers in the field of diffusion in general and that he has had quite an influence on IT diffusion research (McMaster and Kautz 2002). To verify this claim, we investigate whether the group's contributions base their work directly and uncritically on Rogers, are critical of Rogers' work, refer neutrally to Rogers without taking a stand on his work, or do not refer to his work at all.

2.5 Research Approach

To get beyond the simplistic distinction of the positivist and the interpretive research paradigms, we align with Schultze and Leidner (2002) who, when studying the concept of knowledge management in IS, apply Deetz's (1996) framework on scientific discourse and distinguish a normative, interpretive, critical, and dialogical discourse in research. Instead of looking for contradistinctions, which bears little fruit, the intent of the framework is to direct attention to meaningful differences and similarities among different research activities. In the framework, the basic goal of normative research is seen in finding and defining laws, such as like relationships among objects, and in achieving progress. The interpretive research objective is to understand socially constructed constellations and to display cultures and values related to the phenomenon under investigation. Critical research aims to unmask dominance and reform social order while dialogical research strives to reclaim conflict and give space to lost voices.

2.6 Research Method

In line with other researchers performing literature studies (Alavi and Carlson 1992; Barothy et al. 1995; Lai 1996), we classify the contributions in the data material in empirical articles, where the work was based on empirical data and nonempirical articles, which in turn are primarily based on ideas, frameworks and speculation instead of systematic observation and data collection. Empirical IT and IS research has been classified differently by different researchers. Based on the work of Orlikowski and Baroudi (1991), Alavi and Carlson (1992), Cheon et al. (1993), Claver at al. (2000), and Vessey et al. (2001), we distinguish between (1) surveys, also comprising field studies based on questionnaire instruments or interviews, (2) case studies comprising single, multiple, cross-sectional, and longitudinal case studies, (3) action research studies focusing on both scientific results and changes in the units where the research is performed, (4) secondary data studies where the researchers analyze data provided by others, and (5) other empirical methods including laboratory experiments or simulations.

3   RESULTS

The data material consists of the 113 conference contributions, written by more than 170 authors. Only a small group of authors have had more than one article published in the group's proceedings (nine have published two articles, and of these, four have three or more articles). The contributions can be classified in three groups. There is a group of five articles which, from our perspective, do not deal with the diffusion of IT at all but have been accepted for the group's conference series. These articles deal with user engagement, virtual cooperation, the use of a technique for problem analysis, IT strategy, and the IT market. They have not been analyzed further. The second group consists of position statements and experience reports based or not on a research approach, method, or data analysis. This group consists of 19 contributions which were mainly (15 articles) presented at the pilot conference in 1993 where position statements were explicitly welcomed or they were invited lectures in 1997, 2001, and 2002. These contributions are not analyzed using all dimensions. We indicate in the following presentation where they have been taken into account and where not. The third, and by far the largest, group consists of 89 articles, which we classify as analytical or synthetical contributions based on empirical or nonempirical methods; 49 use an empirical method, while 40 are based on nonempirical work. These articles are all analyzed according to dimensions.

Table 1. All Conferences and Contributions (1993–2003)

Conference Number	Place and Year	Topic of the Conference	Number of Contributions	Analytical/Synthesis		Position Statement		Non-Diffusion	
0	Pittsburgh, USA, 1993	Diffusion, Transfer and Implementation of IT	30	15	50%	14	47%	1	3%
1	Oslo, Norway, 1995	Diffusion and Adoption of IT	12	12	100%	0	0%	0	0%
2	Ambleside, UK, 1997	Facilitating Technology Transfer through Partnership: Learning from Practice and Research	22	21	95%	1	5%	0	0%
3	Helsinki, Finland, 1998	Information Systems: Current Issues and Future Changes	8*	8	100%	0	0%	0	0%
4	Banff, Canada, 2001	Diffusing Software Product and Process Innovations	17	13	76%	3	18%	1	6%
5	Sydney, Australia, 2002	The Adoption and Diffusion of IT in an Environment of Critical Change	13	10	77%	1	8%	2	15%
6	Copenhagen, Denmark, 2003	Networked IT: Diffusion and Adoption	11	10	91%	0	0%	1	9%
Total			113	89	78%	19	18%	5	4%

*This conference was a joint IFIP TC 8 WG 8.2/8.6 conference and all contributions that did not have a clear diffusion topic are not considered in our analysis.

3.1 Terminology Used

In the 108 analyzed articles, 30 different terms related to diffusion are used a total of 356 times. One article, although classified as IT diffusion research, uses none of the terms.

Only 23 articles (21 percent) actually define one or more of the terms used. A total of 38 definitions are provided, a number of them referring to other authors such as Rogers, thus the number of definitions developed by the authors themselves is considerable lower.

With regard to the meaning of the terms, one term (adoption) was defined with three different meanings. Adoption—a term that is not mentioned in the original aim and scope—was part of the theme of the first, fifth, and sixth conferences. For the first conference, adoption was defined as having been achieved when the decision to start the usage of an innovation or technology had been taken. Fichman and Kemerer (1994) refer to adoption as "typically defined as the physical acquisition of technical artifacts or as 'commitment' to implement the innovation." This definition is in line with many traditional definitions of adoption in the context of diffusion of innovations as put forward by Rogers (2003). For the second conference, adoption was defined as achieved when the technology was actually used in practice. As Thong and Yap (1996) put it, "adoption of IT is defined as using computer hardware or software applications to support operations, management, and decision making." Finally, for the sixth conference, Bøving and Bødker (2003) defined adoption as achieved when a technology is used in the way its designers intended.

We find that adoption is the most frequently used term. It was found in 75 of the 108 articles. The other four most-used terms are diffusion, implementation, introduction, and transfer. Together these concepts are significantly more-used than the 25 others. The first three are on average used in 50 percent of all articles. It is interesting that the concept transfer, which appears in all declaration scope statements, is only used in a little over 30 percent of the articles.

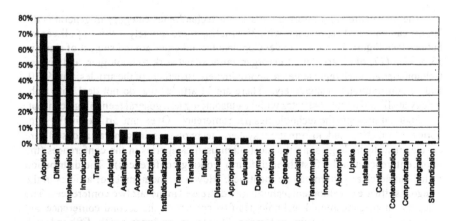

Figure 1. Percentage Use of Terms

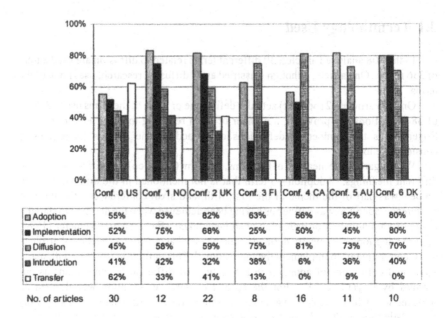

	Conf. 0 US	Conf. 1 NO	Conf. 2 UK	Conf. 3 FI	Conf. 4 CA	Conf. 5 AU	Conf. 6 DK
▣ Adoption	55%	83%	82%	63%	56%	82%	80%
▪ Implementation	52%	75%	68%	25%	50%	45%	80%
▣ Diffusion	45%	58%	59%	75%	81%	73%	70%
▣ Introduction	41%	42%	32%	38%	6%	36%	40%
▢ Transfer	62%	33%	41%	13%	0%	9%	0%
No. of articles	30	12	22	8	16	11	10

Figure 2. Use of Terms by Conference

Looking at the development over the course of the seven conferences and only taking the five most-used terms into account, it appears that the use of adoption, diffusion, implementation, and introduction is somewhat stable over time, with the first three nearly always being used. The use of the term transfer, however, declines significantly over time and is rarely or never used in the last four conferences.

3.2 Types of Technology

The information and information systems technologies category in general is the largest category and represents, with 38 articles, approximately a third of all contributions (see Figure 3). Software development technologies are the subject of study in 25 percent (27) of all articles. Interorganizational, network technologies, and diverse technologies are each represented in approximately 10 percent of the articles, with 9, 10, and 11 contributions, respectively. There are 11 articles that do not deal with technology at all, and a final 2 articles with IT outsourcing as a general technology concept.

Figure 4 presents the technologies per conference. Over time articles in the categories information and information systems technologies in general and software development technologies are the most-often used categories in the conferences (the pilot conference and the first through fourth working conferences). The distribution shifts, but no clear pattern can be identified. However, the number of articles in the category software development technologies decreased in the last two conferences. The category interorganizational technologies first appears in the second conference and increases slightly up to the fifth conference. IT outsourcing appears in the fifth and sixth conferences, but is a rather small category.

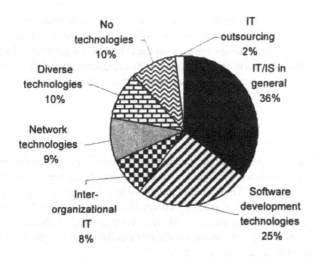

Figure 3. Types of Technology—All Conferences (108 Articles)

Across conferences, the software development technologies category appears in five out of seven conferences (the pilot conference and the second through fifth conferences) and is the dominant category at the fourth conference. This is not surprising as the theme of this conference was "Diffusing Software Product and Process Innovations."

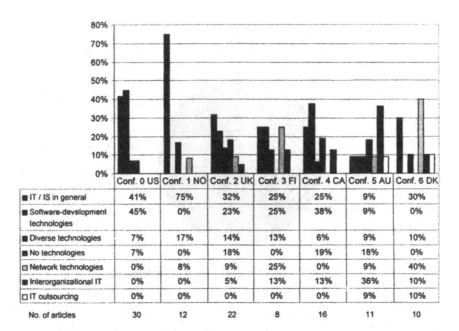

	Conf. 0 US	Conf. 1 NO	Conf. 2 UK	Conf. 3 FI	Conf. 4 CA	Conf. 5 AU	Conf. 6 DK
■ IT / IS in general	41%	75%	32%	25%	25%	9%	30%
■ Software-development technologies	45%	0%	23%	25%	38%	9%	0%
■ Diverse technologies	7%	17%	14%	13%	6%	9%	10%
■ No technologies	7%	0%	18%	0%	19%	18%	0%
▢ Network technologies	0%	8%	9%	25%	0%	9%	40%
■ Interorganizational IT	0%	0%	5%	13%	13%	36%	10%
▢ IT outsourcing	0%	0%	0%	0%	0%	9%	10%
No. of articles	30	12	22	8	16	11	10

Figure 4. Technologies per Conference

The interorganizational IT category dominated the fifth conference, while network technologies, together with information and information systems technologies in general, dominated the sixth, where the topic of the conference was "Networked Information Technology: Diffusion and Adoption." The categories interorganizational IT, diverse technologies, and no technologies are represented at the majority of conferences.

3.3 Unit of Analysis

Organization represents the largest category and accounts for almost two-thirds of all conference contributions (73 articles). All of the other categories are represented with under 10 percent each. They are distributed as follows: others, 8 articles; interorganizational, 7 articles; sector, 6 articles; country, 6 articles; not applicable, 5 articles; region, 3 articles; academia to practice, 3 articles; and individual, 2 articles. The total count of 113 articles exceeds the actual number of published articles as three articles have been classified in several categories.

The unit of analysis *organization* represents by far the largest category at all conferences. However, no trends, neither for the marginal shifts of this category nor for the representation of the other categories, have been found. Perhaps the category *country* deserves special mention here as it appears at the first four but not at the last three conferences.

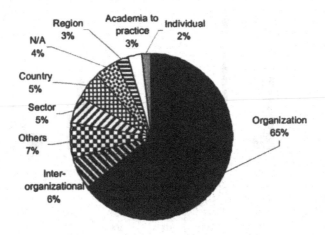

Figure 5. Unit of Analysis for All Conferences

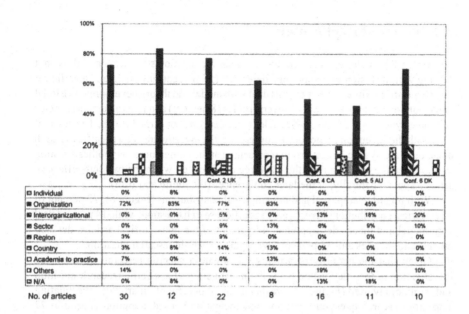

	Conf. 0 US	Conf. 1 NO	Conf. 2 UK	Conf. 3 FI	Conf. 4 CA	Conf. 5 AU	Conf. 6 DK
Individual	0%	8%	0%	0%	0%	9%	0%
Organization	72%	83%	77%	63%	50%	45%	70%
Interorganizational	0%	0%	5%	0%	13%	18%	20%
Sector	0%	0%	9%	13%	6%	9%	10%
Region	3%	0%	9%	0%	0%	0%	0%
Country	3%	8%	14%	13%	0%	0%	0%
Academia to practice	7%	0%	0%	13%	0%	0%	0%
Others	14%	0%	0%	0%	19%	0%	10%
N/A	0%	8%	0%	0%	13%	18%	0%
No. of articles	30	12	22	8	16	11	10

Figure 6. Unit of Analysis per Conference

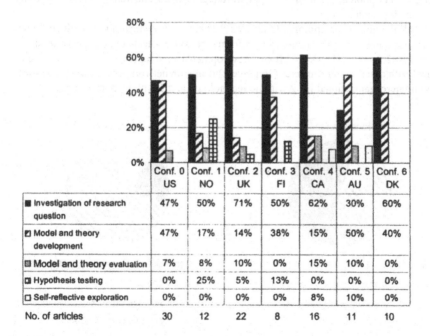

	Conf. 0 US	Conf. 1 NO	Conf. 2 UK	Conf. 3 FI	Conf. 4 CA	Conf. 5 AU	Conf. 6 DK
Investigation of research question	47%	50%	71%	50%	62%	30%	60%
Model and theory development	47%	17%	14%	38%	15%	50%	40%
Model and theory evaluation	7%	8%	10%	0%	15%	10%	0%
Hypothesis testing	0%	25%	5%	13%	0%	0%	0%
Self-reflective exploration	0%	0%	0%	0%	8%	10%	0%
No. of articles	30	12	22	8	16	11	10

Figure 7. Nature of Exploration per Conference

3.4 Nature of Exploration

Of the 89 articles categorized, those discussing position statements and those not dealing with diffusion were not considered, 49 (55 percent) investigate a specific research question, while 26 (28 percent) deal with model and theory development. Model and theory evaluation is a topic of seven articles (8 percent) and five (6 percent) articles test some hypothesis. Finally, two articles (2 percent) are concerned with self-reflection.

With the exception of the fourth conference, the investigation of a specific research question is always the largest group represented at the conferences. Hypothesis testing has not been pursued in any of the last three conferences, while the two self-reflective articles appear, naturally, at the later conferences (the fourth and fifth).

With regard to empirical and nonempirical contributions (Figure 8), 72 percent of all empirical contributions investigate a specific research question, while 14 percent deal with model and theory development; 47 percent of the nonempirical articles develop models and theories and 35 percent investigate a specific research question.

Given that the majority of articles investigate a specific research question, an investigation of the relationship between investigation of a specific research question and terminology used (Figure 9) reveals that in 74 percent of all articles investigating a specific research question the term implementation is used, adoption is used in 72 percent of these articles, while diffusion appears in 69 percent, introduction in 41 percent, and transfer in 33 percent. This means that implementation is used in 36 articles, adoption in 35, diffusion in 34, introduction in 20, and transfer in 16. The other terms play a minor role.

With regard to technology, 15 articles (32 percent) investigating a specific research question deal with information and information system technologies in general, 10 articles (20 percent) focus on software development technologies, 9 articles (18 percent) deal with diverse, and 8 articles (16 percent) deal with network technologies, four deal with interorganizational IT, 2 with no technology, and 1 with IT outsourcing.

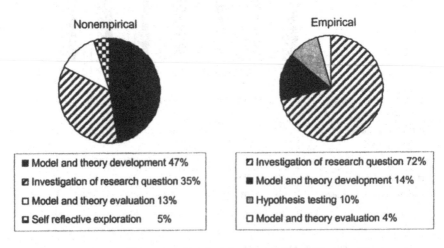

Figure 8. Empirical/Nonempirical Articles According to Nature of Exploration

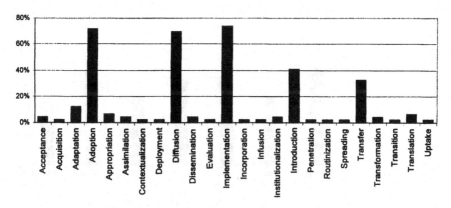

Figure 9. Terminology Used in the 49 Articles
Investigating a Specific Research Question

Finally, the different units of analysis treated in work investigating a specific research question are distributed as follows: 36 are organization, 5 are interorganizational, 5 deal with an industry sector, 2 with a region, 1 with academia to practice diffusion, and 1 with something else. The relationship between investigating a specific research question and research method and approach will be described in the following two subsections.

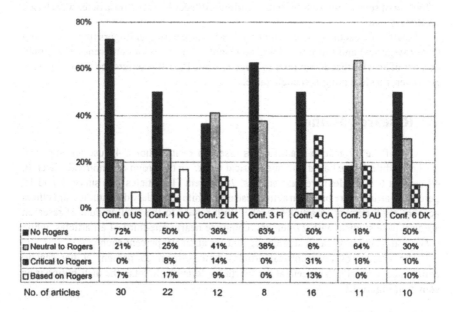

	Conf. 0 US	Conf. 1 NO	Conf. 2 UK	Conf. 3 FI	Conf. 4 CA	Conf. 5 AU	Conf. 6 DK
No Rogers	72%	50%	36%	63%	50%	18%	50%
Neutral to Rogers	21%	25%	41%	38%	6%	64%	30%
Critical to Rogers	0%	8%	14%	0%	31%	18%	10%
Based on Rogers	7%	17%	9%	0%	13%	0%	10%
No. of articles	30	22	12	8	16	11	10

Figure 10. Categorization of Applying Rogers per Conference

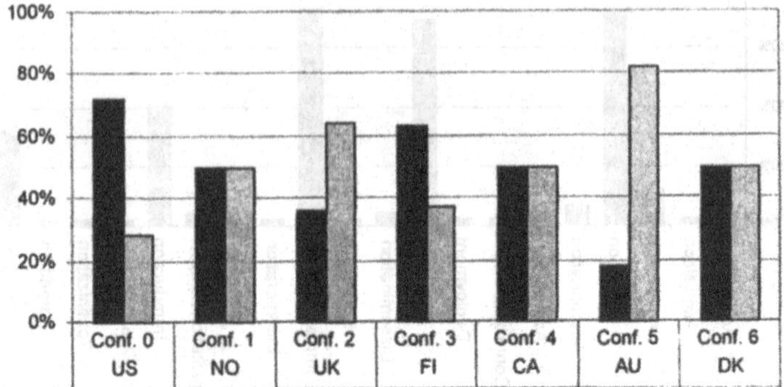

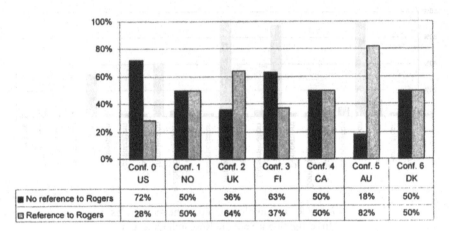

	Conf. 0 US	Conf. 1 NO	Conf. 2 UK	Conf. 3 FI	Conf. 4 CA	Conf. 5 AU	Conf. 6 DK
■ No reference to Rogers	72%	50%	36%	63%	50%	18%	50%
□ Reference to Rogers	28%	50%	64%	37%	50%	82%	50%

Figure 11. Articles Referring/Not Referring to Rogers

Dealing with model and theory development and evaluation the group's treatment of Rogers' work is as follows[1]: the category not referring to Rogers is the largest, with approximately half of all articles (55 out of 108, or 51 percent). The second category is neutral to Rogers, roughly one-third of all articles (31 out of 108, or 29 percent); 12 articles are critical of Rogers (11 percent), and only 9 percent (10 articles) are directly based on his work. At nearly all of the conferences, the first two groups are the largest ones (with the exception of the fourth conference). Articles critical of Rogers appear at five out of seven conferences; at the third and fifth conferences, no articles were based on Rogers' work.

Finally, if we look at the distribution of articles referring to Rogers (the second and third categories) and those not doing so (Figure 11), the pilot conference has a high number of articles that do not refer to Rogers, while the fifth conference is the opposite. However, no clear trend is recognizable.

3.5 Research Method

Out of the 89 articles classified as research contributions, 49 use an empirical method, while 40 are based on nonempirical work. In the group of empirical research, 49 percent (24 articles) are case studies, 20 percent (10 articles) are surveys, and 15 percent (7 articles) are based on action research, while secondary data studies and others account for 8 percent (4 articles) each. With regard to the total amount of research articles, case studies, with 27 percent, comprise nearly one-third of all articles, while surveys and action research studies account for about 10 percent each.

The amount of nonempirical articles swings from 25 percent at the second conference to nearly 70 percent at the fourth conference. In total, the distribution is as shown in Figure 12.

---

[1]Here again, 108 articles, including those comprising position statements, were considered.

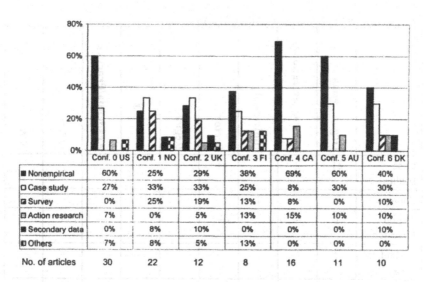

	Conf. 0 US	Conf. 1 NO	Conf. 2 UK	Conf. 3 FI	Conf. 4 CA	Conf. 5 AU	Conf. 6 DK
■ Nonempirical	60%	25%	29%	38%	69%	60%	40%
▢ Case study	27%	33%	33%	25%	8%	30%	30%
▨ Survey	0%	25%	19%	13%	8%	0%	10%
▣ Action research	7%	0%	5%	13%	15%	10%	10%
■ Secondary data	0%	8%	10%	0%	0%	0%	10%
▨ Others	7%	8%	5%	13%	0%	0%	0%
No. of articles	30	22	12	8	16	11	10

Figure 12. Classification of Research Methods per Conference

With regard to applied research method and the nature of exploration (Table 2), the distribution shows a strong dependence between case studies and the investigation of a specific research question.

Looking at research method and unit of analysis (Table 3), again case studies are the majority, especially case studies taking place in organizations.

Table 2. Research Method and Nature of Exploration

	Investigation of a Specific Research Question	Model and Theory Development	Model and Theory Evaluation	Hypothesis Testing
Case studies	18	4	2	–
Surveys	6	–	–	4
Action Research	4	3	–	–
Secondary Data	4	–	–	–
Others	3	–	–	1
Total	35	7	2	5

Table 3. Research Method and Unit of Analysis

	Organization	Interorganizational	Individual	Sector	Region	Country	Academia/Practice	Others	N/A
Case studies	21	2	–	1	–	3		–	–
Surveys	7	–	1	–	1	1	1	–	–
Action Research	7	–	–	–	–	–	–	–	–
Secondary Data	2	1	–	–	1	–	–	–	–
Other	4	–	–	–	–	–	–	–	–
Total	41	3	1	1	2	4	1	–	–

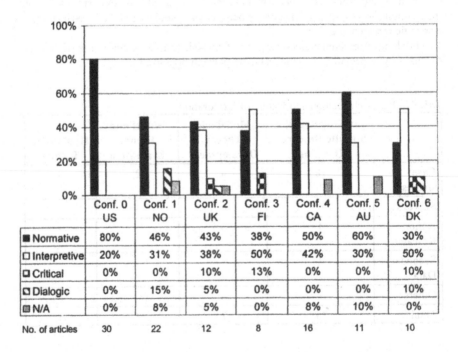

	Conf. 0 US	Conf. 1 NO	Conf. 2 UK	Conf. 3 FI	Conf. 4 CA	Conf. 5 AU	Conf. 6 DK
■ Normative	80%	46%	43%	38%	50%	60%	30%
▢ Interpretive	20%	31%	38%	50%	42%	30%	50%
▢ Critical	0%	0%	10%	13%	0%	0%	10%
▢ Dialogic	0%	15%	5%	0%	0%	0%	10%
▩ N/A	0%	8%	5%	0%	8%	10%	0%
No. of articles	30	22	12	8	16	11	10

Figure 13. Classification of Research Approaches per Conference

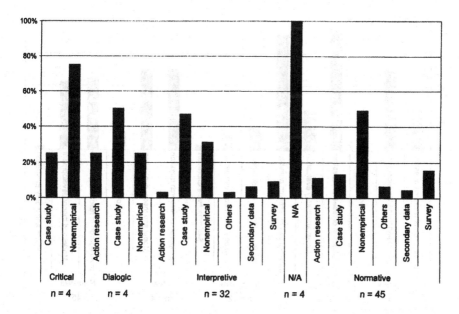

Figure 14. Relationship Between Research Approach and Research Method

3.6 Research Approach

The majority of the 89 research articles presents a normative discourse with 45 articles (52 percent); 32 articles (36 percent) belong to the interpretative discourse. Critical and dialogical discourses appear four times each (4 percent each), while four articles could not be classified according to the chosen framework. Normative and interpretative articles add up to more than 75 percent of all articles at all conferences, with their actual distribution swinging a bit. While the normative discourse dominates the first three conferences, the majority of contributions to the third and sixth conferences, both arranged in northern Europe, comes from the interpretive discourse.

The distribution of research methods within the four research approaches is depicted in Figure 14. In particular, Figure 14 shows that the majority of interpretive articles are case studies (16 articles).

The relationship between research approach and nature of exploration (Figure 15) shows that both investigation of a specific research question and model and theory development are nearly equally dominant in the normative discourse with 44 percent and 42 percent of all 45 contributions respectively while in the interpretive discourse, 72 percent of the 32 contributions deal with one specific research question and only 18 percent with model and theory development.

Finally, the relationship between research approach and unit of analysis (see Table 4) shows that both the normative and the interpretive discourse deal primarily with the organization as the unit of analysis.

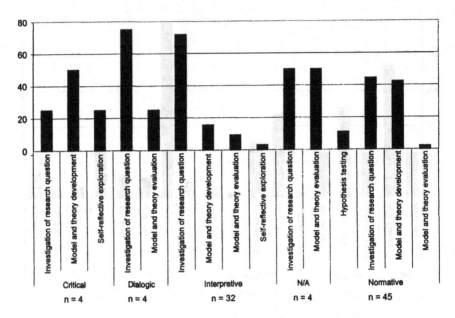

Figure 15. Relationship Between Research Approach
and Nature of Exploration

Table 4. Relationship Between Research Approach and Unit of Analysis

	Organization	Interorganizaational	Individual	Sector	Region	Country	Academia/Practice	Others	N/A
Normative	33	2	2	2	1	2	–	4	–
Interpretive	23	5	–	2	1	2	1	1	1
Critical	3	–	–	–	–	–	–	–	1
Dialogical	4	–	–	–	–	–	–	–	–
N/A	1	–	–	1	–	–	–	–	2
Total	64	7	2	5	2	4	1	5	4

4   DISCUSSION

With the group's aim and scope statement as the starting point and the results presented here, the following discussion attempts to answer two questions: Does the group work with the diffusion, transfer, and implementation of both mature and immature information technologies and systems in organizations and among organizations, sectors, and countries? Does the group work with the development of frameworks, models, and terminology for information technology transfer and diffusion?

Answering question 1, we can conclude that, yes, the group works with diffusion, transfer, and implementation. These terms are used in 62 percent (diffusion), 31 percent (transfer), and 58 percent (implementation) of all articles. Furthermore, these articles analyze implications of diffusion, transfer, or implementation of technology. The group also works with a broad spectrum of information technologies. General information and information system technologies are the largest group, being the subject of 36 percent of all articles, followed by software development technologies the topic in 25 percent.

Along with software process innovations and networked IT, specific technologies appear as topics for two conferences. This approach is in line with the aim and scope statement where, beyond information technologies and systems and software development technologies, no particular technology is mentioned or excluded. Finally, considering the unit of analysis, we can state that again, corresponding to the group's aim and scope, the dominant unit of analysis is the organization, the theme of 65 percent of all contributions, whereas diffusion, transfer, and implementation between organizations (7 percent), in (business and public) sectors (6 percent), and in countries (6 percent) play a minor role.

However, the results also show that the group does more than that. The term adoption, although not mentioned in the aim and scope, is in the title of three conferences and is actually the most-used term in the group's work, appearing in 70 percent of all publications. The term introduction can be found in 33 percent of all articles, making it a more frequently used term than transfer, which, although part of all 10 aim and scope statements, was hardly ever used in the last four conferences. With regard to the overarching question of what the group should do in the future, this question can lead to different conclusions.

The group might want to change its aim and scope statement including terms like adoption and introduction and excluding the term transfer. Such a change would more precisely reflect what the group focuses on in its research.

With regard to the role information technologies play in the group's work, it can be argued that having 10 percent of all articles not dealing with IT at all, but with technology-independent concepts like diffusion, might enrich the group's work, but might also be a sign of a lack of focus. Thus the group might consider no longer accepting work not dealing with IT as it falls outside the group's aim and scope. However, the latter would imply that there would be no room for self-reflection (such as this paper) or theory development independent of particular technological innovations. In this context, it is worth noticing that Rogers, referred to in 49 percent of all articles and by far the most cited author in the analyzed contributions, does not build his diffusion of innovations theory on IT innovations.

Also with respect to the unit of analysis, the group goes beyond its declaration.

Although not regularly and only to a small extent, the individual, the region, diffusion from academia to practice, and from suppliers to customers account for 15 percent of the group's conference contributions. These units might also be explicitly mentioned in an augmented aim and scope statement or excluded from future conferences. Restrictions in unit of analysis could, however, result in important issues related to diffusion and implementation being missed. For future research of the group's work, it would be useful to expand the data to include literature references and affiliation of authors. One particular issue, which could be clarified if affiliation of authors were included, is the share of contributions from practitioners and from researchers from universities and business schools respectively. Practitioners and academics from business schools might be more preoccupied with the supplier-customer relationship whereas researchers from universities might be more interested other issues.

To answer the second question, let us revisit the terms used. In the group's work, 30 different terms related to diffusion are used and 38 different definitions are provided. However, only a little over 20 percent of the articles define the terms they use. For one of the more central concepts, namely adoption, at least three definitions are provided by different authors.

Thus, although it can be argued that the group works with the development of terminology, this seems to be a limited and largely individual, fragmented, and rather uncoordinated endeavor. Parts of this fragmented effort might be explained by the methodological approach of the researchers. Positivists and interpretivists rarely have a common understanding of the deeper meaning of terms and in particular the implications of specific terms. This is clearly illustrated by the example of the term adoption, where the positivist view is represented by Rogers' definition, whereas Bøving and Bødker (2003) represent the interpretivist view on the meaning of the term. However, the methodological stance of the researchers does not excuse that most of the group's work is performed without a definition of the central terms. It would be desirable at the group level to put an effort into a common development of terminology. This is definitely a task that has to be taken more seriously in the future.

The development of frameworks and models can be assessed by looking at the nature of exploration of the group's work. The majority of the articles, 55 percent, is based on investigating a specific research question. While these articles might deal with the development of frameworks or models for a specific aspect of IT diffusion, and thus can be said to contribute to a larger body of knowledge in the field, a comparative analysis of these 49 contributions leading to more general, broader frameworks, models, or theories of IT diffusion has not taken place. Theory development and evaluation including hypothesis testing is the subject of 42 percent of the 89 research-based articles of the group.

In this context it also has to be emphasized that Rogers' framework does not serve the group as a joint starting point or theoretical basis; on the contrary, more than 50 percent of all articles do not even refer to his work. Whether this is out of ignorance or for other reasons cannot be said on the basis of our data. As emphasized earlier, one reason for this could be that Rogers' theory is not directly related to IT innovations.

Again, the argument can be made about the fragmented nature of the group's work and its lack of focus on theory development in the traditional sense. However, although stated in the aim and scope, frameworks, and models, and for that matter traditional theory development, might not be the objective or primary ambition of all group members. Out of the 89 scientific articles, only 52 percent are classified as belonging to the normative discourse with its pursuit of causal logic-based theories, whereas 36 percent subscribe to an interpretive tradition aimed primarily at understanding complex phenomena. Even in the normative approach, theory and model development and the investigation of a specific research question are nearly equally represented, with the latter being, by a small margin (44 percent versus 42 percent), the strongest. This lack of theory can be seen as a weakness of the group, but can also be explained by the relative youth of the field, where the investigation of single questions precedes general methodologies. The group members' interest are mirrored in the interpretive approach, with 32 contributions, where the investigation of a specific research question clearly dominates, with 72 percent, over theory development, with 18 percent. Finally, this is supported by the fact that case studies—usually more associated with understanding than with law like logic (Zmud et al. 1989)—with 27 percent is the research method of nearly one-third of all articles. While not surprising, 48 percent of all interpretive contributions are based on case studies, with 12 percent of the normative articles having a case study background and thus possibly an interpretive element.

With regard to the group's future, this might mean that limiting the group's work to what is more or less explicitly described in the aim and scope is one possibility to deal with the situation. Another way is to broaden the scope by explicitly including theory development in an extension of framework and model development in the aim and scope declaration, but simultaneously clarifying what is meant by theory with regard to the different discourses.

However, as a consequence, this also means that—beyond continuing empirical work and the 22 articles, which were within the normative approach based on nonempirical methods—to further develop the field of IT diffusion theoretically, the group needs to perform more conceptual and theoretical work within the interpretive, critical, and dialogical discourse.

5 CONCLUSION

Based on the above analysis and discussion, we can conclude that the group works toward and within its own aim and scope declaration. There are, however, a number of challenges. The group has no joint terminology and no shared theoretical basis. An expansion of the aims of IFIP WG 8.6 could, therefore, explicitly be to focus on diffusion terminologies and theory development within the realm of IT/IS research.

Like many educational organizations, the group can be considered as a system of loosely coupled individuals, who as semiautonomous participants strive to maintain a degree of independence while working under the name and framework of the organization to pursue their personal goals (Morgan 1986; Weick 1976). As such, a too-exclusive aim and scope statement might hinder the group in extending the body of knowledge. However, beyond researching new technologies like mobile information systems and management fashions and fads like business agility, the group should stay with its roots and work to explicitly contribute to IT diffusion theory and terminology.

To further explore the argument of how deeply the group is actually rooted in the

normative discourse, a more detailed investigation of the authors of normative contributions is necessary to find out whether these authors only pass by the group with one
publication or whether they belong to the kernel of the group. To do this, however, a
clarification of who constitutes the group might be useful, given that only few registered
members publish regularly at the group's conference.

Future research should also look into the degree of internal references within the
group, but in addition study the extent of other common literature references, which
might define a shared and common (back)ground for the group. We have made an
attempt to do so, but the inconsistency of the current data material in this respect does
not yet allow for any conclusions. Thus, here also lies a challenge for the group in its
pursuit of advancing IT diffusion research.

REFERENCES

Alavi, M., and Carlson, P. "A Review of MIS Research and Disciplinary Development," *Journal of Management Information Systems* (3:4), 1992, pp. 45-62.

Ardis, M. A., and Marcolin, B. L. (Eds.). *Diffusing Software Product and Process Innovations*, Boston: Kluwer Academic Publishers, 2001.

Barothy, T., Peterhans, M., and Bauknecht, K. "Business Process Reengineering: Emergence of a New Research Field," *SIGOIS Bulletin* (16:1), 1995, pp. 3-10.

Benbasat, I., and Zmud, R. W. "The Identity Crisis within the IS Discipline: Defining and Communicating the Discipline's Core Properties," *MIS Quarterly* (27:2), 2003, pp. 183-194.

Bunker, D., Wilson, D., and Elliot, S. (Eds.). *The Adoption and Diffusion of IT in an Environment of Critical Change*, Sydney, Australia: Pearson Publishing Service Australia (on behalf of IFIP), 2002.

Bøving, K. P., and Bødker, K. "Where Is the Innovation," in *Networked Information Technologies: Diffusion and Adoption*, J. Damsgaard and H. Z. Henriksen (Eds.), Boston: Kluwer Academic Publishers, 2003, pp. 39-52.

Cheon, M. J, Grover, V., and Sabherwal, R. "The Evolution of Empirical Research in IS: A Study in IS Maturity," *Information & Management* (24), 1993, pp. 107-119.

Claver, E., González, R., and Llopis, J. "An Analysis of Research in Information Systems (1981-1997)," *Information & Management* (37), 2002, pp. 181-195.

Damsgaard, J., and Henriksen, H. Z. (Eds.). *Networked Information Technologies: Diffusion and Adoption*, Boston: Kluwer Academic Publishers, 2003.

Deetz, S. "Describing Differences in Approaches to Organization Science: Rethinking Burrell and Morgan and Their Legacy," *Organization Science* (7:2), 1996, pp. 191-207.

Glasson, B. C. "Toward a National Information Systems and Technology Research and Development Association," in *Diffusion, Transfer and Implementation of Information Technology*, L. Levine (Ed.), Amsterdam: North-Holla,d 1994, pp. 333-345.

Fichman, R. G., and Kemerer, C. F. "The Illusory Diffusion of Innovation: An Examination of Assimilation Gaps," *Information Systems Research* (10:3), 1999, pp. 255-275.

Fichman, R. G., and Kemerer, C. F. "Toward a Theory of the Adoption and Diffusion of Software Process Innovations," in *Diffusion, Transfer and Implementation of Information Technology*, L. Levine (Ed.), Amsterdam: Elsevier Science, 1994, pp. 23-30.

Kautz, K., and Pries-Heje, J. (Eds.). *Diffusion and Adoption of Information Technology*, London: Chapman & Hall, 1995.

Lai, V. S. "An Assessment of Database Research Interest in MIS," *The Data Base for Advances in Information Systems* (27:2), 1996, pp. 37-43.

Larsen, T. J., Levine, L., and DeGross, J. I. (Eds.). *Information Systems: Current Issues and Future Changes*, Laxemburg, Austria: IFIP Press, 1988.

Levine, L. (Ed.). *Diffusion, Transfer and Implementation of Information Technology*, Amsterdam: North-Holland, 1994.

Lyytinen, K., and Rose, G. M. "The Disruptive Nature of Information Technology Innovations: The Case of Internet Computing in Systems Development Organizations," *MIS Quarterly* (27:4), 2003, pp. 557-595.

McMaster, T., and Kautz K. "A Short History of Diffusion," in *The Adoption and Diffusion of IT in an Environment of Critical Change*, D. Bunker, D. Wilson, and S. Elliot (Eds.), Sydney, Australia: Pearson Publishing Service (for IFIP), 2002, pp. 10-22.

McMaster, T., Mumford, E., Swanson, E. B., Warboys, B., and Wastell, D. (Eds.). *Facilitating Technology Transfer Through Partnership: Learning from Practice and Research*, Proceedings of the IFIP TC8 WG8.6 International Working Conference on Diffusion, London: Chapman & Hall, 1997.

Morgan, G. *Images of Organization*, London: Sage Publications, 1986.

Orlikowski, W. J., and Baroudi, J. J. "Studying Information Technology in Organizations: Research Approaches and Assumptions," *Information Systems Research* (2:1), 1991, pp. 1-28.

Perry, J., and Kraemer, K. L. "Innovation Attributes, Policy Intervention, and the Diffusion of Computer Applications Among Local Governments," *Policy Sciences*, April 1978, pp. 179-205.

Prescott, M. B., and Conger, S. A. "Information Technology Innovations: A Classification by IT Locus of Impact and Research Approach," *The Data Base for Advances in Information Systems* (26:2-3), 1995, pp. 20-41.

Rogers, E. M. *The Diffusion of Innovations* (1st ed.), New York: The Free Press, 1962.

Rogers, E. M *The Diffusion of Innovations* (5th ed.), New York: The Free Press, 2003.

Saunders, C. S., Carte, T. A., Jasperson, J., Croes, H., Zheng, W., and Butler, B. S. "Power and Information Technology: A Review Using Metatriangulation," in *Proceedings of the 21st International Conference on Information Systems*, W. J. Orlikowski, S. Ang, P. Weill, H. C. Kremar, and J. I. DeGross (Eds.), Brisbane, Australia, 2000, pp. 339-350.

Schultze, U., and Leidner, D. E. "Studying Knowledge Management in Information Systems Research: Discourses and Theoretical Assumptions," *MIS Quarterly* (26:3), 2002, pp. 213-242.

Swanson, E. B. "Information Systems Innovation Among Organizations," *Management Science* (40:9), 1994, pp. 1069-1088.

Thong, J. Y. L., and Yap, C. S. "Information Technology Adoption by Small Businesses: An Empirical Study," in *Diffusion and Adoption of Information Technology*, K. Kautz and J. Pries-Heje (Eds.), London: Chapman & Hall, 1996, pp. 160-175.

Vessey, I., Ramesh, V., and Glass, R. L. "Research in Information Systems: An Empirical Study of Diversity in the Discipline and ITS Journal," Information Systems Technical Reports and Working Papers, TR106-1 (URL (31-07-2004), Kelley School of Business, Indiana University, 2001 (available online at http://www.kelley.iu.edu/ardennis/wp/tr106-1.doc).

Weick, K. E. "Educational Organizations as Loosely Coupled Systems," *Administrative Science Quarterly* (21), 1976, pp. 1-19.

Wolfe, R. A. "Organizational Innovation: Review, Critique and Suggested Research Directions," *Journal of Management Studies* (31:3), 1994, pp. 405-431.

Zmud, R., Olsen, M. H., and Hauser, R. "Field Experimentation in MIS Research," *The Information Systems Research Challenge: Experimental Research Methods Volume 2*, I. Benbasat (Ed.), Boston: Harvard Business School Research Colloquium, 1989, pp. 97-112.

ABOUT THE AUTHORS

Karlheinz Kautz, Dr. philos, is a professor of Systems Development and Software Engineering in the Department of Informatics at the Copenhagen Business School. Previously, he has been employed as a senior researcher at the Norwegian Computing Center and as a lecturer at universities in Germany, Norway, England, and Denmark. He is the chair of IFIP WG 8.6, Diffusion, Transfer, and Implementation of Information Technology. His research interests are in systems development and system development methodologies in practice, the diffusion and adoption of information technology innovations, the organizational impact of IT, knowledge management, and software quality and process improvement. He has published in these areas in journals including *Information and Software Technology, Information, Technology & People, Scandinavian Journal of Information Systems, Software Process: Improvement and Practice, IEEE Software, Journal of Knowledge Management, Journal of Information Systems, Journal of Informing Science,* and *Journal of Information Technology Cases and Applications.* He is a member of ACM and IEEE. Karl can be reached at Karl.Kautz@cbs.dk.

Helle Zinner Henriksen is an assistant professor in the Department of Informatics at the Copenhagen Business School. She has an M.Sc. in law from the University of Copenhagen and a Ph.D. from the Department of Informatics at the Copenhagen Business School in the field of Management of Information Systems with particular interest on the implications of institutional intervention with respect to interorganizational adoption and diffusion. Her research interests include adoption and diffusion of IT in the private and public sector. Her most recent work focuses on eGovernment and regulation of eGovernment. Helle is involved in the Center for Research on IT and Policy Organizations at the Copenhagen Business School. More details on her research activities and publications can be found at http://web.cbs.dk/staff/hzh/. She can be researched at hzh.inf@cbs.dk.

Toke Breer-Mortensen was a research assistant in the project on which this research article is based. Toke recently graduated from the Copenhagen Business School's Master's program in Computer Science and Business Administration. Toke can be reached at Toke@doek.dk.

Helle Helweg Poulsen was a research assistant in the project on which this research article is based. Helle recently graduated from the Copenhagen Business School's Master's program in Computer Science and Business Administration. Helle can be reached at toke@doek.dk.

3 AGILITY IN INFORMATION SYSTEMS DEVELOPMENT: A Three-Tiered Framework

Kieran Conboy
National University of Ireland
Galway, Ireland

Brian Fitzgerald
University of Limerick
Limerick, Ireland

William Golden
National University of Ireland
Galway, Ireland

Abstract   *The Agile Manifesto was put forward in 2001, and several method instantiations, such as XP, SCRUM and Crystal exist. Each adheres to some principles of the Agile Manifesto and disregards others. This paper proposes that these Agile Manifesto principles are insufficiently grounded in theory, and are largely naïve to the concept of agility outside the field of software development. This research aims to develop a broad, three-tiered framework of ISD agility based on a thorough review of agility across many disciplines. The framework identifies the sources of agility, a classification of agile activities, and the resources utilized by such activities.*

1   THE PROBLEM

The work described in this paper was motivated initially by a concern regarding the lack of integrated and cohesive definitions of agile methods in information systems development[1] (ISD). The formation of the Agile Alliance in 2001 and the publication

---

[1]The terms *information system development* and *software development* are used interchangeably for the purposes of this paper.

of the Agile Manifesto (Fowler and Highsmith 2001) formally introduced agility to the field of ISD. Those involved sought to "restore credibility to the word *method*" (Fowler and Highsmith 2001). The Agile Manifesto presented an industry-led vision for a profound shift in the ISD paradigm through 12 principles. The Manifesto and its principles represent quite pioneering work in coalescing and extending the critique of formalized ISD methods over the past decade or so (Baskerville et al. 1992; Fitzgerald 1994, 1996) and have been well received by practitioners and academics.

However, there are a number of critical issues in the field, all of which revolve around a lack of rigor and cohesion.

- Many different definitions of an agile method exist. Researchers often use the same term to refer to different concepts and different terms to refer to the same concept. However, this is not surprising given that IS researchers cannot even reach consensus on the definitions of the most basic terms such as *information system, method,* and *technique.* In fact, Sharafi and Zhang (1999), Towill and Christopher (2002), and Vokurka and Fliedner (1998) have explicitly illustrated this issue in the case of the term *agility.*

- Many different agile methods exist, such as eXtreme Programming (XP) (Beck 1999), dynamic systems development method (DSDM) (Stapleton 1997); SCRUM (Schwaber and Beedle 2002); Crystal (Cockburn 2002b); agile modeling (Ambler 2002); feature driven design (Coad et al. 1999); lean programming (Poppendieck 2001), and perhaps even the rational unified process (RUP) (Kruchten 2000), all categorized as agile by those that use them. Each of these methods focuses heavily on some of the principles of the agile manifesto and ignore others completely, but yet are portrayed by some not only as an agile method, but as the best agile method.

- Some studies have advocated an *a la carte* approach such as "XP Lite," where an existing agile method is "defanged" (Stephens and Rosenberg 2003) and a subset method used. Others state that "the whole is better than the sum of its parts" and that agile methods are only beneficial when used in their entirety. However, even one of the main supporters of this notion has admitted that the system metaphor concept in XP is rarely, if ever, used (Fowler 2001), a sentiment felt by others in the field (Khaled et al. 2004; Succi and Marchesi 2001). Thus, one could argue that, strictly speaking, any team using XP in this way is not truly agile.

- At the other end of the spectrum, there are some, especially those using more traditional ISD methods, who disregard agile methods, as unstructured, ad hoc, glorified hacking.

- Cockburn (2002a) even dismisses the existence of an agile method altogether, claiming that it is something to which developers can only aspire, and that only hindsight can determine whether an agile method was actually adhered to.

- Finally, there is a perception among the purveyors of the agile method that all prior methods were non-agile. Given that changing requirements were a problem identified over a quarter of a century ago (Boehm et al. 1984), and that methods such as rapid application development were developed to handle such change, it is obvious that some parts of these dated methods at least contributed to agility. "Elements of agility can certainly be found in many processes, but as the saying goes—*one swallow does not a make summer*" (Alleman 2002, p. 54).

One reason for such a lack of consensus in the literature is that the principles of agility expressed in the Agile Manifesto (Fowler and Highsmith 2001) and the various agile methods in existence lack sufficient grounding in management theory, organizational theory, and indeed theory behind all the fields and disciplines which comprise ISD. Consequently, the Manifesto does not consider the evolution of the concept of agility in fields outside ISD. Agility is not a concept unique to software development. Indeed it first appeared in the mainstream business literature in 1991, when a group of researchers at the Iacocca Institute of Lehigh University introduced the term "agile manufacturing" (Goldman et al. 1991). The industry-based report aimed to provide the United States with a weapon to regain its pre-eminence in manufacturing, and described the emerging agile principles being adopted by U.S., European, and Japanese firms as being the way forward. Since then, manufacturing companies across many industries have gained a competitive advantage from such an agile philosophy (Burgess 1994).

However, a review of the agile manufacturing literature indicates that even now, those who study agile manufacturing are having the same problems as those studying agile methods in ISD. There are many diverse and often contradicting definitions of agile manufacturing; the concepts lack a theoretical grounding, and consideration is not given to the differences between overall industry sectors and individual organizations (Burgess 1994).

This suggests that the search for a definitive, all-encompassing concept of agility may not be completed simply through an examination of agility in other fields. Rather the answer it is to be found through an examination of the underlying concepts of agility, namely flexibility and leanness (Sharafi and Zhang 1999; Towill and Christopher 2002) which have much older origins. For example, lean thinking can be traced back to the Toyota Production System in the 1950s with its focus on the reduction and elimination of waste (Ohno 1988), the production of the Spitfire airplane in World War II (Childerhouse et al. 2000), and even as far back as the automotive industry in 1915 (Drucker 1995).

2 RESEARCH APPROACH

In summary, the research approach undertaken and completed thus far is as follows:

- An extensive literature review was carried out to understand the historical evolution and maturation of the ISD field.

- An extensive literature review of agility was undertaken across a number of disciplines such as manufacturing, finance, and organizational behavior. Again, the objective of this review was to gain a better understanding of the historical evolution and maturation of the agile concept.

- The output from the first two stages was used to produce an initial rough draft definition and taxonomy of agility, including headings and subheadings. Criteria for the taxonomy as a whole were that it should aim to be (1) of practical use and practice-connected, (2) inclusive but at the same time parsimonious in its topics and subtopics, (3) of minimal overlap, and (4) reasonably robust in accommodating developments in the field.

3   FOR AND AGAINST A FRAMEWORK FOR THE FIELD

The fields of IS and ISD have always drawn upon many others, such as computer science, organizational theory, linguistics, political science and psychology (Adam and Fitzgerald 1996; Ahituv and Neumann 1990; Avison 1996; Bariff and Ginzberg 1982; Culnan and Swanson 1986; Hirschheim et al. 1994; Vogel and Wetherbe 1984).

It has also been argued that the field cannot be disciplined or controlled by any imposed structure or paradigm, as in the Kuhnian model of scientific advancement, because of its technologically dynamic nature (Banville and Landry 1989). The emergence of agile methods such as XP and the tools such as automated acceptance testing associated with these methods are examples of such dynamism.

A third argument against a common ground, framework, or theory is that a monistic, single view would be restrictive, given the disparate backgrounds and pluralistic interests of those involved in the field (Banville and Landry 1989).

In contrast to the arguments against, there have been many arguments in favor of some unifying framework. For example, it has been argued that without such a framework or underlying theory, a field may be driven by technology or the events of the day (Weber 1987). It has also been said that a framework is needed so that researchers can build upon the development of a consistent set of data, and avoid reinventing the wheel (Grimshaw 1992). In addition, there is historical evidence of certain fields achieving progress at the expense of others through the establishment of a core, theoretical structure (Latour 1988).

A further argument in favor of some kind of framework and structure for a field is that, without it, "progress is but a fortunate combination of circumstances, research is fumbling in the dark, and the dissemination of knowledge is a cumbersome process" (Vatter 1947 p. 31). For example, it has been shown how the production of scientific fact is characterized as a process of creating cognitive order, or some sort of framework, out of disorder (Latour and Woolgar 1979).

4   THE PROPOSED TIERED FRAMEWORK OF ISD AGILITY

In previous research, we have reviewed the literature on agility across many disciplines (Conboy and Fitzgerald 2004a; Conboy and Fitzgerald 2004b; Conboy and Fitzgerald 2004c), and have arrived at the following over-arching, generic definition of agility:

Agility is the continual readiness of an entity to rapidly or inherently, proactively or reactively, embrace change, through high quality, simplistic, economical components and relationships with its environment.

It is beyond the scope of this paper to illustrate the detailed derivation of this definition. However, we believe that it provides a rich enough basis to accommodate even very complex method instances where "just enough method" requires quite a comprehensive and detailed, formalized approach. We discuss and justify the phraseology of this definition next.

4.1 Sources of Change

The definition of agility proposed above places the concept of *change* at its core. In ISD, the emergence of agile methods has been put down to the need to handle change (Cockburn 2002a; Fowler 2000; Fowler and Highsmith 2001). However, there is a tendency in the field of ISD to over-concentrate on system requirements as the overwhelming source of change. The rationale behind agile methods such as XP and SCRUM is their ability to handle requirement changes, and not necessarily all of the changes that an ISD team may have to face. Therefore, the first part of the framework identifies a more comprehensive set of potential sources of change.

- *Customers*: Changing customer requirements was the driving force behind most of the methods proposed since the systems development life cycle. However, customers can be the source of other types of change. For example, a customer may change meeting times with developers, may insist on different deliverables, or may change budget allocations.

- *Technology*: This can refer to the impact a change in hardware and underlying software can have on the principal ISD project. An example would be a necessity to upgrade from Windows 2000 to Windows XP midway through development. However, technology also refers to the methods and processes carried out during development (Schwalbe 2000; Shenhar and Dvir 1995). Furthermore, the probability of change arising as a result of using a method depends on the "newness of that method" (Williams 2002) and any inherent properties it possesses to remove discrepancies between public and private rationality, i.e., varying interpretations of the method and what it entails (Stolterman and Russo 1997).

- *Social Factors*: This is an umbrella term that includes cultural, political, and other similar issues that may drive change in an ISD project. For example, Schein (1965) discusses the concept of the *complex man*, his motives and abilities. He has many needs, arranged in a hierarchy of personal importance, but the hierarchy varies over time. This may change in accordance with different project environments, teams, methods and customers. Furthermore, a person's work involvement may also change in response to a change in these motives. For example, a highly skilled, poorly motivated worker may be as effective and satisfied as an unskilled but highly motivated worker. The implication for project managers is not that there is a single

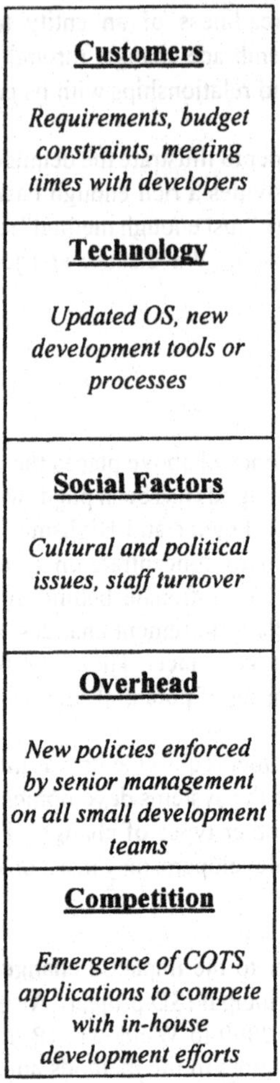

Customers
Requirements, budget constraints, meeting times with developers
Technology
Updated OS, new development tools or processes
Social Factors
Cultural and political issues, staff turnover
Overhead
New policies enforced by senior management on all small development teams
Competition
Emergence of COTS applications to compete with in-house development efforts

Figure 1. Sources of Change

method or strategy to adopt, but that the method must cater for and be adaptable to a variety of abilities and motives which may emerge during the course of a project (Carnall 2002).

• *Overhead*: This refers to any changes imposed by management over and above the ISD team. An example would be that a team within an international consulting organization would be forced to abide by new policies.

• *Competition*: This includes any changes imposed by the need to keep up with competitors and competitor or substitute products (Sharafi and Zhang 1999).

A team should analyze these sources of change and identify which are applicable to them and which are not. Some will always be a source of change, such as customer requirements. However, some depend on the context of the project. For example, a team within a multinational consulting organization will inevitably be subjected to overhead change, whereas an independent team of Web developers may not.

4.2 Classification of Agile Activities

Once an ISD team has identified the potential sources of change it faces, it can conduct an analysis of the ability of its current or future activities to handle such change. However, the literature on agility and its subclassifications is complex and often inconsistent. There tends to be a lot of overlap between the concepts of agility, flexibility, and leanness. At a conceptual level, the following broad classifications of agility have been extracted from the literature:

- *Change Creation*: Agility is not just the ability to adapt to change; it also refers to the ability of an entity to positively impact its environment by initiating such change itself (Gerwin 1993). This suggests that proactive steps may "not just anticipate change, but may create it" (Piore 1989). *Adapt to* implies that change is the driving force and the entity's actions are as a result of that force. Change creation refers to a *two-way process* where the entity not only reacts to change but can also influence it. In an ISD context, this refers to situations where the ISD team is the primary instigator of change, as opposed to a team that is usually passive and change originates from the customer or from levels higher in the organization.

- *Pro-action*: Golden and Powell (2000) discuss the contrast between *proactive* and *reactive* flexibility. This concept recognizes the fact that an entity is not helpless while waiting for change to occur and that steps can be taken *in advance of* change as well as in response to it. The simple example of periodic inspection and preventative maintenance of equipment is a proactive approach to combating machine failure, as opposed to repair and replacement of equipment after failure, which is a reactive one (Gerwin 1993). *Proactive* versus *reactive* strategies have also been described as *offensive* versus *defensive* strategies (Golden and Powell 2000) and *initiative* versus *response* (Goldman et al. 1995). In an ISD context, this is where the ISD team takes actions to elicit changes before they actually occur. Prototyping is a prime example of this. Delaying decisions and staging the investment of resources are also examples of pro-action.

- *Reaction*: Reaction is the most commonly used interpretation of agility, defined as the ability to adapt to change. Even within this relatively simple component of agility, there exist different notions as to what it represents. For example the distinction between defensive and offensive strategies raises the issue that, after change occurs, not only can an entity attempt to return to its original state, but it can take advantage of the change to place itself in a better position (Golden and Powell 2000). *Adapt to* implies that an entity is homeostatic, and that its only objective in the face of change will be to return to its original state. *Embrace* implies that the entity may not only try to return to its original state but may capitalize on the change and improve on its position, hence the use of the term in the earlier definition. Reaction in an ISD context refers to the actions taken by the ISD team in response to a change.

• *Learning*: Although a lot of the earlier concepts such as pro-action and reaction indicated a large overlap between flexibility and agility, the concept of learning seems to make a distinction between them. Agility assumes that change is *continuous*, and embracing it is an ongoing activity. Furthermore, an agile entity should learn how to be more creative, proactive, and reactive over time. This assumption was laid down in the key contribution of Goldman et al. (1995), who described agility in general terms as "a continual readiness to change." The flexibility literature makes no reference to continual change as opposed to a once-off change. Learning in an ISD context is where the project team learns from the change process so as to be more creative, proactive, and reactive during the next cycle.

One component often discussed in the literature on agility, but that does not form part of this proposed framework, is robustness. Hashimoto (1980; see also (Hashimoto et al. 1982) refers to *robustness* or *resilience* as a component of flexibility and agility. Robustness or resilience is the ability to *endure* all transitions caused by foreseen or unforeseen changes, or the degree of change tolerated before deterioration in performance occurs *without* any corrective action (Hashimoto 1980; Hashimoto et al. 1982). This concept indicates that in order to be truly flexible, an entity must not only be able to adapt to change by taking steps, but must also be able to embrace change by taking none. However, this framework does not include robustness as a component of agility. We believe this is justifiable since robustness is not an activity in itself but is a product of pro-action. In other words, proactive activities, if done well, should reduce the need to react. The less reaction required, the higher the level of robustness.

Activities can be analyzed under each of the four classifications of agility outlined above to see how they can contribute to the overall agility of the ISD team. These classifications can be combined with the sources of change identified in section 4.1 to allow a more thorough analysis of activities (see Figure 2)

The framework is not populated as the contents will depend on the specific ISD project and the reason for using the framework. Creative, proactive, reactive, and learning activities can only be aligned with the various sources of change once the project manager has identified the relevant sources of change and subcategories of change applicable to the specific project.

4.3 Resource Utilization

Leanness has been defined as the elimination of waste (Naylor et al. 1999; Ohno 1988; Womack et al. 1990) and doing more with less (Towill and Christopher 2002). Different authors have conflicting opinions regarding the benefits and drawbacks of using a lean approach. However, there is a general consensus that such an approach

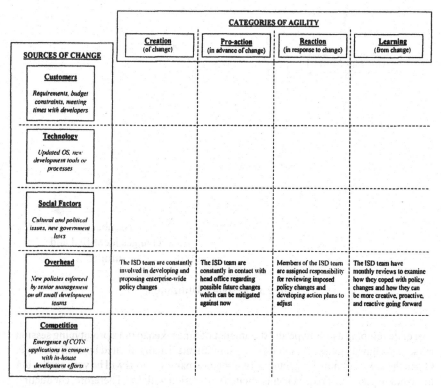

SOURCES OF CHANGE	CATEGORIES OF AGILITY			
	Creation (of change)	**Pro-action** (in advance of change)	**Reaction** (in response to change)	**Learning** (from change)
Customers *Requirements, budget constraints, meeting times with developers*				
Technology *Updated OS, new development tools or processes*				
Social Factors *Cultural and political issues, new government laws*				
Overhead *New policies enforced by senior management on all small development teams*	The ISD team are constantly involved in developing and proposing enterprise-wide policy changes	The ISD team are constantly in contact with head office regarding possible future changes which can be mitigated against now	Members of the ISD team are assigned responsibility for reviewing imposed policy changes and developing action plans to adjust	The ISD team have monthly reviews to examine how they coped with policy changes and how they can be more creative, proactive, and reactive going forward
Competition *Emergence of COTS applications to compete with in-house development efforts*				

Figure 2. Classification of Agile Activities

advocates the utilization of all resources and no unnecessary resources are maintained (Naylor et al. 1999; Ohno 1988; Towill and Christopher 2002; Womack et al. 1990). Some believe that although agility exhibits similar traits to *leanness* in terms of *simplicity* and *quality*, the literature has identified one major difference in terms of *economy* (Young et al. 2001). Ultimate leanness is to eliminate all waste. Agility requires waste to be eliminated, but *only to the extent where its ability to respond to change is not hindered.* This does not remove the need to be economical, only lower its priority.

Identifying and handling change, or in other words being agile, requires resources. The development team faces the task of dealing with change while minimizing the cost, time, and diminished quality required to do so. Figure 3 represents this notion. The x-axis measures the parameterized number of changes identified and fulfilled, the parameter depending on the source of change (refer to Figure 1). For example, the x-axis could be measured by the number of requirement changes, the staff turn-over count, or the number of policy changes introduced. The resources required to fuel the identification and handling of these changes, namely cost, time, and defects, are represented by the y-axis.

This part of the framework dispels the notion that an activity can be labeled as completely agile or non-agile. It depends on the context in which it is used. For example, prototyping is a proactive approach to eliciting customer requirements. The

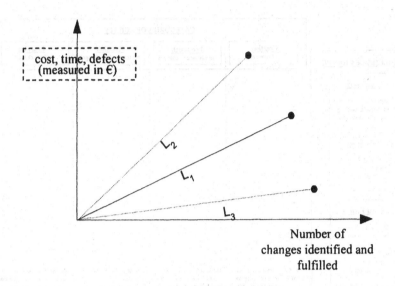

Figure 3. Resource Utilization

cost of developing a prototype and the amount of time taken to run a prototyping session must be weighed against the number of requirements usually elicited by such sessions. Given the law of diminishing returns, running too many sessions will be very costly, but the average number of requirements elicited per session will fall. Therefore, conducting prototyping sessions only contributes to agility if done in moderation. In Figure 3, if too many prototyping sessions are run, the line will rise from L_1 to L_2. The ideal target is to move the line closer to L_3 where there are a large number of requirements identified and handled for the relatively small amount of resources used

A limitation of this part of the framework is the subjective nature of some of the metrics used. Furthermore, it is difficult to estimate the resources utilized by an ISD activity before it takes place and impossible to predict the number of new changes identified as a result. Only in hindsight can the resources utilized be justified by the number of changes elicited and handled. This indicates that there is some element of truth in Highsmith's (1999) notion that only hindsight can determine whether an agile method was actually adhered to.

5   IMPLICATIONS OF THE FRAMEWORK

5.1 In Practice

It is expected that the framework can be used to remove a lot of the inconsistencies in the interpretation and use of agile methods. For example, a developer who believes that agile is a purely reactive capability can see where his/her ideas fit with other, more comprehensive interpretations.

Also, the framework can be used to compare and contrast agile methods with each other, or even with more traditional approaches to determine their true agile content. An ISD team may not necessarily pick the method that ticks the most boxes in the matrix (Figure 2) but may pick the method that best handles the select sources of change that their project may face. Logically, therefore, it can also be used to identify gaps where they have identified sources of change to which they are prone but against which they are not protected.

The various components of agile methods can be individually analyzed, using the framework as a lens. For example, pair programming is proactive in terms of staff turn-over in that it provides overlapping skills between developers should one decide to leave. It is also reactive with regard to errors, where two pairs of eyes are better than one at finding and resolving such bugs (Auer and Miller 2002). Such an individual analysis is useful to ISD teams who wish to adopt an *a la carte* approach to agile methods.

The framework can also be used for training purposes. The team can be made aware of the metrics that are important in terms of agility, such as cost and time reduction and defect prevention.

Finally, the framework can be used retrospectively to determine the agility of an ISD team in hindsight. This is in the same vein of thought as Highsmith's claim that only hindsight can determine whether an agile method was actually adhered to. An analysis can be done to ensure that the correct sources of change were anticipated and that the activities carried out to handle that change had the desired effect.

5.2 In Research and Education

First, the framework is at a relatively higher level of abstraction than most other frameworks of agility, both within ISD literature and outside it. As a result, this framework may provide a foundation to connect other pieces of work which adopt a narrower interpretation of agility. For example, it may allow a researcher who has only focused on the reactive aspect of agility to extend his/her work to the other components such as creation, pro-action, and learning. A big picture view tends to invite the insertion of those pieces that may be missing, or the extra detail that might be needed for a particular purpose or group.

Second, to the extent that a big-picture dialogue is facilitated, it may point to areas of uncertainty and areas where there is a need to know more. For example, a Ph.D. student might use the framework as a top-level roadmap in searching for areas of concern.

Third, this framework is based on literature from many disciplines. This may provide support to researchers who wish to extend this further through divergent research, which draws upon scholarship among different disciplines to address real-world needs (Brown 1992). It may encourage linking with and thinking about other related areas. It facilitates convergent research, developing clearly defined, specific lines of enquiry to validate promising hypotheses. Thus, where divergent research aims to incorporate the big-picture view, the framework may be of value.

By synthesizing the literature and concepts of agility into sources of change, agile classifications, and resource utilization, there may be an opportunity to increase awareness of how important all three are to the overall agility of an enterprise.

Finally, this framework may be applicable outside of the field of ISD to areas such as manufacturing where the same problems regarding inconsistency persist.

6   FUTURE WORK

The next stage of this research is a Delphic survey of leading academics and practitioners in the field of ISD, with a view to testing the three parts of the framework. This will be done by circulating this paper to the aforementioned individuals, and inviting their feedback. The framework will then be revised, based on the feedback from this survey.

Also, once this framework has been refined after practitioner and academic feedback, the next step will be to refine and elaborate the framework. For example, the sources of change may be broken down into a more comprehensive and detailed list of ISD-specific components.

REFERENCES

Adam, F., and Fitzgerald, B. "A Framework for Analyzing the Evolution of the IS Field: Can IS Become a Stable Discipline," in *Proceedings of the 4th European Conference on Information Systems*, Lisbon, June 1996, pp. 17-32.

Ahituv, N., and Neumann, S. *Principles of Information Systems for Management*, Dubuque, IA: Brown, 1990.

Alleman, G. "Agile Project Management Methods for IT Projects," in *The Story of Managing Projects: A Global, Cross-Disciplinary Collection of Perspectives*, E. Carayannis and Y. Kwak (Eds.), Berkeley, CA: Greenwood Press, 2002.

Ambler, S. W. *Agile Modeling: Best Practices for the Unified Process and Extreme Programming*, New York: John Wiley & Sons, 2002.

Auer, K., and Miller, R. *Extreme Programming Applied: Playing to Win*, Upper Saddle River, NJ: Addison-Wesley, 2002.

Avison, D. "The Discipline of Information Systems: IS Teaching, Research and Practice," UK Academy of Information Systems, Cranfield University, 1996.

Banville, C., and Landry, M. "Can the Field of MIS be Disciplined?," *Communication of the ACM* (32:1), 1989, pp. 48-60.

Bariff, M., and Ginzberg, M. "MIS and the Behavioral Sciences: Research Patterns and Prescriptions," *DATA BASE for Advances in Information Systems* (14:1), 1982, pp. 19-26.

Baskerville, R., Travis, J., and Truex, D. "Systems Without Method: The Impact of New Technologies on Information Systems Development Projects," in *The Impact of Computer Supported Technologies on Information Systems Development*, K. Kendall, K. Lyytinen, and J. I. DeGross (Eds.), Amsterdam: Elsevier Science Publishers, 1992, pp. 241-269.

Beck, K. *Extreme Programming Explained*, Upper Saddle River, NJ: Addison Wesley, 1999.

Boehm, B., Gray, T., and Seewaldt, T., "Prototyping Versus Specifying: A Multi-Project Experiment," *IEEE Transactions on Software Engineering* (SE-10:3), 1984, pp. 290-302.

Brown, R. "The State of the Art of Decision Analysis: A Personal Perspective," *Interfaces* (22:6), 1992, pp. 5-14.

Burgess, T. "Making the Leap to Agility: Defining and Achieving Agile Manufacturing through Business Process Redesign and Business Network Redesign," *International Journal of Operations and Production Management* (14:11), 1994, pp. 23-34.

Carnall, C. *Managing Change in Organizations*, Harlow, England: Prentice Hall, 2002.

Childerhouse, P., Disney, S., and Towill, D. "Speeding Up the Progress Curve Towards Effective Supply Chain Management," *International Journal of Supply Chain Management* (5:3), 2000, pp. 176-186.

Coad, P., de Luca, J., and Lefebre, E. *Java Modeling in Color*, Upper Saddle River, NJ: Prentice Hall, 1999.

Cockburn, A. *Agile Software Development*, Upper Saddle River, NJ: Addison Wesley, 2002a.

Cockburn, A. "Agile Software Development Joins the 'Would-Be' Crowd," *Cutter IT Journal* (15:1), 2002b, pp. 6-12.

Conboy, K., and Fitzgerald, B. "A Multi-Disciplinary Literature Review of Agility," paper presented at the Americas Conference on Information Systems, New York, August 6-8, 2004a.

Conboy, K., and Fitzgerald, B. "The Resources Required to Fuel the Agile Fire," paper presented at the Multidisciplinary Software Engineering Conference, Los Angeles, August 21-25, 2004b.

Conboy, K., and Fitzgerald, B. "Towards a Conceptual Framework of Agile Methods," paper presented at the XP and Agile Conference, Alberta, Canada, August 15-18, 2004c.

Culnan, M., and Swanson, E. "Research in MIS 1980-1984: Points of Work and Reference," *MIS Quarterly* (10:3), September 1986, pp. 289-301.

Drucker, P. "The Information That Executives Truly Need," *Harvard Business Review*, January-February 1995, pp. 54-62.

Fitzgerald, B. "Formalized Systems Development Methodologies: A Critical Perspective," *Information Systems Journal* (6:1), 1996, pp. 3-23.

Fitzgerald, B. "The Systems Development Dilemma: Whether to Adopt Formalized Systems Development Methodologies or Not," in *Proceedings of the Second European Conference on Information Systems*, W. Baets (Ed.), Nijenrode, Holland: Nijenrode University Press, 1994, pp. 691-706.

Fowler, M. "Is Design Dead," Chapter 1 in *Extreme Programming Explained*, Upper Saddle River, NJ: Addison-Wesley, 2001.

Fowler, M. "Put Your Process on a Diet," *Software Development*, December 2000, pp. 32-36.

Fowler, M., and Highsmith, J. "The Agile Manifesto," *Software Development*, August 2001, pp. 17-25.

Gerwin, D. "Manufacturing Flexibility: A Strategic Perspective," *Management Science* (39:4), 1993, pp. 395-410.

Golden, W., and Powell, P. "Towards a Definition of Flexibility: In Search of the Holy Grail?," *Omega* (28), 2000, pp. 373-384.

Goldman, S., Nagel, R., and Preiss, K. *Agile Competitors and Virtual Organizations: Strategies for Enriching the Customer*, New York: Von Nostrand Reinhold, 1995.

Goldman, S., Nagel, R., Preiss, K., and Dove, R. *Iacocca Institute: 21st Century Manufacturing Enterprise Strategy: An Industry Led View*, Bethlehem, PA: Iacocca Institute, Lehigh University, 1991.

Grimshaw, D. "Towards a Taxonomy of Information Systems: Or Does Anyone Need a TAXI," *Journal of Information Technology* (7:1), 1992, pp. 30-36.

Hashimoto, T. "Robustness, Reliability, Resilience and Vulnerability Criteria for Planning," *Water Resources Research* (8:1), 1980, pp. 11-47.

Hashimoto, T., Loucks, D., and Stedinger, J. "Robustness of Water Resources Systems," *Water Resources Research* (18:1), 1982, pp. 21-26.

Highsmith, J. *Adaptive Software Development*, New York: Dorset House, 1999.

Hirschheim, R., Klein, H., and Lyytinen, K. "Exploring the Intellectual Structures of IS Development: A Social Action Theoretic Analysis," *Accounting, Management and Information Technology* (6:1), 1994, pp. 1-64.

Khaled, R., Barr, P., and Biddle, B. "System Metaphor in 'Extreme Programming': A Semiotic Approach," in *Proceedings of the International Workshop on Organizationa Semiotics*, Setubal, Portugal: INSTICC Press, August 2004, pp. 152-172.

Kruchten, P. *The Rational Unified Process: An Introduction*, Reading, MA: Addison-Wesley-Longman, 2000.

Latour, B. *The Pasteurisation of France*, Boston: Harvard University Press, 1988.

Latour, B., and Woolgar, S. *Laboratory Life*, London: Sage Publications, 1979.

Naylor, J., Naim, M., and Berry, D. "Leagility: Integrating the Lean and Agile Manufacturing Paradigm in the Total Supply Chain," *Engineering Costs and Production Economics* (62), 1999, pp. 107-118.

Ohno, T. *The Toyota Production System: Beyond Large Scale Production*, Portland, OR: Productivity Press, 1988.

Piore, M. "Corporate Reform in American Manufacturing and the Challenge to Economic Reform," Mimeo, Department of Political Science, Massachusetts Institute of Technology. 1989.

Poppendieck, M. "Lean Programming," *Software Development Magazine* (9:5), 2001, 71-75.

Schein, E. *Organizational Psychology*, Englewood Cliffs, NJ: Prentice Hall, 1965.

Schwaber, K., and Beedle, M. *Agile Software Development with Scrum*, Upper Saddle River, NJ: Prentice Hall, 2002.

Schwalbe, K. *Information Technology Project Management*, Boston: Course Technology, 2000.

Sharafi, H., and Zhang, Z. "A Method for Achieving Agility in Manufacturing Organizations: An Introduction," *International Journal of Production Economics* (62:1-2), 1999, pp. 7-22.

Shenhar, A., and Dvir, D. "Managing Technology Projects: A Contingent Exploratory Approach," in *Proceedings of the 28th Annual Hawaii International Conference on System Sciences*, Los Alamitos, CA: IEEE Computer Society Press, 1995, pp. 494-503.

Stapleton, J. *DSDM: Dynamic Systems Development Method*, Harlow, England: Addison Wesley, 1997.

Stephens, M., and Rosenberg, D. *Extreme Programming Refactored*, Berkeley, CA: Apress, 2003.

Stolterman, E., and Russo, N. "The Paradox of Information Systems Methods: Public and Private Rationality," paper presented at the British Computer Society Annual Conference on IS Methodologies, August 27-29, 1997.

Succi, G., and Marchesi, M. *Extreme Programming Examined*, Reading, MA: Addison-Wesley Longman, 2001.

Towill, D., and Christopher, M. "The Supply Chain Strategy Conundrum: To Be Lean or Agile or To Be Lean and Agile," *International Journal of Logistics: Research and Applications* (5:3), 2002, pp. 4-11.

Vatter, W. *The Fund Theory of Accounting and its Implications for Financial Reports*, Chicago: The University of Chicago Press, 1947.

Vogel, D., and Wetherbe, J. "MIS Research: A Profile of Leading Journals and Universities," *DATA BASE for Advances in Information Systems* (16:1), 1984, pp. 3-14.

Vokurka, R., and Fliedner, G. "The Journal Toward Agility," *Journal of Industrial Management and Data Systems* (98:4), 1998, pp. 165-171.

Weber, R. "Towards a Theory of Artifacts: A Paradigmatic Base for Information Systems Research," *Journal of Information Systems* (1:2), 1987, pp. 3-19.

Williams, T. *Modeling Complex Projects*, New York: Wiley and Sons, 2002.

Womack, J., Jones, D., and Roos, D. *The Machine That Changed the World*, New York: Rawson Associates, 1990.

Young, K., Muehlhaeusser, R., Piggin, R., and Rachitrangsan, P. "Agile Control Systems," *Automobile Engineering* (215:D2), 2001, pp. 189-195.

ABOUT THE AUTHORS

Kieran Conboy is a junior lecturer in Information Systems at the National University of Ireland, Galway, Ireland. His current doctoral research focuses on agile methods for systems development as well as agility across other disciplines. Prior to joining NUI Galway, he was a management consultant with Accenture. Kieran can be reached at kieran.conboy@nuigalway.ie.

Brian Fitzgerald holds the Frederick A Krehbiel II Chair in Innovation in Global Business and Technology at the University of Limerick, Ireland, where he also is a Research Fellow of the University, in addition to being a Science Foundation Ireland Investigator. He has a Ph.D. from the University of London and has held positions at University College Cork, Ireland, Northern Illinois University, United States, the University of Gothenburg, Sweden, and Northumbria University, United Kingdom. His publications include seven books and more than 70 papers, published in leading international conferences and journals. Having worked in industry prior to taking up an academic position, he has more than 20 years experience in the IS field. Brian can be reached at bf@ul.ie.

William Golden is a senior lecturer in Information Systems and a research director of the Centre for Innovation and Structural Change at the National University of Ireland, Galway, Ireland. His current research focuses on how such interorganizational networks enable innovative practices, which enable networked firms, to out perform their rivals. He has coauthored a book, contributed chapters to other texts, and published papers in the areas of electronic commerce and information systems in such journals as *Omega, The International Journal of Management Science, International Journal of Electronic Commerce* and *Journal of End-User Computing.* Willie can be reached at willie.golden@nuigalway.ie.

Part 2

Agile IT Diffusion

4 NAVIGATING SOFTWARE PROCESS IMPROVEMENT PROJECTS

Ivan Aaen
Aalborg University
Aalborg, Denmark

Anna Börjesson
IT University of Gotenburg
Gotenburg, Sweden

Lars Mathiassen
Georgia State University
Atlanta, GA U.S.A.

Abstract   *Software process improvement (SPI) is one of the most widely used approaches to innovate software organizations. In this study, we identify and compare two different tactics for SPI projects. The first tactic, the supertanker, is inspired by centralist thinking. It is driven by process-push, and it aims for efficient process development and diffusion. The second tactic, the motorboat, is inspired by decentralist thinking. It facilitates practice-pull, and it aims for adaptive process development and diffusion. Our analysis of 18 SPI projects at Ericsson in Gothenburg shows how the two tactics lead to different practices and outcomes. We discuss on that basis what SPI tactics to use and identify the presence of muddy and unknown waters as the key characteristic that requires motorboat tactics. We suggest that today's changing business environment calls for agile SPI practices that employ adaptive governance mechanisms at the corporate level and combines motorboat tactics with revised supertanker tactics.*

Keywords   Software process improvement, process implementation, project tactics, agility

1   INTRODUCTION

Software process improvement (SPI) is widely acknowledged as a viable strategy to enhance organizational capability to deliver qualitative software (Grady 1997;

Humphrey 1989; Mathiassen et al. 2002). Many SPI initiatives struggle, however, with low SPI success rates (Aaen 2002; Börjesson and Mathiassen 2004c; Fayad and Laitinen 1997), and several approaches to increase the SPI success rate have been suggested including the use of models for SPI (Paulk et al. 1995), the use of models for process diffusion (Pries-Heje and Tryde 2001), emphasis on SPI change agent capabilities (Humphrey 1989; McFeeley 1996), and management of reactions to change (Weinberg 1997).

The theme of this paper is agility (Dove 2001; Haeckel 1995, 1999). During the last decade, the speed of change in the software industry has increased (Baskerville et al. 2001; Holmberg and Mathiassen 2001). To be successful, software organizations must increasingly be organized, managed, and executed in ways that allow them to effectively sense and respond to unpredictable events in their environment. While the software discipline has focused extensively on software development agility (Abrahamson et al. 2002), there has so far been little focus on software organization agility and agility in SPI (Börjesson and Mathiassen 2004b). To learn more about SPI agility, we identify and compare two different SPI project tactics and study their use and outcome in 18 SPI projects within the telecom company Ericsson AB in Gothenburg, Sweden. One tactic is generic, aiming for the development of organization-level software process elements. We call this the *supertanker* tactic. The other tactic is dedicated, aiming for unique solutions for particular development projects. We call this the *motorboat* tactic. Based on this distinction we focus on the following research questions: *How do different SPI tactics affect the outcome and the ability to navigate in an ever-changing business environment?*

We start by presenting our theoretical framework and research method. Following this, we present and analyze the 18 SPI initiatives at Ericsson. The analysis shows how the two tactics led to different practices and outcomes. We use these experiences to discuss choice of tactics and development of agile SPI practices in software organizations.

2   THEORETICAL BACKGROUND

We first explicate key ideas that underpin the capability maturity model (CMM). We then review the agility mindset and its adoption in software organizations and SPI. Finally, we explicate the two SPI tactics that drive our research into practices at Ericsson.

2.1 The CMM Mindset

The CMM mindset is rooted in the CMM (Paulk, Curtis et al. 1993; Paulk et al. 1995; Paulk, Weber et al. 1993) and the current CMMI–CMM Integration (CMMI Product Team 2002a, 2002b). These models assume that good processes are predictable and will lead to good products.

To Humphrey (1989) a software process is the set of tools, methods, and practices used to produce a software product. Process management strives to produce software according to plan while at the same time improving capabilities. Referring to TQM (total quality management) author Deming, Humphrey identifies statistical process control principles as basic to SPI:

> When a process is under statistical control, repeating the work roughly the same way will produce roughly the same result. To obtain consistently better results, it is thus necessary to improve the process. If the process is not under statistical control, sustained progress is not possible until it is (p. 3).

The focus is on function—what developers should do. The wider context with issues like customer, product, organization, leadership, and commitment plays a dominant role in TQM approaches (Creech 1994). While these issues are discussed in the SPI literature, they play minor roles in the CMM. SPI projects are predominantly viewed as internal to the software organization. In that sense, SPI efforts are done for, with, and by the software developing organization.

Today, the CMMI still portrays process as key to improvement and adopts process modelling as a dominant theme in SPI. Humphrey describes a procedure in a software process as a "defined way to do something, generally embodied in a procedures manual" and he likens this definition with the procedure concept used in programming (p. 158).

This line of thought traces back to Osterweil's (1987) highly influential paper entitled "Software Processes Are Software Too," published around the time Humphrey developed the first version of CMM. The earliest impetus for process programming arose from Osterweil's meetings with Humphrey and his team at IBM in the early 1980s (Osterweil 1997). Osterweil (1987) advocated

> that we describe software processes by "programming" them much as we "program" computer applications. We refer to the activity of expressing software process descriptions with the aid of programming techniques as process programming, and suggest that this activity ought to be at the center of what software engineering is all about (p. 4).

Feiler and Humphrey (1991) adopt a similar view, arguing that processes have many artifacts in common with software and require similar disciplines and methods. They suggest thinking about SPI in software development terms.

These ideas persist in today's CMMI.

- A *process description* is defined as a

> documented expression of a set of activities performed to achieve a given purpose that provides an operational definition of the major components of a process. The documentation specifies, in a complete, precise, and verifiable manner, the requirements, design, behavior, or other characteristics of a process. It also may include procedures for determining whether these provisions have been satisfied (CMMI Product Team 2002a, p. 556).

- A *process element* is "the fundamental unit of a process. A process may be defined in terms of subprocesses or process elements. A subprocess can be further decomposed; a process element cannot" (CMMI Product Team YEAR, PG).

The CMM mindset is rooted in process thinking and modeling with an ambition to create sustainable progress by bringing processes under statistical control. The functional perspective on software practices focuses on internal aspects of software practices and the emphasis on control outweighs a concern for ability to respond to change.

2.2 The Agility Mindset

The increased speed of technology and market change has led to considerable interest in how organizations can manage and respond to unpredictable changes in their environment (e.g., Dove 2001; Gunneson 1997; Haeckel 1995, 1999). The Agility Forum at Lehigh University was formed in 1991 to develop new approaches for production of goods and services based on agile practices. Gunneson (1997) argues that agility is concerned with economies of scope, rather than economies of scale. Where lean operations are usually associated with efficient use of resources, agile operations are related to effectively responding to a changing environment while at the same time being productive. The idea is to serve ever-smaller niche markets and individual customers without the high cost traditionally associated with customization. The ability to respond is the essential and distinguishing feature of agile organizations (Dove 2001).

Agility requires "the ability to manage and apply knowledge effectively, so that an organization has the potential to thrive in a continuously changing and unpredictable business environment" (Dove 2001, p. 9). The two capabilities that are required to practice agility are, therefore, response ability and knowledge management. Response ability is achieved through change proficiency and flexible relationships that are reusable, reconfigurable, and scalable. Knowledge management in turn requires collaborative learning and knowledge portfolio management including the identification, acquisition, diffusion, and renewal of the knowledge the organization requires strategically (Dove 2001).

Haeckel's (1995, 1999) approach to adaptive organization implies radically different forms of governance, institutionalization of new norms of adaptive behavior, and translation of the organization's mission and practices into information that can easily be communicated and interpreted amongst its constituents. There are four basic principles for the adaptive organization. First, the traditional command and control approach that works well in stable, predictable environments is replaced. Instead, organization-specific governance mechanisms are adopted that support a high level of local autonomy, facilitate coordination across individual units, and empower individuals, groups, and organizational units to act on local knowledge while at the same time ensuring a sufficient level of coherent behavior overall. Second, procedures must be supplemented with personal accountability so each business process has two dimensions (Scherr 1993): procedure ("who or what does what to what and with what") and accountability ("who owes what to whom and by when") (Haeckel 1995, p. 11). Third, organizations must implement learning processes on different levels and within different areas. These processes are based on recurrent sense-and-respond cycles (sense–interpret–decide–act). Fourth, the organization must be structured into modular processes. To be highly adaptive, an organization "has to have the ability to snap together modular processes and products as if they were Lego building blocks" (Haeckel 1995, p. 42).

The speed of change has increased within the software industry over the last decade (Baskerville et al. 2001; Holmberg and Mathiassen 2001) and there is consequently a need to adopt agile practices (Börjesson and Mathiassen 2004b). One comprehensive attempt to do so is expressed in the agile software development manifesto (Beck et al. 2001):

- Individuals and interactions over processes and tools
- Working software over comprehensive documentation
- Customer collaboration over contract negotiation
- Responding to change over following a plan

The agility mindset expressed here and in many related agile methods (Abrahamson et al. 2002) is, however, entirely focused on software development on the project level. Agility, though, is an organization-level capability. The challenge is to adopt agility practices broadly in response to unpredictable changes (Börjesson and Mathiassen 2004b). Such efforts must adopt software development agility and SPI agility as integral parts of building agile software organizations.

2.3 Navigating SPI Projects

In order to understand the need for, and approaches to, developing agile practices within SPI, we distinguish between two complementary tactics. The first, the super-tanker tactic, is based on the CMM mindset, whereas the other, the motorboat tactic, is based on the agile mindset.

The supertanker tactic is centralist and top-down: (1) understand the current status of the process relative to CMM (or some other model), (2) create a vision of the desired process relative to CMM, (3) establish a list of required actions, (4) produce a plan for accomplishing these actions, (5) commit resources required to execute, and (6) start over at step 1 (Humphrey 1989, p. 4). Each loop contributes to the standards enforced in the organization.

Humphrey discusses the dilemma of process definition between project-unique circumstances on the one side, and the need for organization-level standardization in order to promote learning, teaching, measuring, and tool support on the other. This dilemma, he suggests, can be solved through tailoring standard software processes to suit specific project needs (p. 248).

To Humphrey, SPI targets a generic process that can be modelled, controlled, measured, and improved. Improvements will only stick if reinforced by careful introduction combined with periodical monitoring:

The actions of even the best-intentioned professionals must be tracked, reviewed, and checked, or process deviations will occur. If there is no system

to identify deviations and to reinforce the defined process, small digressions
will accumulate and degrade it beyond recognition. (p. 22)

In order to achieve organization-level standardization, the supertanker tactic relies
on SPI committees or specialist staff functions. This means a separation of thinkers
from doers with a main focus on organization-wide processes. Key to this tactic is the
process group—a collection of specialists that facilitate the definition, maintenance, and
improvement of processes used by the organization (CMMI Product Team 2002a;
2002b).

The supertanker tactic is, in summary, centralist and top-down with an ambition to
build and enforce organization-level standard processes, with process tailoring as the
response to particular project conditions, with strict process enforcement, and with
separation of thinkers from doers. The SPI governance structure emphasizes overall
coordination of projects and organization-wide institutionalization of standard processes.
Learning primarily takes place on the overall SPI level through continuous sense-and-
respond cycles that identify current weaknesses, initiate new efforts, and implement their
results organization-wide. In many ways this tactic relates to what Weick and Quinn
(1999) call episodic change.

The problem with the supertanker tactic is its focus on procedure (i.e., on the tasks
and decisions involved in producing software according to requirements). The focus on
predictability and planning tends to render the software process bureaucratic based on
command and control thinking.

The motorboat tactic is a critique of the CMM mindset and its deployment of
solitary processes (i.e., one process is provided for any particular task). Kondo (2000)
argues that solitary processes might lead people to feel that they are not responsible for
nonconformance of product quality. Centralism thus might lead to software engineer
alienation. Separating thinkers from doers means a split between insiders and outsiders
in software projects leading to stifled motivation at both ends and to turf guarding if
careers collide in a clash between project interests and general interests in staff functions
or committees. Finally, process perfection will likely be static and fail to seize opportunities for improvement. As Kondo puts it,

since standardized working means and methods have been formulated after
careful consideration of all the angles, they must be the most productive and
efficient means and methods possible, regardless of who uses them—at least
the people who drew up the standards think so. (p. 9)

The motorboat tactic assumes that one size does *not* fit all. Processes are cultivated
taking particular circumstances into account. The tactic includes strong elements of
practice pull from software engineers (Börjesson and Mathiassen 2004c; Zmud 1984)
and change agents work in specific projects to help software engineers help themselves.

Motorboat tactics develop software processes by combining best practices with
experiences shared through networking (Aaen 2002). Processes are emergent and their
use promotes discretion and latitude at the individual and project level in response to
specific circumstances. As in agile approaches such as XP (Beck 2000), software
processes serve primarily as a departure point for defining a common mode of operation

Table 1. Characteristics of the Supertanker and Motorboat Tactics

Issue	Supertanker	Motorboat
Organization	Centralist, top-down	Decentralist, bottom-up
Coordination	Between SPI projects	Between SPI and practice
Process	Generic	Dedicated
Diffusion	Process-push	Practice-pull
Learning	Software organization level	Software project level

in the team. Thinkers and doers work closely together as process experts serve as mentors, coaches, and consultants for a software team—or, they may even join the team for the duration of the project (Kautz et al. 2001).

The motorboat tactic is, in summary, decentralist and bottom-up with an emphasis on project and team level standardization of processes, with a focus on emergent processes that promote discretion and latitude at the level of the engineer, with an emphasis on practice pull to cultivate processes in response to situational opportunities, and relying on facilitation by mentoring and coaching software engineers by embedding change agents directly into software projects. Key to the motorboat tactic is the support of adaptive SPI practices. The governance structure emphasizes coordination between SPI experts and software engineers allowing for local authority in the project. Learning primarily takes place within projects through continuous sense-and-respond cycles that identify current weaknesses, initiate new efforts, and implement these as the project evolves and delivers its results. Thus this tactic relates to organizational change via improvisation (Orlikowski 1996) and to what Weick and Quinn label continuous change.

The problem with the motorboat tactic is that it tends to ignore organization-wide procedures. A sole focus on short-term challenges tends to focus on commitments and to render the software process *ad hoc*. The characteristics of the supertanker and motorboat tactics are shown in Table 1.

3 RESEARCH METHOD

This research is part of a collaborative practice study (Mathiassen 2002) carried out at one of Ericsson's system development centers with more than 20 years of experience developing packet data solutions for the international market.

The authors represent industry and academia in close cooperation to secure relevant data and an appropriate theoretical framing of the study. The authors represent the insider and outsider perspective (Bartunek and Louis 1996). The insider is more connected to the problems than the outsider, while the outsider is more capable of unbiased reflection on the problem. The overall purpose of the research collaboration was twofold. We wanted to improve the understanding of how different SPI tactics at Ericsson affect the outcome, while at the same time contributing to the body of knowledge on SPI. We focused on how different SPI tactics affected the outcome of 18 different SPI projects. Collaborative practice research (Mathiassen 2002) was used to

Table 2. Data Sources

Data Source	Description
Direct involvement	One author was directly involved in 6 of the SPI initiatives and responsible for the remaining 12 initiatives
Participatory observations	One author participated in discussions of problems and results during SPI steering group meetings, training occasions, and informal meetings with software practitioners
SPI project documentation	Project meeting protocols, project presentations, project plans, project decisions, final reports
Minutes of meetings	Formal notes on discussions and decisions made about introduction of the new requirements management approach
Software development tools	Access to the software tools and their databases to understand the actual use of them
SPI survey	A yearly conducted SPI survey made by the SPI unit
Open-ended semi-structured interviews	Informal interviews were made with 10 practitioners to understand and validate the outcome of the initiative

frame this interpretive case study (Yin 1994). As one of the authors has been responsible for and active in the SPI initiatives, this study could also be viewed as action research (Baskerville and Pries-Heje 1999; Galliers 1992; Walsham 1995).

Data were collected and analyzed using a multi-method approach to establish a valid basis for analysis and to develop a thick description of the case (Mingers 2001; Yin 1994). Table 2 summarizes the list of data sources for our study. We used the different data sources to triangulate findings (Yin 1994).

4   THE CASE

Growing from 150 employees in 1995 to 900, in 2001 this particular Ericsson organization was reorganized and downsized during 2002 and 2003 to 550 employees. During this dynamic period, different SPI tactics were used to address and improve software development. The 18 different SPI initiatives were explored from different views as summarized in the Appendix (adapted from Börjesson and Mathiassen 2004c). In retrospect we can divide the 18 initiatives into two groups: The first 11 initiatives executed between 1998 and 1999 employed a supertanker tactic while the remaining 7 initiatives executed between 2000 and 2002 employed a motorboat tactic. We use the following attributes to distinguish between tactics and to understand how they affected outcomes:

   •   Improvement Set-up: How is the initiative organized and coordinated?

- Process Creation: On what basis and with what intentions are processes created?
- Process Diffusion: How are new processes diffused into practice?
- Navigation Ability: What kind of learning takes place in order to sense and respond to changes in the environment?

Our focus is on implementation success—the actual changes in software engineering practice. Implementation success is directly recognizable, unlike SPI success, and although not synonymous with SPI success, implementation success is a prerequisite for SPI success. The next three subsections explore and compare the two tactics.

4.1 The Supertanker

The 11 supertanker initiatives had low or medium implementation success (Börjesson and Mathiassen 2004c). The initiatives targeted key practice areas such as configuration management, requirements management, project tracking, module testing, and subcontract management. Table 3 shows how they were managed.

Table 3. Features of the SPI Supertanker Tactic

Improvement Set-up	*One size fits all*: An organization benefits from centralist SPI initiatives. All product units within the organization can streamline their practices by having one improvement initiative serve common needs. Special interests are served through adaptation and tailoring. Having several product units benefit from one SPI initiative is cost effective.
Process Creation	*High focus on representation in the initiatives*: All SPI decisions are taken in an SPI steering group consisting of representative managers from each unit. The steering group discusses, decides, ensures resources, and follows up on the initiatives. No special attention is devoted to process implementation and use. There is a high focus on good representation from all units. Steering group members prepare and attend steering group meetings and follow up on action points.
Process Diffusion	*Based on the CMM Mindset*: The SPI work is organized through a software engineering process group (SEPG) (Fowler and Rifkin 1990; Humphrey 1989). The SPI group works on a corporate level to support all product units in the organization. CMM is used to assess the organization (identified as level one in 1999) and CMM Light assessments are implemented in ongoing software engineering projects.
Navigation Ability	*High focus on initial requirements*: Serving common needs among product units implies a need to hold on to initial requirements as changes will require negotiations with every stakeholder involved.

In general, supertanker initiatives had high focus on defining a solution, but very little on deployment of the process. For instance, understanding how resistance to change could make SPI initiatives fail received little attention (McFeeley 1996). Serving all product units and their different needs simultaneously made the SPI initiatives spend most of their efforts in the early phases of the improvement work (Börjesson and Mathiassen 2004c). As a result, there was limited interaction between the SPI initiatives and the development projects (except via the representatives participating in the initiative). Interaction was mainly through one-way communication from initiative to software engineers. All initiatives using the supertanker tactic were financed at the organizational level. The development projects did not pay for the solutions they received from the SPI initiatives.

4.2 The Motorboat

The seven motorboat initiatives had high implementation success (Börjesson and Mathiassen 2004c). As with the SPI supertanker initiatives, the motorboat initiatives targeted key practice areas such as requirements management, test, configuration management, and project management. Table 4 shows how the initiatives in the motorboat approach were managed.

In general, there was a high focus on collaboration between the SPI initiative and the software engineers (i.e., the development projects). The initiatives targeted projects as well as concrete activities within projects. The initiatives supported actual work, if necessary by devising new solutions such as editing product requirements into a new database to ensure implementation and use. The initiatives were organized as subprojects within the development projects to ensure close cooperation with end users. Both the SPI initiative and the main engineering project manager in question had the double goal of improving practice and managing the engineering project time schedule. Contacts between the initiative and software engineers were on a daily basis and together they negotiated new requirements and ideas as they came up. The engineering projects financed the SPI initiative. When more than one engineering project was expected to use the result, the main engineering project covered the costs.

4.3 Similarities and Differences

The two tactics had many similarities. Several SPI change agents, managers, and practitioners took part in executing both tactics. Management attention, involvement, and commitment were also high in both cases. The types of products (embedded real-time systems) and improvement areas (requirements management, configuration management, etc.) were the same. In both tactics there was one SPI group responsible for driving the initiatives.

As the outcomes differ between the two tactics, a number of differences stand out. Except for the four attributes we have studied in the previous sections, there are several general differences that may have impacted the outcome. In the motorboat tactic, the SPI change agents worked with only one or a few practices and related tools. In the

Table 4. Features of the SPI Motorboat Tactic

Improvement Set-up	*One size fits one:* A product unit benefits from dedicated SPI initiatives. SPI initiatives are aligned to the extent that the product unit in question works with other organizational units on the same product. Specifically, the dedicated SPI initiative focuses on one engineering project to ensure implementation and use. The initiative focuses on just in time solutions for the engineering projects. Simplicity and relevance makes implementation and use cost effective.
Process Creation	*High focus on implementation and use:* All SPI decisions are taken in an SPI steering group consisting of representative managers from each practice (requirements, design, test, etc.) within the product unit. The steering group discusses, decides, secures resources, and follows up on the initiatives. High attention is devoted to process implementation and use. There is a high focus on having good representation from all practices in the steering group. The project manager is a member of the steering group. Steering group members prepare and attend steering group meetings and to follow up on action points.
Process Diffusion	*Ad hoc mindset:* No special attention is put on any established SPI theory. Serving specific and recognized needs in the product unit are believed to lead to implementation success.
Navigation Ability	*High focus on deployment:* Serving specific and recognized needs in the product unit implies that changing needs can be accommodated subject to particular demands from other organizational units working on the same product.

supertanker approach, the SPI change agents had a wider competence base, but not a very deep one. For SPI change agents, it was easier to collaborate with software engineers when acting as specialists within a process area. When using the supertanker tactic, the change agent role received little attention from management and the SPI group itself. Neither change management nor diffusion of innovations models—the Satir change model (Weinberg 1997) and the diffusion of innovation curve (Rogers 2003)—were known or discussed. When using the motorboat approach, these areas had been identified as important factors for SPI implementation. Management commitment was high in both tactics; however, there were differences in the level of commitment. In both tactics, software managers believed in the value of the improvement work, but only in the motorboat tactic was their attention prominent. In the motorboat tactic, managers joined the SPI steering group, as they knew that if managed sensibly they could really benefit from the initiatives. Conversely, in the supertanker approach, every manager in the SPI steering group knew from the outset that it would be difficult to make the initiative cater for their special needs with so many stakeholders involved.

5   DISCUSSION

During the last two decades, diffusion of technology innovations has increased enormously. Computers in every home and on each desk, mobile phones, Internet connections, and wireless communication are today a fact. When the traditional CMM mindset was in its cradle, a lot of this was hard to imagine. These changes have made the world more maneuverable and things tend to happen much faster as a result. The traditional CMM mindset, which might be efficient in a less-changing environment, has become a supertanker. CMM's basic ideas are still very much the same, but the environment in which the model is used has changed. There are still values in having shared languages, a common ground for learning, and corporate processes for economic reasons. The traditional CMM mindset is, however, no longer ideal to accomplish these values in an ever-changing business environment.

None of the initiatives using the supertanker tactic were successful in implementing and using new practices. Börjesson and Mathiassen (2004c) point out a number of reasons: low process-push and practice-pull, little iteration, little effort spent in the deployment phases, and no consideration of resistance to change. Börjesson and Mathiassen (2004a) offer a more elaborate analysis of process-push and practice-pull issues related to this case study. The CMM mindset of one-size-fits-all does not help SPI change agents to focus on software engineering needs and practices. Too many stakeholders are involved to attain implementation success via high process-push. Such tactics might work well in stable environments, but in our cases there were substantial organizational and project dynamics such as growth followed by downsizing, organizational changes, and numerous project-specific changes of importance for the SPI initiatives. Together, these factors render SPI initiatives based on the CMM mindset into a supertanker that cannot navigate in muddy waters.

The motorboat tactic described in Table 4 was not based on any special theory. The general belief was that a focus on one-size-fits-one would make it possible to set up improvement initiatives where SPI change agents could focus on software engineering needs to assure successful implementation and use. The constantly incoming change requests could be managed, as there were a limited number of stakeholders and, therefore, room for the SPI change agents to sense the ongoing action and respond to changes. The motorboat tactic made it possible to navigate in muddy waters.

The motorboat strategy is a bottom-up approach to improvement. It does, however, not help much in coordinating at the corporate level. One could hope that as people move to new departments and projects, they will bring along their successful processes to new uses and contexts and thereby diffuse new practices. The use of bottom-up strategies may, however, lead to balkanization, confusion, and loss of good experiences in politicized surroundings at the corporate level. Likewise there is no guarantee that bottom-up SPI will result in anything coherent at the corporate level within reasonable time. Great ideas at the local level may not compute at the global level.

Haeckel (1995) offers an elegant solution to the possible conflict between the local and the global. Where the CMM mindset assumes that processes at the global and local level are modeled using similar language (i.e., modeling the local process as a specialization of a global process), the agility mindset lends itself to separate thinking at the two levels. At the local level—the team or project level—procedures and methods are instrumental in negotiating and using common practices. At the global level—the corporate or organizational level—we can adopt Haeckel's ideas, pointing to values, governing principles, and governance models as instrumental in building a common ground for local and global improvement efforts and practices.

Such an agile strategy combines reactive and proactive change proficiency in building efficient and adaptive development processes. It is always important to include efficiency into thinking about SPI practices. In a changing environment, it is, however, as we argue in this paper, equally important to introduce and practice an adaptive mindset. Haeckel (1995) offers governance mechanisms that support enterprise design without leading to command and control structures, but still building corporate coherence in action.

Further research is needed to understand potential combinations of volume, push, pull, target, success, tactic, complexity, etc. for SPI initiatives. There is, of course, a possibility that project volume or combination of push and pull have a greater impact on the result than what is foreseen in this study. Based on available data and the framework used for analysis, our results indicate that SPI tactics significantly affect SPI implementation success, and that the motorboat tactic has led to higher implementation success than the supertanker tactic.

6   CONCLUSION

This study explores and analyzes 18 different SPI initiatives within the telecom company Ericsson in Gothenburg, Sweden. Four attributes— (1) improvement set-up, (2) process creation, (3) process diffusion, and (4) navigation ability—help us identify two different SPI tactics, the motorboat and the supertanker. The supertanker tactic follows a CMM mindset, while the motorboat tactic builds on agile ideas. There is no recognized SPI model supporting the motorboat tactic and this study identifies a need for such. We suggest that a combination of motorboat tactics and modified supertanker tactics is key to successful SPI. We need more research—empirical as well as theoretical—investigating how to build SPI agility by combining bottom-up improvements into coherent practices at the corporate level. Specifically, we need to further investigate *how* adaptive governance approaches and principles on the corporate level can ensure appropriate levels of overall coherence and efficiency.

REFERENCES

Aaen, I. "Challenging Software Process Improvement by Design," in *Proceedings of 10th European Conference on Information Systems* (Volume 1), S. Wrycza (Ed.), Gdansk, Poland, 2002, pp. 379-390.

Abrahamson, P., Salo, O., Ronkainen, J., and Warsta, J. *Agile Software Development Methods: Review and Analysis*, Oulu, Finland: VTT Electronics: Publication #478, 2002 (available online through http://www.inf.vtt.fi/pdf/).

Bartunek, J. M., and Louis, M. R. *Insider/Outsider Team Research*, Thousand Oaks, CA: Sage Publications, 1996.

Baskerville, R., Levine, L., Pries-Heje, J., Ramesh, B., and Slaughter, S. "How Internet Software Companies Negotiate Quality," *Computer* (34:5), 2001, pp. 51-57.

Baskerville, R., and Pries-Heje, J. "Grounded Action Research: A Method for Understanding IT in Practice," *Accounting, Management and Information Technologies* (9:1), 1999, pp. 1-23.

Beck, K. *Extreme Programming Explained: Embrace Change*, Reading, MA: Addison-Wesley, 2000.

Beck, K., Beedle, M., van Bennekum, A., Cockburn, A., Cunningham, W., Fowler, M., Grenning, J., Highsmith, J., Hunt, A., Jeffries, R., Kern, J., Marick, B., Martin, R., Mellor, S., Schwaber, K., Sutherland, J., and Thomas, D. "Manifesto for Agile Software Development," 2001 (available online at http://www.agilemanifesto.org).

Börjesson, A., and Mathiassen, L. "Making SPI Happen: The Road to Process Implementation," in *Proceedings of the 12th European Conference on Information Systems*, T. Leino, T. Saarinen, and S. Klein (Eds.), Turku School of Economics and Business Administration, Turku, Finland, 2004a.

Börjesson, A., and Mathiassen, L. "Organization Dynamics in Software Process Improvement: The Agility Challenge," in *IT Innovation for Adaptablity and Competitiveness*, B. Fitzgerald and E. Wynn (Eds.), Boston: Kluwer Academic Publishers, 2004b, pp. 135-156.

Börjesson, A., and Mathiassen, L./ "Successful Process Implementation," *IEEE Software* (21:4), 2004c, pp. 36-44.

CMMI Product Team. *CMMI for Software Engineering, Version 1.1, Continuous Representation (CMMI-SW, V1.1, Continuous)*, Pittsburgh, PA: Software Engineering Institute Technical Report CMU/SEI-2002-TR-028,), pp. 2002a (available online at http://www.sei.cmu.edu/publications/documents/02.reports/02tr028.html).

CMMI Product Team. *CMMI for Software Engineering, Version 1.1, Staged Representation (CMMI-SW, V1.1, Staged)*, Pittsburgh, PA: Software Engineering Institute Technical Report CMU/SEI-2002-TR-029, 2002b (available online at http://www.sei.cmu.edu/publications/documents/02.reports/02tr029.html).

Creech, B. *The Five Pillars of TQM: How to Make Total Quality Management Work for You*, New York: Truman Talley Books/Dutton, 1994.

Dove, R. *Response Ability: The Language, Structure, and Culture of the Agile Enterprise*, New York: Wiley, 2001.

Fayad, M. E., and Laitinen, M. "Thinking Objectively: Process Assessment Considered Wasteful," *Communications of the ACM* (40:11), 1997, pp. 125-128.

Feiler, P. H., and Humphrey, W. S. *Software Process Development and Enactment: Concepts and Definitions*, Pittsburgh, PA, Software Engineering Institute, 1991.

Fowler, P., and Rifkin, S. *Software Engineering Process Group Guide*, Pittsburgh, PA: Software Engineering Institute, 1990.

Galliers, R. D. "Choosing an Information Systems Research Approach," in *Information Systems Research: Issues, Methods, and Practical Guidelines*, R. D. Galliers (Ed.), Oxford: Blackwell Scientific Publications, 1992, pp. 144-162.

Grady, R. B. *Successful Software Process Improvement*, Upper Saddle River, NJ: Prentice Hall, 1997.

Gunneson, A. O. *Transitioning to Agility: Creating the 21st Century Enterprise*, Reading, MA: Addison-Wesley, 1997.

Haeckel, S. H. *Adaptive Enterprise: Creating and Leading Sense-and-Respond Organizations*. Boston: Harvard Business School Press, 1999.

Haeckel, S. H. "Adaptive Enterprise Design: The Sense-and-Respond Model," *Planning Review* (23:3), 1995, pp. 6-13, 42.

Holmberg, L., and Mathiassen, L. "Survival Patterns in Fast-Moving Software Organizations," *IEEE Software* (18:6), 2001, pp. 51-55.

Humphrey, W. S. *Managing the Software Process*, Reading, MA: Addison-Wesley Publishing Company, 1989.

Kautz, K., Hansen, H. W., and Thaysen, K. "Understanding and Changing Software Organizations: An Exploration of Four Perspectives on Software Process Improvement," *Scandinavian Journal of Information Systems* (13), 2001, pp. 31-50.

Kondo, Y. "Innovation Versus Standardization," *TQM Magazine* (12:1), 2000, pp. 6-10.

Mathiassen, L. "Collaborative Practice Research," *Information, Technology & People* (15:4), 2002, pp. 321-334.

Mathiassen, L., Pries-Heje, J., and Ngwenyama, O. *Improving Software Organizations*, Boston: Addison-Wesley, 2002.

McFeeley, B. *IDEAL: A User's Guide for Software Process Improvement*, Pittsburgh, PA: Software Engineering Institute Handbook CMU/SEI-96-HB-001, 1996 (available online at http://www.sei.cmu.edu/publications/documents/96.reports/96.hb.001.html).

Mingers, J. "Combining IS Research Methods: Towards a Pluralist Methodology," *Information Systems Research* (12:3), 2001, pp. 240-259.

Orlikowski, W. J. "Improvising Organizational Transformation Over Time: A Situated Change Perspective," *Information Systems Research* (7:1), 1996, pp. 63-92.

Osterweil, L. J. "Software Processes Are Software Too," in *Proceedings of the 9th International Conference on Software Engineering*, Los Alamitos, CA: IEEE Computer Society Press, 1987.

Osterweil, L. J. "Software Processes Are Software Too, Revisited," in *Proceedings of the 19th International Conference on Software Engineering*, Los Alamitos: IEEE Computer Society Press, 1997.

Paulk, M. C., Curtis, B., Chrissis, M. B., and Weber, C. V. *Capability Maturity Model for Software, Version 1.1*, Pittsburgh, PA: Software Engineering Institute, 1993.

Paulk, M. C., Weber, C. V., Curtis, B., and Chrissis, M. B. *The Capability Maturity Model: Guidelines for Improving the Software Process*, Reading, MA: Addison-Wesley Publishing Company, 1995.

Paulk, M. C., Weber, C. V., Garcia, S. M., Chrissis, M., and Bush, M. *Key Practices of the Capability Maturity Model, Version 1.1*, Pittsburgh, PA: Software Engineering Institute, 1993.

Pries-Heje, J., and Tryde, S. "Diffusion and Adoption of IT Products and Processes in a Danish Bank," in *Diffusing Software Products and Process Innovations*, M. A. Ardis and B. L. Marcolin (Eds.), Boston: Kluwer Academic Publishers, 2001, pp. 17-34.

Rogers, E. M. *Diffusion of Innovations*, New York: The Free Press, 2003.

Scherr, A. L. "A New Approach to Business Processes," *IBM Systems Journal* (32:1), 1993, pp. 80-98.

Walsham, G. "Interpretive Case-Studies in IS Research: Nature and Method," *European Journal of Information Systems* (4:2), 1995, pp. 74-81.

Weick, K. E., and Quinn, R. E. "Organizational Change and Development," *Annual Review of Psychology* (50), 1999, 361-86.

Weinberg, G. M. *Quality Software Management: Volume 4, Anticipating Change*, New York: Dorset House Publishing, 1997

Yin, R. K. *Case Study Research: Design and Methods*, Thousand Oaks, CA: Sage Publications, 1994

Zmud, R. W. "An Examination of 'Push-Pull' Theory Applied to Process Innovation in Knowledge Work," *Management Science* (30:6), 1984, pp. 727-738.

ABOUT THE AUTHORS

Ivan Aaen is an associate professor of Computer Science at Aalborg University, Denmark. His interests include software engineering and information systems. He holds a Ph.D. in Computer Science from Aalborg University and is a member of the ACM and IEEE Computer Society. Ivan can be reached at aaen@acm.org.

Anna Börjesson is a software process improvement manager at Ericsson AB in Gothenburg, Sweden, and an industrial Ph.D. student at the IT University in Gothenburg. She has over 10 years of software engineering working experience. More than 7 of those years have been dedicated to SPI, change management, and diffusion of innovations. Anna is a member of IEEE and ACM. She can be reached at anna.borjesson@ericsson.com.

Lars Mathiassen is Georgia Research Alliance Eminent Scholar and Professor in Computer Information Systems at Georgia State University. His research interests focus on engineering and management of IT systems. In particular, he has worked with project management, object-orientation, organizational development, management of IT, and the philosophy of computing. Lars can be reached at lmathiassen@gsu.edu.

APPENDIX[1]

#	Improvement Area	Volume	Target	Process Push	Practice Pull	Implementation Success	SPI Tactic
1	Configuration Management	10 weeks 300 person hours 4 participants	Several units	Weak	Weak	Low. The result was considered hard to use. Part of the knowledge gained was used indirectly in other projects.	Supertanker
2	Design Information	21 weeks 400 person hours 6 participants	Several units	Weak	Weak	Medium/Low. The intention was to provide a framework for design. The results were mainly implemented in one project.	Supertanker
3	Estimation and Planning	14 weeks 600 person hours 11 participants	Several units	Weak	Medium	Low. The results were tried out in one project, but it ran into difficulties. Support was weak, and no one helped the project.	Supertanker
4	Historical Data	16 weeks 200 person hours 4 participants	Several units	Weak	Weak	Low. The purpose was to build a database of old data and take action from there, but no interesting data were found.	Supertanker
5	Introductory training	14 weeks 620 person hours 11 participants	Several units	Weak	Strong	Medium. An estimated 50% of managers used the process. Some did not know about it and were not given the opportunity to learn about it.	Supertanker
6	Module Test	12 weeks 400 person hours 10 participants	Several units	Weak	Weak	Medium/Low. The process was used when process engineers were members of a project or when section managers strongly believed in systematic module tests.	Supertanker
7	Project Tracking	9 weeks 300 person hours 7 participants	Several units	Weak	Weak	Medium/Low. The process was used in one project supported by the driver of the SPI initiative.	Supertanker

[1]The table in this Appendix is adapted from Börjesson and Mathiassen (2004c).

#	Improvement Area	Volume	Target	Process Push	Practice Pull	Implementation Success	SPI Tactic
8	Resource Handling	4 weeks 250 person hours 8 participants	Several units	Weak	Medium	Medium. An estimated 75% of managers used the new process. Non-users either did not get the help they needed or did not believe in the approach.	Supertanker
9	Requirements Management	10 weeks 200 person hours 5 participants	Several units	Weak	Weak	Low. The results were hard to use. The members of the SPI initiative mainly used the results as a framework.	Supertanker
10	Requirements Management Implementation	12 weeks 330 person hours 7 participants	Project	Strong	Weak	Medium. The initiative was started because of the low impact of initiative #9. The focus was on one project to suit its needs.	Supertanker
11	Subcontract Management	18 weeks 650 person hours 9 participants	Several units	Weak	Weak	Low. The results needed further adaptation to be useful for different projects, but no effort was made.	Supertanker
12	Requirements Management	30 weeks 1,200 person hours 3 participants	Project	Strong	Strong	High. The process was adapted to a specific project, but needed further adaptation. Process engineers and practitioners solved these problems jointly.	Motorboat
13	Analysis & Design	30 weeks 1,000 person hours 4 participants	Unit	Strong	Strong	Medium/High. This complex area required several iterations of experimenting with processes before the result was satisfactory.	Motorboat
14	Implementation	30 weeks 1,000 person hours 4 participants	Project	Strong	Strong	High. Two slightly different adaptations were made to fit the needs of different products developed on different sites.	Motorboat
15	Test	30 weeks 1,300 person hours 2 participants	Unit	Strong	Strong	High. The result was adapted to a specific project. Process engineers and practitioners solved difficulties together.	Motorboat

#	Improvement Area	Volume	Target	Process Push	Practice Pull	Implementation Success	SPI Tactic
16	Configuration Management	30 weeks 1,650 person hours 6 participants	Unit	Strong	Strong	High. There are many possible solutions for each specific situation. Attention was required to choose one. The dedication of the practitioners was key.	Motorboat
17	Project Management	10 weeks 150 person hours 2 participants	Unit	Strong	Strong	High. The results were used and the project managers' dedication to SPI within project management continued.	Motorboat
18	Process Development Map	30 weeks 200 person hours 2 participants	Unit	Strong	Strong	High. The use of the map is measured in both "hits" and subjective opinions of the need. Measurements are very positive.	Motorboat

5 MAPPING SOCIAL NETWORKS IN SOFTWARE PROCESS IMPROVEMENT: An Action Research Study

Peter Axel Nielsen
Gitte Tjørnehøj
Aalborg University
Aalborg, Denmark

Abstract   *Software process improvement in small, agile organizations is often problematic. Model-based approaches seem to overlook problems. We have been seeking an alternative approach to overcome this through action research. Here we report on a piece of action research from which we developed an approach to map social networks and suggest how it can be used in software process improvement. We applied the mapping approach in a small software company to support the realization of new ways of improving software processes. The mapping approach was found useful in improving social networks, and thus furthers software process improvement.*

Keywords   Software process improvement, agile software development, social network analysis, action research, collaborative practice research

1   INTRODUCTION

Software process improvement (SPI) has long been a concern for software producing companies and researchers. The development of the capability maturity model (CMM) by the Software Engineering Institute sparked a huge interest in the field. The first reports on CMM and similar models were promising; however, in later years an increasing number of failures have been reported by Hansen et al. (2004). According to Hansen et al., very little research on SPI is reflective and critical. The CMM can be taken to be a prototypical example of the formal and model-based approaches. CMM requires many improvements and also improvements of significant complexity (Aaen et al. 2001), and according to Ngwenyama and Nielsen (2003) SW-CMM in particular is based on a rational ideal and the idea of the rational culture for software development.

A small software company, called AlphaSoft here for anonymity, where we conducted the action research, is an organization with fewer than 50 software developers. Along with the company, we have a knowledge interest in software development and SPI in small software companies. Other SPI researchers have a similar interest. Within the SPI community, there has long been the concern that the better known approaches, such as CMM, are not adequate for the improvement issues in small software companies. An early survey shows major concerns that the CMM does not fit small software companies (Brodman and Johnson 1994). There is some agreement on the particular problems facing small companies pursuing SPI: low likelihood of investment in improvement, poor fit with small-company culture, lack of SPI knowledge, lack of action planning, and more sensitivity to changing environments (Cater-Steel 2001; Kelly and Culleton 1999; Villalon et al. 2002; Ward et al. 2001).

Recently, there have been several attempts to develop and test new SPI approaches for small software companies. Some software companies choose to improve software processes in a less formal and less model-driven way. For example, in Kelly and Culleton's (1999) research, company S3 chose an approach informed by the CMM, but based on alternative principles: (1) maximize involvement, minimize disruption; (2) stress quality, not CMM compliance; (3) emphasize the advisory role; and (4) promote efficiency. Reporting on similar efforts, Iversen et al. (1999) and Nielsen et al. (2002) primarily focus on alleviating problems experienced rather than finding discrepancies between software practices and process-maturity models. Villalon et al. (2002) suggest an action package concept to overcome lack of follow-through into action planning and action plan implementation, particularly in small software companies. Richardson (2002) suggests utilizing quality function deployment and has developed a device called the software process matrix to determine the relationships between processes and practices.

Small software companies often face changing environments and, therefore, can easily be more vulnerable than large companies. Ward et al. (2001), addressing software development in small companies, suggest that "the processes by which software is developed are likely to change with circumstances—perhaps even change dramatically—even while general principles like the need for good communication remain constant" (p. 105). Within SPI, Börjesson and Mathiassen (2004) have addressed this desired agility and conclude that, for software development, the agility challenge comprises the need to

- Handle changes in customers' requirements
- Be aware of and respond to technological changes and innovations as well as changes in the market
- Implement software process improvement

Most small software companies focus on the first two challenges. Börjesson and Mathiassen, furthermore, state that an agile software organization needs to balance and coordinate development, improvement and innovation. However, all of these studies on SPI in small software companies found that that is exactly what these companies are *not* doing. They prioritize development over improvement.

Through action research, we are collaborating with a small software company. For almost a year, we joined efforts in trying to follow the rational ideal informed by model-based assessments. Several improvement initiatives suffered premature death and the effort was eventually brought to a halt. Recently, we have tried to recover the SPI process by following an alternative route in which we map social networks, among others. Our initial interest in social networks came partly from the practical desire to understand whether AlphaSoft had an appropriate foundation for a less management-driven SPI approach, and partly from the knowledge that organizational influence processes are hugely important in SPI (Nielsen and Ngwenyama 2002).

Social network analysis is presented in section 2. In section 3, we outline our research approach and in particular we focus on the research process. That leads us to section 4, where we present how we mapped social networks in AlphaSoft and the experience gained from this. In section 5, we discuss the usefulness of the mapping approach in SPI and the implications for SPI and research. The paper ends with section 6, where we draw our conclusions. Altogether, in this paper we address the research question: *To what extent and in which ways is the mapping of social networks useful in SPI in a small company?*

2 SOCIAL NETWORK ANALYSIS

Social network analysis is a framework and a set of techniques applied to study the relationships between organizational actors and their exchange of resources. Organizations are viewed as consisting of actors linked together in networks through action, exchange, and interpretation and sharing of resources such as information and knowledge. Actors are viewed as interdependent. There are relational ties between actors through which resources are exchanged. Network models conceptualize structure as lasting patterns of relational ties (Wasserman and Faust 1994). Wasserman and Faust further define actors as discrete individual, corporate, or collective social units (i.e., not only as a single person). The relational ties can be of varying types: evaluation of one person by another (as with friendship), transfer of material resources, affiliation, authority (as between managers and subordinates), and behavioral interaction, like sending messages and engaging in a discussion (Wasserman and Faust 1994, p. 18).

Social network analysis is not a new approach. It has been developed and applied in a large number of organizational studies. (For historical accounts, see Scott 2000; Tichy et al. 1979; Wasserman and Faust 1994.) The framework does not give the unit of analysis and data may be collected about many different kinds of actors and relational ties. It is, however, common to collect data about the contents of the relational ties as well as their intensity and reciprocity. Having collected the data, the approach requires the study of network properties and structural characteristics are considered crucial. The structural characteristics are, for example, network size, density, clustering, reachability, centrality, star, liaison, bridge and gatekeeper. Tichy et al. (1979) define these as

- Density: the number of actual relational ties in the network as a ratio of the number of possible relational ties
- Centrality: the degree to which relations are guided by the formal organization
- Star: the individual with the highest number of relational ties (also called the central actor)

These are just a few of the analyses that can be performed on the total network. The analyses all have a foundation is graph theory (Borgatti and Everett 1992; Scott 2000; Wasserman and Faust 1994), but the interpretation and the semantic implication of these analyses remain specific to the setting where the data were collected.

Social network analysis has been applied in information systems research. Zack (2000) argues that social network analysis can be used to explore the impact of information systems on organizational forms. Temdee and Korba (2001) apply social network analysis to measure the appropriateness of computer-based systems supporting cooperative work. In studies of computer-supported collaborative learning, social network analysis has been applied to logs of interaction between learners (Martínez et al. 2003). Social network analysis has also been used in the study of exchange of information (Haythornthwaite 1996).

Our application of social network analysis focuses on the social networks through which software process improvement may happen. We have chosen to apply interactional analysis. Tichy et al. claim that it is easy to gather data for interactional analysis and that it has all the benefits of the other analyses (positional, reputational, and decisional). They describe interactional analysis as an approach that focuses on interactions, influence, feedback and power.

3   ACTION RESEARCH APPROACH

The research is part of a national research project on software process improvement and knowledge management. The project involves three software companies and researchers from three research institutions. The research approach has been action research of the type that is called collaborative practice research (Iversen et al. 2004; Mathiassen 2002). Collaborative practice research is action research supplemented with field experiments and practice studies.

A software process improvement project was created in AlphaSoft as an action research project. Serving a dual purpose is a core characteristic of action research (Hult and Lennung 1980; McKay and Marshall 2001). In this case, the researchers' intervention in AlphaSoft served the dual purpose of collaborative problem solving focused on software processes and contributing to SPI research. Action research was chosen because it was the intention to create immediate linkage between theories and practice for the benefit of practical problem solving and for the benefit of testing and building practice-based theories. Action research at its best does exactly that: it validates findings through immediate action.

The research reported in this paper is a small part of the whole collaborative practice research effort. The action research process follows the process outlined by Iversen et al. (2004) and McKay and Marshall (2001).

The action research process is specifically directed at assessing the usefulness of mapping social networks in SPI in a small software company. We did not design this process before, or even at the beginning of, our intervention. The process came about after several unsuccessful attempts at facilitating improvement of the software processes in AlphaSoft. The appreciation of the problem situation led to a study of the relevant literature (see section 1). We realized only gradually that social network analysis might

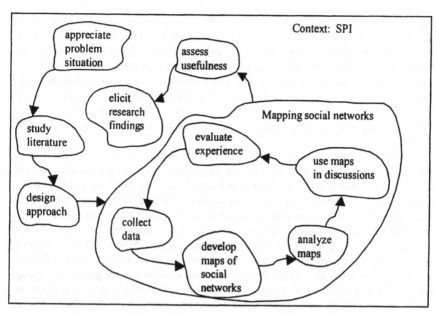

Figure 1. The Action Research Process (based on
Iversen et al. (2004) and McKay and Marshall (2001))

offer insights that our clients, and we, needed. That led us to study the literature on social network analysis (see section 2). Based on this, we designed an approach through which we could collect the necessary data, develop the maps of social networks, analyze the maps, use the maps in discussions and evaluate the resulting experience (see Figure 1). In the following sections, we present the applied approach: a description of the situation that we entered (section 4.1); the data collection (section 4.2); the different maps and how they were developed (sections 4.3, 4.4, and 4.5); the action researchers' analysis of the maps (section 4.6); and the use of the maps in a discussion with an SPI manager and the joint evaluation of the experience (section 4.7).

The action research and the mapping approach was later assessed in terms of the six criteria form Iversen et al.: roles, documentation, control, usefulness, theory, and transfer (see section 5).

4 MAPPING SOCIAL NETWORKS IN SPI

The mapping of social networks followed the approach in Figure 1.

4.1 The Situation Appreciated

AlphaSoft is a small software company with two departments. The ERP department develops a large ERP system and maintains it at a number of customer sites. The tasks are characterized by long-term and close contacts with few customers. The software developers have much domain knowledge within logistics in the particular area where their customers operate. The head of this department is also responsible for the quality system and the ISO9000 certificate. He was a key actor in the SPI group, where the head of the tailor-made department was also a member. The tailor-made department develops several tailored systems for many different customers. Their products range from traditional administrative systems to Web portals. The application domains vary and the developers' primary expertise lies within software engineering and project management.

Previously, improvements in software development were informal and spread through collaboration and informal contacts with colleagues. A few significant improvements attracted management's attention and were taken to be company improvements. One such improvement even turned into an internal software development project. Most improvements, however, remained personal or local between a few colleagues.

When the action research began, the company was introduced to basic SPI approaches and soon top management announced the slogan "CMM level three—in three years." This is a quite common slogan for newcomers to SPI. An SPI group was formed and a developer from each of the departments was appointed to the group. The group took on the responsibility of assessing the current practices, planning improvement initiatives, and implementing these. Successful improvements were also supposed to be added to the existing quality system. The manager of the ERP department later characterized the whole set-up as a complete failure. His perception is that some developers felt pushed aside and that others stopped focusing on improvements, waiting for the results from the SPI group. The group lacked time and resources and organized only one improvement initiative. Add to this market decline and consequently low sales figures, which led the company to shift its focus toward sales work and the monthly sales figures.

Despite these setbacks, AlphaSoft's management recognized the value of their previous improvements as vital for their business success and found it necessary to proceed. The two department managers' perception was that future improvements must be rooted in a strategy that provides faster feedback as well as visible and immediate benefits for software developers. It was in this atmosphere that the mapping of social networks was initiated.

4.2 Social Network Analysis of SPI

For the purpose of mapping social networks, we collected the data following the principles of the interactional methods in social network analysis (see section 2). The data consist of developers' and managers' individual perceptions of their communication on issues of improvement in the company during the last six months in retrospect. They were asked to identify and characterize the communication as they remembered it. For each interaction, they were asked to assess whether the communication had been

- Formal or informal
- Written or oral
- Downward, upward, or lateral

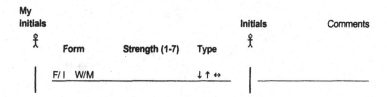

Figure 2. Graphical Questionnaire (Extract)

The first two we refer to as the form of communication. The last refers to the direction of the organizational influence as described by Kotter (1983). The developers and managers were also asked to assess the weight of the communication on a scale from 1 to 7 where 1 is very low (e.g., receiving an e-mail) and 7 is very high (e.g., collaboration or continuous dialogue). We developed a graphical questionnaire as an aid to be filled in by the developers and the managers (see the extract, Figure 2).

We loaded the data into NetDraw. NetDraw is a tool for social network analysis that can display graphs with actors as nodes and relationships as edges. Both nodes and edges can have attributes. The data is stored as an Ucinet dataset and can be loaded directly into the tool.

The tool offers various display features and analyses automatically performed by graph algorithms. We used the tool to analyze and keep an overview of the data (e.g., to select parts of the graph, show different attributes and weights, identify central actor, cut-point, etc.) using graphical elements to visualize structures in the social networks. We performed a systematic analysis of the data to elucidate the following network structures:

- Centrality, peaks, and blocks
- Components, k-cores, and cut-points
- Ego-networks, distribution of strengths, form, and influence in the social networks

In the presentation of the maps that follows we focus on the most important structural features disregarding maps that were neither important nor relevant in understanding the specific SPI effort in AlphaSoft.

4.3 The Basic Map

We chose a basic map as a starting point and maintained the same layout in all maps in order to increase visual comparability.

The basic map of social networks is shown in Figure 3. Diamonds are actors in the ERP department; circles are actors in the tailor-made department; actors are numbered for anonymity; managers are prefixed with an M; M-9 is the CEO. The basic map shows only one *component*, as a path exists between all actors with at least one tie. The ties between the two departments are few, but within the departments the networks are dense and almost evenly distributed. M-19 is the *central actor* as he is the actor with the highest degree, i.e., the numbers of ties: (11). M-19 is also a *peak* as he is more central

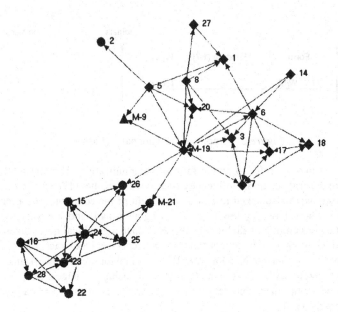

Figure 3. Basic Map of Social Network of SPI Activity

than any other actor to which he is connected. Developer #6, although highly connected with a degree of 8, is not a peak as he is connected directly to M-19. This is not surprising as M-19 is the manager of the ERP department and responsible for the quality system, the ISO9000 certificate, and a key actor in the SPI group. He is connected to the top manager, M-9, and all connections between the ERP department and tailor-made goes through him.

M-21, the manager of the tailor-made department, is far from central and not a peak. He shares the contact with the ERP department with developer #26. In the tailor-made department, developer #24, with a degree of 8, is the only peak and he is connected to all in the department. The path from any of the managers to any of their developers is less than or equal to 2 edges. In the ERP department, this is due to the central role of the manager, and in the tailor-made department, to developer #24.

4.4 The Maps of *3k*-Cores, Cut-Points and Components

Figure 4 shows three maps that contribute to the understanding of the overall social networks. The 3k-core displays the actors with a degree greater than or equal to 3. This map is not significantly different from the basic map as only three developers in the ERP department are cut out. The 3k-core map shows the connectivity of the network and that the inner coherence of the company seems relatively strong. Actors M-19 and #5 are *cut-points* because if just one is removed from the network it will break into two components. Developer #5 is a marginal cut-point as he will only cut out one other actor. M-19, on the other hand, is important because he is the cut-point between the ERP depart-

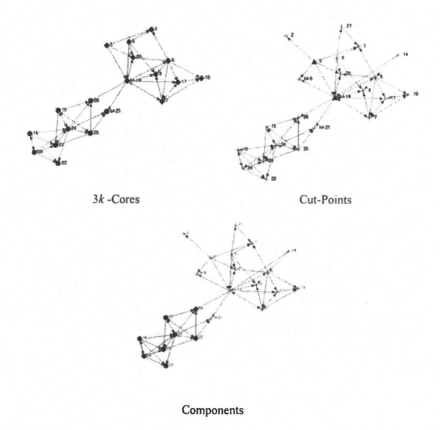

3*k* -Cores   Cut-Points

Components

Figure 4. Three Different Maps Based on Graph Analysis

ment and the tailor-made department. The components map shows a similar tendency for the network to break into two since the two identified components coincide with the departments. The only exception to this is that manager M-21 of the tailor-made department, from a graph theoretical viewpoint, has a stronger tie to the ERP department than to his own department.

4.5 The Maps of Attributes

Figure 5 shows the attributes of communication. Communication is mostly informal and all actors are involved in informal communication. Formal communication is only found around the two peaks and between the two departments. Written communication department has a stronger presence in the tailor-made department and around the manager of the ERP department. Oral communication is widespread and every actor participates in oral communication. It is worth noticing that communication between the departments is formal but oral.

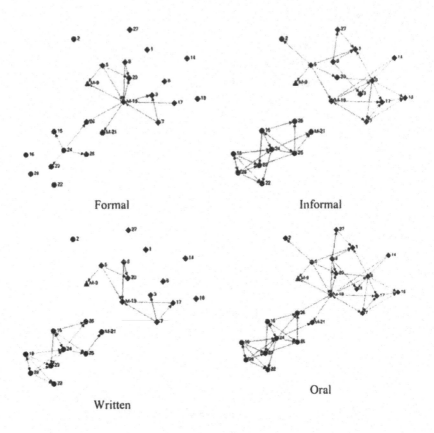

Formal

Informal

Written

Oral

Figure 5. The Maps of Attributes in the Social Networks

Figure 6 shows two maps resulting from analysis of weights. The highest weights map shows the highest weight reported for all ties. Overall, the high weights seem evenly distributed over the departments, but weights are rather low between the departments. The only communication of weight 7 is between the manager of the ERP department and developer #6 (who is very well connected in that department). The rest of the ties involving M-19 are somewhat weaker. If developer #6 and M-19 are both removed from the map, the department falls apart; they are the backbone of the department.

4.6 The Researchers' Analysis

We, the action researchers, produced the following analysis of all of the maps. This analysis was presented to the SPI manager during the next step in the approach.

The overall picture of social networks shows two departments with an informal, mostly oral and widespread interaction within the departments, but with sparse contact

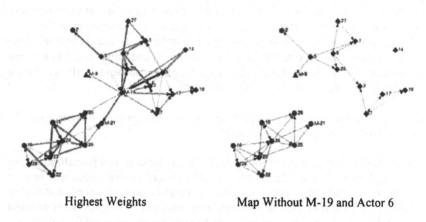

Highest Weights   Map Without M-19 and Actor 6

Figure 6. Two Maps Based on Analysis of Weights

between departments and to top management. The ERP department has a central manager, M-19, "gatekeeping" the department against all the other actors in the company in a more formalistic way than usual in the company. He controls the communication on improvements both within his own department and also at the management level and he is the only middle manager with contact to the top management.

The tailor-made department seems to have an internal central player in developer #24 keeping the department together and communicating intensively with many. The manager of the department, M-21, only plays a small role in SPI as he has few ties and partakes in lightweight communication. He only connects to the whole department through developers #24 and #25. It looks like widespread delegation of responsibility for SPI.

Misfits between the underlying social networks and a centralized strategy largely explain the failure of the previous centralized SPI initiative. The underlying social networks are uneven and, in the ERP department, developers are unaccustomed to written communication, while in the tailor-made department, the networks are lateral thus less disposed to acting on formal management directive. A centralized strategy is management-driven, communicated in writing, and formal. Either the social networks must change or another strategy must be chosen.

The following ought to concern an SPI manager wanting to embark on an alternative strategy for SPI:

- The remarkably weak ties between the two departments certainly are a hindrance for the central and cross-departmental SPI approach.

- A serious management commitment to SPI will be very difficult to exercise with so little communication on SPI involving the top manager. Maybe the lack of management involvement shows that SPI is not of strategic importance to the company's business strategy.

- As long as only sparse and formal ties through managers connect the two departments, few improvements will spread easily from one department to the other. Closer ties need to be built between the two departments and at the level of the developers. If this seems impossible or undesirable, one could choose to view the departments as separate social networks and organize independent SPI activities in both, deliberately decreasing knowledge sharing.

- Any SPI initiative in AlphaSoft will benefit from stronger collaboration among the managers and with the CEO involved.

- The ERP department could benefit from decentralization, less formalization, and delegation of responsibilities. M-19 could very well be overloaded with responsibilities. If that is the case, he is a bottleneck that stops improvements and hinders knowledge sharing and communication in the company. Management commitment to SPI is based on real involvement and focus, not too much work, and too few resources to deal with it. On the other hand, rather than aiming at central control, AlphaSoft could base this control on mutual adjustment between peers.

- The analyses do not display network structures that hinder ideas and improvements from being communicated among peers (except for the weak ties between departments).

4.7 The Discussion with the SPI Manager

A session with the SPI manager, M-19, was organized to present the maps and the researchers' analysis. The main purpose of this session was to push the SPI initiative forward by helping the company to discuss possible ways to support SPI through their social networks. The session followed this agenda:

1. Present and validate the maps of social networks
2. Present the researchers' analysis
3. Discuss the analysis
4. Facilitate the manager's own analysis of the maps
5. Decide which actions should be taken

The maps were presented and explained to the manager as done in sections 4.2 through 4.5. This part of the session was primarily dedicated to the validation of the data underneath the maps. For example, the manager wondered if it was differences in understanding the questionnaire that led to the big difference in written communication between the two departments—or if that really could be the case. He also noticed that a developer with whome he had worked closely was peripheral in the social network—and he wondered why. He found both well-known structures in the maps and surprising structures. It was concluded that the data were sufficiently valid for the present session, but that similar sessions involving more managers and developers should be based on a broader coverage of actors.

Next, the researchers presented their analysis of the maps as done in section 4.6. This led to a discussion of both the extent to which the analysis fitted the manager's understanding and the possible ways of supporting SPI through social networks in future. Throughout, the manager listened to the outside view and studied the maps. Gradually, the discussion led the manager to formulate new views on the social networks, and suggestions for how to proceed with SPI.

The discussion did not lead to a specific plan for the next SPI initiative, but it did lead to the recognition that the company needed to work more on analyzing the situation to become successful with the new SPI initiatives. On the one hand, a pure centralized SPI strategy had not worked in the past. On the other hand, a pure peer-driven strategy may not fit the company either. Maybe a mixed strategy could be implemented, but in either case the existing social networks would be insufficient and a change process would have to be considered.

The actions agreed upon were

- Increase the data coverage by making sure that all actors responded to the questionnaire. The mapping of social networks should even be extended to cover the third department, which so far had not been engaged in SPI.

- Immediately organize a similar session with the department managers, M-19 and M-21, and the CEO, M-9. The discussion should be based on the broader coverage.

- Plan, prepare, and realize a seminar for the entire company where the maps were again discussed. The intention should be to arrive at suggestions for how to improve the social networks to form a better foundation for SPI.

5 DISCUSSION

In the discussion of the approach to mapping social networks, we first focus on the validity of the research, then on the approach itself, the lessons we have learned about it, and its usefulness in SPI. Second, we focus on the wider research implications and how the approach relates to the existing research on SPI in small and agile companies. Together the discussion covers the six criteria for evaluating action research found in Iversen et al. (2004): roles, documentation, control, usefulness, theory, and transfer. For brevity, only the latter three are emphasized.

5.1 Usefulness and Lessons Learned

Let us first establish the basis for the action research in terms of the criteria from Iversen et al.

- *Roles:* Two researchers were active in the research reported here. Both researchers had been involved in the collaboration with the company at the time the idea of social network analysis was introduced. The researchers were responsible for developing the approach and for carrying out most activities. They facilitated the activities "use maps in discussions" and "evaluate experience" with the SPI manager as the main contributor.

- *Documentation:* Data about the action research (not to be confused with the data about social networks) were collected by the researchers through the maps (as in Figures 3 through 6), and the analyses of maps documented in the researchers' notes and diaries from their meetings with the SPI managers.

- *Control:* The use of social network analysis was initiated by the researchers, but came about during existing collaboration between the researchers and the software company. Authority remained at all times with the company's SPI managers. The action research was governed by an overall contract committing the researchers and the company to collaborate on SPI, but the contract was not detailed and did not stipulate the use of social network analysis.

We have assessed the usefulness of mapping social networks in SPI based on the criterion that the actors acknowledged that learning had occurred, insights had been gained, or even that actions had been taken. In using this pragmatic criterion we concur with several action researchers (e.g., Checkland 1981; Mathiassen 2002).

First, the two researchers and the SPI manager all found that the session in which they used the maps of social networks was valuable. The session advanced the SPI process in several ways.

- The participants came away with a sense of progress similar to that experienced in all problem solving when a better problem definition is reached (explained well by Schön 1983).

- A profound understanding was reached during the session—more profound than what had previously emerged implicitly in discussions among the researchers and the SPI manager.

- Decisions were taken—perhaps not radical decisions, but decisions all the same—that had the potential for making the SPI activity forward. These decisions led to actions being taken to the effect of first involving the other managers, and later involving all developers, in a similar session.

Second, the SPI manager expressed explicitly that the maps were very useful. Not only did the maps show what he already knew, they also contained angles, pointers, and clues that he had never thought about before. He genuinely found the maps interesting as a kind of mirror in which he could now see his own organization in a new light. This was not expressed out of politeness as he had on several previous occasions expressed dissatisfaction with the researchers' ideas and did not have any academic or theoretical interest.

Third, the two researchers found the approach and the maps useful. The maps aided in understanding why several previous attempts at improving software processes had failed. The maps also indicated how the researchers could become more successful as facilitators of process improvement.

In addition to this general assessment of usefulness, there are a number of specific lessons learned about the approach.

- Maintaining that the maps are a means for discussion and debate among the actors involved is crucial; they do not represent real-world social networks. Hence, the data's objectivity or accuracy is not of paramount importance; it is sufficient that the data reflect actors' perceptions of their communication about improvement.

- The data collection for the maps can be very fast and efficient. In our data collection, we did not cover the entire company, but full coverage could be achieved efficiently. On the other hand, if the data collection becomes too relaxed, the actors involved may not want to discuss the maps, or they will not take action based on the maps. That will seriously jeopardize the mapping approach.

- Collecting data about actors' perceptions of communication with other actors, and even based on the recollection of activity for the last six months, does not signal validity of data. In the validation we experienced, it did not become an issue. On the other hand, it is possible to reduce the reliance on recollection by tracking actors' perceptions of communication over a period.

- The tool we used, NetDraw, has been very helpful in the process. After some initial problems with data formats, it has consistently supported not only the drawing of maps based on the data, but also a number of the most common algorithmic analyses that can be performed on social networks. The tool works well with small amounts of data when there is a need for visualization. It is not likely to be as valuable with large amounts of data, as large social networks are not easy to visualize.

5.2 Implications for SPI in Small Companies

Our mapping approach relates to the existing theories of SPI in small companies in the following ways. First, the mapping of social networks, as in the approach we used at AlphaSoft, seems particularly relevant for understanding SPI activity in small companies. Small software companies are less likely to favor a formal, centralized SPI approach as discussed in the introduction. AlphaSoft conforms to earlier reports (Cater-Steel 2001; Kelly and Culleton 1999; Villalon et al. 2002; Ward et al. 2001) in that

1. They did not want to invest as much in SPI as the companies following the CMM.
2. The formal and centralized SPI approach did not fit their small company culture.
3. They to some extent lacked SPI knowledge.
4. Actions were less planned.
5. They were very sensitive to their changing environment (i.e., market segment changes).

In this setting, mapping fits well as a low-budget approach to assess strengths and weaknesses in the social networks. This is an important part of the infrastructure for informal SPI because such companies lack the economical inclination to invest in a formal, rational, centralized infrastructure. It enables companies to discuss and exploit the possibilities that already exist and to focus on necessary improvements.

Second, the ability to change with a changing environment is an agile property of a software company. The ability to change requires, among other things, well-functioning communication (Ward et al. 2001). It is thus desirable to analyze the social network of communication to ensure this important principle is the basis for constantly changing processes and, hopefully, improvements.

Third, agile software development requires particular activity to implement SPI (Börjesson and Mathiassen 2004), but most small software companies focus on agile properties directly related to development activities (e.g., changing requirements, technology, and innovation). As we see it, changing requirements, technologies, and markets may well demand more improvement. In the small software company, this activity again ought to be supported by the same kind of social networks. Further, Börjesson and Mathiassen state that an agile software organization needs to balance and coordinate development, improvement, and innovation. However, all of the studies of SPI in small software companies mentioned in the introduction found that that is exactly what they are not doing—and with good reasons. Like AlphaSoft, they prioritize development over improvement. Therefore, while studying the social networks of communication about SPI in AlphaSoft, we began to wonder what the networks of development looked like and if we, instead of improving and building SPI social networks, could piggyback on the working, and probably more stable, social networks supporting development. We could map the social networks of communication on development and perhaps investigate if, and how, the small company could do SPI while primarily attending to development.

Our mapping approach could be transferred to other, similar situations. Based on our, so far, limited experience with the mapping approach, we suggest that it will work for small companies, but not large ones. To facilitate discussions that bring the process forward, the maps of social networks must show the networks in a highly visual way that can be grasped by the actors involved without them being experts on social network analysis.

Consideration of whether practitioners can use the approach independently (i.e., without the researchers' presence) is always relevant for approaches stemming from action research. Actors who possess a theoretical and practical competence in social network analysis may develop maps, while those possessing more general process facilitation skills lead the activities in which maps are used to spark discussion.

Very little in the mapping approach is specific to AlphaSoft. The data collection methods and development, analysis, and use of maps in discussions are all transferable to other small, agile software organizations. For these parts, we claim some generality. What cannot be transferred to other organizations are the specific maps, the analyses of AlphaSoft through maps, and the specific outcomes of the discussions. For that, we claim no generality.

6 CONCLUSION

We have tried here to answer the research question: *To what extent and in which ways is the mapping of social networks useful in SPI in a small company?* In this paper, we have addressed this by outlining an approach for mapping social networks that may be used in SPI initiatives. Through action research, we have shown how we used the approach in AlphaSoft, and we have discussed its usefulness, relation to theory in the field, and circumstances under which it may be transferred to other situations.

There are several limitations in our action research and use of social network analysis. Further research needs to be done to

1. Improve the mapping approach, particularly how to efficiently collect valid data and decide which maps to develop and bring to the discussion

2. Test the approach further; it is particularly relevant to test the approach in other small software companies showing a wide range of characteristics

3. Develop implications for SPI that can be drawn from the maps of social networks

REFERENCES

Aaen, I., Arendt, J., Mathiassen, L., and Ngwenyama, O. "A Conceptual MAP of Software Process Improvement," *Scandinavian Journal of Information Systems* (13), 2001, pp. 81-101.

Borgatti, S. P., and Everett, M. G. "Notions of Position in Social Network Analysis," *Sociological Methodology* (22) 1992, pp. 1-35.

Brodman, J. G., and Johnson, D. L. "What Small Businesses and Small Organizations say about the CMM," in *Proceedings of the 16th International Conference on Software Engineering*, Sorrento, Italy, 1994, pp. 331-340.

Börjesson, A., and Mathiassen, L. "Improving Software Organizations: The Agility Challenge," unpublished manuscript submitted to a journal, 2004.

Cater-Steel, A. P. "Process Improvement in Four Small Software Companies," in *Proceedings of the 2001 Australian Software Engineering Conference*, Los Alamitos, CA: IEEE Computer Society Press, 2001, pp. 262-272.

Checkland, P. *Systems Thinking, Systems Practice*, Chichester, England: Wiley, 1981.

Hansen, B., Rose, J., and Tjørnehøj, G. "Prescription, Description, Reflection: The Shape of the Software Process Improvement Field," paper presented at the UK Association of Information Systems Conference, Glasgow Caledonian University, Glasgow, Scotland, 2004.

Haythornthwaite, C. "Social Network Analysis: An Approach and Technique for the Study of Information Exchange," *Library and Information Science Research* (18), 1996, pp. 323-342.

Hult, M., and Lennung, S.-A. "Towards a Definition of Action Research: A Note and Bibliography," *Journal of Management Studies*, May 1980, pp. 241-250.

Iversen, J. H., Mathiassen, L., and Nielsen, P. A. "Managing Risk in Software Process Improvement: An Action Research Approach," *MIS Quarterly* (28:3), 2004, pp. 395-433.

Iversen, J., Nielsen, P.A., and Nørbjerg, J. "Situated Assessment of Problems in Software Development," *The DATABASE for Advances in Information Systems* (30:2), 1999, pp. 66-81.

Kelly, D. P., and Culleton, B. "Process Improvement for Small Organizations," *Computer* (32:10), 1999, pp. 41-47.

Kotter, J. P. "Power, Dependence, and Effective Management," in *Organizational Influence Processes*, R. W. Allen and L. W. Porter (Eds.), Glenview, IL: Scott, Foresman and Company, 1983, pp. 128-143.

Martínez, A., Dimitriadis, Y., Rubia, B., Gómez, E., and de la Fuente, P. "Combining Qualitative Evaluation and Social Network Analysis for the Study of Classroom Social Interactions," *Computers & Education* (41), 2003, pp. 353-368.

Mathiassen, L. "Collaborative Practice Research," *Information Technology & People* (15:4), 2002, pp. 321-345.

McKay, J., and Marshall, P. "The Dual Imperatives of Action Research," *Information Technology & People* (14:1), 2001, pp. 46-59.

Ngwenyama, O., and Nielsen, P. A. "Competing Values in Software Process Improvement: An Assumption Analysis of CMM from an Organizational Culture Perspective," *IEEE Transactions on Engineering Management* (50:1), 2003, pp. 100-112.

Nielsen, P. A., Iversen, J. H., Johansen, J., and Nielsen, L. B. "The Adolescent Effort," in *Improving Software Organizations: From Principles to Practice,* L. Mathiassen, J. Pries-Heje, and O. Ngwenyama (Eds.), Reading, MA: Addison-Wesley, 2002.

Nielsen, P.A., and Ngwenyama, O. "Organizational Influence Processes in Software Process Improvement," European Conference on Information Systems, Gdansk, 2002.

Richardson, I. "SPI Models: What Characteristics Are Required for Small Software Development Companies?," *Software Quality Journal* (10:2), 2002, pp. 101-114.

Schön, D. *The Reflective Practitioner: How Professionals Think in Action,* New York: Basic Books, 1983.

Scott, J. *Social Network Analysis: A Handbook* (2nd ed.), London: Sage Publications, 2000.

Temdee, P., and Korba, L. "Of Networks, Interactions and Agents: An Approach for Social Network Analysis," in *Proceedings of the Sixth International Conference on Computer Supported Cooperative Work in Design,* Ottawa: NRC Research Press, 2001, pp. 324-329.

Tichy, N. M., Tushman, M. L., and Fombrun, C. "Social Network Analysis for Organizations," *The Academy of Management Review* (4:4), 1979, pp. 507-519.

Villalon, J., Agustin, G. C., Gilabert, T. S. F., Seco, A. D., Sanchez, L. G., and Cota, M. P. "Experiences in the Application of Software Process Improvement in SMES," *Software Quality Journal* (10:3), 2002, pp. 261-273.

Ward, R. P., Fayad, M. E., and Laitinen, M. "Software Process Improvement in the Small," *Communications of the ACM* (44:4), 2001, pp. 105-107.

Wasserman, S., and Faust, K. *Social Network Analysis: Methods and Applications,* Cambridge, England: Cambridge University Press, 1994.

Zack, M. H. "Researching Organizational Systems using Social Network Analysis," in *Proceedings of the 33rd Hawaii International Conference on Systems Science,* Los Alamitos, CA: IEEE Computer Society Press, 2000.

ABOUT THE AUTHORS

Peter Axel Nielsen is an associate professor in Information Systems at the Department of Computer Science at Aalborg University. Over the past years he has been engaged in understanding information systems development practice and the use of methodologies. His research interests include analysis and design techniques, object-orientation, and software process improvement. He is coauthor of a book on object-oriented analysis and design and a book on software process improvement. Peter can be reached at pan@cs.aau.dk.

Gitte Tjørnehøj is an assistant professor and Ph.D. student at the Department of Computer Science, Aalborg University, Denmark. She is a member of the SPV research project in Denmark. Her research is rooted in 10 years experience working in the IT industry. Her main research interests are management of IT and IS development focused on organisational change. Gitte can be reached at gtj@cs.aau.dk.

6 ORGANIZATIONAL INFORMATION SYSTEM ADOPTION: A Network Perspective

Dirk S. Hovorka
Kai R. Larsen
University of Colorado
Boulder, CO U.S.A.

Abstract   *As distributed organizations increasingly rely on technological innovations to enhance organizational efficiency and competitiveness, interest in agile environments that enhance the diffusion and adoption of innovations has grown. Although Information Systems has confirmed that social influence factors play an important role in the adoption of technological innovations by individuals, less is understood about the mechanisms within social communication networks that facilitate the flow of social influence and knowledge and about the organizational capacity to acquire and absorb new knowledge. This exploratory study helps to specify interactions and feedback within social communication networks and organizational capacities in a network organization environment. We use an exploratory case study design to document how the flow of knowledge within social communication networks affected the adoption of a large-scale software system in several counties within New York state. Data from decision makers in two comparable network organizations were analyzed for differences in social communication networks and the organization's capability to absorb and exploit new knowledge. The data suggest that information system adoption was influenced by communication processes that reinforced social influences and supported knowledge transfer, and hampered when those processes were absent. Implications for the development of theory about the relationship between social information processing and the ability of an organization to absorb and adopt new technology are discussed.*

Keywords   Information system adoption, organization, social network communication theory, social information processing, absorptive capacity, case studies, network organizations

1   INTRODUCTION

As investment in computer and information technologies in modern organizations has continued to increase, there has been persistent interest by the Information Systems community in developing models of information systems diffusion and adoption. Traditionally, adoption of information systems is viewed as a slow process involving sequential adoption and implementation stages (Lyytinen and Damsgaard 2001). There is, however, increasing interest in the creation of agile environments that facilitate the adoption of information systems.

Both social networks and capabilities to acquire and exploit new information have been identified as important components of innovation adoption. In the sprit of looking beyond the dominant adoption paradigm (Fichman 2004), the key question this research examines is whether organizational form can create an environment in which organizations can increase agility by strengthening social communication networks and increasing their capacity to acquire and exploit new knowledge. Agility has been defined as "the ability to detect opportunities for innovation and seize...opportunities by assembling requisite assets, knowledge, and relationships" (Sambamurthy et al. 2003, p. 245). Agility, in this sense, is closely aligned with an organization's absorptive capacity or its ability to acquire, assimilate, transform, and exploit new knowledge (Cohen and Levinthal 1990; Zahra and George 2003). In this exploratory case study, we examine the influence of the strategic implementation of an organizational network form on organizational-level information system adoption. Network organizations are characterized by flexibility, decentralized planning and control, and lateral ties with a high degree of integration of multiple types of socially important relations across formal boundaries (Baker 1992; van Alstyne 1997).

By empirically examining an information systems adoption setting within a network organization form, this paper accomplishes two goals: (1) it demonstrates how network characteristics can influence system adoption by affecting the flow of social and informational influence and (2) it proposes an integrated model of select communication network processes and the organizational construct of absorptive capacity. The study examined the voluntary adoption of a state-advocated information system in two network organizations based on consortia. Each consortium was organized by the state government to distribute knowledge in a phased manner from a lead organization to local organizations within the same consortia. This network form is consistent with many large, distributed organizations or cooperative groups desiring to disseminate information. Adoption was identified by the purchase and use of all or part of the state-advocated information system. A network with a high level of adoption and a network with a low level of adoption provide empirical data to examine communication network characteristics, social information processing, and the absorptive capacity construct leading to the development of an integrated organizational adoption model.

2   THEORETICAL BACKGROUND

Research on information systems adoption is often divided into insular domains divided by unit of analysis (individual, group, or organizational) and by differences

between variable studies and process or stage approaches (Gallivan 2001). Adoption
research is frequently based on Roger's (2003) diffusion of innovation framework (for
a review see Fichman 2000), which has a broad focus on how communication channels
and opinion leaders shape adoption, but does not illuminate the network mechanisms by
which variables and constructs interact and become important during adoption. A
preponderance of adoption studies based on the technology acceptance model (for a
review see Venkatesh et al. 2003) focus on the characteristics of individual adopters,
theories of individual behavior, and antecedent variables, but do not address the
theoretical underpinnings of the communication networks in which the individuals are
embedded (Monge and Contractor 2003). It has been well established that individual
behavior is affected by social and informational influence within networks (Sussman and
Siegal 2003; Triandis 1980), and research has confirmed the importance of networks in
the diffusion process (Swan et al. 1998). But there is little research on process
interaction or mechanisms by which social factors become influential in adoption
success or failure (Gallivan 2001; Paré and Elam 1997). In addition, some research has
questioned the applicability of the diffusion concepts (Larsen 2001) and the conjectures
underlying the diffusion model (Lyytinen and Damsgaard 2001), particularly when
examining organizational adoption. Adoption of innovation is enabled by access to new
ideas (Swan et al. 1998) and reduction of knowledge barriers (Chau and Tam 1997), and
recent research views adoption as a socially constructed process with greater proactive
participation by adopters than previously conceived (McMaster 2001). Investigation of
the network processes that support system adoption is critical, because it provides
another level of explanation from an organizational perspective, and further examines
the importance of organizational agility in a system development and adoption setting.

The guiding theories selected in this study specifically apply to the context of the
knowledge acquisition and absorption that occurs during an adoption process. We
examine characteristics of communication networks, social information processing, and
absorptive capacity, which are closely aligned with the flow of knowledge, social and
informational influence, and capacity to acquire and utilize new knowledge within and
among organizations.

2.1 Characteristics of Social Communication Networks

Social communication networks are frequently viewed purely as an emergent
characteristic (Grandori ad Seda 1995; McKelvey 1997). However, social
communication networks can also be strategically formed and supported to encourage
knowledge transfer between organizations (Gulati et al. 2000). Network organization
forms may be implemented with the intention of strengthening social communication
networks to improve knowledge acquisition and transfer. Communication contacts may
be formal (with planned meetings, reporting structures, and training) or informal (with
social connections through conferences, unplanned discussions, and similar
mechanisms). The strength of ties is often defined as the frequency of communication
and the degree of the network is defined as the number of direct links with other network
members (Monge and Contractor 2003). We posit that social influence variables
identified in previous research become important predictors only in the presence of

formal and/or informal network ties and formulate question 1: *Are the strength and degree of network connections positively correlated with system adoption?*

2.2 Social Information Processing

Social information processing (SIP) is defined as the concept "that individuals may be influenced by cues from others about what to attend to, how to value salient dimensions of workplace phenomenon and how others perceive the same phenomenon" (Rice and Aydin 1991, p. 220). Contact provided by communication networks is the mechanism by which people and organizations are exposed to information, attitudes, and behavior. This exposure increases the likelihood that members of the network will acquire and assimilate knowledge, attitudes, and behaviors from others in the network (Rice 1993). SIP predicts that "socially constructed meaning about tasks, individual's past experiences about tasks, and objective characteristics of the work environment, all influence perceptions, assessments, attitude formation and behaviors" (Rice 1990, p. 34).

Previous studies have identified network-related antecedent variables to adoption intention, for example, subjective norms, social factors, social influence, social norms, or images (Kraut et al. 1998; Venkatesh et al. 2003). Social and informational influence, salient referent groups (Compeau and Higgins 1995) and managerial- and organizational-level support for computer use (Thompson et al. 1991) influence an individual's adoption intention only through the communication network in which the actor is embedded. These factors form a class of *social influence* variables grounded in SIP theory as well as theories of individual behavior. It is this class of variables that can be used to tie individual adoption studies to organizational-level system adoption through mechanisms defined in network theories.

Transmitted attitudes may have a positive or negative valence (Stuart et al. 2001), leading to processing of the information by potential adopters. Social information may be in different forms but lead to informational influence (Sussman and Siegal 2003) regarding system adoption. We suggest that the characteristics of the communications network itself will determine, in part, the effect of informational influence, social norms, and attitudes leading to question 2: *Does the communication network affect adoption by influencing positive or negative social information processing regarding the information technology?*

2.3 Absorptive Capacity

Absorptive capacity (ACAP) can be conceptualized as a set of organizational abilities to manage knowledge. ACAP relies on both external connections and internal social networks, and thus provides a contrast to the previous theories. Zahra and George (2003) identify four distinct dimensions: acquisition, assimilation, transformation, and exploitation. Within the organization, these dimensions are linked via social integration mechanisms, which can facilitate the distribution and exploitation of knowledge. Social integration may occur informally in social networks, or formally through the use of co-ordinators. In the context of system adoption, an organization's absorptive capacity is built on network mechanisms for identifying and sharing knowledge and for rewarding the transfer of knowledge. The time and resources organizations dedicate to acquiring and distributing information may be critical components for positive adoption. Prior knowledge, diversity of knowledge sources, comprehension, and learning are all indicators of the acquisition and assimilation of knowledge (Cohen and Levinthal 1990; Zahra and George 2003).

Prior work has identified the porosity of firm boundaries and formal and informal network structures that identify responsibilities and competencies (Matusik and Heeley 20045) and previous experiences of individuals (Cohen and Levinthal 1990; Taylor and Todd 1995) as contributing to organizational absorptive capacity. These variables emphasize the contribution of network influences and may be incorporated into theoretical network mechanisms leading to question 3: *Do communication networks foster overall absorptive capacity leading to information system adoption?*

3 STUDY ENVIRONMENT

Probation departments are a part of the criminal justice system and provide an alternative to incarceration for criminals whose crimes or family situations justify community inclusion. Traditionally, funding for criminal justice activities has gone to law enforcement, the prison system, and parole. A result is that probation departments historically have lacked the technology needed to improve the efficiency and effectiveness of their core operations.

In June 1996, a survey by the state of New York's probation agency showed that most probation departments relied on paper forms or limited personal computer use. Many probation departments were involved in uncoordinated and nonstandardized information systems development efforts. To encourage electronic record sharing, caseload management, and standard reporting information, as well as other probation activities, a state-wide probation IS project aimed at small- to mid-sized departments was initiated. After extensive network readiness surveys, requirements analysis, and review of proposals from vendors, a specific information system named PROBER was selected for implementation.

In 1997, the 50 local probation departments were organized into eight geographically contiguous networks, called *consortia,* to facilitate the adoption process. The consortia were intended to support knowledge distribution and sharing, and to make available the expertise about the process required to successfully adopt the system. Two lead departments were chosen to help customize, document, and provide final acceptance of the selected vendor's software. Both lead departments were encouraged to schedule meetings, provide support by distributing solutions to problematic processes, and involve the counties of their consortium in the process of preparing for the new system.

4 METHOD

The two consortia selected for comparison in this study had different levels of system adoption (see Figure 1). Although the grouping of counties was designed to create

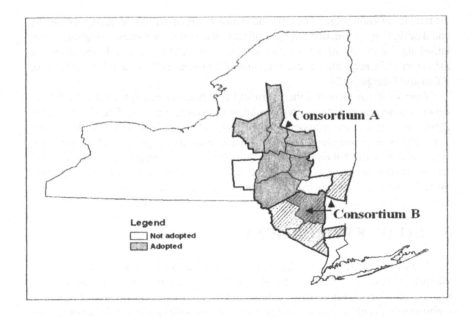

Figure 1. Adoption by Counties Within Each Consortium

consortia with similar characteristics, the difference in percentage of counties of each consortium which adopted the system (78 percent versus 17 percent) raises questions regarding why the differences occurred. These consortia were the first two involved in the adoption process and had the longest involvement with the consortia network that initiated the adoption effort.

.The two consortia were also similar in how they tested the software and incorporated the software into organizational processes. Data were collected from the 7-year (1996 to 2002) records of the probation information systems project. The data included presentations given by the project director, an extensive set of project documents, observations of meetings, the project director's monthly reports, and 37 interviews with all of the primary decision makers. The interviews lasted 1.25 hours on average.

4.1 Research Design

The primary method of data gathering was through 37 semi-structured interviews conducted in 2002. Interview questions included the frequency and type of communication with other probation departments during the adoption process, and the influences and factors that guided the information system decision process. A second line of questions probed the capacity and preparedness of the departments to acquire and utilize knowledge, and determined what mechanisms in the network supported or hindered efforts to exploit the knowledge. Although the interviews were guided by prepared questions, a large degree of flexibility was incorporated to allow the researchers to pursue relevant issues that arose during the interview, and to allow subjects open-ended answers. Two adjacent consortia, referred to as consortium A and consortium B, with nine and six departments, respectively, were compared. Figure 1 shows the geographical distribution of the counties in the two consortia and indicates which county probation departments adopted the information system.

Interviews were conducted with the probation directors in each county in the study, as well as with senior probation officers and senior staff members who were directly involved with the adoption decision. Both the current and former state project directors were also interviewed. In addition, a former director of one of the consortium departments was interviewed due to her involvement with the early stages of the project. This range of interviews provided direct contact with the primary decision makers in all 15 departments in the study.

4.2 Data Analysis

Data analysis was divided into six distinct steps.

- **Code-book development**: A tree structure of codes was developed from the theoretical perspectives selected for this study. Codes were chosen to mark the existence of an item (e.g., system adopted) and the directionality of attributes, where applicable (e.g., positive social information processing or negative social information processing).

- **Database creation**: A database of all transcribed interviews, documents, and presentations was created. All transcripts and documents were named and formatted, and the database was constructed by using QSR NVIVO software.

- **Knowledge-base development**: Coding of the transcribed interviews and documents was performed following established standards (Miles and Huberman 1994). Multiple analysis phases applied predetermined codes and allowed codes to emerge during coding. Two researchers coded a selection of the interviews to test consistency of the coding scheme. Reliability testing determined that there were very few disagreements regarding application of the codes. Consequently, samples of the coded transcripts were double-checked for omitted codes by the second researcher, with no major omissions noted.

- **Retrieval of coded text**: The data were partitioned into different sets based upon system adoption. Text relevant to the hypotheses was retrieved from initial large-scale sets of data from consortium A and consortium B. As analysis proceeded, other sets were created to allow different comparisons of codes, co-occurrences, and text-strings. Examples of the different data configurations examined include adopters versus non-adopters in the entire database, and non-adopters versus adopters within each consortium.

- **Text segment comparison**: Documents created from retrieved text segments were compared for the occurrence, frequency, and meaning of text segments related to each research question. Relationships among specific coded texts were mapped to expose processes and reveal patterns in data. Research questions were addressed through deductive inference closely following the scientific methodology of controlled deductions in qualitative case studies outlined by Lee (1989).

- **Reexamination of data**: Comments, notes, and maps developed during the previous steps were used to reexamine the data and create codes for phenomena that had not been predicted. Patterns of responses were examined in the light of extant literature to determine whether other theoretical stances needed to be included in the explanation. Exemplars of particular evidence chains were sought, and other relationships among the variables were examined.

The final stage of analysis involved integrating the networking processes and proposing how these relationships were formed. An integrated model of the processes indicates how the relationships that emerge in the communication network can explain the differences between system adoption outcomes.

5   FINDINGS

As a group, consortium A was considered to have adopted the information system, with seven of nine participating counties adopting the system. In contrast, only the lead county of the six counties in consortium B adopted the system. Lead counties in each consortium were appointed by the state probation department on the basis of their agreement to adopt.

5.1 Findings: Question 1

The data indicate that the strength and degree of the social communications network is positively correlated to adoption success. In these consortia, the social communications network was characterized by both central ties from local departments to the lead department and lateral ties between members of the consortium. Changes in frequency of communication between dyads were aggregated to a comparative measure between the two consortia for central and lateral ties. Changes in the degree, or number of possible central and lateral ties, were determined prior to the start of the consortia and again as a single measure for the period during which the consortia were active. Table 1 shows the differences between consortium A and consortium B in the degree of lateral and central ties (out of all possible ties) and the changes in frequency of communication of those ties.

In both consortia, network strength increased after the network organization form was initiated. This increase was greater in consortium A for both formal, central ties and for informal, lateral connections between local departments. In consortium A, a total of six formal consortium meetings were held in the five years since the beginning of the

Table 1. Comparison of Central and Lateral Network Ties

		Prior to Consortia Formation	During Consortia Period	
		Network Degree Existing ties of (Possible ties)	New ties created	Network Strength Ties that Increased in communication frequency of (possible ties)
Consortium A (high adoption)	Central Ties	5 of (8)	3	8 of (8)
	Lateral ties	18 of (28)	4	9 of (28)
Consortium B (non-adoption)	Central Ties	2 of (5)	3	2 of (5)
	Lateral ties	4 of (10)	0	0 of (10)

system implementation. All eight of the local departments of consortium A reported an increase in contact with the lead department and roughly one-third of the potential lateral ties increased in communication frequency. At the consortium network level, both frequency of communications and number of possible connections increased.

In contrast, no formal activities were held in consortium B after the initial planning meetings. Department directors traveled to other counties to examine the software, but no meetings among all consortium members were organized. None of the departments in consortium B reported an increase in the number of lateral connections. The network-level changes in strength and degree of connections in consortium B were less than was observed in consortium A.

Formal meetings appear to have provided one mechanism through which informal connections could be initiated. Notably, the greatest difference between the two consortia is in number and strength of lateral ties. This direct communication among local member organizations may represent a *tertius iungens* orientation toward linking people by facilitating coordination between connected network members (Obstfeld 2005) and may provide a mechanism by which knowledge is transferred.

5.2 Findings: Question 2

Data indicate that the social communication networks influenced system adoption by social information processing related to the PROBER project. All departments involved in the project reported both positive and negative comments about the PROBER system. In consortium A, almost all of the directors commented on a specific benefit the system would provide. These included managing caseloads, increasing efficiency for probation officers, financial benefits from automating restitution, and involving officers more directly in the cases. The statement that best captures the most common attitude was that benefits "on the positive side, I think outweigh [the negative]."

The directors acknowledged that they had heard negative comments, but these were mostly minor implementation difficulties, complaints from officers about having to perform clerical work, and resistance to change, rather that substantive doubts about the system. For example,

> *There was a lot of input, we're not data-entry clerks, we're used to dictating our words, or writing out our letter long-hand and give it to the secretary, and some of us can't type, and if you're hunting and pecking when you input this information, it's going to take a long time. It changes the job-requirement a little bit; it changes the skills you need to bring to the job. In the past, you didn't have to know how to type to be a probation officer; nowadays it sure helps. There was a lot of frustration.*

In contrast, directors in consortium B were far more ambivalent about the project and reported vague comments about what they had heard (e.g., "some people like it and some didn't like it"). Even in cases where they reported hearing positive attitudes, they included a negative counterpoint, such as wanting to wait until the bugs were fixed, expressing concern that the system wouldn't support departmental processes, or worrying that the system was too complex, inflexible, or limited in function.

Negative social information processing can also impact members of a strong communication network. Directors who were critical of the PROBER system argued for an alternative automation system developed by a department in the eastern part of the state. This alternative system was less expensive, currently available, and purportedly met state reporting standards.[1] The proposal to adopt the alternative system included information critical of the PROBER system and resulted in a resolution to stop further development and deployment of PROBER. Considerable discussion of the alternative system caused controversy and confusion and required that meetings be arranged to resolve the confusion.

5.2 Findings: Question 3

In general, stronger social communication networks increased organizational ability to acquire, assimilate, and exploit new knowledge. A general assessment of ACAP for each department was estimated and compared using characteristics representative of the ability to acquire, assimilate, and exploit knowledge (Table 2). Computer experience and use of other information systems were the surrogate measures for prior knowledge. Whether the department obtained the necessary hardware prior to obtaining the software, the existence of local IS department support, the interest level of the officers and staff, and sufficient time for training were characteristics related to a department's ability and willingness to assimilate and exploit new knowledge. Table 2 summarizes the ACAP items aggregated within consortia A and B.

---

[1] An independent evaluation subsequently revealed that the alternative system was subject to system crashes, did not meet state standards, nor did it allow electronic reporting.

Table 2. Absorptive Capacity (ACAP) Characteristics

ACAP Items	Consortium A (high adoption) Number of counties of classification/total counties	Consortium B (non-adoption) Number of counties of classification/total counties
User computer experience	High 2/9; Mixed 4/9; Low 3/9	High 0/6; Mixed 3/6; Low 3/6
Prior or current use of similar systems	had used or are currently using some type of automation systems 5/9	Had used or are currently using some type of automation systems 6/6
IS department support	Good 6/9; Limited 3/9	Good 0/6; Limited 3/6; Low 1/6; using external contactor 2/6.
Obtained hardware prior to software	Purchased or upgraded PCs 5/9	Purchased or upgraded PCs 4/6

As expected, the presence of prior knowledge in the form of computer experience was positively associated with adoption. In consortium A, a majority (six of nine) of directors rated their employees as having high computer experience (two departments) or as having a mixture of experienced and inexperienced computer users (four departments). The opposite was reported in consortium B with all of the six departments considering their employees' computer experience to be mixed or low.

When previous or current use of automation systems used in probation departments (e.g., spreadsheets developed in-house, the previous County Automation Project, the Correction Project, and the Youth Assessment Project) was examined, there was no apparent relationship with adoption of the PROBER system. Consortium B actually had a higher proportion of departments that had used or were currently using some type of information system.

IS department competence was also correlated with adoption. In consortium A, six of the nine departments had good relationships with competent MIS departments. Interestingly, the three departments who felt their MIS support was limited did adopt the system, indicating that this was not necessarily a roadblock to adoption. Therefore, the limited MIS support reported in consortium B does not explain the non-adoption behavior.

Finally, a majority of departments in both consortia obtained sufficient computer and network hardware, indicating that this was not a factor for the differences between the consortia.

5.4 Summary of Findings

Considered individually, the theories informing the three research questions could be used to explain some of the observed adoption differences between the consortia.

But these data also reveal that there are interactions within the communication network that enhance or mitigate the impact of each theory. Illuminating these interactions allows for a richer explanation of the processes by which the social communication network contributes to organizational adoption. For example, network degree (number of possible network connections) increases the variety of knowledge sources. Network strength (frequency of contact) increases the exposure to knowledge, attitudes and behaviors of network members. Together, these network characteristics increase social information processing which, in turn, increases or decreases network strength depending on the valence of the social information processing. In addition, dimensions of absorptive capacity can cross organizational boundaries when a strong communication network is present, so that the capacities of network members are enhanced. Network members who have positive attitudes and behaviors are more likely to provide knowledge and technical support to other network members and network members who received support generally exhibited positive attitudes. This feedback between social information processing and absorptive capacity within the social communication network points to the opportunity for these theories to be integrated into a more fully explanatory model.

6   INTEGRATED MODEL

Our data suggest that the two networks studied had dramatically different adoption outcomes. As with any study of real-world phenomena, many possible explanations exist for the observed differences. But an examination of the fixed attributes of the probation departments, including the size, number of employees, number of clients served, budget, and distance from other probation departments in the same consortia, did not reveal any patterns that could explain the difference in outcome between the consortia. The number of counties in each consortium was not a determining factor, given that three counties in a four-county consortium in the eastern part of the state adopted the system. In that consortium, the lone non-adopting county had a functioning information system prior to the start of the state consortium initiative.

An integrated organizational adoption model (Figure 3) shows the interactions of the processes examined in this research. This model presents a set of propositions about the specific relationships among network strength, social information processing, absorptive capacity, and organizational adoption.

In a distributed organizational environment, the use of formal communications structures and the subsequent creations of informal ties can result in a strong, dense network with central and lateral ties that provide the connections through which social influence and knowledge flow. The content of the social influence variables has a positive or negative valence. In this case, positive content is supportive of system adoption, whereas negative content contains information opposing system adoption. The strength and density of the communication network alters the potential of social influence variables to affect adoption via social information processing. Stronger network connections increase the likelihood that particular social influence variables will be received from different sources, and also increase the frequency with which such transfers occur. In consortium A, one director commented that

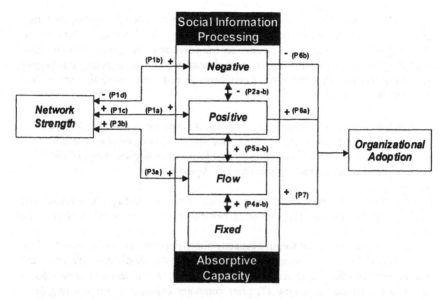

Figure 2. Integrated Organizational Adoption Model

[The consortium] creates an environment where directors can have a forum to discuss the issues, the goods and the bads about it, and be able to go back to their county and make some decisions along with the people that they have to make those decisions with. I mean, that's the best piece about it, as far as I'm concerned, because you go to a meeting and I can get some pretty good information about the system, and then come back to my own county and say, well this is how it works, this is what it can do for us.

Simultaneously, knowledge transfer in the form of social influence, norms, and attitudes strengthens or weakens communication network ties, depending on its valence. Generally, positive knowledge flows tend to increase network strength, and negative knowledge flows result in fewer connections with less frequent communications.

The integrated model represents SIP as composed of positive and negative valences that interact. Strongly positive components are those that support adoption, whereas negative components are those that oppose adoption. In this case study, some directors were strongly affected by negative attitudes. In one instance, a director in consortium A noted that even though negative comments had affected his personal opinion, other directors had disregarded the comments

You know, I can remember who had a lot of complaints about it, but I can't remember what [the complaints] were. And the person that had a lot of complaints is a person i respect and I know wouldn't steer counties wrong, so I put a lot of credibility into that person's comments...but yet another director heard those same comments at the same meeting, and went ahead and purchased the software knowing full well that there were these alleged problems with it.

But during an extended adoption process, social information processing supported by a strong network can result in individuals altering their attitudes. Exposure to frequent positive attitudes, or similar attitudes from diverse sources, can overcome initial negative attitudes adopted from even respected sources. The same director quoted above altered his decision when the positive comments he had heard eventually outweighed the negative comments.

> *I talked to my data processing director and the plan for us was to wait a year or so to see how the counties in the pilot project did and maybe some other counties...what they thought of it....I had heard enough good things about it last year I went and tried to get it for our department.*

This indicates that the transfer of attitudes and social influences of a positive valence can supplant negative attitudes and vice versa, particularly in a dense network with strong ties.

We propose that each absorptive capacity dimension can be linked to aspects of the communication network. Greater network density increases the diversity of sources and is consistent with the acquisition dimension of ACAP. Assimilation of knowledge is linked to the attitude regarding IT, prior computer experience, and learning (e.g., training). The transformation dimension requires the internalization of knowledge as reflected by changes in internal processes. Knowledge exploitation is supported by social integration mechanisms within the organization and interorganizational networks that increase employee interaction and promote problem solving.

Our data indicate that departments relied on knowledge from members of their communication networks for both the decision to adopt and for the assimilation and exploitation of the software. This suggests that the previous conceptualization of ACAP as fixed within the organization is incomplete. Elements that enable an organization to assimilate, transform, and exploit knowledge can be transferred through a social communication network and comprise *dynamic ACAP*. The mobility of dynamic ACAP through a network differentiates it from *fixed ACAP*, which resides within the organization and cannot easily be shared. The ability of organizations to augment internal ACAP deficiencies by obtaining knowledge from the network increases the chances of a positive adoption result. In one case, a senior officer stated

> *But I deal with the counties all over, anyone who has a question about the system and [my director] has been willing to send myself and [my coworker] to go anywhere that people need assistance.*

Fixed ACAP is comprised of prior information system experience, interest, computer competence, and computer resources. High levels of these capacities provide the potential to extend dynamic ACAP with problem solving, training, and system support through network connections. Conversely, network members can overcome deficiencies in fixed ACAP through communication network connections. Advice about specific problems and recommended changes in organizational procedures to better utilize the system can overcome low user computer experience. Thus, capacities grounded in the organization, such as technical and problem-solving support, can become knowledge exchange processes that move through the network and increase an organization's ability to assimilate and exploit the system. By increasing experience, knowledge, and problem-solving capacities in the beneficiary organization, dynamic ACAP increases the fixed ACAP of the recipient. All of the adopting counties in consortium A relied heavily on other consortium members for advice and help. One director reported that the departments that impacted his decision were "probably those counties that were into the system and had initiated it and I was able to get some answers from; they had some experience going through the system."

As shown in Figure 3, a reciprocal relationship exists between the processing of social information (SIP) and the organizations' ability to acquire, assimilate, and exploit knowledge (ACAP). The ability of SIP and knowledge transfer to overcome a low ACAP dimension was demonstrated by the decision to adopt the software in the three departments in consortium A that had mixed levels of interest in the system. These three departments all had poor experiences with prior software systems for other functions, yet through their interactions with departments in the consortium, they had acquired knowledge leading to a positive adoption result. In consortium B, where there were fewer network ties and most of those were weaker, negative experience with prior software and negative comments regarding the PROBER system were not overcome by positive SIP and ACAP support flowing through the network.

Organizations processing positive social influence variables are potentially more likely to contribute dynamic ACAP to network members. At the same time, the flow of ACAP in the network increases the amount of positive information processed by network members. For example, a network member who is receiving problem-solving or technical help will likely communicate positive attitudes and normative behaviors to other network members. This is exhibited in comments such as

> *I think what the consortium does, it gives the other probation directors some kind of feeling that there are other people out there willing to help them out when they are having a problem. The biggest fear, and it is a major decision, whether you are going to commit your department to an automation system, either this one or that one, and whenever you can feel secure that, number one, there are other people you respect who are doing it and have made that decision, you feel a little bit better about your own decision. And, then when you need it, those people are there and you can call on them for help; it makes you more willing to be a willing participant in the process.*

The positive or negative valence of the content of social information that is processed has a direct influence on the likelihood of adoption. Positive attitudes and supporting norms increase adoption; negatively oriented information decreases adoption likelihood. Typical of the evidence of the impact of negative SIP

> *There was a point in the process where two directors got disenchanted with the PROBER process, and they were significant directors, they are people who could influence people heavily. One of them went to the meeting and made a comment like, "You have to be nuts to implement PROBER"....he was also very energetic and sometimes he speaks before he realizes the implications of*

what he's talking about. So, he made that comment, he scared off [a probation department]. [The director of that department] definitely was thinking about PROBER and now they scared [the director] so much she didn't know what to do, so she was going to go with the alternative system.

An organization's ability to acquire, assimilate, transform, and exploit knowledge determines its overall absorptive capacity. System adoption is frequently a complex process requiring new information, learning, and assimilation of new skills, as well as changes in internal processes and organizational structures. The capacity to accomplish these goals is directly related to the willingness and ability to adopt a new information system.

The integrated model identifies some of the processes and interactions inherent in social communication network theories and provides a more complete explanation of the differences within and between the networks than any of the theories alone. The model reflects our belief that organizational-level adoption can be subsumed under general network theories regarding interactions of network processes that support or weaken system adoption initiatives.

7   CONCLUSIONS

By examining communication processes and interactions of organizations from the perspective of the social communication network, this study demonstrates how networks can influence the agility of organizations to acquire and assimilate new ideas and adopt innovations such as information systems. This research identifies the interaction of network characteristics, social communication processes, and organizational capabilities and shows that strong and dense communication networks facilitate knowledge flows that enhance social information processing and support the flow of elements of absorptive capacity in the network.

Social information processing of pro-adoption social influence, social norms, attitudes, and behaviors can increase the chance of positive adoption outcomes. Social information processing is a crucial aspect of the adoption process during which supporting or discouraging knowledge interacts as decisions regarding system adoption are made. Network members may attend to different information, depending on the specific source, the variety of sources, or the frequency of exposure to the information. Supporting knowledge transferred through the network may displace negative attitudes toward adoption. The opposite process, in which negative attitudes, beliefs, and behaviors are transferred and negatively influence adoption, can also occur. The strength and density of the social communication network partially determines the influence of social information processing.

An organization's agility is based, in part, on it's ability to acquire, assimilate, transform, and exploit knowledge, and can be increased through strong and dense network ties to other organizations. Interorganizational networks can also reinforce deficient absorptive capacity dimensions in connected organizations. In the case of organizational IS adoption, this dynamic ACAP may take the form of technical support, implementation procedures, transfer of knowledge pertaining to software customization, and problem solving. This extension of the ACAP construct across organizational boundaries supplies a mechanism by which communication networks can support IS adoption across organizational boundaries. In groups of autonomous organizations, the fixed ACAP of a specific member can be enhanced by dynamic ACAP from other members.

The integrated adoption model presented in this research proposes interactions within the network adoption process by which social influence variables become important. The interactions shown in this model indicate that these social communication network theories are not separate, independent processes, but are actually intertwined. When applied to the adoption process, network communication theories must be considered together in order to fully understand the knowledge flows that increase the abilities of an organization to acquire and exploit new knowledge leading to organizational information system adoption.

REFERENCES

Baker, W. E. "The Network Organization in Theory and Practice," in *Networks and Organizations: Structure Form and Action,* N. Nohria and R. G. Eccles (Eds.), Boston: Harvard Business School Press, 1992, pp. 397-429.

Chau, P. Y. K., and Tam, K. Y. "Factors Affecting the Adoption of Open Systems: An Exploratory Study," *MIS Quarterly* (21:1), March 1997, pp. 1-24.

Cohen, W. M., and Levinthal, D. A. "Absorptive Capacity: A New Perspective on Learning and Innovation.," *Administrative Science Quarterly* (35), 1990, pp. 128-152.

Compeau, D. R., and Higgins, C. A. "Computer Self-Efficacy: Development of a Measure and Initial Test," *MIS Quarterly* (19:2), 1995, pp. 189-211.

Fichman, R. G. "The Diffusion and Assimilation of Information Technology Innovations," in *Framing the Domains of IT Management: Projecting the Future...Through the Past,* R. W. Zmud (Ed.), Cincinnatio, OH: Pinnaflex Educational Resources, Inc., 2000, pp. 105-127.

Fichman, R. G. "Going Beyond the Dominant Paradigm for Information Technology Innovation Research: Emerging Concepts and Methods," *Journal of the Association for Information Systems* (5:8), 2004, pp. 314-355.

Gallivan, M. J. "Organizational Adoption and Assimilation of Complex Technological Innovations: Development and Application of a New Framework," *Data Base for Advances in Information Systems* (32:3), 2001, pp. 51-85.

Grandori, A., and Soda, G. "Inter-firm Networks: Antecedents, Mechanisms and Forms," *Organization Studies* (16:2), 1995, pp. 183-205.

Gulati, R., Nohria, N., and Zaheer, A. "Strategic Networks," *Strategic Management Journal* (21:3), 2000, pp. 203-215.

Kraut, R., Rice, R. E., Cool, C., and Fish, R. "Varieties of Social Influence: The Role of Utility and Norms in the Success of a New Communication Medium," *Organization Science* (9:4), 1998, pp. 437-453.

Larsen, T. J. "The Phenomenon of Diffusion: Red Herrings and Future Promise," in *Diffusing Software product and Process Innovations,* M. Ardis and B. Marcolin (Eds.), Boston: Kluwer Academic Publishers, Boston, 2001, pp. 35-50.

Lee, A. S. "A Scientific Methodology for MIS Case Studies," *MIS Quarterly* (13:1), March 1989, pp. 33-49.

Lyytinen, K., and Damsgaard, J. "What's Wrong with the Diffusion of Innovation Theory?," in *Diffusing Software Product and Process Innovations,* M. Ardis and B. Marcolin (Eds.), Boston: Kluwer Academic Publishers, 2001, pp. 173-190.

Matusik, S., and Heeley, M. B. "A Multilevel Theory of Absorptive Capacity in the Software Industry," *Journal of Management*, 2005 (forthcoming).

McKelvey, B. "Quasi-Natural Organization Science," *Organization Science* (8:4), 1997, pp. 352-380.

McMaster, T. "The Illusion of Diffusion in Information System Research," in *Diffusing Software Product and Process Innovations*, M. Ardis and B. Marcolin (Eds.), Boston: Kluwer Academic Publishers, 2001, pp. 67-83.

Miles, M. B., and Huberman, A. M. *Qualitative Data Analysis: An Expanded Sourcebook* (2nd ed.), Beverly Hills, CA: Sage Publications Ltd., 1994.

Monge, P. R., and Contractor, N. *Theories of Communication Networks*, New York: Oxford University Press, 2003.

Obstfeld, D. "Social Network, the Tertius Iungens Orientation, and Involvement in Innovation," *Administrative Science Quarterly*, 2005 (forthcoming).

Paré, G., and Elam, J. J. "Using Case Study Research to Build Theories of IT Implementation," in *Information Systems and Qualitative Research*, A. Lee, J. Liebenau and J. I. DeGross (Eds.), London: Chapman & Hall, 1997, pp. 542-568.

Rice, R. E. "Individual and Network Influence on the Adoption and Perceived Outcomes of Electronic Messaging," *Social Networks* (12:1), 1990, pp. 27-55.

Rice, R.E. "Using Network Concepts to Clarify Sources and Mechanisms of Social Influence," in: *Progress in Communications Science*, W.J. Richards and G. Barnett (eds.), Ablex, Norwood, 1993, pp. 43-62.

Rice, R. E., and Aydin, C. "Attitudes toward New Organizational Technology: Network Proximity as a Mechanism for Social Information Processing," *Administrative Science Quarterly* (36:2), 1991, pp. 219-244.

Rogers, E. *Diffusion of Innovations* (5th ed.), New York: Free Press, 2003.

Sambamurthy, V., Bharadwaj, A., and Grover, V. "Shaping Agility Through Digital Options: Reconceptualizing the Role of Information Technology in Contemporary Firms," *MIS Quarterly* (27:2), June 2003, pp. 237-263.

Stuart, W. D., Russo, T. C., Sypher, H., Simons, T. E., and Hallberg, L. K. "Influences of Sources of Communication on Adoption of a Communication Technology," in *Diffusing Software Product and Process Innovations*, M. Ardis and B. Marcolin (Eds.), Boston: Kluwer Academic Publishers, Boston, 2001, pp. 191-204.

Sussman, S. W., and Siegal, W. S. "Informational Influence in Organizations: An Integrated Approach to Knowledge Adoption," *Information Systems Research* (14:1), March 2003, pp. 47-65.

Swan, J., Newell, S., and Robertson, M. "Interorganizational Networks and Diffusion of Information Technology: Developing a Framework," in *Information Systems Innovation and Diffusion: Issues and Directions*, T. J. Larsen (Ed.), Hershey, PA: Idea Group Publishing, 1998, pp. 220-250.

Taylor, S., and Todd, P. "Assessing IT Usage: The Role of Prior Experience," *MIS Quarterly* (19:4), 1995, pp. 561-570.

Thompson, R. L., Higgins, C. A., and Howell, J. M. "Personal Computing: Toward a Conceptual Model of Utilization," *MIS Quarterly* (15:1), March 1991, pp. 125-143.

Triandis, H. C. "Values, Attitudes, and Interpersonal Behavior," in *Nebraska Symposium on Motivation: Beliefs, Attitudes, and Values*, Lincoln, NE: University of Nebraska Press, 1980, pp. 195-259.

Van Alstyne, M. "The State of Network Organization: A Survey of Three Frameworks," *Journal of Organizational Computing* (7:3), 1997, pp. 83-152.

Venkatesh, V., Morris, M. G., Davis, G. B., and Davis, F. D. "User Acceptance of Information Technology: Toward a Unified View," *MIS Quarterly* (27:3), 2003, pp. 425-478.

Zahra, S. A., and George, G. "Absorptive Capacity: A Review, Reconceptualization and Extension," *Academy of Management Review* (27:2), April 2003, pp. 185-203.

ABOUT THE AUTHORS

Dirk S. Hovorka is a Ph.D. candidate at the Leeds School of Business, University of Colorado, Boulder. His research includes influences of social networks on knowledge exchange, information systems in science, and the philosophical foundations of IS research.

Kai R. Larsen is an assistant professor of Information Systems in the Leeds School of Business, University of Colorado, Boulder. His research interests center around interdisciplinary approaches to information systems implementation and interorganizational networks.

7 CROSSING THE CHASM IN SOFTWARE PROCESS IMPROVEMENT

Anna Börjesson
Fredrik Martinsson
Magnus Timmerås
Ericsson AB and
IT University of Gothenburg
Gothenburg, Sweden

Abstract   *Software process improvement (SPI) is a well-known approach to enhance software quality and business efficiency. The approach has been widely used, discussed, adopted, and criticized within the software community since Watts Humphrey's introduction of SPI in 1989. SPI is a particular instance of diffusion of innovations. One challenging difficulty within diffusion of innovations is crossing the chasm between early adopters and early majority. To explore this issue in relation to SPI, we have studied an initiative implementing a new change request process and tool at the telecom company Ericsson AB in Gothenburg, Sweden. An action research approach was adopted with the double purpose of supporting the SPI initiative toward success while at the same time learning about tactics that SPI change agents can adopt to successfully cross the chasm. The study identifies a tactic, the guerrilla tactic, that SPI change agents can use to successfully cross the chasm and it discusses lessons from practicing this tactic in relation to the SPI and diffusion of innovation literature.*

Keywords   Software process improvement, diffusion of innovations, the chasm, SPI change agent tactics

1   INTRODUCTION

Software process improvement (SPI) is a particular instance of diffusion of innovations. Both SPI and diffusion of innovations are approaches widely used in practice and elaborated in research. Several different models for how to organize and drive SPI work are available. The capability maturity model (Paulk et al. 1995), the IDEAL model (McFeeley 1996), and the plan-do-act-check cycle (Grady 1997) are some of the more familiar models. Far too many SPI efforts do, however, fail (Bach 1995; Bollinger and McGowan 1991; Börjesson and Mathiassen 2004b; Fayad and Laitinen 1997; Humphrey and Curtis 1991) and the indicated reasons are many. Established SPI and diffusion of innovation literature recognizes SPI change agents and their different tactics as important factors to avoid failure (Grady 1997; Humphrey 1989; Kautz et al. 2001; McFeeley 1996; Pries-Heje and Tryde 2001; Rogers 2003). Other reasons are the danger of not using structured approaches to change (Paulk 1999) such as the chasm (Moore 2002) and not recognizing and addressing it in the technology adoption curve (Rogers 2003). Moore (1999) claims that failure to diffuse a new technology can stem from not recognizing and understanding the challenges with the chasm. Moore identifies a special tactic for crossing the chasm called "down the bowling alley."

We have studied and participated in an SPI initiative at the telecom company Ericsson AB in Gothenburg, Sweden, over a 10-month period. The SPI initiative focused on definition and implementation of a new change request solution for a product development unit consisting of 500 employees. The main question raised was, what tactics can SPI change agents use to cross the chasm? In the early stages of the SPI initiative, there was an idea by the SPI change agents driving the initiative to use a tactic where focus was put on establishing a trustworthy reference group and working closely with these people, both as a group and individually. The tactic, called the *guerrilla tactic*, was built on Moore's "down the bowling alley" tactic.

Delone and McLean (1992) observe that information technology use is the most frequently reported measure of IT implementation success and, therefore, it is used as an indicator for IT diffusion success. In accordance to this, the implementation and use of the new change request handling is used in this study as an indicator for SPI success. The new change request solution was successfully diffused into the organization and the chasm was crossed. The study explores the tactics that were adopted to achieve this. It discusses these in relation to Moore's (1999) ideas, and it discusses practical lessons learned in this particular SPI initiative with respect to crossing the chasm.

The study is presented as follows. The first section presents the theoretical context, mainly focusing on SPI change agent tactics and the chasm in the technology adoption curve. The next section describes the action-based research approach. In the fourth section, we present data from the SPI initiative according to Susman and Evered's (1978) cyclical action research approach and discuss the contributions of the research. Finally, our conclusions are presented in the fifth section.

2   THEORETICAL CONTEXT

This section presents the basic theoretical framework for this paper. First, we present SPI change agent tactics. Second, we review the technology adoption curve (Rogers 2003), the concept of the chasm (Moore 2002), and Moore's (1999) down-the-bowling-alley strategy for crossing the chasm.

2.1 SPI Change Agent Tactics

Humphrey (1989) stresses that enthusiastic, technically and politically capable, and dedicated resources with the management's confidence are necessary means to reach successful SPI. Humphrey calls these dedicated resources SPI change agents. Dedicated resources are needed to assure that practitioners overcome resistance, that practitioners are provided with adequate training and support, and that projects receive necessary consultation. SPI change agents need to use different tactics to accomplish these tasks. Several other SPI experts also recognize the need of SPI change agents to assure successful SPI. McFeeley (1996) stresses the importance of committing dedicated resources to drive the SPI work. Fowler and Levine (1993) identify the SPI change agent role and their tactics as one of five key factors for successful diffusion of an innovation. Pries-Heje and Tryde (2001) provide a practical framework for how SPI change agents can organize planning to assure successful process implementation. This strategy also includes other acknowledged implementation tactics (Eason 1988). Pries-Heje and Tryde's work has been successfully adopted and used by Volvo IT in Gothenburg, Sweden (Andersson and Nilsson 2002).

We interpret the roles presented by Kautz et al. (2001) as *tactics*. In this light, the work of Kautz et al. can be seen as an SPI change agent that uses tactics from four different perspectives (technical expertise, facilitating participation, political agency, and individual therapy) to contribute more to the SPI result. The tactics do not preclude each other. The first tactic, *technical expertise*, provides insight to fully understand the problem area with help from a formal assessment. This tactic assumes that the organization can be completely controlled by introducing procedures and standards to perform work processes. The second tactic, *facilitating participation*, bases work on the assumption that the world is socially constructed. The focus is more on the change agent performing a consulting and facilitating role where the members of the organization discover the improvements and solutions themselves. The third tactic, *political agency*, resolves structural conflicts among different stakeholder groups in the organization. The change agent, using the tactic political agency, strives for change through influencing the tensions and contradictions among organizational members. The change agent believes in radical change. The fourth tactic, *individual therapy*, assumes that reality is socially constructed. The change agent, using this tactic, works with the different individual subjects' attitudes and opinions, because the agent recognizes that the world is created by the individual.

SPI has been viewed by many of these authors as a particular instance of diffusion of innovations (Rogers 2003). Humphrey, McFeeley, and Grady all agree and argue that SPI will not happen if dedicated people do not drive the change. This is also further elaborated and emphasized by Börjesson and Mathiassen (2004b), who point out several different SPI change agent tactics to be used to accomplish successful SPI. Rogers claims that SPI change agents would not be needed in the diffusion of innovations if there were no social and technical chasms between the change agency and the client system. This is, however, not the case and Rogers defines five different generalizations (i.e., SPI change agent tactics) for how SPI practitioners can interact with the clients to achieve positive diffusion effects. The success of the SPI change agent in securing the adoption of processes by clients is positively related to the following:

- The extent of the SPI change agent's effort in contacting clients
- Client orientation, rather than a change agency orientation
- The degree to which a diffusion program is compatible with clients' needs
- Empathy with clients
- Credibility in the clients' eyes

2.2 Crossing the Chasm

It is well established within SPI literature that there is a gap between acquired and deployed technologies (Fichman and Kemerer 1999) and several theories have been presented to explain reasons for this gap (Abrahamsson 2001; Börjesson and Mathiassen 2004b; Weinberg 1997). Moore's (2002) chasm emphasizes the gap. The chasm framework was originally developed to understand marketing and deployment of high-technology products over a population of profit-making firms. The chasm has also been discussed and used as an overall framework for understanding change (Paulk 1999). Paulk argues that the use of structured tactics to cope with change increases the likelihood of successful change. Moore's (1999) suggestion for how to cross the chasm, "down the bowling alley," is such a tactic. Moore's chasm is built upon Rogers' recognized technology adoption curve, which consists of five different groups of people, each group having its specific profile (see Figure 1). The first group, *innovators*, tends to seek out the new technology before formal marketing. The innovators usually are very technology focused. The second group, *early adopters*, accepts new products very early in the technology life cycle. The early adopters find it easy to imagine, understand, and appreciate the potential benefits with the new technology. The third group, *early majority*, is driven by a strong sense of practicality. The early majority wants well-established references from relevant market segments before committing themselves. The fourth group, *late majority*, shares all of the concerns of the early majority, but they do not feel comfortable in their ability to manage the new technology. They wait until a new technology has become a well-established standard. The fifth and final group, *laggards*, simply do not want anything to do with the new technology. When they accept a new technology, they probably do not know it is there.

One main idea when diffusing an innovation is to create a bandwagon effect where each convinced group can be used as a reference for the next group to keep momentum when marketing of a new technology (Rogers 2003). Between any of these groups, there is a gap. This gap symbolizes the difficulty any group will have in accepting a new technology if it is presented in the same way as it was to the group to its immediate left (Moore 2002). The important gap is the gap between early adopters and early majority (see Figure 1), which is called the chasm (Moore 2002). Moore claims that this chasm is extremely dangerous if it goes unrecognized. The innovators and the early adopters are prepared to bear with the bugs and glitches that the new technology entails. The early majority wants technology to enhance, not overthrow, the established ways of working. Because of these incompatibilities, the early adopters do not make a good reference for the early majority. The early majority does, however, need good references to assure a minimal disruption of the established way of working. Moore (2002) defines this as a catch-22 problem.

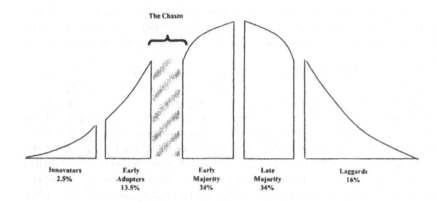

Figure 1. The Technology Adoption Curve (Rogers 2003)
and the Chasm (Moore 2002)

To solve the catch-22, Moore (1999) presented his down-the-bowling-alley tactic for crossing the chasm. Each market niche, or group of would-be adopters, is represented by a bowling pin and the goal is to strike down one pin so that it helps to knock the next one over. In this way, momentum is built up as more and more pins are knocked over by each other. Moore claims that the selection of pins to target is an important task. The initial selected pins should meet two criteria; the would-be adopters should have a compelling need for the solution, and competition should be scarce in that area. There is also a need for applying a customer-oriented tactic. The innovation supplier ensures that they can deliver the whole product to the selected target (i.e., instead of trying to satisfy the requirements of the whole market, focus is put on meeting one target customer's expectations). Moore identifies the whole product as the bare minimum requirements one specific customer has to purchase the innovation. Momentum is built up through first selecting the pins within the same market segment with the same whole product needs, and then further developing the product to reach new market segments. At this point, the chasm has been crossed and the early majority market is about to be penetrated.

3 RESEARCH APPROACH

This SPI initiative had the dual goal of both improving the change request handling and understanding what tactics SPI change agents can use to cross the chasm and assure successful SPI. Mathiassen's (2002) collaborative practice research (CPR) supports the possible realization of this dual goal. Another important part of CPR is the insider and outsider perspective (Bartunek and Louis 1996). The authors of the current study have been working within Ericsson in the SPI unit. Two of them have been driving the initiative as SPI change agents and have taken the insider role (i.e., they have been directly involved in action). The third author has been responsible for the initiative, but has taken the outsider role through regular analysis, discussions with the SPI change agents, reflection, and interviews with SPI initiative participants. The initiative has also been discussed, analyzed, and reflected upon in the monthly SPI forum (Börjesson 2004).

The study is based on action research (Baskerville and Pries-Heje 1999; Davison et al. 2004; Galliers 1992) with a focus on understanding what tactics SPI change agents can use to cross the chasm and, by doing so, assuring SPI success. The research question is, what tactics can SPI change agents use to cross the chasm? Baskerville and Pries-Heje (1999) argue that the fundamental contention of action research is that a complex social process can be studied best by introducing changes into that process and observing the effects of these changes. Recent research by Davison et al. (2004) elicited a set of five principles and associated criteria to ensure and assess both rigor and relevance of canonical action research (CAR). The term *canonical* is used to formalize the association with the iterative, rigorous, and collaborative process-oriented model developed by Susman and Evered (1978). Susman and Evered's model has been widely adopted in the social sciences and, hence, has gained "canonical status" (Davison et al. 2004). The five proposed principles and the adoption of these in this study are described in Table 1.

Both the study and the structure of the paper have followed the cyclical action research approach by Susman and Evered, including the five phases of diagnosing (identifying the problem), action planning (considering alternative courses of action for solving the problems), action taking (selecting a course of action), evaluating (studying the consequences of the actions taken), and specifying learning (identifying general indicators for SPI success).

Table 1. The Principles of CAR (Davison et al. 2004) and its Adoption in This Study

Principle	Adoption in This Study
The principle of the researcher–client agreement (RCA)	The researchers and clients are the same individuals. One of the three researchers has taken the academic role through the commitment to an ongoing industrial Ph.D. program.
The principle of the cyclical process model (CPM)	The study used Susman and Evered's (1978) cyclical action research method.
The principle of theory	Established theories as the technology adoption curve (Rogers 2003), the chasm (Moore 2002) and "down the bowling alley" (Moore 1999) are used.
The principle of change through action	One of the main goals of the study is to change the current way of working and to improve practice. CPR (Mathiassen 2002) is adapted.
The principle of learning through reflection	Meetings for reflections on the ongoing progress have been regularly pianned and executed. Also, the initiative has been regularly analyzed and reflected upon in the monthly SPI forum (Börjesson 2004).

Table 2. Data Collected Throughout the Initiative

#	What	Explanation
1	Direct involvement	All three authors have been directly involved or responsible for the management and outcome of the SPI initiative. This participation gives primary access to the organization, personal opinions, coffee break discussion, etc. that cannot be reached in any other way.
2	SPI initiative data	The two SPI change agents driving the initiative collected data about reference group meetings (time, participants, disagreements, decisions, outcome, etc.).
3	Participatory observations	The author taking the outsider role participated in some reference group meetings to observe and reflect.
4	SPI forum content	The papers and ongoing SPI initiatives that were studied, discussed, and reflected upon.
5	SPI forum reflections	Comments, ideas, and reflections during the SPI forum were written down and stored by one of the authors on the internal SPI unit Web.
6	SPI unit survey 2003 and 2004	60 questions with six scale answers were asked through a Web questionnaire in the yearly SPI unit survey in 2003 and 2004 to all software engineers in the development unit.
7	Tool data	Access to data in the tool such as change request registrations, who and how many entering data in the tool, and how the change requests were managed according to the process.
8	Final interviews with eight of the participants in the reference group.	Each interview lasted for 30 minutes (occasionally longer) and two of the authors were present at each interview.

The authors collected data for 10 months throughout the initiative as summarized in Table 2. Triangulation of data (Yin 1994) has been important to avoid bias and to secure validity of the research. The combination of many different data sources has made triangulation possible.

4 ACTION LEARNING

The SPI initiative follows Susman and Evercd's (1978) five phases. The first phase identifies and defines the problem with the current change request handling situation and the difficulties with assuring SPI implementation and use. The second phase describes the plan to solve the problem by implementing a new solution for change requests and

Table 3. The Change Request Process and Tool Situation in Late 2003

CCB	Process	Tool
Development project A	Project specific process A	No tool (spreadsheet A)
Development project B	Project specific process B	No tool (spreadsheet B)
Development project C	Project specific process C	Local version C
Unit X	Unit specific process X	Local version X
Unit Y	Unit specific process Y	No tool (spreadsheet Y)

it also describes a new tactic to address the difficulties with process implementation and use. The third phase describes which actions were taken according to the plan. The fourth phase discusses the evaluation of the actions taken. Finally, phase five discusses general indicators for successful SPI in relation to the theoretical context presented in the second section.

4.1 Diagnosing

The software development unit studied develops and maintains parts of 3G mobile networks. It is located in Gothenburg, Sweden, and has approximately 500 employees. There is an SPI group, responsible for driving SPI initiatives, consisting of six people. In late 2003, the change request procedures were identified as a major risk for development projects and the organization as a whole. Over 150 employees were directly affected by these procedures. The degree and pace of changes within software organizations have increased over the past years as indicated by the notions of fast-moving software organizations (Baskerville et al. 2001; Börjesson and Mathiassen 2004a; Holmberg and Mathiassen 2001) and radical IT-based innovations (Lyytinen and Rose 2003). Software organizations and their ongoing development projects constantly need to react to new or changed customer requirements as a result of a changing business environment. The studied organization has several different change control boards (CCB), supporting either a development project or a specific organizational unit with management of the change requests. All CCBs used different processes for change-request handling and most of the processes lacked tool support. Table 3 shows the change-request process and the tool situation in late 2003.

A number of problems were identified. Each CCB had its own process for change-request handling, and its own way of storing the data. Each time a CCB was set up, effort was spent on defining these issues. Change requests that needed to be handled by more than one CCB became very complex from an administration and follow-up point of view, with the risk of loosing track of decisions and information when a change request moved between the CCBs.

With the exception of the complexity of the improvement initiative, there was an identified problem regarding successful deployment of new solutions. Through extensive SPI initiative participation, theory studies, discussion, and reflection (Börjesson 2004), the SPI unit acknowledged a major difficulty when starting a wider deployment

Table 4. Data from SPI Unit Survey 2003 and 2004

How important is it that you participate to assure successful SPI?	Not Important		Important	
	2003	2004	2003	2004
I am the leader of the process work	72%	71%	28%	29%
I am a part of the group defining the new way of working	40%	38%	60%	62%
I give feedback to the new way of working in order to get it good enough	16%	14%	84%	86%

of a new or changed process (Börjesson and Mathiassen 2004b; Fichman and Kemerer 1999; Humphrey 1989; Weinberg 1997). Users of new practices did not accept new solutions in the same way as the SPI change agents driving the initiatives. Many of the potential users were driven by a strong sense of practicality and they wanted clear proof that the new solution would be beneficial for them.

Furthermore, data from two consecutive SPI surveys show that people want to be involved to assure a successful SPI (see Table 4). Almost 3 out of 10 employees wanted to lead the work. More than 6 out of 10 employees wanted to be a part of defining the new way of working. More than 8 out of 10 wanted to review the new way of working to assure it was good enough. It is, however, practically impossible to fulfill these desires in a large organization. This data indicates the importance of having a trust-worthy reference group on which people can rely.

4.2 Action Planning

In late 2003, the organization decided to start an SPI initiative to improve the change-request process and tool situation. The plan was to define a new process (based on previous experience) in close collaboration with the development project just starting up and the unit controlling the product features on an overall level. The other CCBs would align as new development projects started and the old one finished its release. There was a decision to use the tool ClearQuest. This was a natural choice as this was Ericsson's choice as a corporation for change-request handling. Two of the CCBs had used ClearQuest as a support tool before and ClearQuest has connections to other tools already used in the organizations (such as RequisitePro and ClearCase).

In parallel, the SPI unit decided to use previous learning on how to manage successful SPI initiatives (Börjesson and Mathiassen 2004b). The SPI change agents dedicated to the SPI initiative also decided to try out a new tactic to make users accept the solution faster. As the identified problems were closely related to the chasm (Moore 2002), the down-the-bowling-alley tactic was used for setting up the guerrilla tactic. The guerrilla tactic consists of two main parts: choosing a dedicated reference group with a compelling need for the solution and having a tactic for close collaboration between the SPI change agents and the reference group. The SPI initiative will benefit from having a reference group upon which all potential users can rely. The reference group should consist of people driven by a sense of practicality who will become natural references for the majority of users. The reference group needs to consist of members that cover all affected organizational areas. The typical member of the reference group must be experienced in the specific practice, understand the big picture, and be well known and respected in order to facilitate the deployment of the SPI initiative. The SPI change agents, representing the group of people that easily understand and appreciate the potential benefits of the new practice, should work in close collaboration with the reference group to become their natural reference. The SPI change agents should influence the most strategic individuals in the reference group in order to get commitment at reference group decision meetings and to elaborate ideas with its members.

The collaboration between the reference group and the SPI change agents can be described as influencing a group by influencing its core members. The tactic for close collaboration consists of SPI change agents who personally brief and discuss upcoming decisions with some of the members of the reference group in between reference group decision meetings. The member that needs to be addressed before a decision meeting varies, since that is dependent on the decisions to be discussed in the upcoming meeting. Collaboration with strategic reference group members addresses problems and uncertainties but also new ideas for how things should be solved before the actual decision meeting takes place.

The first bowling pin in the guerrilla tactic is the reference group (see Figure 2). This first pin will help to knock the next one over (i.e., get the other users to use the new solution). It is, therefore, extremely important to choose and collaborate with the reference group in a way that ensures their commitment and dedication to the solution.

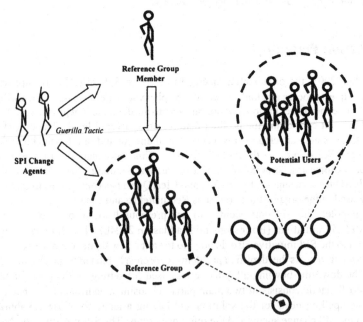

Figure 2. SPI Change Agents Using the Guerrilla Tactic

4.3 Action Taking

A first action was to set up the reference group. A number of strategic people (nine individuals) responsible for or involved in the CCB work were asked by the SPI change agents to participate in the reference group. In parallel, the SPI change agents learned how to master the ClearQuest tool for the advanced technical development of the solution. One important success factor for accomplishing high process push is to have not only committed SPI change agents, but also competent SPI change agents (Börjesson 2004; Humphrey 1989; McFeeley 1996).

Between reference group meetings, the SPI change agents addressed strategic individuals in the reference group in order to prevent unnecessary disagreements and thus improve the solution. Events that triggered the SPI change agents to address a strategic individual could be if they believed that this person had in-depth knowledge, was poorly informed, felt overrun, or if they believed this person could impact the other people in the group to understand the big picture. Table 5 shows date and purpose, meeting preparations that were made between reference group meetings and the outcome of these meetings.

In early May, the new change request solution was presented and deployed. The SPI change agents conducted a number of courses to all potential users and reference group members participated in each course. The reference group members could defend and explain the solution and, as they were active users of the new solution, they became well-established references. The SPI change agents also conducted start-up meetings for the affected CCBs in order to support them in the early phases of introducing the new work methods. Again, reference group members played a central deployment role as they both were regular members of the CCBs and had been a part of the SPI initiative. Finally, as the SPI change agents were phased out of deployment activities, the reference group members stayed current in their regular roles, where use of the new solution was natural. In these roles, the reference group members could continue the day-to-day deployment and support the new solution.

4.4 Evaluating

In mid-June 2004, eight active users were interviewed about their experiences and opinions concerning the SPI initiative and solution in order to further understand how the guerrilla tactic affected the outcome of the initiative. This tactic was unknown to the reference group at the time the interviews were conducted. The active users represented the three target CCBs, CCB chairmen, project managers, and senior engineers working with change requests in their daily work. The results of the interviews are summarized in Table 6.

When the solution was released, the reference group members and CCB members were immediately given access to the tool. Table 7 shows the growth of users entering data in the tool and the amount of data in the database. The numbers in the table are accumulated from the date (May 10, 2004) the database was opened for use. The numbers show individuals that actually updated information in the tool. It has not been possible to measure users only reading information.

Table 5. Reference Group Meeting Data

Reference Group Meeting	Meeting Preparations	Meeting outcome
#1: 2004-01-15 Present time plan and purpose of the reference group and the change request handling	The SPI change agents collaborated individually with four reference group members	Agreement and necessary decisions taken.
#2: 2004-01-30 Present overall change request solution and concept	No collaborations performed	No agreement. Most of the reference group members had their own opinion about a potential solution.
#3: 2004-02-06 Present overall change request solution and concept	The SPI change agents collaborated individually with five reference group members	Agreement and necessary decisions taken.
#4: 2004-02-20 Present change request process and detailed solution	The SPI change agents collaborated individually with three reference group members	Agreement (after smaller adjustments) and necessary decisions taken.
#5: 2004-03-05 Peer review of detailed solution, two new participants in the reference group	No collaborations performed	No agreement. The two new reference group members objected, as they did not fully understand the earlier agreements.
#6: 2004-03-12 Formal review of detailed solution and peer review of tool interface	The SPI change agents collaborated individually with seven reference group members	Agreement (after smaller adjustments) and necessary decisions taken.

The SPI initiative was carried out according to the time plan. Six reference group meetings were held within the planned time frame. The rollout of the solution was originally planned to match the need of a new engineering project in week 18, but as the engineering project was a few weeks late, the rollout of the new change request solution was moved to week 21.

This SPI initiative aimed to cover the entire organization; however, all employees are not required to work with change request handling. The calculation of the total target group is based on the main technical stakeholders (project managers and requirements engineers, approximately 90 employees) having an 80 percent usage and peripheral technical stakeholders (design and test engineers, approximately 325 employees) having a 25 percent usage. The 80-percentage number is based on that most, but not all, main technical stakeholders are working with change requests, while the 25-percentage number is based on the prerequisite that only team leaders and senior engi-

Table 6. Compiled Results of the Interviews

#	Questions	Yes	No	Not Applicable	Positive Answers
1	The result was generally positive	6	2	0	75%
2	The decisions were generally handled in a positive way	6	1	1	75%
3	The SPI change agents' process push was generally positive	5	1	2	63%
4	The rollout was generally considered as positive	7	0	1	88%
5	The users' response have generally been positive	6	2	0	75%
6	The attitude is, in the end, generally positive	6	2	0	75%
7	It was generally positive with a tight time schedule	5	1	1	71%
8	The result was generally received positively	5	1	2	63%

Table 7. Active Users and Data in the Change Request Database

Measurement	2004-06-02	2004-07-05	2004-09-02	2004-10-04
Number of change requests submitted since the start	24	99	170	258
Number of unique users having updated change requests since the start	19	43	54	65

Table 8. Distribution of Potential Users Between Groups

Group	Percentage according to Rogers	152 × Rogers' percentage
Innovators	2.5%	4
Early Adopters	13.5%	20
Early Majority	34%	52
Majority	34%	52
Laggards	16%	24
Total sum	*100%*	*152 (88 × 08 + 326 × 0.25)*

neers are working with change requests. Groups that are not expected to work with change request handling have not been counted (approximately 100 employees). Table 8 shows the distribution of the population of expected change request users and what role they take in Rogers' diffusion of innovation curve.

4.5 Learning

As indicated from the interviews (Table 6) and tool measurements (Table 7), the SPI initiative was successful in implementation and use. In all, 75 percent of the interviewees believed the initiative was successful. Also, within a period of 5 months period from the start, nearly half of all potential users had accessed and entered data in the change request tool. The main question now is to understand what effects the guerrilla tactic had on this positive outcome.

The two SPI change agents did not believe they could determine problems and solutions for the new solution by themselves. They used tactics to work in close collaboration with strategic users of the new process and they tried to solve conflicts, not only as they occurred but also through preventive actions. The two SPI change agents used tactics combining facilitating participation and political agency (Kautz et al. 2001). The tight and focused collaboration between SPI change agents and the reference group is identified by Rogers as one of five key features for SPI change agents to succeed in securing adoption of the innovation.

The two SPI change agents identified a reference group consisting of (probable) individuals from the early majority, who could become natural references and facilitate for the rest of the early majority to cross the chasm (Moore 2002; Rogers 2003). This is closely related to the important selection of the first pin in the down-the-bowling-alley tactic (Moore 1999). Having individuals in a reference group that do not want to overthrow the current way of working before they feel convinced requires special treatment. The identification of the first pin is, according to Moore, crucial. Moore claims that every other pin is derived from this head pin. In this study, we have identified the importance of the reference group in capturing new users. The reference group members defended and explained the solution and they became well-established references. The selection of the reference group has been crucial for crossing the chasm. Most users were derived from the reference group. The SPI change agents also used tactics for collaboration with the individuals in the reference group, both one by one and in the group, to manage the special needs each reference group member had. This part of the tactic supports Moore's ideas about building up a momentum where one pin helps to knock the next one over (see Figure 2). Furthermore, the SPI change agents collaborated with the reference group to listen, understand and identify the key features for the users to be willing to use the solution. This part of the tactic is well aligned with Moore's (1999) identification of "the whole product." SPI is a special instance of diffusion of innovations and the guerilla tactic is partly an instance of the down-the-bowling-alley tactic. Table 9 explains how the down-the-bowling-alley and guerrilla tactics relate to each other.

Data from Table 5 shows a high correlation between high use of guerrilla tactics and high acceptance of the solution suggested by the SPI change agents. The reference

Table 9. The Relations Between Down-the-Bowling-Alley and Guerrilla Tactics

	Down the Bowling Alley (Moore 2002) (Each market niche, or group of would-be adopters, is represented by a bowling pin and the goal is to strike down one pin so that it helps to knock the next one over.)	**Guerrilla** (Identification and collaboration with respected practitioners who can understand and appreciate the new practice and become natural references for the majority of users.)
How to choose first target group	Choose an initial pin with a compelling need for the solution. Assure scarce competition in the selected pin area.	Choose a dedicated reference group that will become natural references for the majority of potential users. The reference group needs to consist of members that cover all affected organizational areas. A typical member of the reference group is experienced in the change area, understands the big picture and is well known and respected.
How to meet customer require-ments	Assure that the innovation supplier ensures they can deliver the whole product to the selected target, i.e. instead of trying to satisfy the requirements of the whole market, focus is put on meeting one target customer's expectations. Moore (1999) identifies the whole product as the bare minimum requirements one specific customer has for purchasing the innovation.	The SPI change agents should work in close collaboration with the reference group to become their natural reference. The SPI change agents should carefully listen, understand, and identify the key features for the users. The SPI change agents should influence the most strategic indi-viduals in the reference group in order to get commitment at refer-ence group decision meetings.

group meetings that were prepared through individual collaboration resulted in a more positive results than those which had not. The success of a decision meeting consisted of a tendency to agree on important issues in order to proceed. Table 7 shows a regular growth of users in the ClearQuest tool since the start and five months after the rollout: 65 individuals have been captured (i.e., have started to use the solution). To capture the whole group up to early majority, 76 individuals are needed according to Rogers' percentages (see Table 8). The early majority was achieved five months after the rollout. These data indicate that the chasm has been crossed. Note that these numbers do not visualize individuals that only read information in the tool.

The users' responses to the new solution have been generally positive (see Table 6). There has been no identified turmoil requiring extra, unplanned efforts to manage reactions to change or to capture the early majority group. The reference group has been working in the daily business where the new solution has been used and they have been able to function as natural references for the rest of the early majority group. Not one single project or line manager expressed dissatisfaction with the solution during rollout. The chasm was successfully crossed and the new solution was implemented and used, which indicates SPI success (DeLone and McLean 1992). The study indicates that the guerrilla tactic had a positive impact on the SPI outcome (i.e., there are specific tactics that SPI change agents can use to cross the chasm).

There are a number of factors, other than the guerrilla tactic, that could have influenced the outcome of the SPI initiative in a positive direction. Two experienced SPI change agents led the work, which is an important success factor (Humphrey 1989). The SPI change agents also had previous experience with the ClearQuest tool. Most change-request processes defined in the organization over the years have had the same basic features, which could indicate that this is a relatively non-political improvement area. Furthermore, the use of a tool can itself be an enforcing factor. There is no way to bypass the process, since all information is handled within the tool. The presence of both the non-political improvement area and the organization's wish for a common solution indicate a strong pull from the practitioners (Börjesson and Mathiassen 2004b). Further research is necessary to identify the impacts of these factors.

Practitioners and researchers are advised to try out and study further tactics that SPI change agents can use to cross the chasm. We need to understand and learn more about the perils of the chasm to accomplish successful implementation and use of new innovations.

5   CONCLUSIONS

This research focuses on an SPI tactic to accomplish successful SPI implementation. The study carefully analyzes an SPI initiative within Ericsson AB to improve the change-request process and tool. Moore's (2002) chasm is used as a framework from which a special SPI change agent tactic, called the guerrilla tactic, is adopted. The guerrilla tactic identifies how SPI change agents can choose a target group and meet its requirements to cross the chasm. The authors view the guerilla tactic as a specific instance of Moore's down-the-bowling-alley tactic, which SPI change agents can use to assure successful SPI implementation. The result from measurements based on tool use, interviews with practitioners, and extensive participation by SPI change agents in the initiative indicates that the use of the guerrilla tactic facilitated crossing the dangerous chasm and made successful SPI implementation possible. Further research is necessary to understand and learn more about the use of different SPI change-agent tactics for crossing the chasm.

REFERENCES

Abrahamsson, P. "Rethinking the Concept of Commitment in Software Process Improvement." *Scandinavian Journal of Information Systems* (13), 2001, pp. 69-98.

Andersson, I., and Nilsson, K. "Improving Diffusion Practices in a Software Organization," in *Proceedings of the 35th Annual Hawaii International Conference on System Science*, Volume 8, IEEE Computer Society Press, Los Alamitos, CA, 2002.

Bach, J. "Enough About Process: What We Need Are Heroes," *IEEE Software* (12:2), 1995, pp. 96-98.

Bartunek, J. M., and Louis, M. R. *Insider/Outsider Team Research, Qualitative Research Methods*, Thousand Oaks, CA: Sage Publications, 1996.

Baskerville, R., Levine, L., Pries-Heje, J., Ramesh, B., and Slaughter, S. "How Internet Software Companies Negotiate Quality," *IEEE Computer* (14:5), 1999, pp. 51-57.

Baskerville, R., and Pries-Heje, J. "Grounded Action Research: A Method for Understanding IT in Practice," *Management and Information Technology* (9), 1999, pp. pp. 1-23.

Bollinger, T. B., and McGowan, C. "A Critical Look at Software Capability Evaluations," *IEEE Software* (8:4), 1991, pp. 25-41.

Börjesson, A. "Improve by Improving the Improvers," paper presented at the 27th Information Systems Research in Scandinavia Working Conference on Learn, Know and Move IT, Falkenberg, Sweden, 2004.

Börjesson, A., and Mathiassen, L. "Organization Dynamics in Software Process Improvement: The Agility Challenge," in *IT Innovation for Adaptablity and Competitiveness*, B. Fitzgerald and E. Wynn (Eds.), Boston: Kluwer Academic Publishers, 2004a, pp. 135-156.

Börjesson, A., and Mathiassen, L. "Successful Process Implementation," *IEEE Software* (21:4), 2004b, pp. 36-44.

Davison, R., Maris, M. and Kock, N. "Principles of Canonical Action Research," *Infomation Systems Journal* (14), 2004, pp. 65-86.

Delone, W., and McLean, E. "Information Systems Success: The Quest for the Dependent Variable," *Information Systems Research* (3:1), March 1992), pp. 60-95.

Eason, K. *Information Technology and Organizational Change*, London: Tyler & Francis, 1988.

Fayad, M. E., and Laitinen, M. "Process Assessment Considered Wasteful," *Communications of the ACM* (40:11), 1997, pp. 125-128.

Fichman, R. G., and Kemerer, C. F. "The Illusory Diffusion of Innovation: An Examination of Assimlation Gaps," *Information Systems Research* (10:3), 1999, pp. 255-275.

Fowler, P., and Levine, L. "Technology Transition Pull: A Case Study of Rate Monotonic Analysis, Part 2," Working Paper CMU/SEI-93-TR-031, ADA275637, Software Engineering Institute, Carnegie Mellon University, 1993.

Galliers, R. D. "Choosing an Information Systems Research Approach," in *Information Systems Research: Issues, Methods, and Practical Guidelines*, R. D. Galliers (Ed.), Oxford: Blackwell Scientific Publications, 1992, pp. 144-162.

Grady, R. B. *Successful Software Process Improvement*, Upper Saddle River, NJ: Prentice Hall, 1997.

Holmberg, L., and Mathiassen, L. "Survival Patterns in Fast-Moving Software Organizations.," *IEEE Software* (18:6), 2001, pp. 51-55.

Humphrey, W. S. *Managing the Software Process*, Reading, MA: Addison Wesley, 1989.

Humphrey, W. S., and Curtis, B. "Comments on a Critical Look at Software Capability Evaluations," *IEEE Software* (8:4), 1991, pp. 42-46.

Kautz, K., Hansen, H. W., and Thaysen, K. "Understanding and Changing Software Organisations: An Exploration of Four Perspectives on Software Process Improvement," in *Diffusing Software Product and Process Innovations*, M. A. Ardis and B. L. Marcolin (Eds.), Boston: Kluwer Academic Publishers, 2001, pp. 87-109.

Lyytinen, K., and Rose, G. M. "Disruptive Nature of Information Technology Innovations: The Case of Internet Computing in Systems Development Organizations," *MIS Quarterly* (27:4), December 2003, pp. 557-595.

Mathiassen, L. "Collaborative Practice Research," *Information, Technology & People* (15:4), 2002, pp. 321-345.

McFeeley, B. "IDEAL. A User's Guide for Software Process Improvement," Handbook CMU/SEI-96-HB-001, The Software Engineering Institute, Carnegie Mellon University, 1996.

Moore, G. *Crossing the Chasm: Marketing and Selling Technology Products to Mainstream Customers* (revised ed.), New York: HarperCollins Publishers, 2002.

Moore, G. *Inside the Tornado: Marketing Strategies from Silicon Valley's Cutting Edge* (revised ed.), New York: HarperCollins Publishers, 1999.

Paulk, M. C. "Structured Approaches to Managing Change," *Crosstalk—The Journal of Defense Software Engineering* (12:11), 1999, pp. 4-7.

Paulk, M. C., Weber, C. V., Curtis, B., and Crissis, M. B. *The Capability Maturity Model: Guidelines for Improving the Software Process*, Reading, MA: Addison-Wesley, 1995.

Pries-Heje, J., and Tryde, S. "Diffusion and Adoption of IT Products and Processes in a Danish Bank," in *Diffusing Software Product and Process Innovations*, M. A. Ardis and B. L. Marcolin (Eds.), Boston: Kluwer Academic Publishers, 2001, pp. 17-34.

Rogers, E. M. *Diffusion of Innovations* (5th ed.), New York: Free Press, 2003.

Susman, G., and Evered, R. "An Assessment of the Scientific Merits of Action Research," *Administrative Science Quarterly* (23), 1978, pp. 582-603.

Weinberg, G. M. *Quality Software Management Volume IV: Anticipating Change*, New York: Dorset House Publishing, 1997.

Yin, R. *Case Study Research*, Newbury Park, CA: Sage Publications, 1994

ABOUT THE AUTHORS

Anna Börjesson is a software process improvement manager at Ericsson AB in Gothenburg, Sweden, and an industrial Ph.D. student at the IT University in Gothenburg. She has over 10 years of software engineering working experience, with more than 7 years been dedicated to SPI, change management and diffusion of innovations. Anna is a member of IEEE and ACM. She can be reached at anna.borjesson@ericsson.com.

Fredrik Martinsson is a software process improvement manager at Ericsson AB in Gothenburg, Sweden. Fredrik is in parallel working as a change agent with special focus on requirements management, change request handling and project management. He has been working both for Ericsson and for Volvo Trucks with quality assurance, change management, and SPI. Fredrik can be reached at fredrik.martinsson@ericsson.com.

Magnus Timmerås is an SPI change agent at Ericsson AB in Gothenburg, Sweden. Magnus has nearly 10 years of experience working with SPI and SPI-related areas. Magnus has been appointed a senior engineer within SPI and his engineering skills cover areas such as CMM, RUP, software metrics, quality assurance, process adaptation work, and process implementation theories. He can be reached at magnus.timmeras@ericsson.com.

8 FOOLING AROUND: The Corporate Jester as an Effective Change Agent for Technological Innovation

Tom McMaster
University of Salford
Salford, United Kingdom

David Wastell
University of Manchester and
Nottingham Business School
United Kingdom

Helle Zinner Henriksen
Copenhagen Business School
Copenhagen, Denmark

Abstract   *In this reflective paper, we examine the roles and attributes of the change agent in the context of the organisational innovation adoption process. Various skills and qualities are required and expected of such a role, however wit and humor are not among those qualities typically emphasized in the subject literature. Yet these may be essential ingredients in the successful management of change. We examine the role of humour in the workplace in particular, as an empowerment tool on one hand, and as a display of subversion on the other. We note that the traditional role and attributes of the court jester exude those very qualities that might be missing in traditional descriptions of the change agent: deep insight, wit, and the ability to exert strong influence through humor. We consider the notion of the corporate jester and discuss whether such a role may hold any merit for the process of change management.*

1 INTRODUCTION

Jester wanted. Must be mirthful and prepared to work summer weekends. Must have own outfit (with bells). Bladder on stick provided if required.

The Times, August 5, 2004

The above advertisement appeared on August 5, 2004, in the situations vacant section of *The (London) Times* newspaper. It was placed by English Heritage, a government-sponsored agency charged with the protection of historical buildings and monuments, and they were seeking a juggling, joke-telling, part-time entertainer for summer weekend events sponsored and promoted by them. Since no official "state jester" has been employed in the United Kingdom since Archie Armstrong, Jester to Charles I (a role Cromwell abolished in 1649 following Charles' execution), English Heritage claimed it as the first state jester appointment in England for more than 350 years.

The jester is thus by no means dead. In this theoretical and reflective paper, we review relevant research literature on the subject (drawing on the work of Ackoff [1993], Otto [2001] and Welsford [1935] in particular) to explore the role of the (corporate) jester as a change agent in organizational innovation in general, and technological change in particular. Ackoff first mooted the idea of the corporate jester in relation to change in the journal *Systems Practice* in 1993, but the paper is a short one and the idea is given limited development. Here we push the concept further as we consider the role of humor as a catalyst for diffusing the resistance that goes hand-in-hand with uncertainty around the prospect of organizational change, especially where the implementation of new technology is involved. Although we will address the general role of humor, there will be a particular concern with the idea of the corporate jester. Lest confusion arise, we emphasize that in talking of such comedic figures, we do not in the first instance mean those informal clowns and buffoons that inhabit most workplace environments. Instead, we are primarily thinking of a kind of officially endorsed and empowered role that finds parallels in the appointed court jesters of medieval Europe and elsewhere. This being said, much of what we have to say applies to self-appointed folk figures as well as the formally sanctioned fool.

The subject of humor is gaining ground (as we shall see) as a worthy field of study amongst organizational scholars. There is a sporadic discourse on emotion within IS research, e.g., around anxiety and organizational learning (Wastell 1999, see below), and more recently on the influence of moods on understanding and action (Ciborra 2002). However, the topic of humor has not been specifically addressed (to our knowledge) in relation to the adoption and implementation of information technologies. Nonetheless, it is our general contention that technological innovation is essentially a process of organizational change, and so the topic of humor and the role of jesters are well worth considering within our domain. A simple technological example will feature in our reflections. We will discuss the role of the Microsoft paperclip as a kind of techno-logical jester, albeit a jester that signally hinders rather than facilitates. While we have specific concerns for the information systems domain, nevertheless some of the messages here have general implications for the wider field of organizational studies and behavior.

In the next section, we will discuss some of the problems associated with change. In section 3, we consider the generic role of the change agent, while in section 4 we raise the topic of humor in organizational settings. In section 5, we return to the theme of the jester and the attributes required, and we consider the "virtual" jester made possible by technology. In the final section, we discuss implications for the manage-ment of change and technological innovation, along with our conclusions.

2   ANXIETY AND HUMOR IN ORGANIZATIONAL CHANGE

The notion of *business agility* is one that evokes images of a firm with the capacity to embrace change quickly, and at short notice, for the express purpose of gaining or maintaining competitive advantage where firms might operate in such arenas. Other organizations, for example not-for-profit institutions such as local government agencies, may also have an interest in agility, although for different ideological motivations. Information technologies are seen by some as enablers of the change process, and are considered to be the very platform upon which business agility is predicated (Sambamurthy 2004). Business process reengineering (BPR) explicitly champions the potential of IT to effect revolutionary change in organizational structures and processes. Davenport (1993) speaks of *process innovation* in order to highlight the radical, transformational potency of IT. Despite this rhetoric, much IT-enabled change results in failure (Chang and Powell 1998; Wastell 1999). Software process innovation is a domain of special interest to IFIP WG8.6. Here the implementation of new tools and methodologies commonly evidences substantial resistance and frequent rejection (Hardgrave et al. 2003; Iivari 1996; Orlikowski 1993). The critical studies of Kautz and McMaster (1994) and Wastell (1996) provide telling insights into the problematics of methodological change, narrating the failure of two organizations to implement structured methods.

We contend that failed change efforts reflect a failure to "unfreeze" (Dent 1999; Lewin 1947), i.e., to abandon the old institutional order. Organizations seek to preserve their current identities, unless there a powerful reason to do otherwise. Threats and crises drive change. Gersick's (1991) notion of discontinuous change as *punctuated equilibrium* reflects the idea that the *status quo* will prevail in organizations unless there is a perceived need for change. Wastell et al. (2003), for instance, attribute the absence of a sense of urgent crisis as explaining the apparent resistance of local authorities in the United Kingdom to the modernizing imperatives of the eGovernment agenda. "Shocks" are required to overcome this organizational inertia: "only when people reach a threshold of sufficient dissatisfaction with existing conditions [will] they initiate action to resolve their dissatisfaction" (Van de Ven 1995). The notion of "problematization" within actor-network theory (Latour 1987) similarly reflects the need for innovations to align around a perceived sense of threat as the first critical stage in the process of technological innovation. McMaster et al. (1997) portray the rejection of a structured IS methodology in terms of the failure to "problematize" the situation in such a way as to portray the methodology as the accepted solution to the troubles and difficulties besetting the organization.

Extant organizational structures and processes provide members of business enterprises and other organizations with a sense of identity and security (Hirschhorn 1988; Menzies-Lyth 1988; Wastell 1999). Such psychological fortifications will not readily be given up. Hence the paradox that projects explicitly aimed at change often result in a perpetuation or indeed a strengthening of the *status quo* (Molinsky 1999). Change requires organizational energy (Benjamin 1993), with a strong collective sense of crisis serving to align and engage key stakeholder groups in the innovation process (Benjamin 1993; Latour 1987). Defensive reactions often occur (Wastell 1999; Wastell et al. 2003) when severe threats are confronted. The threat-rigidity hypothesis (Barnett and Pratt 2000) portrays a state of internal paralysis (strengthened internal control, restriction of information) elicited by crises that threaten to overwhelm the organization's repertoire of coping responses. Rigidity is one reaction to change, innovation is another. All forms of crises provide innovatory opportunities: to deal with problems, to unfreeze old behaviors, to develop new ways of understanding and acting (Kovoor-Misra et al. 2001).

The threat of change engenders unconscious processes within individuals (Bovey and Hede 2001) with these processes serving to provide protection from the feelings of anxiety that change evokes. These defenses can obstruct individuals from adapting to change, or they may function adaptively as part of a positive engagement with reality (Wastell 1999). Examples of negative defenses, such as denial, disassociation, projection, and acting out, are typically emphasized in psychodynamic accounts of change; however, there are positive defenses too. Humor is one such coping mechanism, which can help individuals embrace the need for change and to work through the anxieties it can produce. Bovey and Hede (2001) recently examined the relationship between humor and organizational change. In a survey of nine organizations undergoing major change efforts, they found humor to be associated with a "ready and willing" orientation to change. The maladaptive defenses, on the other hand, were associated with a resistive disposition.

In this paper, we develop the discourse on innovation and resistance by focusing on the psychological dynamics that underlie the process of organizational change. Since organizations continually shape (and are themselves in turn shaped by) social power relations, emotional and political forces are highly relevant in relation to the possibilities for, and defenses against change (Vince 1996). Specifically, we examine the role of humor as either a facilitative or a subversive agent. In particular, we will examine how humor might be expressed and realized in the workplace through the actions of agents of change. As Dyer (1984) noted two decades ago, change agent traits, including voice, appearance, and other physical and psychological attributes, will have consequences on the outcome of the implementation project.

3   THE CHANGE AGENT

The role of the change agent is assumed to be critical to the successful implementation of new technologies (Rogers 1995). The change agent acts as a link between the change agency (those promoting the innovation), and the client system (the potential adopters of the innovation). As a professional protagonist, be it teacher, consultant, public health worker, development worker, or salesperson (ibid., pp. 336-370), the change agent thus occupies a privileged position in the process and the situation.

3.1 Attributes of the Change Agent

The term *change agent* has been in use since at least the early 1960s (Nielson 1961; Rogers 1962) and the role is deemed by many to be critical in the innovation-adoption process. Despite this, there has been remarkably little research on the subject of change agents or of the qualities and attributes they might be expected to possess and exude. Detailed definitions, attributes, and descriptions tend therefore to be thin on the ground.

Somewhat bizarrely, in two book with the phrase "change agent skills" in the titles (Egan 1988a, 1988b), no entry for "change agent" appears in the indexes. Nor does there appear to be any reference to the phrase in the books! Seemingly aimed at the in-house practitioner, these books present models composed of prescriptive sequences of action that the author says companies need to implement if they seek and expect to attain successful change toward a notion of excellence. They are not specifically about change agents.

Eisenstein's wonderfully entitled *The Printing Press as an Agent of Change: Communications and Cultural Transformations in Early-Modern Europe* (1979) and Laver's *Information Technology: Agent of Change* (1989) similarly have no index entries for change agent. However, these two scholarly works at least have the respective merits of suggesting, if only in their titles, that change agents need not be limited to human beings but (consistently with actor-network theory) might just as easily be nonhuman.

Some attributes for change agents are inferred from the roles described by Rogers (1995, pp. 336-337), and these are that the change agent should

- possess "superior" technical knowledge of the innovation to that of client
- develop a need for change
- establish information exchanges
- diagnose problems
- create an intent to change
- translate that intent into action
- stabilize adoption (prevent discontinuance of the innovation)
- achieve a terminal relationship with the client (meaning that after adoption, he is no longer required)

Further insights are derived from other sources. For example, Clarke (1994) says that other functions of the change agent are

- to destabilize the *status quo* (before any organization can change, it must first be unfrozen from its current ingrained practices, as noted above)
- to induce a level of anxiety in the would-be adopter regarding the possibility of not changing that exceeds the natural increases in anxiety induced by the prospect of change: in other words creating the perception that the current ways are not working
- breaking rules; this is an essential part of innovation, and means heading in a direction that is quite opposite to that of everyone else

Turner et al. (1996), in discussing the project manager as change agent, require adoption of the roles of internal consultant, team leader, and ambassador. Dyer (1984) suggests the change agent might be called a facilitator, consultant, OD practitioner, or some other title, but that the essential qualities for success are leveling (honesty) and sharing (communicating) with the client. He adds that personality traits and voice and other physical attributes of the change agent will affect the change process, although exactly how and in what kinds of ways are not clear.

In this paper, we broadly concur with Dawson (2003), who supports the claims of Buchanan and Story (1997), that the notion of a singular change agent role is ultimately flawed, as there are both multiple agents of change and multiple players who enter and are drawn into the political arena of change management. Moreover, in line with Bacharach and Baratz (1962), while certain explicit activities can be identified as political, these actions may only represent the tip of the political iceberg, for it is the decisions that are not made, the options that never arise, and the voices that are never heard that form an integral part of the political process, if not its primum mobile.

In short, all stakeholders in the system into which it is planned that change be introduced are strictly change agents and these will have an effect on the process. While this is so, we will be primarily concerned here with those individuals formally appointed to the role. They may be human or they may not be. But by whatever means the change agent is described in the literature, qualities that quite positively do NOT routinely emerge from the descriptions (yet may be critical for the successful implementation of change) are those of humor and wit.

4   HUMOR AND ORGANIZATIONAL CHANGE

Although the role of humor in organizational life is a neglected area, we have noted the recent upsurge in research on humor in organizational studies. The broad view that has emerged sees humor as essentially functional for the individual, i.e., that humor is used by individuals for a range of practical purposes (Thomas and al-Maskati 1997). The work of Kahn (1989) has been particularly influential in summarizing much previous research. Kahn identifies six principal functional roles for humor in organizational settings (paraphrased from Thomas and al-Maskati).

- *Coping.* Humor enables people to detach themselves from potentially threatening situations, enabling them to maintain their self-image. Faced by collective threats, humor serves to generate cohesion within the group; laughing together forms an immediate social bond.

- *Reframing.* Humor allows people to separate themselves from dominant and conventional definitions of reality, constructed through prevailing power relations. By presenting alternative interpretations of situations, it becomes possible to envisage change to the *status quo.*

- *Communicating.* Humor enables painful or difficult messages to be conveyed in nonthreatening ways. Because humor has a frivolous face, serious messages that might have negative consequences for either or both parties may be transmitted safely.

- *Expressing hostility.* Humor may be used to express aggression, hinting indirectly at hostile feelings that would be inappropriate or dangerous to express openly.

- *Constructing identities.* Humor can contribute to the formation of in-group culture, helping members to maintain their identities and their distinctiveness from others.

In general, Kahn contends that humor serves to enable individuals to manipulate psychological distance. Faced with an external threat, for example, humor helps individuals cope by both increasing the members' distance from the threat and by bringing members closer together. In organizational settings, humor thus enables members to deal with the ambiguous, uncertain, and political character of organizations as well as the tensions that arise from their engagement in alienating organizational systems.

Humor can certainly play a key role in facilitating organizational change. British Airways' much-publicized employment (see below) of a corporate jester provides a pertinent example (Westwood 2004). Another illustration is provided by the employment of a "humor consultant" by one firm to run staff workshops when they laid off 40 percent of their employees. The egregious claim is made that this device helped minimize the negative responses normally associated with downsizing (ibid). Overall, the published literature of whatever provenance tends to emphasize the pro-managerial virtues of humor, whether it be stimulating creativity, improving decision making, enhancing morale, improving group performance, or reinforcing corporate culture. Barsoux (1996), for instance, enthusiastically alludes to the "dividends of humor" as follows:

> humor closes the communication gap between leaders and followers, it makes organizational confusion more bearable, it draws attention to areas in need of change, it facilitates change and encourages plurality of vision. In short, it breaks down barriers between people and makes an organization more participative and responsive. It follows that an environment which is amenable to humor will also facilitate organizational learning and renewal.

5 CORPORATE JESTER AS CHANGE AGENT

At the beginning of this paper, we referred to English Heritage and the advertisement it placed in *The Times* on August 5, 2004, along with the claims it made for the appointment being the first of its kind for over 350 years. Intriguing as such a claim sounds, it is, alas, untrue: English Heritage is hardly the "state" for one thing. As fanciful and unencumbered by the inconvenience of fact as this may be, it nonetheless did have the instant effect of attracting world-wide media attention. Subsequent coverage in articles in newspapers, magazines, and on television and radio stations across the globe was extensive. It was a very successful public relations exercise. Nonetheless and despite this, there are a number of professional jesters in civic and/or mayoral employment across the United Kingdom.

For example, Jonathan the Jester, awarded the title European Jester of the Year in 1999 by the UK's National Guild of Jesters, was appointed in 1997 as jester to the mayor (and thus the people) of Salisbury, a medieval town in Wiltshire, southwest England. His duties are to the communities of Salisbury, and to fund-raising for charitable causes. Other cities have also appointed official jesters. These include

Sylvester the Jester of Leicester,[1] Justin Andrews, jester to the city of Oxford, and
Peterkin the Fool, to the city of Bristol.

The National Guild of Jesters, for which Jonathan the Jester currently holds the
office of secretary and acts as its spokesperson, has over 30 full-time professional
members. They estimate that there may be as many as 200 jesters currently working in
England (many of these are talented part-time enthusiasts, including Nigel Roder, a.k.a.
Kester the Jester, the successful candidate for the post advertised by English Heritage).
In addition to the annual Titling Ceremony, the Guild organize frequent *moots* (convo-
cations of jesters) in specific locations where they are happy to exercise their skills in
return for a few jars of ale, and they act as an official voice for the disparate jester
communities of England.

5.1 The Corporate Jester

There have been advocates for the appointment of corporate jesters for at least a
decade-and-a-half (Ackoff 1993; Kets de Vries 1990), and real-life appointments of
corporate jesters have indeed taken place. These include, for example, Paul Birch,
appointed in 1994 as Corporate Jester to British Airways by Colin Marshall, former
CEO of that organization, in order to "stir things up" (Sittenfeld 1998). Paul used his
appointment to promote creativity, show managers that just because they were boss did
not mean they were right, and to say the things that most people are generally afraid to
say, at least publicly on record within their own organizations.

According to Ackoff (1993), the corporate Jester must be able to

- stimulate and disrupt the *status quo*
- recreate and provide the pauses that refresh the pursuit of change
- inspire creative transformations and help sustain them
- apply incisive and humorous revelations of the truth of their organizations and
  those who manage them
- ask questions that others dare not ask
- provide unexpected answers and be able to reject commonly held assumptions
  about their social systems
- seek power "to influence" rather than power "over" those who can bring about
  change
- express opinions authoritatively, based on acute observation and sound theory
- be corporate conscience, constructive critic, and thorn in the side of management through wit and humor

The role of the corporate jester is not dissimilar to that of the "sage fool" of older
times. Such comic individuals exercised a check on kingly hubris by reminding the
monarch of the transience of sublunary power and the fallibility of all human authority.
Attention was drawn to the pursuit of foolhardy actions, offering the king a counter view

---

[1]For readers who may not know, Leicester is pronounced "Lester."

to the sycophancy of fawning courtiers. As Kets de Vries (1990) has argued, the relationship of the corporate jester to organizational leadership is the same: to balance the hubris of the latter and engage with senior executives in an organizational drama dealing humanely and wisely with fundamental issues of human nature.

Shakespeare's fools provide familiar literary examples of the sage-fool genre. In a classic essay on the fool in King Lear, Knights (1959) observes that the fool "speaks to (and out of) a quite different order of apprehension: his function is to disturb with glimpses of confounding truths that elude rational definition." The comic garb of the fool's banter provides an obfuscating wrapping (another distancing device) around messages that, had they been directly delivered, risk bringing indignant wrath upon the head of the impertinent critic. The following exchange from the play provides a neat illustration:

Fool: The Lord that counseled thee to give away thy land,
           Come place him here by me, do thou for him stand:
           The sweet and bitter fool will presently appear,
           The one in motley here, the other found out there.

Lear: Does't thou call me fool boy?

Fool: All thy other titles thou hast given away; that thou was born with.

Kent: This is not altogether fool my lord.

Fool: No, faith, great lords and men will not let me; if I had a monopoly
           out, they would have part on't; and ladies too, they will not let me
           have all the fool to myself; they'll be snatching.

Unpalatable truths are imparted, but in a facetious, tangential manner that allows the fool to dance cleverly out of reach. A dangerous thing indeed to dub a king a fool, and the fool nimbly treads a dangerous line whilst pressing home his critique.

5.2 Virtual Jesters?

We earlier commented that change agents need not be human. Can we assume, then, the same of jesters? The answer is yes, and one that immediately springs to mind is Ronald McDonald, a virtual corporate clown who is as essential a trade mark to the McDonald Corporation as the large yellow "M" that spans the globe.

Another of interest to us is the Microsoft paperclip, which combines some of the traditional attributes of the jester, namely wisdom (it guides us through our own ignorance to "correct" behavior) and humor. We have more to say about this virtual technological jester in the next section.

5.3 The Significance of the Jester in a Technology Setting

Here we will again make analogies to the notion of a kingdom and the court jester. The kingdom is portrayed as the personal computer (PC), granting the user the role of the monarch. In the realm of the PC, the court jester is portrayed as the Microsoft paperclip.

The objective of this exercise is to illustrate how the developers of the Microsoft office package have reinvented the formalized role of a teaser with the intention of making it a part of our daily work. The Microsoft paperclip accommodates many of the features which characterize the court jester, as noted above. Additionally, the paperclip purports to take the role of a change agent. The recommendations provided by the clip intend to help the user make better use of the software application, in the place of the normal tutorials where the user is in charge of when to get instruction on how to use the software application The paperclip activates itself when it assesses that the user can usefully benefit from getting advice on how to make the best use of the software.

Contrary to the sage fool and the corporate jester, it is dubious if the paperclip jester supports successful implementation, or if it is rather a hindrance. No challenge to the *status quo* is offered, no alternative realty held up to the user, although there is clearly an invitation to explore more of the dominant one provided by the application. Although there are traces of wisdom in the suggestions the Microsoft paperclip imparts to the user, most (if not all) users of the Microsoft office package known to the authors find the feature extremely annoying. They immediately choose the option "Hide" to avoid getting advice on how to make the best use of their software applications!

From this perspective, the efforts of IT jester as a change agent have failed. At the first possible chance, the user will discontinue the information exchange relationship, which is one of the first steps necessary in the process of supporting further acceptance of an innovation (Rogers 2003, p. 369). As an exercise in humorous change agency, it is an act, like an unfunny clown, that dies on its feet.

5.4 The Jester as Change Agent

It is arguable that jesters can operate as change agents, or at least that the two roles can learn from each other. In this section, we consider the respective qualities and characteristics further, through mapping the attributes of the change agent as described by Rogers (1995) and Clarke (1994) against the attributes of the corporate jester specified by Ackoff (1993). We include these in Table 1.

There are many general similarities and some significant differences in the attributes of each, although we would argue that those of the corporate jester represent a far richer, more human personification (apart from the fact and beside which they are a lot more fun!). By comparison, the picture that emerges of the change agent, especially as described by Rogers, is a somewhat dry and sober one, although Clarke's contributions introduce a far more radical element than would otherwise be the case.

It is when considering the difference phases of a change effort that the clearest differences emerge. Change involves questioning of the extant order, the envisaging of a new reality, followed by the technical work involved in building the new vision. It is

Table 1. Attributes of the Change Agent and the Corporate Jester

The Change Agent	The Corporate Jester
Destabilize the *status quo* (Clarke 1994)	Stimulate and disrupt the *status quo*
Develop need for change (Rogers 1995)	Recreate and provide the pauses that refresh the pursuit of change
Create an intent to change (and) translate that intent into action (Rogers 1995)	Inspire creative transformations and help sustain them
Establish information exchanges (Rogers 1995)	Apply incisive and humorous revela-tions of the truth of their organizations and those who manage them
Diagnose problems (Rogers 1995)	Ask questions that others dare not ask
Break rules—essential for innovation: head in opposite direction to everyone else (Clarke 1994)	Provide unexpected answers and be able to reject commonly held assump-tions about their social systems
Achieve a terminal relationship with the client (Rogers 1995)	Seek power to influence rather than power over those who can bring about change
Superior technical knowledge (Rogers 1995)	Express opinions authoritatively, based on acute observation and sound theory
Induce a level of anxiety in the would-be adopter system related to *not* changing (Clarke 1994)	Be the corporate conscience, construc-tive critic and thorn in the side of management through wit and humor

the latter area where the roles most clearly diverge. The jester is not, *par excellence*, an implementer. His is not the mundane business of detailed plans, new management structures, targets, and deliverables—the quotidian banalities of project management. Doubtless comedic talents ease the fears and anxieties that surface during implemen-tation, as we have argued above. But it is as critic and visionary where the jester most clearly scores, i.e., the use of humor to provoke debate and challenge the *status quo*.

6   DISCUSSION AND CONCLUSIONS

The role of the jester in human society appears to be one that is universally recognized and embraced by all cultures and in all times, a role that clearly has considerable social value and importance. Otto (2001) provides many anecdotal accounts of jesters from ancient Persia, from China, from the native peoples of the Americas and Australasia, plus the European court jester with which many of us are familiar. Welsford (1935), too, provides accounts of jesters from history, and fictional jesters from literature. Modern jesters have become stars of the cinema (e.g., Charlie Chaplin) or stand-up comedians. It can be no coincidence that three of the world's highest paid television personalities in recent times are successful jesters. Ray Romano is currently the highest paid TV star (Sibbald 2004). Before him, Kelsey Grammer held the title, he in turn succeeding Jerry Seinfeld.

The general thrust of academic as well as practitioner writing tends to promote a broadly benign view of organizational comedy. Its subversive side is seldom mentioned. Westwood (2004) addresses this seditious aspect, using the example of a corporate comedian to explore this darker role. Westwood's account stresses the limited prerogative of such hired jesters. Whether traditional jester or corporate comic, the fool presents an alternative reality, a different way of framing the prevailing situation. So much of humor works in this way; indeed, that is arguably its primary psychological dynamic, the questioning of the dominant reality, the *status quo*, by whatever comedic form it assumes: lampoonery, satire, farce, irony, slapstick. But herein lies its subversive limit. To work as humor, there must be relief after the tension, the discomfort created must be resolved, with a return to the dominant reality. For a moment, the veil is lifted, but normality must be restored if laughter is to erupt. Think of the clown gesticulating a gun at the circus audience. The gun is fired, and a flag pops out emblazoned with the word "Bang." Were the gun real and people killed, there would be no humor, only tragedy.

Writers such as Westwood thus contend that humor is inevitably and symbiotically contained by the dominant reality. Its subversive power is ever constrained. The corporate jester and the sage fool are hired hands, operating under the license of those in power. They cannot go too far in poking fun and challenging the authority on which they depend, biting the hand that feeds them. Lear's Fool well shows this, and by avoiding confrontation, he is ultimately impotent to deflect the King from the folly of his intended purpose. Equally, we would hardly expect Microsoft's paperclip to give the real advice some would say it should impart around the use of the company's products! The subversion of humor then, in Westwood's view, is exactly the opposite: it reinforces power relations rather than undermining them. The licensed banter of the fool only serves to remind the audience who is really in charge! Ironically, then, the prevailing hierarchy tends to be strengthened by comedic performance, however irreverent.

But is this always so? Can humor never be a weapon, a subversive agent? Where the fool is licensed, the humor sanctioned by the ruling group, this will surely be the normal outcome. But in conflictual situations, the articulation of an alternative reality and the attack on the *status quo* can undermine the dominant elite. Taylor and Bain (2003) reject the view that humor always contributes to organizational harmony. They describe the case of a call center where satire and joking not only served to provide relief from the routine of call center life, but contributed to the development of a vigorous counterculture that conflicted with corporate aims and priorities. A group of activists exploited humor to help make trade unionism a popular idea and to weaken managerial authority.

In conclusion, humor (and its formal embodiment in human or nonhuman jesters) plays an important role in human life. In organizational settings, although it may sometimes question the prevailing power relations and the dominant ontology, overall it is constrained in this critical function, tending inevitably to reinforce the *status quo*. Change agents invariably operate under the sanction and management of the existing hierarchy; their role is not to overturn the dominant regime. If change occurs, it is the transformation sought by the ruling clique. As an instrument of the established order, humor thus generally works to promote organizational harmony. In this role, it can clearly ease the dynamics of change, which is therapeutically valuable in these turbulent times emblematized by the agile business. The beneficial value of "fun at work" as a means of diffusing organizational stress is advocated by Redman and Mathews (2002), who recount the attempt of a major retail organization to instil such a "fun culture" (through humorous newsletters, fancy dress events). While some success is claimed, there are obvious cautions in looking to such crude attempts to manipulate culture in order to resolve deep-seated organizational malaise and realize sustainable improvements in performance. Nonetheless, the authors conclude that "the idea of the postmodern manager and the management consultant [i.e., the generic change agent role] as the corporate jester is not without its immediate appeal."

The natural state of any organization is that of autopoetic reproduction, which inevitably entails resistance to change (Porra 1990). As we noted above, organizations are held together by powerful forces which tend to maintain the *status quo*. The imperative to change inevitably evokes insecurity and stress, and humor can help allay the anxieties associated with innovation, overcoming the inertial forces embedded in the social defense structure of the organization, but at the same time creating a shared fund of cathartic stories to maintain social cohesion in times of stress and upheaval. Humor in organizations is above all a palliative, not a subversive force. In relation to technological change, this role is clearly manifest in the burgeoning corpus of computer jokes directed at an array of predictable targets. Searching the Internet with "jokes and Microsoft" as keywords yields (as might well be imagined) a good crop of mirthful images and verbal banter, in which the much-abused paperclip receives its deserved share of ridicule (e.g., the egregious offer of help to the writer of a suicide note!).

Humor thus provides a welcome distraction from the threats to jobs and security that are associated in the popular imagination with technological change. There is clearly a cathartic role for the jester (and humor in general) in easing the pain of change, although inept implementations (such as the paperclip) provide a cautionary tale. Innovators need also to be aware of the subversive role of humor to draw together and mobilize forces of resistance. This is a particular problem for our field where the widespread prevalence of spectacular IS failures provides a fecund source of humorous atrocity stories to be told with a wry, subversive edge. Humor though, in whatever form it might take, is a natural part of being human—enhancing joy, ameliorating pain, and building social bonds. It is a neglected area of study in our field, and one that would clearly benefit from further research (especially of an ethnographic character) to bring out the role humor plays (formally and informally) in facilitating or hindering change and innovation. By way of ending, we will give the final word to Thomas Sydenham, 17th century physician and philosopher:

> *The arrival of a good clown exercises a more beneficial influence upon the health of a town than of twenty asses laden with drugs.*

REFERENCES

Ackoff, R. L. "The Corporate Jester," *Systems Practice* (6:4), 1993, pp. 333-334.

Bacharach P., and Baratz, M. "Two Faces of Power," *American Political Science Review* (56), 1962, pp. 641-651.

Barnett, C. K., and Pratt, M. "From Threat-Rigidity to Flexibility: Toward a Learning Model of Autogenic Crisis on Organizations," *Journal of Organizational Change* (13), 2000, pp. 74-88.

Barsoux, J-L. "Why Organizations Need Humor," *European Management Journal* (14:5), 1996, pp. 500-508.

Benjamin, R. "Managing IT-Enabled Change" in *Human Organizational and Social Dimensions of Information Systems Development*, D. Avison, J. E. Kendall, and J. I. DeGross (Eds.), Amsterdam: North Holland, 1993, 381-298.

Bovey, W. H., and Hede, A. "Resistance to Organizational Change: The Role of Defense Mechanisms," *Journal of Management Psychology* (16:7), 2001, pp. 534-548.

Buchanan, D., and Story, J. "Role-Taking and Role-Switching in Organizational Change: The Four Pluralities" in *Innovation, organizational change and Technology*, I. McLoughlin and M. Harris (Eds.), London: International Thompson Business Press, 1997.

Chang, L-J., and Powell, P. "Towards a Framework for Business Process Re-Engineering in Small and Medium-Sized Enterprises," *Information Systems Journal* (8), 1998, pp.199-215.

Ciborra, C. *The Labyrinths of Information: Challenging the Wisdom of Systems*, Oxford: Oxford University Press, 2002.

Clarke, L. *The Essence of Change*, Upper Saddle River, NJ: Prentice Hall International, 1994.

Davenport, T. *Process Innovation: Reengineering Work Through Information Technology*, Boston: Harvard Business School Press, 1993.

Dawson, P. *Reshaping Change: A Processual Perspective*, London: Routledge, 2003.

Dent, E. B. "Challenging Resistance to Change," *Journal of Applied Behavioral Science* (35), 1999, pp. 25-41.

Dyer, W. G. *Strategies for Managing Change*, Reading, MA: Addison Wesley Publishing Company Inc., 1984.

Eisenstein, E. L. *The Printing Press as an Agent of Change: Communications and Cultural Transformations in Early-Modern Europe* (Volumes 1 and 2), Cambridge, UK: Cambridge University Press, 1979.

Egan, G. *Change-Agent Skills A: Assessing and Designing Excellence*, San Diego, CA: University Associates Inc., 1988a.

Egan, G. *Change-Agent Skills B: Managing Innovation and Change*, San Diego, CA: University Associates Inc., 1988b.

Gersick, C. "Revolutionary Change Theories: A Multi-Level Exploration of the Punctuated Equilibrium Paradigm," *Academy of Management Review* (16), 1991, pp. 10-36.

Hardgrave, B. C., Davis, F., and Riemenschneider, C. K. "Investigating Determinants of Software Developers' Intentions to Follow Methodologies," *Journal of Management Information Systems* (20), 2003, pp. 123-151.

Hirschhorn, L. *The Workplace Within: The Psychodynamics of Organizational Life*, Boston: MIT Press, 1988.

Iivari, J. "Why Are CASE Tools Not Used?," *Communications of the ACM* (39:10), 1996, pp. 94-103.

Kahn, W. "Toward a Sense of Organizational Humor: Implications for Organizational Diagnosis and Change," *The Journal of Applied Behavioral Science* (25), 1989, pp. 25: 45-63.

Kautz, K., and McMaster, T. "The Failure to Introduce System Development Methods: A Factor-Based Analysis" in *Diffusion, Transfer and Implementation of Information Technology*, L. Levine (Ed..), Amsterdam: Elsevier/North-Holland, 1994, pp. 275-287.

Kets de Vries, M. F. R. "The Organizational Fool: Balancing a Leader's Hubris," *Human Relations* (43:8), 1990, pp. 751-770.

Knights, L. C. *Some Shakespearean Themes*, Stanford, CA: Stanford University Press, and London: Chatto and Windus, Ltd., 1959.

Kovoor-Misra, S., Clair, J. A., and Bettenhausen, K. L. "Clarifying the Attributes of Organizational Crises," *Technology Forecasting and Social Change* (67), 2001, pp. 77-91.

Laver, M. *Information Technology: Agent of Change*, Cambridge, UK: Cambridge University Press, 1989.

Latour, B. *Science in Action*, Boston: Harvard University Press, 1987.

Lewin, K. "Frontiers in Group Dynamics," *Human Relations* (1:1), 1947, pp. 5-41.

McMaster, T., Vidgen, R., and Wastell, D. "Technology Transfer: Diffusion or Translation," in *Facilitating Technology Transfer Through Partnership: Learning from Practice and Research*, T. McMaster, E. Mumford, E. B. Swanson, B. Warboys, and D. Wastell (Eds.), London: Chapman and Hall, 1997, pp. 64-75.

Menzies-Lyth, I. *Containing Anxiety in Institutions: Selected Essays*, London: Free Association Books, 1988.

Molinsky, A. L. "Sanding Down the Edges: Paradoxical Impediments to Organizational Change," *Journal of Applied Behavioral Science* (35:1), 1999, pp. 8-24.

Nielson, J. *The Change Agent and the Process of Change*, Michigan State University, 1961.

Orlikowski, W. "CASE Tools as Organizational Change: Investigating Incremental and Radical Changes in System Development," *MIS Quarterly* (17:3), September 1993, pp. 309-340.

Otto, B. K. *Fools Are Everywhere: The Court Jester Around the World*, Chicago: University of Chicago Press, 2001.

Porra, J. "Colonial Systems," *Information Systems Research* (10:1), 1999, pp. 38-69.

Redman, T., and Mathews, B. P. "Managing Services: Should We Be Having Fun?," *Services Industries Journal* (22:3), 2002, pp. 51-62.

Rogers, E. M. *Diffusion of Innovations*, New York: The Free Press, 1962.

Rogers, E. M. *Diffusion of Innovations* (4th ed.), New York: The Free Press, 1995.

Rogers, E. M. *Diffusion of Innovations* (5th ed.), New York: The Free Press, 2003.

Sambamurthy, V. "IT as a Platform for Competitive Agility," in *IT Innovation for Adaptability and Competitiveness*, B. Fitzgerald and E. Wynne (Eds.), Boston: Kluwer Academic Publishing, 2004, pp. 467-468.

Sibbald, V. "Romano Wonders if Everyone Will Love Mooseport," *Movie News*, February 9, 2004.

Sittenfeld, C. "He's No Fool (But He Plays One Inside Companies)," *Fast Company*, November 19, 1998, p. 66.

Taylor, P., and Bain, P. "Subterranean Worksick Blues: Humor as Subversion in Two Call Centres," *Organization Studies* (24:9), 2003, pp. 1487-1509.

Thomas, A. B., and Al-Mashati, H. "I Suppose You Think That's Funny! The Role of Humor in Corporate Learning Events," *International Journal of Human Resource Management* (8:4), 1997, pp. 519-538.

Turner, J. R., Grude, K. V., and Thurloway, L. (Eds.). *The Project Manager as Change Agent*, London: McGraw-Hill, 1996.

Van de Ven, A. H. "Managing the Process of Organizational Innovation" in *Organizational Change and Redesign*, G. Huber and W. Glick (Eds.), Oxford: Oxford University Press, 1995, pp. 269-294.

Vince, R. *Managing Change: Reflections on Equality and Management Learning*, Cambridge, UK: The Policy Press, 1996.

Wastell, D. G. "The Fetish of Technique: Methodology as a Social Defense," *Information Systems Journal* (6:1), 1996, pp. 25-40.

Wastell, D. G. "Learning Dysfunctions in Information Systems Development: Overcoming the Social Defenses with Transitional Objects," *MIS Quarterly* (23:4), December 1999, pp. 581-600.

Wastell, D., Kawalek, P., and Newman, M. "Plus ça Change: Defensive Translations and Resistance to IT-Enabled Change in Local Government" in *Proceedings of the 11th European Conference on Information Systems,* M. Martinez, M. D. Marco, C. Ciborra, A. Carignani, and R. Mercurio (Eds.), Naples, Italy, 2003.

Welsford, E. *The Fool: His Social and Literary History*, London: Faber and Faber, 1935.

Westwood, R. "Comic Relief: Subversion and Catharsis in Organizational Comedic Theater," *Organizational Studies* (25:5), 2004, pp. 775-795.

ABOUT THE AUTHORS

Tom McMaster is a lecturer in the Information Systems Institute in the University of Salford, Manchester, UK. Tom has a variety of research interests including technology transfer. He is a member of IFIP 8.2 and a founding member of IFIP 8.6, for which he co-organized the 1997 Ambelside event. Tom can be reached at t.mcmaster@salford.ac.uk.

David Wastell is Professor of Information Systems at Nottingham Business School. His current research interests are IT-enabled innovation, public sector reform and electronic government, and the human factors design of complex systems. He has published over 100 journal articles and conference papers in information systems, human factors, and health informatics, after an early research career in cognitive and clinical psychophysiology. He is on the editorial board of the *European Journal of Information Systems* and *Information and Management* and has co-organized two IFIP conferences (WG 8.6 in 1997 and WG 8.2 in 2004). Dave has considerable consultancy experience, especially in the public sector. He can be reached at dave_wastell@hotmail.com.

Helle Zinner Henriksen is an assistant professor in the Department of Informatics at the Copenhagen Business School. She has an M.Sc. in law from the University of Copenhagen and a Ph.D. from the Department of Informatics at the Copenhagen Business School. Her Ph.D. is in the field of Management Information Systems with particular interest in the implications of institutional intervention with respect to interorganizational adoption and diffusion. Her research interests include adoption and diffusion of IT in the private and public sectors. Her most recent work is focused on eGovernment and regulation of eGovernment. Helle is involved in the Center for Electronic Commerce and the Center for Research on IT in Policy Organizations, both at the Copenhagen Business School. More details on her research activities and publications can be found at http://web.cbs.dk/staff/hzh/. Helle can be reached at hzh@inf.cbs.dk.

Part 3

IT Infrastructures Agility

9 AN EMPIRICAL INVESTIGATION OF THE POTENTIAL OF RFID TECHNOLOGY TO ENHANCE SUPPLY CHAIN AGILITY[1]

Anthony Vance
Brigham Young University
Provo, UT U.S.A.

Abstract   *This empirical study examines the potential of RFID technology to increase the business agility and coordination of inventory supply chain systems. The bullwhip effect is a logistics management phenomenon in supply chain systems that is characterized by a lack of business agility. This study examines the potential of radio frequency identification (RFID) technology to increase the business agility and coordination of inventory supply chain systems, greatly reducing the bullwhip effect through timely information provided throughout the supply chain. An experiment of one group of 15 teams using a simulated RFID-enabled supply chain system compared mean team costs with those of a control group of 15 teams, providing empirical evidence that RFID-technology can increase a supply chain's business agility, as manifested by a reduction in inventory holding and stockout costs.*

1 INTRODUCTION

This study examines the potential of radio frequency identification (RFID) technology to increase the business agility of inventory supply chains by mitigating what is known in supply chain management literature as the "bullwhip effect" (Lee et al. 1997b). RFID technology has received much attention in recent years as retailers and manufacturers such as Wal-Mart, Gillette, and Target have committed themselves to implementing this technology into their supply chain information systems. Logistics literature suggests that RFID technology increases the agility of supply chain systems and gives companies a competitive advantage (Kinsella 2003). RFID tags are analogous

---

[1]This research was sponsored by the Kevin and Debra Rollins Center for eBusiness at Brigham Young University.

to barcodes that wirelessly transmit their serial number to in-store scanning machines (Atock, 2003; Robertson, et al. 1999). This automatic self-identification process is a great improvement over traditional barcodes. Traditional barcodes typically require employees to physically scan each item. Because traditional barcodes require a line-of-sight view of a barcode in order to scan the serial number, barcode scanning is labor-intensive and is usually only performed at the checkout register (Sarma et al. 2001). RFID chips add a nominal cost to each item but enable supply chain information systems to easily scan items throughout the supply chain, potentially enabling managers to visualize exactly how much inventory exists in the supply chain, and therefore know how much more inventory needs to be purchased or produced.

Proponents claim that RFID technology can potentially enable supply chain managers to overcome problems caused by imperfect or insufficient information inherent in current inventory management systems (RFID Forum 2003). The bullwhip effect is a well-known problem within supply chain management literature that directly relates to business agility from an Information Systems standpoint (Bowersox et al. 2000; Lee et al. 1997b). Information systems can increase business agility by providing businesses with current, relevant information from which managers can make better informed decisions. The bullwhip effect is a supply chain phenomenon in which imperfect inventory information is amplified as it is transmitted through the supply chain, resulting in increasingly inefficient inventory order levels. In a supply chain system with low coordination, suppliers gauge consumer demand by observing orders made by retailers. However, retailer orders are usually inflated due to safety stock—an inventory buffer used to allow for fluctuations in consumer demand (Sterman 1989). Retailer orders then offer a distorted view of consumer demand. The distortion of actual consumer demand worsens as each successive tier in a supply chain adds its own level of safety stock to the orders it requests. By the time the information reaches the top of the supply chain, the information is grossly distorted and most adversely affects top-level manufacturers (Lee et al. 1997a). In the bullwhip analogy, top-level manufacturers represent the tip of the bullwhip that is finally cracked.

The term *bullwhip effect* was coined by Proctor and Gamble management who noticed an amplification of information distortion as order information traveled up the supply chain (Lee et al. 1997b). However, amplification of information distortion was known to supply chain management researchers long before the term bullwhip effect came into common use. For example, in 1958, Forrester presented a number of simulated case studies detailing the distortion of order information that occurs along a supply chain. In one computer-simulated study, a 10 percent increase in retail sales caused retailers to increase inventory orders by 10 percent, which in turn was matched by a 16 percent and 28 percent increase in orders by distributors and warehouses respectively. Finally, the manufacturers increased output by 40 percent (Forrester 1958). Forrester concluded that the variation amplification observed in supply chains was due in part to communication delays and distorted information. More recent studies have also pointed to imperfect information as the root cause of the bullwhip effect. One study involved a series of experiments using a role playing game called the Beer Distribution Game, which was developed at Massachusetts Institute of Technology (Sterman 1989). In this study, Sterman used the Beer Distribution Game to show how using incomplete data to make inventory ordering decisions leads to wide inventory fluctuations in the supply chain. More recently, a study dealing with mathematical econometrics showed that demand signal processing, the practice of gauging demand from the order information of the next downstream supply chain member, is a significant factor of the bullwhip effect (Lee et al. 1997a). The above-mentioned studies show that imperfect information in the form of distortion or delays contributes significantly to the bullwhip effect.

Although the technical merits of RFID are well documented, the technology is still emerging and there is little available information that examines the capability of RFID technology to mitigate the bullwhip effect. On the other hand, while many of the studies cited above present theoretical models and simulations examining the bullwhip effect, these studies do not take into account the advantage of the added information now available through RFID technology.

The purpose of the present study was to empirically link previous research on the bullwhip effect to the potential of RFID supply chain information systems to increase supply chain agility and thereby reduce the bullwhip effect. This research employs a simulation intended to reveal the extent of RFID technology's impact on a vertical supply chain system. In so doing, this study helps to establish principles of RFID technology that can be further added to and expanded. RFID technology has the potential to overcome the bullwhip effect's amplified inventory information distortion by providing each tier of a supply chain with accurate, real-time information of inventory allocation within the supply chain. Because this study examines the affect of enhanced information, the proposed experiment does not involve RFID tags. Instead, a simulation is proposed that mimics an inventory supply chain system that is enabled with RFID technology.

2 OPERATIONALIZING THE CONSTRUCT OF INVENTORY MANAGEMENT EFFICIENCY

Because imperfect information is so central to the occurrence of the bullwhip effect, this study proposes that additional information available through the use of RFID technology will enable inventory managers to achieve the construct of regulating inventory stock within an appropriate range, that is, setting "the inflow rate so as to compensate for losses and usage and to counteract disturbances which push the stock away from its desired value" (Sterman 1989, p. 322). In order to operationalize the construct of appropriate inventory regulation, this study used the following two measures:

1. The cost of foregone revenue or stockout costs. Sterman defines stockout costs as "the cost for having a backlog of unfilled orders" (p. 326). Stockout costs are determined as the total lost sales revenue for every inventory unit on back order.

2. The cost of unnecessary inventory holding costs, determined as the holding cost of all inventory units that are not sold during a given sales period (Sterman 1989).

Combined, the above measures help operationalize the appropriate regulation of inventory because, in order to minimize stockout and holding costs, a firm must keep inventory levels within the optimum range. The more efficient a supply chain, the less the combined cost of holding costs and stockout costs. Conversely, the less efficient an inventory supply chain is, the higher the holding and stockout costs will be. This study's construct related question is: *Will the use of RFID chips enable supply chains to better regulate inventory levels within the optimum (most cost efficient range)?*

The operational question that follows the construct is: *Will use of RFID chips enable supply chains to minimize the inventory holding and stockout costs?*

Supply chain systems with additional information resulting from the usage of an RFID technology application should have statistically significant lower-average inventory stockout costs as well lower-average inventory holding costs than those managers with traditional barcode systems and limited inventory information. Further, RFID-enabled supply chain systems should not experience the amplification of order information distortion that is typical of the bullwhip effect (Lee et al. 1997a). Higher-tier supply chain members such as wholesalers and manufacturers should have roughly equal levels of inventory holding and stockout costs. A more equal variance in inventory stockout and holding costs among supply chain tiers should be reflected by a lower standard deviation of individual supply chain tier holding and stockout costs than the standard deviation of supply chain systems without RFID technologies. Therefore, the present study proposes the following hypotheses:

H0: RFID-enabled supply chain systems that track and display inventory information to member supply chain tiers **will not** have lower mean inventory costs than traditional supply chain systems.

H1: RFID-enabled supply chain systems that track and display inventory information to member supply chain tiers **will** have lower mean inventory costs than traditional supply chain systems.

3   METHOD

To test the above hypothesis, this study employed the Beer Distribution Game, a popular simulation in supply chain literature used to demonstrate how poor information and low coordination of supply chain members causes the bullwhip effect to occur. The Beer Distribution Game was developed at MIT to simulate the bullwhip effect in an experiment, and has been used widely for nearly four decades (Munson et al. 2003).

According to Sterman, the Beer Distribution Game is a "simulated inventory distribution system which contains multiple actors, feedbacks, nonlinearities, and time delays. The interaction of individual decisions with the structure of the simulated firm produces aggregate dynamics which systematically diverge from optimal behavior" (p. 321). In short, the Beer Distribution Game repeatedly demonstrates how the bullwhip effect can result from imperfect information. This study involves an experiment that employs a traditional Beer Distribution Game as used by Sterman for the control group, and a modified version of the Beer Distribution Game for the experimental group.

3.1 Control Group

The Beer Distribution Game consists of a simplified four-tier supply chain in which a team of four human subjects each play the part of inventory manager for one of four supply chain tiers: retailer, wholesaler, distributor, and factory. Each tier inventory manger orders inventory independently from the other supply chain tier managers using only the inventory order information from the immediate downstream supply chain member. The game is typically played on a board with markers representing inventory evenly distributed throughout the supply chain. However, for this experiment, both control and experimental versions of the Beer Distribution Game were played using a real-time, Wb-based network that allowed four students at four separate computer workstations to act as an integrated supply chain. The level of inventory demand by consumers is simulated by a predefined level of consumer demand that is the same for each instance the Beer Distribution Game is played. As retail inventory levels are depleted through customer sales, the retail inventory manager orders more inventory from the distributor. The distributor in turn orders more inventory from the factory warehouse, and so on. Each tier manager can only use the order information available from the downstream supply chain member. Given varying customer demand, each tier must order a level of safety stock so that costly stockouts do not occur. However, if too much safety stock is on hand, the tier will incur a per-item inventory holding cost. The holding cost for each item of inventory is $2, while the stockout cost per inventory item is $4. The object of the game is to minimize holding and stockout costs as a team, or in other words, become an efficient supply chain.

In administering the game, each subject is randomly assigned a role as a retailer, wholesaler, distributor, or factory. After the rules of the game are explained, the game's distribution channel is initialized in equilibrium. Each tier has an inventory of 12 cases, and the supply chain throughput is four cases per week to match consumer demand that is also initially four cases per week. During the first four rounds, consumer demand remains the same as the subjects become accustomed to ordering for their respective tier. For the first three rounds, the subjects are instructed to order four cases; in the fourth round subjects can order any nonzero amount. However, in the fifth round, there is an unannounced increase in consumer demand to eight cases. This increase in demand creates a disequilibrium in the supply chain to which the subjects must adjust. In the game's instructions, the subjects are told the game will continue for 50 rounds; however, Sterman suggests halting the game after round 30 to avoid horizon effects.

Each tier has only local information available: each subject can only see the order size of the next downstream tier. In Sterman's study of 48 teams (consisting of 192 subjects), invariably customer demand information represented by retail orders became distorted as each successive tier added a measure of safety stock to the order. The information distortion within the supply chain caused broad swings in inventory levels from inventory shortages to surpluses, with always the top-most tier (factory) being most affected. At the end of all of the rounds, the holding costs and stockout costs are tallied for the team as a whole (all four tiers) and recorded.

From the above description of the mechanics of the Beer Distribution Game, five contributing factors to the occurrence of the bullwhip effect can be seen. These are

- Delay in signal. The time required for an inventory order to arrive at the next upstream tier (four rounds).

- Delay in inventory to arrive. The time required for ordered inventory to reach the next downstream tier (an additional four rounds).

- Limited global information. Subjects are ignorant of how much inventory is available at other tiers as well as the level of demand facing other tiers.

- An unexpected 100 percent increase in customer demand. The inventory demanded by the consumer jumps from four units of inventory to eight where it subsequently remains until the end of the game.

- Uncoordinated order decisions. Subjects cannot communicate with one another, thereby preventing team strategies to form.

Each of the above five factors contributes to the occurrence of the bullwhip effect and together make the occurrence of the bullwhip effect almost inevitable and practically impossible to mitigate. In fact, in Sterman's observations of performing the Beer Distribution Game over the span of multiple decades revealed that the bullwhip effect always occurred to some degree when the game was administered.

3.2 Experimental Group

The experimental group played the Beer Distribution Game in precisely the same manner of execution as the control group, with the exception that the experimental computer program simulated the use of RFID technology by displaying the flow of all inventory cases from the lowest supply chain tier (retailer) to the highest tier (factory). Not only does this added information provide each supply chain member with real-time inventory information, but in effect a continuous consciousness of the whole supply chain is created. This full awareness of the supply chain should greatly increase the agility of the supply chain as a whole as inventory managers are able to make better inventory decisions. Because of the above advantages, it is hypothesized that the bullwhip effect in the experimental group will be much less acute than in the control group.

By simulating an RFID-enabled supply chain within the model of the Beer Distribution Game, two of the five factors contributing to the occurrence of the bullwhip effect are removed: limited global information and, following as a natural consequence, the delay of signal. Given the current literature on the potential of RFID technology to provide both instantaneous and global supply chain information (Kinsella, 2003; Sarma et al. 2000), removing these two factors seems consistent with the capabilities of proposed RFID-enabled supply chain systems.

However, the remaining three contributing factors to the occurrence of the bullwhip effect are held constant, namely the delay in the receipt of inventory, the unexpected increase in consumer demand, and the requirement that inventory ordering decisions be made independently, without communication among fellow supply chain tier members.

These three factors significantly contribute to the occurrence of the bullwhip effect and, therefore, the utility of the Beer Distribution Game to produce the bullwhip effect should remain.

3.3 Sample

The sample for this study was 120 undergraduate students at a private university in the western United States drawn from two large introductory classes in Accounting and Information Systems. Each student was randomly placed in a team with three other students. Because both experimental and control group versions of the Beer Distribution Game were played using networked computers, subjects did not know who their teammates were. Altogether, the subjects were organized into 30 teams of four—15 teams for the control group and 15 teams for the experimental group.

4 RESULTS

At round 30, each team's combined holding and stockout costs were totaled for all supply chain tiers for all previous rounds. This aggregation produced one single inventory cost total for each team. An independent samples f-test revealed that mean costs for the experimental group simulating the RFID technology approach were significantly less than those in the control group (f = 4.706, p = .039). Table 1 presents the exploratory statistics for the two; note the difference in the means and standard deviations.

The resulting mean for the control group was affected by an outlier team with an unusually high score that raised the control group's mean substantially, from approximately $76,000 dollars to nearly $168,000 dollars. However, despite this outlier

Table 1. Exploratory Statistics

Group		Statistic	Std. Error
Experimental	Mean	$17,536.67	2886.36
	Median	$12,480.00	
	Std. Deviation	$11,178.81	
	Minimum	$6,340.00	
	Maximum	$42,860.00	
	Range	$36,520.00	
Control	Mean	$167,927.47	93109.72
	Median	$54,638.00	
	Std. Deviation	$360,612.40	
	Minimum	$16.090.00	
	Maximum	$1,447,702.00	
	Range	$1,431,612.00	

Table 2. F-Test of Experimental and Control Group Differences

	Group	N	Mean	Std. Deviation	F	Sig.
Costs	Experimental	15	$17,536.6667	$11,178.80509	4.706	.039
	Control	15	$167,927.4667	$360,612.40109		

and resulting greatly increased within-group variance, the f-test found significant between-group difference at the .05 level (see Table 2).

5   DISCUSSION

This study indicates that RFID technology has significant potential to increase business agility in supply chain systems. From the results, it is apparent that the RFID-simulated experimental group was enabled to better adapt to the change in consumer demand as well as to each supply chain member's independent inventory orders. Because of continuous supply chain information available from the production of inventory to its eventual sale, the experimental RFID-simulated group was able to act more closely as an integrated whole rather than four disjointed units or parts. Without this added information, it was difficult for control group supply chain members to achieve any level of coordination.

From the perspective of business agility, RFID-technology holds tremendous promise for manufacturing supply chains. Managing inventory through several distinct and often divergent supply chain tiers is a major challenge. With such conditions, any coordination among supply chain tiers is a victory. However, given the volatile market place and increasing pressure from competitors, inventory supply chains must become increasingly agile in order to remain competitive and relevant to the consumer's needs. The promise of RFID technology is to enable a supply chain to act as a cohesive unit—to readily provide inventory information throughout the supply chain, from inventory creation to its final sale to the consumer (Atock, 2003; Kinsella, 2003; Robertson et al. 1999).

The validity of above study is necessarily limited by the relatively small team sample size. A planned expansion of the provided sample may help to strengthen the conclusion and internal validity of this study. Similarly, studies of RFID-technology applied to different business applications would certainly strengthen this study's external validity. As an abstract simulation, the RFID-enabled Beer Distribution Game is obviously limited in its generalizability. However, on this point, Sterman gave this insight into his initial research utilizing the Beer Distribution Game:

> The experiment, despite its rich feedback structure, is vastly simplified compared to the real world. To what extent do the experimental conditions and results apply? First, would subjects' behavior differ if customer demand follows a more realistic pattern, e.g. noise and seasonality? The order decisions of many subjects were in fact noisy and cyclic. (p. 326)

Sterman also explains that although managers in the real world have access to more inventory information than the subjects in the experiment, "information in the real world is often out of date, noisy, contradictory and ambiguous" (p. 326). Therefore, the generalizability of this study, although limited, may be greater than it ostensibly appears.

A further limitation to the validity of the present study is the lack of real-world, RFID-enabled supply chain data to verify the results of the simulated RFID-enabled supply chain of the experimental group. The validity of the traditional Beer Distribution Game in describing the bullwhip effect has been strengthened by agreement with expert opinion of supply chain domain professionals and data observed from the bullwhip effect in actual supply chains. The findings of the present study can also be strengthened by similar calibration to data provided by actual RFID-enabled supply chain systems when such systems become more widely implemented.

Given the above-mentioned expectation for RFID technology to revolutionize the supply chain system, some may find little surprise with the above results. Indeed, the idea that timely and pertinent information can enhance the efficiency of a supply chain is not only intuitive, but also foundational to logistic information systems and the field of Information Systems in general. However, despite how axiomatic the above results may appear, the potential of RFID technology to increase business agility in supply chains should nevertheless be explored and empirically studied. If the above-stated predictions are even partially accurate, RFID technology merits a thorough under-standing through empirical study as use of this technology unfolds. Without such carefully tested knowledge, RFID technology may fall into the category of a fad and be misapplied, and the promise of greater business agility of a supply chain as a whole may take longer to realize.

REFERENCES

Atock, C. "Where's My Stuff?," *Manufacturing Engineer* (82:2), 2003, pp. 24-27

Bowersox, D. J., Closs, D. J., and Stank, T. P. "Ten Mega-Trends that Will Revolutionize Supply Chain Logistics," *Journal of Business Logistics* (21:2), 2000, pp. 6-10.

Forrester, J. W. "Industrial Dynamics: A Major Breakthrough for Decision Makers," *Harvard Business Review* (4:36), July-August 1958, pp. 37-66.

Kinsella, B. "The Wal-Mart Factor," *Industrial Engineer* (35:11), November 2003, pp. 32-36.

Lee, H. L., Padmanabhan, V., and Whang, S. "The Bullwhip effect in Supply Chains," *Sloan Management Review* (38:3), 1997a, pp. 93-102.

Lee, H. L., Padmanabhan, V., and Whang, S. "Information Distortion in a Supply Chain: The Bullwhip Effect," *Management Science* (43:4), 1997b, pp. 546-548.

Munson, C. L., Hu, J., and Rosenblatt, M. J. "Teaching the Costs of Uncoordinated Supply Chains," *Interfaces* (33:3), 2003, pp. 24-39.

RFID Forum. *Logistics & Transport Focus* (5:1), July-August 2003, p. 49.

Robertson, I. D., Blewett, M., Amin, J., Butt, I., Donnelly, F., Harwood, P., and Woolven, A. "A Simple Radio-Frequency System for Asset Tracking Within Buildings," *IEE Colloquium* (23), October 25, 1999, pp. 29-34.

Sarma, S., Brock D. L., and Ashton, K. "The Networked Physical World: Proposals for Engineering the Next Generation of Computing, Commerce, and Automatic-Identification," Massachusetts Institute of Technology Auto-ID Center White Paper, October 1, 2000 (available online at http://www.autoidlabs.org/ whitepapers/MIT-AUTOID-WH-001.pdf).

Sarma, S., Brock, D. L., Engels, D. "Radio Frequency Identification and the Electronic Product Code," *IEEE Micro* (21:6), 2001, pp. 50-54.

Sterman, J. "Modeling Managerial Behavior: Misperceptions of Feedback in a Dynamic Decision Making Experiment," *Management Science* (35:3), 1989, pp. 321-339.

ABOUT THE AUTHOR

Anthony Vance received a master's degree from Brigham Young University in Information Systems Management in 2004. Currently, Anthony works as a consultant in Deloitte's Enterprise Risk Services division where he performs Sarbanes-Oxley IT assessments as well as fraud prevention data analyses in relation to SAS 99. Anthony lives in Atlanta with his wife Sarah and their one-year-old son, Ryan. Anthony can be reached at Anthony.Vance@byu.edu.

10 DIFFICULTIES IN IMPLEMENTING THE AGILE SUPPLY CHAIN: Lessons Learned from Interorganizational Information Systems Adoption

Akos Nagy
Tilburg University
Tilburg, THE NETHERLANDS

Abstract   *Agility is becoming an important component in the continuous struggle to increase overall supply chain performance. The need to react speedily to sudden changes in demand or supply necessitates the sharing of a large amount of high quality information in a timely manner between trading partners. Electronic data interchange (EDI) and other interorganizational systems (IOS) are able to support these goals; however, the diffusion of these systems throughout the supply chain is by no means guaranteed. We borrow from the IOS adoption literature to explain reasons of failure to adopt. We use the adoption position model to analyze three short case studies and we corroborate that, in these cases, the relative power of a firm and its intent of adoption toward a specific IOS together determine its position in the decision. By combining the adoption positions of the trading partners, we can effectively predict the decision of the outcome. At the end of the paper, we propose strategies to overcome these barriers which hinder the realization of an agile supply chain.*

Keywords   Agile supply chain, interorganizational information system, adoption, adoption position, power

1 INTRODUCTION

1.1 The Agile Supply Chain

Establishing effective supply chain strategies became paramount in today's market environment where technological developments, increasing competition, and ever more demanding customers necessitate the supply chain to be more efficient. The reduction of costs by eliminating waste and delays and the simultaneous improvement of customer satisfaction is the goal of supply chain performance initiatives (Christopher and Towill 2001). This philosophy is the center point of the lean approach, which was extended by Womack and Jones (1996) to include the suppliers of an organization where they envisioned the seamless flow of goods throughout the whole value chain, eventually creating a *lean enterprise*.

The lean concept works well where demand is relatively stable and hence predictable and where variety is low. However, where demand is volatile and the variety of customer requirements is high, an agile design is needed (Christopher 2000). Agility has been defined in many different ways in the literature and often the difference between agility, leanness, and flexibility is not clear. We adopt the definition of Conboy and Fitzgerald (2004) on agility, which is the result of a meta-analysis and reflects the differences between these terms:

> Agility is the continual readiness of an entity to rapidly or inherently, pro-actively or reactively, embrace change, through high quality, simplistic, economical components and relationships with its environment.

According to Mason-Jones et al. (2000), the agile design of a supply chain is most important where not the costs, but the service level decides on who the market winner is. Lee (2004) goes further and states that being agile is only one of the three qualifiers of a sustainable advantage next to being able to adapt over time to changing market conditions and to align interests of all firms in the supply network.

1.2 From Information Technology Diffusion to Adoption

In order to realize agility in supply chains, companies have to adapt a different mindset where they have a high priority on production schedule and where they utilize the concepts of quick response and continuous replenishment (Christopher et al. 2001). Such practices are able to diminish the bullwhip effect (Morell and Ezingeard 2002), which is the amplification of demand order variability as orders move up the supply chain (Lee et al. 1997). This approach requires that communication at all levels of the supply chain must be effective and timely; therefore, information systems become necessary components of a successful supply chain design. Interorganizational information systems (IOS), refer to computer and telecommunications infrastructure developed, operated, and/or used by two or more firms for the purpose of exchanging information that supports a business application or process (Li and Williams 1999). IOS enable higher visibility between trading partners and support the struggle to lower demand uncertainty. In the context of supply chains, they enable integration between trading partners through faster, more-efficient, and more-accurate data exchange, thus offering ample benefits for companies (Bakos 1998; Banerjee and Golhar 1994; O'Callaghan et al. 1992; Vlosky et al. 1994; Von Heck and Ribbers 1999).

The diffusion of a technology is the process by which an innovation is communicated through certain channels over time among the members of a social system

(Rogers 1995). Diffusion speeds up in the presence of positive network effects (Teo et al. 2003) or an industry-wide regulatory body or when a critical mass of adopters (Somasundaram 2004) is reached. The ideal scenario of supply-chain-wide diffusion of IOS, however, does not happen very often.

To find the reasons behind these failures, we seek understanding through the adoption decision of each individual organization. By utilizing the model of Nagy (2004) on IOS adoption, we try to answer the following research questions through case studies:

- Why does the adoption of IOS fail in supply chains?
- What strategies could help firms to overcome the barriers of adoption of the IOS in order to realize an agile supply chain?

2 ADOPTION IN THE IOS LITERATURE

Research on the adoption of IOS already has a long history. Electronic data interchange (EDI) has been used for more than 30 years now (Stefansson 2002) to exchange structured data electronically in a standardized format between organizations (O'Callaghan and Turner 1995) and has been intensively researched since the mid-1980s (Chan and Swatman 1998; Somasundaram and Karlsbjerg 2003).

The diffusion of IOS can be analyzed at three different levels: the micro level analysis focuses on characteristics of individuals and/or organizational units, the macro level on industry-wide or national regulatory bodies, while the meso level in between the two concentrates on networks of interacting agents (Damsgaard and Lyytinen 1998). What makes IOS an interesting technology to study is that it requires two or more organizations to agree upon its implementation; therefore, an adoption decision depends heavily on the other parties (Chan and Swatman 1998), necessitating co-adoption of the technology (Nelson et al. 2002). Socio-political factors, such as interfirm power relationships and trust, come in to play an important role in the decision-making process.

This paper focuses on the dyadic relationships of trading partners (placing the research on the meso level) and on the reasons of success and failure to co-adopt IOSs.

As competition moves from individual firm level to the level of supply chains, there is an increasing need for a seamless flow of information between supply chain partners. Unfortunately, the assumption of unproblematic IOS integration often found in modular supply chain research (Von Liere et al. 2004) is unrealistic. Firms act strategically when they decide not to adopt a certain IOS (Bouchard 1993); therefore, we assume that companies act rationally and estimate not only the benefits (Chwelos et al. 2001; Jones and Beatty 1998), but also the perceived costs (Nagy et al. 2004) and perceived risks (Kumar and van Dissel 1996) of an IOS project. The costs and risks of IOS implementation have often been cited as potential barriers of adoption just as well as social factors such as lack of trust (Hart and Saunders 1997) and lack of coordination and cooperation (Tan and Raman 2002).

In recent years, research on the role of power in information systems has gained momentum as the interest of researchers increased to study behavioral factors as well as purely rationalistic ones (Jasperson et al. 2002). Power relations have been studied on the individual, group, organizational, and interorganizational levels. In this paper, we are interested in the last category and define power as a firm's ability to influence change in another organization that is dependent upon that firm's resources (Hart and Saunders 1998).

Nagy (2004) criticizes the IOS literature for not handling the role of power relations between supply chain partners properly. His main critique is that power in the literature always appears to have a positive effect on adoption (as external pressure), however an inhibiting effect could also be theorized. This paper develops the adoption position model, which tries to overcome this biased view on the role of power and give a more complete explanation on the adoption phenomenon. We are going to apply this model through case studies to show how the (lack of) co-adoption of an IOS contributes to the realization of an agile supply chain.

3   THE ADOPTION POSITION MODEL

3.1 Description of the Model

The main advantage of the model is that it takes into account both the economic and social factors of the decision-making process and by doing this it becomes possible to separate the intention of adoption from the actual ability of the firm to control that decision. Firms do not operate in a vacuum they are part of a larger supply network where certain power structure is present (Cox et al. 2002). Power is defined as the capability of a firm to exert influence on another firm to act in a prescribed manner (Hart and Saunders 1997). This influential effect, however, has only been utilized in IOS research as an enabler to adoption and it is mostly part of the intention construct (Chwelos et al. 2001), giving an incomplete view on adoption.

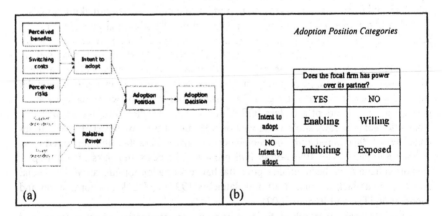

Figure 1. The Adoption Position model (Source: A. Nagy, "The Effect of Power on the Adoption of Interorganizational Information Systems: The Adoption Position Model," *Proceedings of the 12th European Conference on Information Systems,* 2004)

Figure 1a presents the model. The adoption decision is the function of the combined adoption position of the two trading partners that are negotiating over a proposed IOS. There are four possible adoption positions into which a company can be categorized based on its intention to adopt and its relative power over its partner (Figure 1b). An *enabling* firm is interested in the adoption and has influence over its trading partner; therefore, even when the partner is resistant, it can use its power in different ways to *try* to make the implementation come true. Note that being in an enabling position does not guarantee that the IOS adoption will occur; instead it only gives the possibility for the firm to try to start the project.

A firm that is interested in the adoption of a certain IOS but has no power over its trading partner is termed as being in a *willing* adoption position. The willing firm perceives a net positive return on the investment and is willing to share information through the intended electronic linkage, but it is not able to force its trading partner into the adoption. A firm with an *inhibiting* position sees no interest in implementing and using the proposed IOS and it has the power to create a barrier to adoption. Those firms that fall into the last quadrant are less fortunate; they see no interest in the adoption and they have no leverage over the trading partner; therefore, they are dependent on the partner's position. Their adoption position is called *exposed*.

Having determined the adoption position of a focal firm, however, still does not make it possible to predict the outcome of the adoption decision. The cause of this ambiguity is the way power positions are categorized between two firms. Cox (1997) proposes the so-called power matrix as a typology of power relationships between two firms. Next to the two cases where one of the partners dominates (supplier dominance or buyer dominance), the parties involved can be also interdependent or independent. This means that knowing that the buyer has power is still not enough information to decide whether it is a case of buyer dominance or interdependence. This method, therefore, necessitates the analysis of dependence from both sides of the dyad.

When we apply the adoption position model to both parties in a dyadic relationship, we get 16 possible combinations on the position of the supplier and the buyer (see Figure 2). This typology is addressed in a pair-wise way, such as enabling–willing or inhibiting–enabling where the words signify the adoption position of the supplier and the buyer, respectively.

		Buyer's adoption position			
		Enabling	Willing	Inhibiting	Exposed
Supplier's adoption position	Enabling	+	+	+/-	+
	Willing	+	+	–	?
	Inhibiting	+/-	–	–	–
	Exposed	+	?	–	–

Figure 2. Adoption Positions in a Dyadic Relationship and Propositions for the Outcome of the IOS Adoption

At the intersection of each combination is a proposition for the success of the IOS adoption. A "+" sign means that the particular adoption position pair will hypothetically support the adoption, while a "–" marked pair does not. In the case of "+/–" the interdependent parties have opposing intentions and the decision is not straightforward. The "?" sign refers to the equivalently ambiguous outcome of the decision when the parties have opposing intention but neither has the leverage to influence the other.

3.2 Operationalization of the Constructs

Intent to adopt is operationalized as perceived benefit (the anticipated advantages that the IOS can provide for the organization) (Chwelos et al. 2001), perceived risks (Kumar and van Dissel 1996), and switching costs. Switching cost is defined as the cost incurred by the organization when deciding to adopt a new IOS compared to the current technological and operational level. We distinguish costs incurred from the infra-structure, application, and business process levels (Nagy et al. 2004).

Relative power is operationalized based on Cox et al. (2002), where the authors combine the work of Emerson (1962) with the resourced based view (Barney 1991) to determine critical assets in an organization. These critical assets are defined as supply chain resources that combine high utility with relative scarcity in a buyer-supplier exchange and in a market context. We use the concept of critical assets to measure dependence and to determine the power relationship between the trading partners. For a listing of the detailed operationalization of the constructsm see Appendix A.

3.3 Reasons of Failure

According to this model, the adoption of IOS and, therefore, the closer integration of a dyadic section of a supply chain could fail in two basic scenarios: (1) one party has no intention to adopt the technology and the other has no power to coerce or otherwise impose its will on its partner; (2) one party has no intention to adopt the IOS and is not dependent on the initiator; therefore, that party has the power to say no and act as an inhibitor.

Several factors can lead to the lack of intention: the company does not see the benefits in the technology or it does not perceive added value by adopting another IOS in the case where it already has a different system in place with other trading partners. Costs of implementing an IOS could discourage firms, especially when it necessitates change in business processes. The perception that the investment has a high risk on the technical, operational, or strategic level negatively affects the intention to adopt as well (Hughes et al. 2004). Such risks are that the technology will become obsolete (Kumar and van Dissel 1996), the trading partner will act opportunistically, the IOS has a high asset specificity (Williamson 1979), and the possibility of getting locked in (Lonsdale 2001).

4   COMPARATIVE CASE STUDIES

In this section, we are going to apply the adoption position model in a qualitative way through case studies (both from primary and secondary source) to show how the (un)successful co-adoption of an IOS led to the (un)successful realization of agility in supply chains.

4.1 Case 1: Inhibiting–Willing Relationship

The description of the case is based on the case study by Ribbers (1995). Lumiance BV is a supplier of lighting fixtures in the Netherlands. Its core activities are design, purchasing of piece parts, and distribution. The assembly of the fixtures had been sourced out to another company. The total assortment comprised 500 article numbers. The piece parts were bought from 100 suppliers.

Technische Unie (TU) was one of Lumiance's most important customers in the Netherlands, purchasing all 500 articles. The TU-initiated EDI project first failed because of the lack of technical readiness at Lumiance. The project had been delayed by two years. In 1992, the second run met with another problem. Lumiance could not introduce the purchase order confirmation message because it did not have the right organization for inventory control. Inventories for Dutch and international customers were not separated, neither physically nor at the information level. The key was to implement the standard EAN barcoding system to be able to universally identify the stock items. The company would not mind introducing the EAN code, although it had its own four-digit article code. It was planned to expand the system to Lumiance's own suppliers.

To make the system work smoothly, it was important to get the suppliers to adopt the EAN coding system and standard packaging units also had to be introduced. Lumiance's suppliers, however, were strongly opposed to the EAN code system due to their already installed bar coding systems and information systems. Compliance with the EDI proposal would have required substantial investments in changing their infrastructure, applications, and business processes. Therefore, there was clearly no intention to adopt the system. Lumiance did not have the power to make the suppliers invest more in additional systems and change the existing business processes in either a coercive or a persuasive way. The opposition of a powerful supplier (inhibiting position) hindered Lumiance's integration efforts (willing position).

4.2 Case 2: Willing–Inhibiting Relationship

This example of a failed supply chain integration is based on Gregor and Menzies (2000). In the Australian beef industry, supply chain management requires producers to commit to the production of quality meat according to agreed specifications, including documented feeding strategies and animal health inputs, trace-back procedures, and even taste tests to ensure their product meets the expectations and the promise of the retailer.

Effective supply chain management in the beef industry would put the industry in a better position to compete with other industries, such as pork and chicken.

The need for compliance with the individually identifiable cattle regulation has forced the implementation of the National Livestock Identification Scheme (NLIS), which will enable greater trace-back to property of origin in case of disease or chemical residue scares. Such a system necessitated the implementation of EDI. Within the processing industry, there are a number of hardware and software systems currently in use. A number of privately owned companies had established their own methods of collecting information, but there was still little interconnectivity between processors and farms.

The establishment of the national identification system was stalled because the processors were not willing to provide feedback as part of that system. Processors did not wish to cooperate because it would provide the producer with increased data analysis and comparison opportunities that could work to the disadvantage of the processors. Also, the meat processors were using computer systems that did not transmit in the industry standard file format.

There is a buyer dominant power structure in the Australian beef industry, where the main source of power is that a large supplier pool of small firms is faced by a small pool of large buyers. Switching and searching costs for buyer are low and, in this sector, vertical integration is also a threat. The perceived benefit of a higher level of integration is low for the powerful buyer, because more extensive information sharing and visibility would shift the power toward the supplier. The lack of an industry body that owns the problem forced the less powerful producers to initiate the project (willing position), but they could not make the buyers (inhibiting position) integrate their systems or create a more effective supply chain.

4.3 Case 3: Exposed–Enabling Relationship

The previous cases were examples of failures of IOS adoption that caused the supply chain to be less effective than it could have been. Individual interests of supply chain members sometimes work against the interest of the supply chain in which they operate when the power structure enables them to do so. Power relationships can also be in favor of establishing a more agile supply chain when the dyads form supportive adoption positions (see Figure 2). We conducted this case study during the year 2002.

Bakkersland Easy Bakery is a large producer of bread and bakery products and also cake, deep-frozen, and fast-food products in the Netherlands. It employs 2,700 people. The market for bakery products consists of 6.8 percent of the total food industry. The company owns 26 plants in the Netherlands and has a sales organization in several European countries (Belgium, Germany, France, Spain and Italy) and it also exports to the United States.

Bakkersland has over 100 suppliers of raw materials, mainly from the Netherlands and from Belgium, and a few others for packaging material from outside the Benelux countries. On the customer side, distribution creates an even more complex network not only because of the number of customers (approximately 60), but also the existence of different distribution channels. Most of the products are shipped to distribution centers owned by the supermarket chains. There are 20 supermarket chains operating in the Netherlands and all of them have their own warehouses. Third-party logistics service providers carry out the transportation. Other distribution channels include independent warehouses, sales agents (across Europe and in the United States), direct sales to restaurants, and sales through company-owned retail pastry stores and outlets. Approximately 85 percent of all the production goes to retail.

A large retailer (call it Retailer) was the first retail chain in the industry that initiated the implementation of EDI with its suppliers. Retailer pushed the suppliers to adopt EDI through a value-added network, but it employed a persuasive strategy where Retailer demonstrated the use of the system to the suppliers. Retailer wanted to minimize its inventory level in the stores to virtually zero. In order to achieve this, it wanted to implement the concept of vendor managed inventory (VMI) under the so called "comakership policy," where the supplier gains access to inventory levels and control over replenishment.

Bakkersland, however, did not see the benefits of the system. With their current information systems in place, they have already achieved a 99.4 percent service level and they did not believe that the new process was well suited for their current ERP system. From Bakkersland's viewpoint, the VMI would only put additional burdens on them in the form of costs and responsibility.

The relationship was clearly buyer dominance despite the size of Bakkersland. About 25 percent of their total sales went to Retailer, which in fact has the largest market share in the Netherlands. The product is highly substitutable on a very competitive market. The EDI system was eventually implemented.

We can conclude that Bakkersland and Retailer formed an exposed–enabling adoption position pair, which led to the adoption of the system and the realization of a more agile supply chain, despite the fact that the supplier did not have the intention to do it.

5   REMEDIES AND STRATEGIES

What strategies are available for an organization that wishes to introduce higher agility in its supply chain, but has not been able to do so, because it failed to implement an IOS with its trading partner(s)? We can use the adoption position model to answer this question as well. Figure 2 showed those adoption position pairs supportive of an IOS adoption decision. The company that wishes to implement a system with its trading partner, therefore, first has to evaluate the relationship and position itself and its partner in the matrix of Figure 1b. There are two ways to change the unfavorable position to a favorable one: either the focal firm has to persuade its trading partner to use the system or it has to increase its power level.

By increasing the benefits or lowering the barriers of adoption, the focal firm can positively change the intention of its trading partner. Piderit (2000) found that lowering barriers is more effective. Barriers, such as switching costs of the partner (Nagy et al. 2004), to the new system can be lowered by using standardized applications that can integrate more easily into existing IT architecture or by jointly planning shared business processes, which will require less business process redesign (Nelson and Shaw 2003).

The second strategic direction for an initiator of an IOS project is to increase its power base or to increase the dependence of the partner firm. This is much harder to achieve as it is often requires the redesign of the supply chain (vertical integration, disintermediation of intermediaries) or making significant changes in one's own business (higher value proposition for partner through increased commercial or operational importance; Cox et al. 2002) or by introducing new governance mechanisms (quasi integration and participation in joint decision making; Subramani and Venkatraman 2003).

It is important to note that higher power does not necessarily mean that it has to be used coercively. Power can be exercised in a persuasive way as well or the mere potential of having power can influence adoption (Hart and Saunders 1997). Helping suppliers develop the necessary capabilities to adapt to new business requirements (Krause et al. 1998) will establish trust in the relationship. This increased trust will lower the perceived risks of the IOS and create a positive intention toward adoption.

Thus a self-assessment of relative power of a firm will result in different negotiation strategies. A relatively more powerful firm might choose to coercively influence the behavior of its trading partner or it could try to persuade with a softer approach. A weaker firm could anticipate the requirements of a more powerful partner and employ a proactive strategy (Webster 1995). So far, the paper assumes a single relationship between supply chain members; however, these relationships are often multi-faceted (Wiseman 1988). In such situations firm A might be dependent on firm B on one side, but could have the upper hand on another. Negotiation strategies become even more important in these cases, but a further discussion is beyond the scope of this paper.

6 CONCLUSION

Information technology is an essential component of effective supply chain management; therefore, by studying interorganizational systems we can contribute to the agility literature.

We have demonstrated through three short case studies that the adoption of IOS can have significant effects on the efficiency of supply chains. The cases suggest that the electronic exchange of information between trading partners not only depends on their intention to adopt the system, but on the underlying power structure as well. A conflict of interest in IOS adoption coupled with an unsupportive power structure could lead to inefficiencies in the supply network and can indirectly thwart the efforts to realize an agile supply chain. These preliminary results suggest that research on agility should not neglect the effect of power relations in business networks.

Using the adoption position model, we were able to explain why the co-adoption of IOS fails or succeeds. However, the small number of cases does not validate completely our model, therefore further case studies need to be conducted to tests the hypotheses.

By estimating the adoption position of both parties in a dyadic relationship, one could predict the outcome of the adoption decision. This has important implications for both researchers and practitioners: Researchers would be able to map entire supply chains and examine the prospect of supply-chain-wide diffusion of a technology. Practitioners could benefit from the model by establishing a clearer view over their company's position in the supply chain and evaluating project proposals on different IOSs.

REFERENCES

Bakos, Y. "The Emerging Role of Electronic Marketplaces on the Internet," *Communications of the ACM* (41:8), 1998, pp. 35-42.

Banerjee, S., and Golhar, D. Y. "Electronic Data Interchange: Characteristics of Users and Nonusers," *Information and Management* (26:2), 1994, pp. 65-74.

Barney, J. "Firm resources and sustained competitive advantage," *Journal of Management* (17:1), 1991, pp. 99-120.

Bouchard, L. "Decision Criteria in the Adoption of EDI," in *Proceedings of the 14th International Conference in Information Systems*, J. I. DeGross, R. P. Bostrom, and D. Robey (Eds.), Orlando, FL, 1993, pp. 365-376.

Chan, C., and Swatman, P. M. C. "EDI Implementation: A Broader Perspective," in *Proceedings of the 11th International Conference on Electronic Commerce*, Bled, Slovenia, 1998, pp. 90-108.

Christopher, M. "The Agile Supply Chain: Competing in Volatile Markets," *Industrial Marketing Management* (29:1), 2000, pp. 37-44.

Christopher, M., and Towill, D. "An Integrated Model for the Design of Agile Supply Chains," *International Journal of Physical Distribution and Logistics Management* (31:4), 2001, pp. 235-246.

Chwelos, P., Benbasat, I., and Dexter, A. S. "Research Report: Empirical Test of an EDI Adoption Model," *Information Systems Research* (12:3), 2001, pp. 304-321.

Conboy, K., and Fitzgerald, B. "Toward a Conceptual Framework of Agile Methods," paper presented at XP Agile Universe, Calgary, Alberta, 2004.

Cox, A. "On Power, Appropriateness and Procurement Competence," *Supply Management*, October 1997, pp. 24-27.

Cox, A., Ireland, P., Lonsdale, C., Sanderson, J., and Watson, G. *Supply Chains, Markets and Power: Mapping Buyer and Supplier Power Regimes*, London: Routledge, 2002.

Damsgaard, J., and Lyytinen, K. "Contours of Diffusion of Electronic Data Interchange in Finland: Overcoming Technological Barriers and Collaborating to Make it Happen," *Journal of Strategic Information Systems* (7:4), 1998, pp. 275-297.

Emerson, R. M. "Power-Dependence Relations," *American Sociological Review* (27), 1962, pp. 31-41.

Gregor, S., and Menzies, D. "Electronic Data Interchange and Supply Chain Management: A Case Study of the Beef Industry," working paper, Central Queensland University, 2000.

Hart, P., and Saunders, C. "Emerging Electronic Partnerships: Antecendents and Dimensions of Edi Use from the Supplier's Perspective," *Journal of Management Information Systems* (14:4), 1998, pp. 87-111.

Hart, P., and Saunders, C. "Power and Trust: Critical Factors in the Adoption and Use of Electronic Data Interchange," *Organization Science* (8:1), 1997, pp. 23-41.

Hughes, M., Powell, P., Panteli, N., and Golden, W. "Risk Mitigation and Risk Absorption in IOS: A Proposed Investigative Study," in *Proceedings of the 12th European Conference on Information Systems*, T. Leino, T. Saarinen, and S. Klein (Eds.), Turku, Finland, 2004, pp. 1-8.

Jasperson, J., Carte, T. A., Saunders, C., Butler, B. S., Croes, H. J. P., and Zheng, W. "*Review*: Power and Information Technology Research: A Metatriangulation Review," *MIS Quarterly* (26:4), 2002, pp. 397-459.

Jones, M. C., and Beatty, R. C. "Towards the Development of Measures of Perceived Benefits and Compatibility of Edi: A Comparative Assessment of Competing First Order Factor Models," *European Journal of Information Systems* (7:3), 1998, pp. 210-220.

Krause, D. R., Handfield, R. B., and Scannel, T. V. "An Empirical Investigation of Supplier Development: Reactive and Strategic Processes," *Journal of Operations Management* (17:1), 1998, pp. 39-58.

Kumar, K., and van Dissel, H. G. "Sustainable Collaboration: Managing Conflict and Cooperation in Interorganizational Systems," *MIS Quarterly* (20:3), 1996, pp. 279-300.

Lee, H. L. "The Triple-A Supply Chain," *Harvard Business Review*, October 2004, pp. 1-13.

Lee, H. L., Padmanabhan, V., and Whang, S. "The Bullwhip Effect in Supply Chains," *Sloan Management Review* (38:3), 1997, pp. 93-102.

Li, F., and Williams, H. "New Collaboration Between Firms: The Role of Interorganizational Systems," in *Proceedings of the 32nd Hawaii International Conference on System Sciences*, Los Alamitos, CA: IEEE Computer Society Press, 1999, pp. 1-10.

Lonsdale, C. "Locked-in to Supplier Dominance: On the Dangers of Asset Specificity for the Outsourcing Decision," *The Journal of Supply Chain Management* (37:2), 2001, pp. 22-27.

Mason-Jones, R., Naylor, J. B., and Towill, D. "Engineering the Agile Supply Chain," *International Journal of Agile Management Systems* (2:1), 2000, pp. 54-61.

Morell, M., and Ezingeard, J.-N. "Revisiting Adoption Factors of Inter-Organizational Information Systems in SMEs," *Logistics Information Management* (15:1), 2002, pp. 46-57.

Nagy, A. "The Effect of Power on the Adoption of Interorganizational Information Systems: The Adoption Position Model," in *Proceedings of the 12th European Conference on Information Systems*, Turku, Finland, 2004.

Nagy, A., Orriens, B., and Fairchild, A. "The Promise and Reality of Internet-Based Interorganizational Systems," in *Proceedings of the IADIS International Conference e-Society*, Avila, Spain, 2004, pp. 886-890.

Nelson, M. L., and Shaw, M. J. "The Adoption and Diffusion of Interorganizational System Standards and Process Innovations," in *Proceedings of the MIS Quarterly Special Issue Workshop*, Seattle, WA, 2003, pp. 258-301.

Nelson, M. L., Shoonmaker, M., Shaw, M. J., Shen, S., Qualls, W., and Wang, R. "Modularized Interoperability in Supply-Chains: A Co-adoption Study of RosettaNet's XML-Based Inter-Organizational Systems," in *E-Business Management: Integration of Web Technologies with Business Models*, M. J. Shaw (Ed.), Boston: Kluwer Academic Publishers, 2002, p. 480.

O'Callaghan, R., Kaufmann, P. J., and Konsynski, B. R. "Adoption Correlates and Share Effects of Electronic Data Interchange Systems in Marketing Channels," *Journal of Marketing* (56:2), 1992, pp. 45-56.

O'Callaghan, R., and Turner, J. A. "Electronic Data Interchange: Concepts and Issues," in *EDI in Europe: How it Works in Practice*, H. Krcmar, N. Bjørn-Andersen, and R. O'Callaghan (Eds.), Chichester, England: John Wiley & Sons Ltd.., 1995, pp. 1-19.

Piderit, S. K. "Rethinking Resistance and Recognizing Ambivalence: A Multidimensional View of Attitudes Toward an Organizational Change," *Academy of Management Review* (25:4), 2000, pp. 783-794.

Ribbers, P. M. "Purchasing Through EDI: The Case of Technische Unie in The Netherlands," in *EDI in Europe: How it Works in Practice*, H. Krcmar, N. Bjørn-Andersen, and R. O'Callaghan (Eds.), Chichester, England: John Wiley & Sons Ltd.., 1995, pp. 47-84.

Rogers, E. M. *Diffusion of Innovations* (4th ed.), New York: Free Press, 1995.

Somasundaram, R. "Operationalizing Critical Mass as the Dependent Variable for Researching the Diffusion of e-Marketplaces: Its Implications," in *Proceedings of the 17th Bled eCommerce Conference*, Y-H Tan, D. Voge, J. Gricar, and G. Lenart (Eds.), Bled, Slovania, June 2004, pp. 1-14.

Somasundaram, R., and Karlsbjerg, J. "Research Philosophies in the IOS Adoption Field," in *Proceedings of the 11th European Conference on Information Systems*, C. Ciborra, R. Mercurio, M. De Marco, M. Martinez, and A. Carignani (Eds.), Napoli, Italy, 2003, pp. 1-11.

Stefansson, G. "Business-to-Business Data Sharing: A Source for Integration of Supply Chains," *International Journal of Production Economics* (75:1-2), 2002, pp. 135-146.

Subramani, M., and Venkatraman, N. "Safeguarding Investments in Asymmetric Inter-organizational Relationships: Theory and Evidence," *Academy of Management Journal* (46:1), 2003, pp. 46-62.

Tan, M., and Raman, K. S. "Interorganizational Systems and Transformation of Interorganizational Relationships: A Relational Perspective," in *Proceedings of the 23rd International Conference on Information Systems*, L. Applegate, R. Galliers, and J. I. DeGross (Eds.), Barcelona, Spain, 2002, pp. 877-884.

Teo, H. H., Wei, K. K., and Benbasat, I. "Predicting Intention to Adopt Interorganizational Linkages: An Institutional Perspective," *MIS Quarterly* (27:1), 2003, pp. 19-49.

Vlosky, R. P., Smith, P. M., and Wilson, D. T. "Electronic Data Interchange Implementation Strategies: A Case Study," *Journal of Business and Industrial Marketing* (9:4), 1994, pp. 5-18.

Von Heck, E.., and Ribbers, P. M. "The Adoption and Impact of EDI in Dutch SME's," in *Proceedings of the 32nd Hawaii International Conference on System Sciences*, Los Alamitos, CA: IEEE Computer Society Press, 1999, pp. 1-9.

Von Liere, D., Hagdorn, L., Hoogeweegen, M., and Vervest, P. H. M. "Organizational Performance of a Firm in a Modular Business Network," in *Proceedings of the 12th European Conference on Information Systems*, Turku, Finland, 2004.

Webster, J. "Networks of Collaboration or Conflict? Electronic Data Interchange and Power in the Supply Chain," *Journal of Management Information Systems* (4:1), 1995, pp. 31-42.

Williamson, O. "Transaction Cost Economics: The Governance of Contractual Relations," *Journal of Law and Economics* (22:2), 1979, pp. 233-261.

Wiseman, C. *Strategic Information Systems*, New York: McGraw-Hill Professional, 1988.

Womack, J. P., and Jones, D. T. *Lean Thinking: Banish Waste and Create Wealth in Your Corporation*, New York: Simon & Schuster, 1996.

ABOUT THE AUTHOR

Akos Nagy is a Ph.D. candidate in the Department of Information Systems and Management at Tilburg University, The Netherlands. He holds a M.Sc. in Information Systems from the Graduate School of the Center for Economic Research in Tilburg University. His research work has been presented at several international conferences. His current research interests are interorganizational information systems, supply chain management and performance, and the role of power in business networks. Akos can be reached at A.Nagy@uvt.nl.

APPENDIX A: OPERATIONALIZATION OF THE CONSTRUCTS

Constructs/Variables	Source

Perceived Benefits
Direct
    Reduced transaction costs
    Improved cash flow
    Reduced inventory
Indirect
    Improved information flow
    Improved internal operations
    Improved service
    Improved trading partner relations
	Chwelos et al. 2001
	Jones and Beatty 1998)

Perceived Risks Relation specific assets risk Relation specific processes risk Post contractual dependence Information asymmetry risk Loss of resource control risk Loss of ordering elasticity Use of sub-optimal practices Risk of opportunism (Trust) Technology risk	Hughes et al. 2004 Kumar and van Dissel 1996 Lonsdale 2001

Switching Cost
Compatibility/Readiness
    Infrastructure compatibility
    Application compatibility
    Business process compatibility
Specificity
    Infrastructure change specificity
    Application change specificity
    Business process change specificity
    Training
	Nagy et al. 2004

Supplier's Dependence on Buyer
Resource utility
    Operational importance
    Commercial importance
Substitutability
    Buyer pool
    Supplier's switching cost
    Search cost
Threat of backward integration
Threat of intermediation
Cartel of buyers
	Barney 1991
	Cox et al. 2002
	Emerson 1962

Constructs/Variables	Source

Buyer's Dependence on Supplier
Resource utility
    Operational importance
    Commercial importance
Resource Scarcity
    Imperfect imitability
    Substitutability
Threat of forward integration
Threat of intermediation
Cartel of buyers
	Barney 1991
	Cox et al. 2002
	Emerson 1962

11 AGILITY THROUGH IMPLEMENTATION: A Case from a Global Supply Chain

Magnus Holmqvist
Volvo and Viktoria Institute
Göteborg, Sweden

Kalevi Pessi
Göteborg University and Viktoria Institute
Göteborg, Sweden

Abstract   *This case is based on sharing empirical experiences and results from several years of collaborative research. The focus is on implementation projects with solutions for spare parts distribution in the automotive industry.*

The origin is a Volvo initiative with a Web portal for selling spare parts over the Internet. The journey will start with the creation of a platform for distribution of spare parts and continue with the process of introducing Web services and building new relations.

The new structure relies on the development of integration between legacy and a new information technology platform. The study followed the development of the platform as well as innovations that emerged in the new business structure. The paper describes the difficulty of creating a new platform and the even-more difficult establishment of new relations. However, the case also illustrates that continuous implementation projects deliver innovation in new relations and new channels, thereby displaying the unprecedented agility with which IT enables business value. The leverage for this is high and it is easier to roll out the new channels after the first implementation. Agility is achieved by working continuously with scenario development and by keeping implementation projects comprehensive, involving both technology and relations between supply chain actors.

Keywords   Agility, implementation, IT management, supply chain, Web services

1   INTRODUCTION

Agility is the ability to respond rapidly to unpredictable changes in demand. New technologies as well as business concepts have always been used to alter demand., but implementers need to be aware of the existence of considerable installed bases and existing relations. In-depth experiences from implementation projects in aftermarket logistics at Volvo provide unique knowledge of information technology and business development in a world that increasingly requires agility. Globalization and market demands have made logistics one of the most critical business issues. The case presents the active collaboration between the researchers and industry over a number of years. It summarizes and expands research presented earlier focusing on aftermarket logistics and theoretical scenarios (Holmqvist et al. 2001), the characteristics of e-business in logistics (Holmqvist and Enquist 2001), actual e-business consequences for spare part distribution (Holmqvist et al. 2003), and process integration and Web services (Holmqvist and Pessi 2005).

One objective of the case is to highlight results and experiences from business-to-business integration and how stakeholder relations, existing business, and IT context as well as endurance during implementation influence agility. The process illuminates how unforeseen and unintended results can be turned into valuable actions and innovations.

Theoretical reflections include IT management (Magoulas and Pessi 1998), systems development issues such as complexity of boundaries (Jackson 2003), and aspects of Web services such as composition and synchronisation (Christensen et al. 2001). Technology transfer and diffusion is a challenge, not least in terms of managing the duality of, first, exploring new technology then exploiting it in a global business context (Changsu and Galliers 2004; Finnegan et al. 2003; Huang et al 2003; these articles provide insights relating to agility from both the business and technology perspectives). Supply chain theories range from both supply to demand concerns (Ericsson 2003) and concepts from logistics that address agility (Christopher and Towill 2000).

We briefly describe the case context, followed by a summary of the research method. We then focus on specific implementation projects and their relation to agility. The paper concludes with comments on IT management and agility as delivered through implementation.

2   CASE CONTEXT AND AFTER-MARKET LOGISTICS

This case is anchored in the real business context of after-market logistics at Volvo, together with a perspective that has connections to current theories and research on IS/IT management. Volvo is a world-class provider of transport solutions, services, and products. With global presence and sales exceeding 170 billion SEK, its more than 70,000 employees focus on business-to-business operations in the areas of trucks, buses, construction equipment, marine and industrial engines, and Aero (www.volvo.com).

Logistics is a complex operation characterized by intensive information exchange between several stakeholders. Spare parts distribution at Volvo involves thousands of suppliers and tens of thousands of distribution points with hundreds of thousands of end-customers. The industrial product families contain hundreds of thousands of parts, which demand handling with both a long-term service responsibility and complicated supersession chains.

The parts also increase in complexity, as they are no longer just physical but also digital as well as part of service arrangements and wider business solutions. The fierce competition in the transport sector pushes the business-to-business relations to focus on bottom-line results in a reality of diminishing margins. This at the same time that exploiting core competencies and finding new business propositions through innovations seems to be even more important.

IT management is not easy when there are highly dynamic factors. Multiple interrelations on the one hand and significant differences between actors on the other are common in the field of logistics. To be agile, have flexible yet not costly over capacity, is a term that has been used to describe a desired capability. In this sense, there is a similarity and natural attraction to the loosely coupled architecture that surrounds Web services. Web services are currently being widely addressed in IT management discussions.

Actual implementation experiences and results from advanced Web services are, so far, scarce. However, the commercial value and interest are vivid. For example, IBM is using one of the implementation projects within this case as a case study for Web services as well as presenting it in their "Company of the Month" section (http://www-306.ibm.com/software/ebusiness/jstart/casestudies/volvo.shtml).

Although IBM shares some of the project work from one specific implementation, it gives a simplified and commercialized view of the objective, the implementation itself and not the origin of the overall development. This case has the objective of sharing several implementations as well as enriching the context and highlighting challenges.

3   RESEARCH METHOD

The characteristics of this Volvo case are, in terms of size, scope, and content, relevant (Yin 1984). The in-depth knowledge and open access to the research context provides information that can contribute to a discussion of IS/IT management issues. The first author of this paper has an extensive background within Volvo, thus enhancing the relevance to practice. There is an advantage to having extensive access to the case context, a factor that is crucial when studying complex situations that need comprehensive descriptions.

This paper reports from the study of three implementation projects.

(1) Establishing platform and approaching truck dealers and end-customers in selected European markets

(2) Refinements for bus key customers and standalone truck importers

(3) Developments for truck dealers and end-customers in Asia and East Europe

The first specific Web service implementation project for this case originated in late 2001 and the third implementation was deployed during the spring of 2003.

The methodology basically involves interpretive case study (Walsham 1995). In this case, the data collection has mainly been carried out through observations, semi-structured interviews, and workshops with stakeholders, decision makers, designers, and developers. All implementation projects have involved interviews with the steering group chairman, the project sponsor, and the person in charge of the pilot site (these represent the CIO, the after-market management, the dealer principal or equivalent). On several occasions, other representatives have been interviewed in order to include all supply chain actors.

User feedback from each implementation project has been collected and analyzed. As projects have been deployed, the first structured feedback has been conducted via a user satisfaction survey after three months and then continuously executed.

It may be argued that case studies in general lack replicability, that generalizations are difficult to make, that self-criticism is omitted, and that the research rigor is easy to question. However, the main objective of this case is to increase the understanding of agility and Web service implementation by sharing experiences of a practical context. The research in this paper is based on collaborative involvement and, together with a rigorous process, the objective is to provide contributions to both organizational development and scientific knowledge (Applegate 1999; Braa and Vidgen 1999; Mathiassen 2002).

We now present current developments and Web service implementations, reflecting on agility both in terms of technology and business.

4   IMPLEMENTATION PROJECTS AND AGILITY

The implementation projects that are the focus of this case originated in the review and development of an e-business strategy initiated in 2000. The business-to-business relations were challenged in many ways. Still, in a mature and large-scale industry, things do not change over night. Overall, the business-to-business relation is strongly driven by business focus rather than consumer behavior (i.e., productivity and bottom-line results matter more than image and appearance). At the turn of the millennium, Volvo decided it was time to change their Internet solutions from being just a place on the Web where customers could find information about products and services into a tool for conducting business with customers and dealers.

A main driver for starting the project was a common view in the whole automotive industry that the Internet, as a new technology, enabled an opportunity to create a new, efficient channel to reach and conduct business with customers. Three main incentives were identified which justified the project.

- Competitors: other truck manufacturers but also new entrants. Special focus and attention was set on possible third party Internet companies that wanted to sell spare parts. This was a significant potential threat for the after-market business.

- Cost reductions: Internet and e-business could increase productivity in existing processes and improve support given to customers but especially to dealers with services like online training for mechanics, information and document distribution, and spare part look-up.

- New services to broaden and expand the total offer such as simplified telematics services, load matching, and spare parts replenishment.

The result of the project was an initial implementation of two portals, one for customers and one for dealers. These portals include services on the Internet that support the customers' and dealers' total business cycle. This cycle ranges all the way from getting information about services and products, to being able to order spare parts (this service was called Parts Online and is a focus for this case), to operation and follow-up of the vehicle fleet, and, in the end, to resell, for example, an old truck. (The entry screens for the portal can be viewed at www.volvotrucks.com/onlineservices.) However, what can not be seen, and what was initially widely underestimated, was the challenge to establish the basic platform. The platform was part of the original implementation project and, therefore, the range of initial services that would support the total business cycle was limited. There was an awareness that establishment of a new channel with new technology would meet resistance and difficulties. Consequently, the goal was to include a valuable service in each part of the business cycle and expand gradually rather than to embrace everything at once. This was a major success factor, although the original implementation was generally regarded (especially in the first year) as too costly and delivering too little.

For Parts Online, the original goal was to increase sales to customers with accessories and consumable parts as well as spare parts for those customers operating their own workshop—within selected markets in Europe. Parts Online is a user-friendly system where customers can search for and order spare parts 24 hours a day, 7 days a week (24/7). An example of a screen from the Web portal is shown in Figure 1. Originally, the functionality was organized into categories of find parts, order parts, and use parts. However, as mentioned, in the original implementation, the functionality was rudimentary but has evolved gradually. The context was characterized by a lot of dynamics, thus the scope of the project was kept comprehensive in order to secure deliveries. At the same time, this created a situation where it would be possible to adapt rapidly to new issues. To be agile was characterized by one business manager as "the elephant cannot be a ballerina" and, on a follow-up question, he explained that the traditional strategic projects were usually like large elephants in order to give impact, but were not able to balance and fine tune during implementation.

The business value objectives in terms of cost reduction potential was realised, but the number of users was highly overestimated. Dealers saved time and had less administrative work on the phone with customers. A big issue was to solve the relation between dealers, customers, and Volvo where the main obstacle was to reassure the dealers that the solution was built to support their business and not to by-pass them. This was solved by letting the customer register and make the business agreement with a dealer and buy spare parts directly from them. During the implementation a concept of win-win-win arose, where a beneficial set-up for Volvo, the dealers and the customers could be designed.

One of the largest advantages that followed from keeping the initial implementation project limited was not only that it became comprehensive but also that much knowledge was gained from getting practical at an early stage. In combination with an initial value chain analysis and assessment actors, a number of theoretical scenarios had been developed. These scenarios have provided much of the knowledge base, contributing to an

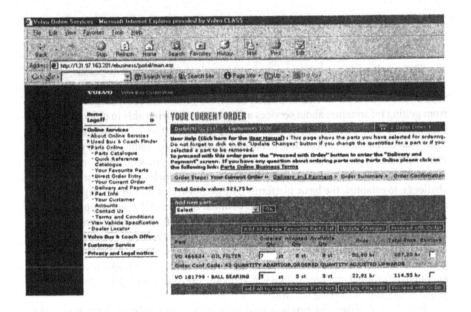

Figure 1. Example of the Web Portal Screen from Parts Online

architectural agility but ultimately leveraging the experiences gained during implementation in relation to follow-on projects. Four scenarios were developed for the imminent
introduction of the online services project, including a spare parts portal as seen in
Figure 2. The arrows show the physical distribution path based on the order flow and
access to the customer order point, for example the "Today" scenario showed that there
was no online connection between the dealer and end-customer workshop and consequently no management of the distribution between them (therefore the dashed arrow).

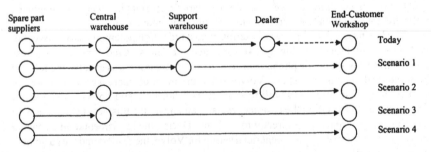

Figure 2. Original Scenario Development
(Adapted from M. Holmqvist, O. Hultkranz, G. Stefansson, and A.
Wingqvist, "Consequences of E-Commerce on Physical Logistics: A
Theoretical Scenario for Spare Part Distribution," *Proceedings of the
9th World Conference on Transport Research,* 2001)

Scenario 1: The spare parts are distributed directly from the support warehouse to the end-customer, which is the customer's workshop in all scenarios.

Scenario 2: The spare parts are shipped directly from the central warehouse to the dealer and then from the dealer to the end-customer.

Scenario 3: The shipment is sent directly from the central warehouse to the end-customer, bypassing both support warehouse and dealer.

Scenario 4: The spare parts are sent directly from the supplier to the end-customer, bypassing all traditional distribution centers.

4.1 Initial Implementation

Volvo, similarly to other vehicle manufacturers, has come to play a major role in the after-market supply chain. Their dominating position originates from the control of product development and sourcing as well as influence upon the distribution network, dealers and customers. From the perspective of Volvo, the spare parts manufacturer represents the supplier from which spare parts are bought. Dealers are the actors that buy spare parts from the vehicle manufacturer and then sell them on to vehicle owners, thus they are sometimes also referred to as retailers. Consequently, vehicle manufacturers refer to vehicle owners and operators as customers or even end-customers who may have their own workshops.

The scenario analysis provided the original implementation project with a set of different possibilities. At that time, however, only one scenario had been justified for implementation. The most viable seemed to be to strengthen the relationship between the dealer and the customer by providing an additional channel for spare parts. Volvo would then also further build upon the relation with its dealers and, by improving the performance of the dealer offer, would gain in the competitive market place. This implementation reinforced an ultimate goal and overall business strategy intended to attract end-customers from their own workshops to the dealer workshops. Referring to the scenarios depicted above, this can be described as building upon Scenario 2 (as depicted in Figure 3).

The original implementation project provided the means to reach customers where the main impacts were the commercial relations, the technical platform, and extending the supply chain with delivery options as well as ordering systems to customers.

Figure 3. Original Implementation Project: Reaching End-Customers

The technical challenges in deploying an infrastructure had mainly difficulties with single sign-on, multi-language, 24/7, security, business process synchronization, and legacy connectivity.   Nevertheless, the vast work did result in a platform that could actually be easily extended and respond in an agile way to increasing business demands with more functionalities to support the total business cycle.

This combined business and technology agility was a major benefit and, at the time, an innovation that would prove to deliver much more value than originally estimated. This would not have been possible without the first implementation. Furthermore, the first scenario had significant challenges with central involvement in very local relationships. Market companies and dealers as well as the global functions have not been used to collaborate in a cross-functional or cross-hierarchical way. Consequently, this is still an emerging area.

4.2 Continuous Implementation and Innovation

Even with the obstacles to overcome both in terms of technology and relations, the established platform provided opportunities for follow-on implementation projects. A second project was launched to deliver the enhanced technological features for a group of more-established relations: importers. Importers mainly exist in small markets on the international scene. They represent a company that usually sells to dealers and manages importation of spare parts.

The thought was also, in some rare and minor cases ,to extend directly to end-customers. However, still involving the close proximity and human relation of the dealers, the system and logistics connection goes from a central warehouse to end-customers. This case would only be valid if certain criteria are fulfilled, such as end-customers maintaining their own workshops for the foreseeable future and as long as distribution points and volumes are justifiable.

This first follow-on implementation, related to Scenario 3 and seen in Figure 4, enforced a win-win-win situation between end-customers, dealers, and Volvo. This was a profound innovation and a clear delivery of the existing agility. This has been a unique situation where global functions, market establishments, and dealers have collaborated both cross-functionally and between different levels. Furthermore, it has had a very high return in relation to the minor follow-on investment required.

After the second implementation, new possibilities were focused based on the positive results of the second project. Focus was put on new geographical areas out-side Europe, such as Asia, as well as extending the capabilities of support warehouses to

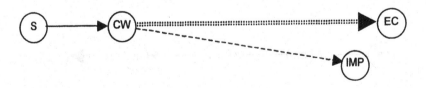

Figure 4. Continuous Implementation: Restructuring Relations

Figure 5. Continuous Implementation: Extending Reach

deliver to end-customers. Technically the platform needed minor adaptations and the objective was to extend logistical capabilities. Utilizing the capabilities leveraged agility and provided business value.

The second follow-on implementation (i.e., the third implementation project) correlates to Scenario 1 (see Figure 5). Based on the experiences gained during the first two implementations the challenge was to deploy a more decentralized structure (i.e., several support warehouses). This was possible to manage even though it required close analysis and monitoring during roll-out. Technically more-advanced Web services could be developed, primarily because a critical mass of practical competence had been built-up but also as platform stability was established. Still, difficulties were encountered, especially upon alignment for business process synchronization.

The overall impression about the development is that all the work that was completed during the initial implementation project paid off, gave payback in follow-on implementations. Both the cost and the lead-time were lowered in later versions. The largest benefits have been the agility that has enabled innovations both in terms of functionality and technical and business set-up as well as ability to manage relations between stakeholders. Table 1 provides a summarized view.

Table 1. Summarized View of Implementation Projects (Adapted from M. Holmqvist, O. Hultkranz, G. Stefansson, and A. Wingqvist, "Consequences of E-Commerce on Physical Logistics: A Theoretical Scenario for Spare Part Distribution," *Proceedings of the 5th Logistics Research Network Conference,* 2003.)

	Original Implementation	First Follow-On Implementation	Second Follow-On Implementation
Development Cost (relative size)	1	1/5	< 1/20
Lead time (relative)	1	½	1/4
Challenges			
– Project process	Complex, many functions involved —but good focus	Easier, since follow-on learning curve	Poor focus, since less management attention
– Technology	New, Complex	Stabilizing	Established
– Commercial relations	Existing but new collaboration	Emerging but new	Experience from former set-ups
– Logistics	Not focused	New	Existing
Results			
– Cost/Benefit	Emerging	Great	As expected
– Innovation		Win-win-win relations	Extended reach and features

Before providing some concluding comments, it must be emphasized that no general governance model for agility will be delivered. At the most, the scenario development may been seen as a guideline but, due to the business dynamics , it will not be possible to strictly control strategic developments. Thus thoughts of strategic alignment (Henderson and Venkatraman 1993) are too inhibiting while, at the same time, just allowing drift (Ciborra 2000) may lose the ability to drive progress.

Consequently, agility is nurtured by action through implementation, based on a strategic awareness, and with comprehensive projects it is possible to lead development.

5 CONCLUDING COMMENTS

The new structure for spare parts distribution at Volvo relies on the development of integration between legacy and a new IT platform as well as development of relationships between stakeholders. The case shows that implementation projects on a solid platform designed to meet agile business demands bring innovations that have enabled a new business structure.

The creation of a new platform is problematic and the establishment of new relations is even more difficult. The main challenges are: single sign-on, process synchronization, multi-language, 24/7, security, and legacy connectivity. However, areas that have been less illuminated are single sign-on and business process synchronization and these are highlighted here as a main concern. Consequently, they are presented as areas for further research.

Finally, this case has summarised but also expanded findings from research that has been presented in earlier papers. It is important to see the continuation of results through a holistic review of IT management. Specifically, continuous implementation projects can deliver innovation in new relations and new channels, especially when agility has been addressed from the beginning. It is easier to roll out the new channels after the first implementation; it is beneficial to start in areas where established relations exist, it is favorable to wait with development of advanced Web services until the technical platform is stable and key business relations are established—then the leverage constitutes the agility that provides a high business value.

Agility is achieved by working continuously with scenario development and by keeping implementation projects comprehensive. These involve both technology and relations between supply chain actors.

REFERENCES

Applegate, L. "Rigor and Relevance in MIS Research—Introduction," *MIS Quarterly* (23:1), Special Issue, March 1999, pp. 1-2.

Braa, K., and Vidgen, R. Interpretation, Intervention, and Reduction in the Organizational Laboratory: A Framework for In-Context Information System Research," *Accounting Management & Information Technologies* (9), 1999, pp. 25-47.

Changsu, K., and Galliers, R. "Deriving a Diffusion Framework and Research Agenda for Web-Based Shopping Systems," *Journal of Electronic Commerce Research* (5:3), 2004, pp. 199-215.

Christopher M, Towill D. "Supply Chain Migration from Lean and Functional to Agile and Customized," *Supply Chain Management* (5:4), 2000, pp. 206-213.

Christensen, E., Curbera, F., Meredith, G., and Weerawarana, S. "Web Services Description Language (WSDL) 1.1," *WC3 Note*, Ariba, International Business Machines Corporation, and Microsoft, March 15, 2001 (available online at http://www.w3.org/TR/2001/NOTE-wsdl-20010315).

Ciborra, C. (Ed.). *From Control to Drift*, Oxford: Oxford University Press, 2000.

Ericsson D. "Supply/Demand Chain Management: The Next Frontier for Competitiveness," in *Global Logistics*, D. Waters (Ed.), London: Kogan Page, 2003.

Finnegan, P., Galliers, R., and Powell, P. "Applying Triple Loop Learning to Planning Electronic Trading Systems," *Information Technology and People* (16), 2003 pp. 461-483.

Henderson, J., and Venkatraman, N. "Strategic Alignment: Leveraging Information Technology for Transforming Organizations," *IBM Systems Journal* (32:1), 1993, pp. 4-16.

Holmqvist, M., and Enquist, H. "IT Is Not New vs Old, Yet Real e-Logistics," in *Proceedings of the 24th IRIS Conference*, Bergen, Norway, 2001, pp. 445-458.

Holmqvist, M., Hultkrantz, O., Stefansson, G., and Wingqvist, A. "Consequences of E-Commerce on Physical Logistics: A Theoretical Scenario for Spare Part Distribution," in *Proceedings of 9th World Conference on Transport Research*, Seoul, Korea, 2001.

Holmqvist, M., Hultkrantz, O., Stefansson, G., and Wingqvist, A. "Consequences of E-Commerce for Spare Part Distribution," in *Proceedings of 5th Logistics Research Network Conference*, London, 2003, pp. 196-216.

Holmqvist, M., and Pessi, K. "Process Integration and Web Services," *Scandinavian Journal of Information Systems*, 2005 (forthcoming).

Huang, J., Makoju, E., Newell, S., and Galliers, R. "Opportunities to Learn from 'Failure' with Electronic Commerce: A Case Study of Electronic Banking," *Journal of Information Technology*, (18), 2003, pp. 17-26.

Jackson, M. *Systems Thinking: Creative Holism for Managers*, New York: John Wiley & Sons, 2003.

Magoulas, T., and Pessi K. *Strategisk IT-management*, Ph.D. Thesis, Göteborg University, 1998.

Mathiassen, L. "Collaborative Practice Research," *Scandinavian Journal of Information Systems* (14), 2002, pp. 57-76.

Walsham, G. "Interpretive Case Studies in IS Research: Nature and Method," *European Journal of Information Systems* (4), 1995, pp. 74-81.

Yin, R. *Case Study Research: Design and Methods*, Thousand Oaks, CA: Sage Publications, 1984.

ABOUT THE AUTHORS

Magnus Holmqvist (M.Sc.) is an Industrial Ph.D. candidate at the Göteborg University and currently works with Business Innovation at Volvo Information Technology (www.gu.se, www.volvo.com). He has extensive experience with global supply chain management, specializing in after-market business. Magnus' research interests are in the integration of complex systems and he has been a frequent guest lecturer in subjects such as business process development and project management. Magnus can be reached at Magnus.Holmqvist@volvo.com.

Kalevi Pessi (Ph.D.) leads the Business Technology research group at the Viktoria Institute (www.viktoria.se). He is head of the IT Management Master's program at the IT University in Göteborg (www.ituniv.se). Kalevi's Ph.D. thesis was in IT management; his current research interests are in the areas of business value and architectural design. He has been the managing director of the Viktoria Institute and Knowledge Management Director at Guide, a large Swedish consultancy firm, and has broad experience from trade and industry. Kalevi can be reached at pessi@informatik.gu.se.

Part 4

Agile Development

12 A STUDY OF THE USE OF AGILE METHODS WITHIN INTEL

Brian Fitzgerald
University of Limerick
Limerick, IRELAND

Gerard Hartnett
Intel Communications Europe
Shannon, IRELAND

Abstract   *This study investigated the use of the agile methods, eXtreme programming (XP) and Scrum, at the Intel Network Processor Division engineering team based in Shannon, Ireland, over a three-year period. The study is noteworthy as it is based on real industrial software projects involving experienced software engineers, with continuous reflection and monitoring of the application of these approaches. It provides evidence that agile methods are far from anti method; rather, they require disciplined application and careful customization to the particular needs of the development context. The study also shows how XP and Scrum can complement each other to provide a comprehensive agile development method, with XP providing support for technical aspects and Scrum providing support for project planning and tracking. The manner in which XP and Scrum have been customized to suit the needs of the development environment at Intel Shannon is described, as are the lessons learned. The XP practices that were applied did lead to significant benefits, with pair-programming leading to reductions in code defect density of a factor of seven, and one project actually achieving zero defect density. However, some observed limitations of pair-programming are described. Intel Shannon also found that not all XP practices were applicable in their context. Thus, the study suggests that, contrary to suggestions that XP is not divisible or individually selectable, a la carte selection and tailoring of XP practices can work very well. In the case of Scrum, some local customization has led to a very committed adoption by developers themselves, in contrast to many development methods whose use is decreed mandatory by management. The success of Scrum is significant. Projects of six-month and one-year duration have been delivered ahead of schedule, which bodes well for future ability to accurately plan development projects, a black art in software development up to now.*

1   INTRODUCTION

Despite 50 years of software development experience, the vast majority of software projects continue to exceed budget and development schedule, and are often of poor quality when completed. In recent times, agile approaches have emerged as an apparently revolutionary new practice-led paradigm that can address these central problems. The agile approaches comprise a broad range—eXtreme Programming (XP) (Beck 2000), dynamic systems development method (DSDM) (Stapleton 1998), Scrum (Schwaber and Beedle 2002); Crystal (Cockburn 2001); agile modeling (Ambler 2002); feature driven design (Coad et al. 1999); lean programming (Poppendieck 2001), and perhaps even the rational unified process (RUP) (Kruchten 2000), although there is considerable disagreement on whether or not RUP is an agile method. These approaches differ significantly from traditional approaches to software development, emphasizing development productivity rather than process rigor, and seeking to deliver business value quickly, while also accommodating changing user requirements.

It is important to emphasize that agile approaches are not anti method; rather, they operate on the lean principle of "barely sufficient methodology" (Highsmith 2002). The change in emphasis from the traditional approaches is summarized in the following value-tradeoffs:

- Individuals and interactions over processes and tools
- Working software over comprehensive documentation
- Customer collaboration over contract negotiation
- Responding to change over following a plan

Advocates of the agile approaches recognize that both sides of these value statements are relevant to software development. However, they choose to emphasize the first part of each statement as more important than the second part. The overall principles underpinning the agile approaches are summarized in the agile manifesto (www.agilemanifesto.com).

The use of agile approaches is growing rapidly, estimated to be in use in two-thirds of all IT development companies in 2002 (Sliwa 2002). Practice is ahead of research in this area, but much of the evidence offered thus far has been anecdotal in nature. Thus, the study reported on here in Intel Shannon is particularly useful as the findings are based on intensive investigation of the agile initiatives that have been implemented. Two of the most popular and widely used agile methods are XP and Scrum, and both of these are in active use in Intel Shannon. Hence, a brief background summary of each of these approaches is provided here.

1.1 eXtreme Programming (XP)

The eXtreme Programming (XP) approach explicitly acknowledges that it is not a magic "silver bullet" of revolutionary new techniques; rather, it is a set of tried and trusted principles that are well-established as part of the conventional wisdom of software engineering, but which are taken to an extreme level—hence the name eXtreme

Programming. XP has been pioneered by Kent Beck, and has its origins in a project to develop an internal payroll system at Chrysler in 1996-97. It is comprehensively described in Beck (2000, p. xv), where he describes it as "a light-weight methodology for small-to-medium-sized teams developing software in the face of vague or rapidly-changing requirements." XP comprises five key values, *communication, feedback, simplicity, courage*, and *respect*. These are underpinned by 12 key practices, summarized in Table 1.

A marked feature of XP is that several of the practices overlap to some extent and thus serve to complement and reinforce each other—refactoring, simple design, collective ownership, and coding standards, for example. However, while XP is acknowledged as not being a "one size fits all" approach suited to every development context, there is by no means unanimous agreement on where the limits of its applicability lie. Thus, its application in Intel Shannon is especially pertinent as it represents an industrial product development setting with experienced software engineers. Many of the reported benefits of XP to date have been in academic university environments (e.g., Hedin et al. 2003; Muller and Tichy 2001) and, therefore, lessons learned from its application in a real software development context are invaluable, as quite few such studies have been published (Heim and Hemphill 2003). Also, McBreen (2003, p. 88) identifies the importance of "continuous reflection" on the application of XP practices, and this was very much a feature of the Intel Shannon context.

1.2 Scrum

Scrum (Schwaber and Beedle 2002) is a simple, low-overhead process for managing and tracking software development. While it is very much influenced by Boehm's (1988) spiral model, it has its origins in a project by Jeff Sutherland at the Easel Corporation in 1993 where it was used in the development of an object-oriented analysis and design tool. While XP is used in Intel Shannon for the technical engineering aspects of development, Scrum is used for the project management aspects, for which it is better suited. Scrum differs from traditional approaches in that it assumes that analysis, design, and development processes are largely unpredictable. At its heart, Scrum comprises a number of stages which, building on its underpinning metaphor of a rugby scrum, also follow a sporting theme.

* First, the **pre-game** phases:
  - **Planning**: This phase involves the definition of a new release of the system based on the currently known backlog of required modifications, along with an estimate of its schedule and cost. If a new system is being developed, this phase consists of both conceptualization and analysis. If an existing system is being enhanced, this phase consists of limited analysis.
  - **Architecture**: This phase includes system architecture modification and high-level design as to how the backlog items will be implemented.

Table 1. Key Practices of XP (Adapted from K. Beck, *Extreme Programming Explained*, Addison-Wesley, 2000)

The Planning Game
A quick determination of the scope of the next software release, based on a combination of business priorities and technical estimates. It is accepted that this plan will probably change.

Small Releases
Put a simple system into production quickly, then release new versions on a very short cycle.

Metaphor
Guide all development with a simple shared story of how the whole system works.

Simple Design
The system should be designed as simply as possible at any given moment in time.

Testing
Programmers continually write tests which must be run flawlessly for development to proceed. Customers write function tests to demonstrate the features implemented.

Refactoring
Programmers restructure the system, without removing functionality, to improve nonfunctional aspects (e.g., duplication of code, simplicity, flexibility).

Pair-Programming
All production code is written by two programmers at one machine.

Collective Ownership
Anyone can change any code anywhere in the system at any time.

Continuous Integration
Integrate and build the system every time a task is completed—this may be many times per day.

40-Hour Week
Work no more than 40 hours per week as a rule.

On-Site Customers
Include an actual user on the team, available full-time to answer questions.

Coding Standards
Adherence to coding rules which emphasize communication via program code.

- Following this is the main **game** phase:
  - **Sprints**: This involves development of new release functionality, with constant respect to the variables of time, requirements, quality, cost, and competition. Interaction with these variables defines the end of this phase. There are multiple, iterative development sprints, or cycles, that are used to evolve the system.

- Finally, there is the **post-game** phase:
  - **Closure:** Here the focus is on preparation for release, including final documentation, pre-release staged testing, and release.

The first and last Scrum phases (planning and closure) consist of defined processes, where all processes, inputs, and outputs are well defined. The knowledge of how to do these processes is explicit. The flow is linear, with some iteration in the planning phase.

Sprints are nonlinear and flexible. Where available, explicit process knowledge is used; otherwise tacit knowledge and trial and error is used to build process knowledge. Sprints are used to evolve the final product. The project is open to the environment until the closure phase. The deliverable can be changed at any time during the planning and sprint phases of the project. The project remains open to environmental complexity, including competitive, time, quality, and financial pressures, throughout these phases.

One of the most interesting aspects of Scrum is the daily meeting of the project team. The daily meeting is kept short, typically 15 minutes. Everyone answers three questions.

- What did you do in the last 24 hours?
- What roadblocks did you encounter that you need someone to remove?
- What is your plan for the next 24 hours?

Within Intel Shannon, quite a lot of experimentation has been done using Scrum on projects of different sizes and complexity. Despite the claim by its proponents that Scrum has been used on "thousands of Scrum projects" (Schwaber and Beedle 2002), there have been few accounts of the use of Scrum in real-world projects (Abrahamsson et al. 2003), a notable exception being the study by Rising and Janoff (2000).

The remainder of the paper is structured as follows: In the next section, contextual background information is provided in relation to Intel Shannon. Following this, the case study research method and the personal interview process employed in this study is discussed. In the next section, the actual implementation of XP and Scrum and the lessons learned are discussed. Finally, the conclusions from the study are presented.

2 BACKGROUND: INTEL SHANNON DEVELOPMENT CONTEXT

Intel Shannon is based in the west of Ireland and is part of the Intel's Infrastructure Processor Division. The main Intel plant in Ireland near Dublin employs 4,200 people.

The Intel Shannon organization employs close to 100 people, and about 70 are involved in engineering, software development, and silicon design. The products under development are network processors for networking equipment typically for SMEs, the small office/home (SOHO), and 3G wireless markets. For these products, requirements analysis is typically done in the United States, the software and silicon design is done in Shannon. Intel Shannon has seen significant growth in their workforce over the past few years. They are now striving to institute a repeatable engineering process whereby they will have multiple products under development in parallel in different phases. In the past, their portfolio has been characterized by a startup/single-product focus.

In terms of software development, Intel Shannon has been formally assessed at Level 2 on the capability maturity model (CMM). While this has led to some discipline in the development process, the rapid time-to-market pressures have led Intel Shannon to consider agile methods. Further, they are a company that embraces innovation and seeks to rigorously assess new techniques and methods that could meet their market needs. Intel Shannon has been deploying a range of agile methods over the past three years, principally two flavors of agile methods: XP for the technical engineering aspects of software development and SCRUM for the project planning and tracking.

While the move to CMM certification was driven more as a top-down mandate within the organization, in contrast, Scrum and XP were introduced at a grassroots engineering level as optional techniques. As such, their adoption has grown organically over time. They were not mandated or compulsory as the techniques were being introduced in parallel with CMM implementation. While many tend to view CMM and agile methods as axiomatically incommensurable, this has been cogently shown to be an oversimplification (Paulk 2001).

Agile methods are also finding use in the wider Intel software engineering community. The company now has an internal wiki Web site and diverse teams meet on a regular basis to share experiences with different agile methodologies. Again, this community is driven by grassroots engineering.

The lessons learned have been significant and are discussed in section 4, but first the research method employed in this study is described.

3   RESEARCH METHOD

Given that the agile methods area is a relatively new research area, research of an exploratory and descriptive nature is needed, and any research method chosen should reflect this. Marshall and Rossman (1989) propose a framework for matching research purpose with research methods and data capture techniques. In the case of research which has a descriptive and exploratory focus, a combination of case study and in-depth interviewing is deemed appropriate according to their framework.

3.1 The Case Study Method

The case study is not viewed in a similar fashion by all researchers (see Smith 1990). However, according to one of the more common interpretations, it describes a single situation, and usually involves the collection of a large amount of qualitative information (see Benbasat et al. 1987; Lee 1989; Yin 1994). Case studies can be very valuable in generating an understanding of the reality of a particular situation, and can provide a good basis for discussion. There is neither an attempt at experimental design nor any control of variables. However, since the information collected is often specific to the particular situation at a particular point in time, results may not be generalizable.

Notwithstanding this limitation, the case study was chosen as the research method for this study, as its advantage in providing thick description was seen as outweighing its limitations. Also, the project manager responsible for the deployment of agile methods subsequently became a coauthor of the paper. Thus, the findings are further strengthened through the direct validation of those responsible for the process being studied.

3.2 In-Depth Personal Interviews

The purpose of the personal interview is to encourage the interviewee to relate experiences and attitudes relevant to the research problem (Walker 1988). It is a very flexible technique in that the interviewer can probe any interesting details that emerge during the interview, and concentrate in detail on particular aspects.

It should be noted that a reflexive approach was deliberately allowed in the interview phase adopted in this study. This has been identified as important in exploratory research (Trauth and O'Connor 1991) as it allows for refocusing as the research progresses, in that responses to certain questions can stimulate new awareness and interest in particular issues which may then require additional probing. Eisenhardt (1989) also recommends such a strategy, labeling it *controlled opportunism.*

In this study, a series of formal and informal interviews were conducted over a one-year period with the project manager and key staff responsible for agile deployment at Intel Shannon. Interviews were generally of one- to two-hour duration. Informal interviews were used to clarify and refine issues as they emerged. Also, as one of the primary sources of information became a coauthor of the paper, the correctness of the researchers' interpretation was less of an issue than in the traditional model whereby exclusively external authors interpret the research findings.

4   USE OF XP AND SCRUM AT INTEL SHANNON

4.1 XP

Intel Shannon has been using XP for five years. However, even though they have been committed users of XP, they have been quite pragmatic in choosing only those aspects of XP which they perceived as relevant to the needs of their development context. The XP practices that have been deployed, however, have been carefully monitored and the implications measured. These practices were pair-programming, testing, refactoring, simple design, coding standards, and collective ownership. Their experiences with each are discussed in turn below.

Scrum has also been used for five years. Again, the documented technique has been tailored locally.

Scrum has seen more enthusiastic adoption at the individual team level than eXtreme Programming. The reasons for this are discussed in more detail below.

4.1.1   Pair-Programming

Pair-programming is perhaps the best known of the XP practices, with generally positive reports on its usage, although Muller and Tichy (2001) suggest that it decreases overall productivity. While most of the other XP practices have been applied across all of the individual software teams at Intel Shannon, pair-programming has been selectively applied. Most teams consist of between two and six software engineers with a wide range of experience. Pair-programming was applied initially by two teams on two components of the software for the IXP2XX network processor. On the later IXP4XX network processor, it was again employed by two teams.

Pair-programming was perceived as having a number of significant advantages at Intel Shannon. First, it was estimated that the required code quality level was achieved earlier. On the IXP2XX project, the pair-programmed components had the lowest defect density in the whole product. The defect densities were a factor of seven below the component with the highest density. On the IXP4XX project, two of the three Intel Shannon based teams used pair-programming. One of the teams achieved zero defect quality. The team with the highest defect density was the team that did not. The three teams all had similar experience profiles. With pair-programming, developers did not get stuck wondering what to do next. If one person was unsure, the other probably did know. Developers also believed that they learned quite a lot from each other and that they remained more focused on the job at hand, and less likely to go off on a tangent.

The essential nature of pair-programming, where one person is effectively looking over the other's shoulder, meant that minor errors were caught early, saving considerable debugging time. Also, it was useful for testing and debugging, as a fresh viewpoint could spot the obvious flaw which was not obvious to the pair partner. The overall process also ensured that more than one developer gained a deep understanding of the design and code, thus facilitating collective ownership (discussed below). Developers suggested that they had more fun, and found the work more interesting. They also seemed more enthusiastic about their work.

However, there were a number of problematic aspects associated with the use of pair-programming also. For example, it was found to be unsuitable for simple or well-understood problems, which could be fixed as quickly as a single developer could type. In a similar vein, when doing lots of small changes (e.g., eliminating To-Do's), it tended to get frustrating.

Some developers found pair-programming could break their flow of concentration as they needed to pause to communicate nonobvious ideas to the pair partner. Indeed, some developers expressed the view that it was difficult to reflect and concentrate with someone by their side.

Overall, Intel Shannon has documented a number of lessons which will guide its future use of pair-programming.

- Some basic rules of pair working etiquette are required, e.g., no keyboard wrestling.
- Consideration needs to be given to neighbors to keep background noise to a minimum.
- Use large fonts.
- Set clear objectives at the start of a programming session.
- Planning and coordination may be necessary to prioritize programming over other activities (e.g., helping other engineers, phone calls, meetings), otherwise both people may not be free simultaneously.
- Pair-programming was not seen as valuable during sustaining activities on the project when the amount of coding is not as significant.

4.1.2 Testing

Intel Shannon also implemented a test-code development strategy (i.e., writing the unit-test code while writing production code). They found this had a number of advantages. It set a direction for the immediate development, namely to get the test case working. It also helped developers get a better understanding of the functionality required of the software from a client point of view. The unit-tests are also implemented as part of a regression test suite and all component unit tests are run on the code repository nightly. Integration tests are also developed to test the individual components in concert and "smoke tests" are run daily with external test equipment in the weeks leading up to a release.

4.1.3 Refactoring

Refactoring was another XP technique that was quite widely used at Intel Shannon. They found it worked best when it was done early, as it eliminated a lot of bugs that would have taken up a lot of debugging time otherwise. Refactoring also became akin to a continuous design activity, which is discussed next.

4.1.4 Simple Design

In this case, design was done on a whiteboard before each block of code was written. As a result, the design document emerged on an ongoing basis in parallel with the code implementation. Quite significantly, however, they have not subscribed to the XP concept of the code being the design as documentation is an integral part of the product deliverable at Intel Shannon. Simplicity increasingly became the guiding principle and, over time, developers stopped trying to second-guess the client code and just implemented the requirements. As already mentioned, this practice was very closely linked to refactoring.

4.1.5   Collective Ownership

This practice led to a number of benefits. First, it ensured that several members of
the project team knew the code well enough to make changes, so if one person was busy,
another person could make the requested change. Also, in the Intel Shannon context,
changes in team composition were quite common. In the past, this meant that developers had to choose between bringing any code they wrote with them and continuing to
maintain it, or spending time teaching the code to someone else and handing over
responsibility. Collective ownership allowed management more flexibility as it resulted
in teams being able to maintain the code base as several of the original members would
know it well enough to maintain it.

However, Intel Shannon found that collective ownership was only appropriate on
a single team basis. Code ownership across multiple teams was not applied. The
software engineering team on the whole product could be as many as 30 engineers and
the team felt collective ownership could not scale to this wide a population.

4.1.6   Coding Standards

Intel Shannon defined a C-coding standard early in the project and referred to it
extensively during coding and code inspections. Coding standards were already a very
strong feature of their development environment prior to the application of XP.

4.1.7   Unused XP Practices

XP pioneers have suggested that it cannot be applied with piecemeal cherry-picking
of individual practices. As Schwaber (2001, p. 8) puts it, "[XP] values and their underlying practices and techniques are not divisible and individually selectable; they form
a coherent, whole process." However, a number of XP practices were not applied at
Intel Shannon as they felt they were not applicable to their development context. The
unused practices include the planning game, small releases, continuous integration, 40-
hour week, metaphor, and on-site customers. The reasons for lack of adoption of these
practices were as follows:

The planning game was not used as many aspects of planning are covered by the
Scrum technique, discussed later. From a business priority perspective, a product-
marketing team has the responsibility for deciding feature priorities. They are in a
separate organization, most of whom are not physically colocated. In future, however,
they intend to use some prioritization aspects of the planning game.

The XP practice of small releases is not feasible early in the product schedule as in
this business the software releases are tied to silicon availability. Once silicon is
available, the team typically delivers minor releases every four to six weeks and major
releases every two quarters.

While continuous integration is practiced for each component, given the complexity
of the overall software and the need for external test equipment, full system integration
is done only in the fortnight leading up to a release.

The 40-hour week was seen as a great aspiration but it was not consistently achievable in the Intel Shannon development context, where the discrepancy in time zones between Europe and the United States serves to extend working hours.

On-site customers are not available. These projects are tied to the design of silicon and in many cases do not have specific customers during the early conceptual stages. The product marketing group acts as a customer proxy, prioritizing features based on potential revenue.

Metaphor was not explicitly used, but at a high level the software components do correspond to the interfaces on the silicon and have common patterns of functions on the APIs.

4.1.8   Overall Lessons on XP Practices

Overall, Intel Shannon is quite happy with the XP experience. Some of the practices, such as simple design and testing, are now used across the board on all development teams. Testing is also integrated into the development environment.

Despite its success, pair-programming has not grown to the same extent as Scrum, for example. This dichotomy will be discussed below.

In general, where pair-programming was adopted, it tended to lead to a smaller code base and, as defect rate is directly correlated with code length, this has led to more efficient use of resources.

As a thought experiment, the developers tried to imagine how the software would have turned out if a more traditional development process had been followed. They believed it would have taken in or around the same time—any discrepancies would be lost in the noise of overhead. However, they felt the traditional code would probably have been quite a bit more complex and long to cater for situations that would probably never occur. As mentioned above, since the defect rate is a constant, this would equate to more bugs.

4.2 Scrum

Scrum has been used for three years at Intel Shannon although some of the engineers had used it for almost five years in their previous organizations. Scrum has really only been documented in book form since 2002 (Schwaber and Beedle 2002). Up to then the technique was documented on a number of Web sites (e.g., http://www.jeffsutherland.org/scrum/index.html and http://www.controlchaos.com/scrum.pdf). The Intel team also employed a number of techniques from EPISODES (Cunningham 1995), the precursor to eXtreme planning.

Scrum was initially piloted by one team and its use has grown organically to the extent that it now is used by most of the teams in Intel Shannon. They believe the key reason for this enthusiastic embrace of the technique is due to one of the customizations this initial team made. The daily Scrum meeting took place around a board covered with yellow post-it notes. The team recorded tasks for the 24-hour period on post-its. This made Scrum very visible in the organization, and curiosity from other teams helped the

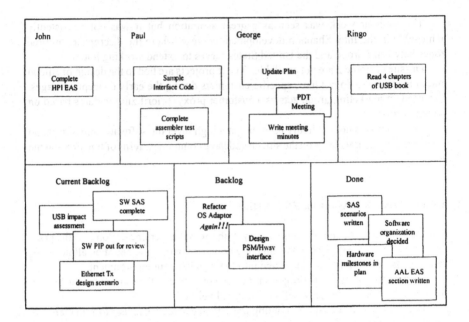

Figure 1. Sample Scrum Daily Meeting Post-It Record

initial spread of the technique. Figure 1 illustrates a sample meeting record with post-its attached.

Team members arrive at the daily meeting with their new post-its for the next 24 hours. The post-its in their named area are the tasks that were committed to at the last meeting. If a task is too big for the next 24 hours, they write a subset of it on a new post-it. During the Scrum meeting, the team members move completed tasks into the "done" area. Moving the post-its around helps achieve a shared group visualization of the tasks and project progress.

They have also experimented with other innovative practices. For example, one team member took notes and then published the tasks on a Web page. However, they found this was a significant overhead for that team. They also tried running the meeting with each individual taking notes in a personal notebook, but this reduced the shared group visualization of the project. Overall they found the shared post-it board the most useful.

The post-its encourage people to prepare more thoroughly in advance for the daily meeting. Continuous preparation happens as developers stick new post-its to their PC screens during their work in the interim between daily meetings.

Until recently, all teams were geographically colocated so the simple low-tech post-it technique has worked very well. Interestingly, they now have one distributed team, which has commenced using the technique by employing a shared spreadsheet and net-worked meeting software. It is too early to report on the results of this project, but early indications are promising, thus indicating that some agile methods may be more appli-cable to distributed development than has been suggested up to now (McBreen 2003).

| effective number of engineers | | 2.6 | 2.6 | 2.7 | 2.8 | 2.8 | 2.6 | |
Sprint Tasks	Baseline	Sprint 1	Sprint 2	Sprint 3	Sprint 4	Sprint 5	Sprint 6	Unassigned
Atmd HLD workshops	12.0							12.0
Aai5/Aai0/Aai2 workshops	2.0							2.0
Fpath	64.5							64.5
QMgr	43.5							43.5
Atmd	111.5							111.5
Aai5Acc.FuncSpec.Draft/Review	10.0							10.0
Aai5Acc.DesignSpec	7.0							7.0
Aai5Acc.Code	6.0							6.0
Aai5Codelet.Spec	7.5							7.5
Aai5Codelet.Code	7.0							7.0
Total	271	0	0	0	0	0	0	271.0
Fixed Overhead								
Holidays.Public	4.0							4.0
Holidays.Vacation	45.0							45.0
Training	4.0							4.0
Total	53	0	0	0	0	0	0	53.0
		0	0	0	0	0	0	

Figure 2. Scrum Planning

4.2.1   Scrum Planning

Intel Shannon has made some modifications to the planning process as well. They use two planning stages, one at the start of each sprint and one at the start of the project.

Planning is kept simple. There is no complex Gantt chart with complex inter-dependencies between tasks. The overall plan is a series of sprints (see Figure 2). Internal or external milestones can be lined up with sprint completions, but the dependencies between the tasks within the sprint are not worked out in advance.

Each team lead does a plan outlining all of the sprints to the end of the project. Initial meetings are conducted by the engineers to get high-level estimates that can be allocated and distributed across a number of sprints. In one of the projects, the wide-band Delphi technique was used to generate the estimates (Linstone and Turoff 1975). Dependencies between teams are made between end-of-sprint milestones.

In terms of deliverables, the team lead provides a list of sprint milestones and the contents of each sprint to the overall project lead.

Intel Shannon does not use sprint time boxing which is part of some implementations of Scrum. The high-level tasks are split to distribute them across sprints. They then continue to distribute and split tasks until the duration of each sprint is at most 20 working days. Contingency is built into the plan and effort estimates are done based on ideal engineering effort. The contingency factor is tuned as the project progresses.

At the start of each sprint, the team decides which tasks are going to be done in the next sprint. They look at the start of project sprint plan and look at any new backlog items that may have come up during the last sprint. Tasks are allocated to individuals to spread the load. The sprint protects the team from the environment surrounding it for a meaningful amount of time.

At the end of the sprint, the team lead writes a wrap-up report, listing the tasks completed including extra tasks that were not part of the original sprint plan. The report will also contain lessons learned and a measurement of the actual effort expended in the sprint versus the estimate at the start-of-project. Other end-of-sprint deliverables could include a demo, a project review, or a release.

4.2.2   Overall Lessons on Scrum

Project teams have had excellent success delivering projects on time and within budget. An early project of 5.5 months duration with four team members delivered their final release within three days of the original plan. The IXP4XX release 1.0 software was delivered one week ahead of schedule on a project with an original planned duration of over a year. The team consisted of 5 teams and over 30 engineers. All teams used Scrum.

The key advantages of Scrum that the team observed were

- Planning and tracking become a collaboration involving the whole team
- Excellent communication builds up within the team, thus building morale and helping the team to gel
- The team lead has more bandwidth for technical work
- Enables the team to deliver on-time

The early adoption of Scrum has led to the formulation of internal training courses and in short time the use of Scrum has reached critical mass. In the case of XP, pair-programming was not as visible and did not reach the same critical mass. In general, most of the engineers acknowledge the utility and advantages of pair-programming but are still slow to apply it. They are not making a conscious decision not to use it and maybe the technique needs some renewed internal promotion.

Another possible factor limiting the spontaneous adoption of pair-programming at the individual engineer level may be the perception that individual ownership of code components is of more value when performance reviews are being evaluated.

5   CONCLUSIONS

Overall, there are many lessons from this research at Intel Shannon. The study is useful in being solidly based on the rigorous and disciplined implementation of agile approaches in a real development context involving experienced software engineers, with a careful reflection on subsequent results. The study confirms that both XP and Scrum have merit and are very complementary in that XP provides good support for the more technical aspects of development while Scrum provides a very good framework for project planning and tracking. Also, it is clear that these approaches are not anti method but require a disciplined approach and indeed need to be tailored to the needs of the development context. Notwithstanding this, developers themselves have embraced these techniques and use has grown over time, in stark contrast to many organizations where the use of development methods is mandated by management, which leads to far less actual usage of these methods (Fitzgerald 1998).

Intel Shannon did not find that all of the XP practices were applicable in their context. Pair-programming, testing, refactoring, simple design, coding standards, and collective ownership were all applied to good effect. However, while they found pair-programming to have significant benefits, in terms of code quality for example, its use is not increasing, but this may be explained by the need for other management support mechanisms to support its use. Several XP practices were not considered applicable, such as the planning game, small releases, continuous integration, metaphor, on-site customer, and 40-hour week. While XP advocates reasonably point to the fact that the practices form a coherent whole, this does not mean that selective relevant practices cannot be applied to good effect. Intel Shannon certainly derived value from a subset of the practices. Also of interest is the fact that the XP principle that the code is the documentation did not feature at Intel Shannon since documentation is an integral part of the product deliverable.

Intel Shannon has also achieved significant benefits through the use of Scrum. Again, they have adapted it very much to their needs with the highly visible daily meeting report. Also, the use of Scrum has led to consistent meeting of development schedules on very complex projects with long project durations, but with no degradation in product quality. Scrum has been more robust than XP over time, when sustained on just grassroots engineering sponsorship. Finally, the deployment of Scrum on a distributed development project suggests that some agile approaches may be more amenable to distributed development than has been assumed up to now. This will be the focus of further study.

REFERENCES

Abrahamsson, P., Warsta, J., Siponen, M., and Ronkainen, J. "New Directions on Agile Methods: A Comparative Analysis," in *Proceedings of 25th International Conference on Software Engineering*, New York: ACM Press, 2003, pp. 244-254.

Ambler, S. *Agile Modeling: Effective Processes for Extreme Programming and the Unified Process*, New York: Wiley & Sons, 2002.

Beck, K. *Extreme Programming Explained*, Upper Saddle River, NJ: Addison-Wesley, 2000.

Benbasat, I., Goldstein, D., and Mead, M. "The Case Research Strategy in Studies of Information Systems," *MIS Quarterly* (11:3), September 1987, pp. 369-386.

Boehm, B. "A Spiral Model of Software Development and Maintenance," *IEEE Computer* (21:5), 1988, pp. 61-72.

Coad, P., Lefebvre, E., and DeLuca, J. *Java Modeling in Color with UML*, Upper Saddle River, NJ: Prentice Hall, 1999.

Cockburn, A. "Crystal Light Methods," *Cutter IT Journal*, 2001 (available online at http://alistair.cockburn.us/crystal/articles/clm/crystallightmethods.htm).

Cunningham, W. "EPISODES: A Pattern Language of Competitive Development Part I," 1995 (available online at http://c2.com/ppr/episodes.html).

Eisenhardt, K. "Building Theory from Case Study Research," *Academy of Management Review* (14:4), 1989, pp. 532-550.

Fitzgerald, B. "An Empirical Investigation into the Adoption of Systems Development Methodologies," *Information and Management* (34), 1998, pp. pp. 317-328.

Hedin, G., Bendix, L., and Magnusson, B. "Introducing Software Engineering by Means of Extreme Programming," in *Proceedings of 25th International Conference on Software Engineering*, New York: ACM Press, 2003, pp. 586-593.

Heim, C., and Hemhill, D. "Extreme Programming and Scrum: A Local Experience Report from Gearworks," Object Technology Users Group, St. Paul, MN, October 2003 (available online at http://www.otug.org/meeting/200310.html).

Highsmith, J. "Does Agility Work?," *Software Development*, June 2002, pp. 28-36.

Kruchten, P. *Rational Unified Process: An Introduction*, Reading, MA: Addison-Wesley, 2000.

Lee, A. "A Scientific Methodology for MIS Case Studies," *MIS Quarterly* (13:1), 1989, pp. 33-50.

Linstone, H., and Turoff, M. *The Delphi Method: Techniques and Applications*, Reading, MA: Addison-Wesley, 1975.

Marshall, C., and Rossman, G. *Designing Qualitative Research*, Thousand Oaks, CA: Sage
    Publications, 1989.
McBreen, P. *Questioning Extreme Programming*, Boston: Addison-Wesley, 2003.
Muller, M., and Tichy, W. "Extreme Programming in a University Environment," in
    Proceedings of 23rd International Conference on Software Engineering, New York: ACM
    Press, 2001, pp. 537-544.
Paulk, M. "Extreme Programming from a CMM Perspective," *IEEE Software* (18:6), November-
    December 2001, pp. 19-26.
Poppendieck, M. "Lean Programming," *Software Development*, June 2001, pp. 71-75.
Rising, L., and Janoff, N. "The Scrum Software Development Process for Small Teams," *IEEE
    Software* (17:4), July-August 2000, pp. 26-32.
Schwaber, K. "Will the Real Agile Processes Please Stand Up", *Cutter Consortium Executive
    Report* (2:8), 2001, pp. 1-22.
Schwaber, K., and Beedle, J. *Agile Software Development with Scrum*, Upper Saddle River, NJ:
    Prentice Hall, 2002.
Sliwa, C. "Agile Programming Techniques Spark Interest," *ComputerWorld*, March 14, 2002
    (available online at http://www.computerworld.com/softwaretopics/software/appdev/story/
    0,10801,69079,00.html).
Smith, N. "The Case Study: A Useful Research Method for Information Management," *Journal
    of Information Technology* (5), 1990, pp. 123-133.
Stapleton, J. *Dynamic Systems Development Method: The Method in Practice*, Reading, MA:
    Addison-Wesley, 1998.
Trauth, E., and O'Connor, B. "A Study of the Interaction Between Information, Technology
    and Society," in *Information Systems Research: Contemporary Approaches and Emergent
    Traditions*, H-E. Nissen, H. K. Klein, and R. A. Hirschheim (Eds.), Amsterdam: Elsevier
    Publishers, 1991, pp. 131-144.
Walker, R. *Applied Qualitative Research*, Hampshire, England: Gower, 1994.
Yin, R. *Case Study Research: Design and Methods* (2nd ed.), Thousand Oaks, CA: Sage
    Publications, CA, 1994.

ABOUT THE AUTHORS

Brian Fitzgerald holds the Frederick A Krehbiel II Chair in Innovation in Global Business
and Technology at the University of Limerick, Ireland, where he also is a Research Fellow of the
University, in addition to being a Science Foundation Ireland Investigator. He has a Ph.D. from
the University of London and has held positions at University College Cork, Ireland, Northern
Illinois University, United States, the University of Gothenburg, Sweden, and Northumbria
University, United Kingdom. His publications include seven books and more than 70 papers,
published in leading international conferences and journals. Having worked in industry prior to
taking up an academic position, he has more than 20 years experience in the IS field. Brian can
be reached at bf@ul.ie.

Gerard Hartnett is a software architect in Intel's Infrastructure Processor Division focusing
primarily on new products. He has been with Intel for five years, in which time he has focused
on architecture and engineering management on Intel's entry-level and mid-range network processors. He is coauthor of the forthcoming book, *Designing Embedded Networking Applications*,
from Intel Press. Prior to Intel, he worked for many years in the telecommunications industry on
GSM, ATM, voice, and network management products. He has an M.Sc. from University
College Cork and a B.Eng. from the University of Limerick.   Gerard can be reached at
gerard.hartnett@intel.com.

13   HOW AGILE IS AGILE ENOUGH?
Toward a Theory of Agility in Software Development

Kalle Lyytinen[1]
Case Western Reserve University
Cleveland, Ohio U.S.A.

Gregory M. Rose
Washington State University
Vancouver, Washington U.S.A.

Abstract   *This paper outlines a theory of software development agility that draws upon a model of IT innovations. We examine how both exploration and exploitation impact software development agility. We propose a sequential model of learning in which agility is driven by exploration versus exploitation needs and development agility is influenced by learning focus. Organizations need to balance multiple conflicting goals including speed, quality, cost, risk and innovative content. The value of the model is illustrated by probing how software organizations controlled their agility in Internet computing between the years 1997 and 2003.*

1   INTRODUCTION

In software, *agility* can be defined as developers' ability to sense and respond nimbly to technical and business opportunities in order to stay innovative in a turbulent environment. An *agile* software development organization has the capability to respond to unexpected environmental changes and increase its process speed. In the past, the Information Systems literature sought to control the outcome quality and reliability by submitting to virtues of system engineering: the system must be flawless, user friendly,

---

[1]Author order is alphabetical; the authors contributed equally to this paper.

or scalable. This logic pervaded debates around the "software crisis" and motivated the development of approaches such as structured methodologies and process improvement frameworks.

This worldview faced a reality check when new economy rebels changed the idea of system development. Software had to be developed at, and for markets in, a fast pace (Baskerville et al. 2001; Carstensen and Vogelsang 1999; Cusumano and Yoffie 1999; Lyytinen and Rose 2003; Pressman 1998). The key to competitiveness was agility and this echoed well with research in strategy on dynamic capability (D'Aveni 1994; Teece et al. 1997) and rapid product development (Kessler and Chakrabarti 1996). However, it is not clear what agility in software means. Is it the speed at which some type of running system is available? Is it the change in ratio between delivered functionality and the elapsed time? Or is it the client's increased velocity? All these speeds are distinct aspects of *agility* and dictate different ramifications on how to improve it. Another issue relates to antecedents of agility, and to what extent the organizations can manipulate them. There is a huge difference in changing the speed in doing X when compared to changing the speed in which the organization moves from doing X to doing Z. Finally, we must better understand how agility relates to other process outcomes such as risk or how agility varies during technology diffusion (Baskerville et al. 2001, Lambe and Spekman 1997).

This paper develops a model that accounts for differences in the relative change and types of *agility* that organizations can achieve at different stages of technology diffusion. We show that the need for agility must be balanced with other desirable process features such as innovative content, risk, quality, and cost and how process outcomes are valued in competitive environments. We validate the model by a multisite case study of software development in seven organizations that adopted Internet computing over a 5-year period. The study illustrates how organizations changed and controlled their agility over the study period by changing their perceptions of agility and the need for it. These changes were outcomes of continued attempts to balance agility with other process features such as innovative content, cost, quality, and risk. The remainder of the paper is organized as follows. Section 2 formulates the development model and reviews the related literature. Section 3 describes the field study, while section 4 reports the main findings of the study.

2   RELATED LITERATURE AND SOFTWARE DEVELOPMENT AGILITY MODEL

The goal of the software development agility model is to detect dependencies between specific environmental, organizational, and market factors that affect how agility and other process factors relate to one another. The model draws on Swanson's (1994; see also Lyytinen and Rose 2003) model of IT innovation and March's (1991) exploration–exploitation dichotomy. According to the model, software organizations are engaged in both exploration and exploitation while innovating with information technology. During periods of fast transition (e.g., the shift to Internet computing), the exploration speed (absorptive capability of technical potential) and development speed

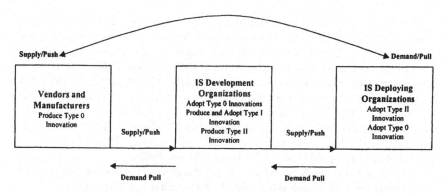

Figure 1. IT Value Chain and Realms of IS Innovation

(fast exploitation) must be combined to harness the new technology. Yet, exploration and exploitation set up quite different demands and contexts for agility. To understand this process, the context of innovation must be understood.

2.1 Model of IT innovation

The concept of IT innovation has remained poorly developed despite the vast literature on IT-based innovation (Lyytinen and Rose 2003; Swanson 1994). IT innovation has multiple sources and a broad scope in the IT value chain (Swanson 1994). As a consequence, innovation within system development (such as agility) is not a singular event, but subsumes a chain of events which all portray significant departures from existing practices. An IT innovation normally traverses a complex ecology of innovative events (see Figure 1) (Lyytinen and Rose 2003; Swanson 1994).

Figure 1 shows three value activities in the IT domain: (1) *creation of IT base technologies* such as operating systems by vendors (we call this base innovation a *Type 0 innovation*), (2) *creation of processes, technologies and organizational arrangements* that enable better or more reliable delivery of software in organizational contexts (called a *Type I innovation*), and (3) *development and adoption of new types of IT solutions* (called a *Type II innovation)*. The arrows in Figure 1 show how downstream organizations adopt innovations produced by companies upstream so as to increase their overall scope and quality of IT deployment. Hence, IT innovation means many things (Lyytinen and Rose 2003): breakthroughs in computing capability (Type 0 innovation), departure from current methods to develop applications (Type I innovation), or novel applications (Type II innovation). The connection is not causal: many Type II innovations do not necessarily affect other parts. The case for such Type 0 innovations is much rarer, but still possible. The value chain also suggests that innovations can take place in any part of the chain and by doing so they can affect other innovations upstream or downstream.[2]

---

[2]Swanson calls these strong and weak order effects.

Due to the technology dependent nature of software innovation, organizations adopting significant Type 0 and Type I innovations *together* can *produce* radically new applications (Type II) and thereby engage in *disruptive IT innovations* (Lyytinen and Rose 2003). These disruptions are outcomes of radical breaks in the IT base, where components in the computing base are reassembled (Henderson and Clark 1990). For example, Internet computing was a disruptive innovation created by (Type 0) architectural change (TCP/IP-based tools and n-tier computing), which was made radical with the addition of browsers, data formatting standards, and software platforms (J2EE, .Net, etc.). This enabled the development of radically new services (Type II) which were demanded by faster speed (Type I) (Lyytinen and Rose 2003).

We can now investigate the extent to which changes in Type 0 innovation *can* lead to innovations in Type I, such as agile development, and the consequent *fast* adoption of Type II innovations (business agility). We conjecture that the agile innovation is produced by two capabilities: (1) the capability of software organizations to adopt Type 0 innovations and (2) their capability to successfully *transform* and *hone* these capabilities into Type I innovations. This is dependent on the mobilization of two related capacities. The first capability—*technology absorption*—reflects an organization's ability to sense, acquire, and absorb new base technologies through *exploration*. The second capability reflects a software organization's (1) ability to use new IT deployments for process improvement and (2) to effectively learn from such occasions in order to formalize process knowledge. This latter process we call *exploitation*. Successful software innovators need to effectively and continuously identify and match strategic opportunities for their process improvement with emerging technical capabilities.

2.2 Exploration and Exploitation

In the management literature, *exploration* and *exploitation* have been established as two fundamental responses to environmental challenge (March 1991). These archetypes help distinguish two distinct modes in which organizations compete and adapt, and how they organize, strategize, and execute. Through exploitation, organizations refine by trial-and-error learning their competencies through repeated actions over of time. Exploitation is about harnessing "old certainties" through refinement, implementation, efficiency, production, and selection. Exploration, in contrast, is about discovering new opportunities where organizations create new competences through search, discovery, experimentation, risk taking, and innovation (Henderson and Clark 1990; March 1991; Tushman and Anderson 1986).

Exploration requires substantially different structures, processes, strategies, capabilities, and culture (Tushman and Anderson 1986). Exploration leans toward organic structures, loose couplings, improvisation, chaos, and emergence. Exploitation deals with mechanistic structures, tight coupling, routinization, bureaucracy, and stability. Returns with exploration are uncertain, highly variable, and distant in time, while exploitation yields returns that are short term, have higher certainty and lower variance (March 1991). Due to their fundamental differences, exploration and exploitation pose a continuous tension for management (Levinthal and March 1993). These tensions create dysfunctional learning outcomes when either exploration or exploitation is preferred (March 1991). Trial-and-error learning can bias management to focus too much on current capabilities—at the expense of new opportunities—thus causing capacities to become core *rigidities*, and creating learning myopias and competency traps (Levinthal and March 1993; March 1991). In contrast, when organizations engage in excessive exploration, continued "failure leads to search and change, which lead failure which lead to even more search and so on" (Levinthal and March 1993, p. 98). Organizations' learning becomes chaotic: managers love to explore but fail to allocate resources to exploit their new competencies.

This invites us to understand how organizations learn to tack between exploration and exploitation and consequently change their resource bases through acquisition, integration, recombination, and the removal of capabilities (Eisenhardt and Martin 2000). In doing so, they must relentlessly integrate, reconfigure, gain, and release resources as a response to changes (D'Aveni 1994; Teece et al. 1997). Such dynamic capability embodies a learning related meta-capability by which software organizations learn to blend exploration and exploitation across different stages of IT innovation.

2.3 Exploration and Exploitation in Software Development Organizations

The general logic of exploration and exploitation during IT innovation stages is depicted in Figure 2. Exploration processes result in IT development firms adopting

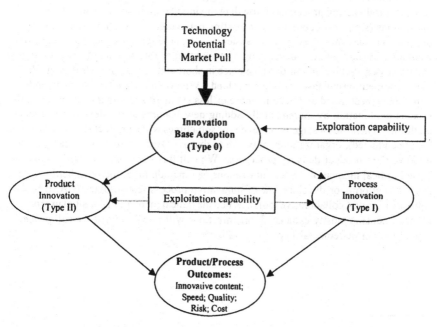

Figure 2. A General Model of IT Innovation as Exploration and Exploitation

Type 0 base innovations that lead to production of new Type II and Type I innovations (Lambe and Spekman 1997; Lyytinen and Rose 2003). An example of Type II innovations would be the organizations' ability to create a capability to produce totally new types of applications, while the innovation of Type I would be adopting new process technologies that help deliver the same software functionality in half of the time. Exploration agility as *absorptive capacity* (Cohen and Levinthal 1991) means two things: (1) the software organization must adopt new Type 0 and Type I technologies faster than its peers, and (2) it must use these technologies to develop Type II innovations (explorative process innovation) faster. If the organization is successful, this will change the organizations' innovations in its products (Type II innovations) and processes (Type I innovations). The more the former deviate from the current product mix, the more *innovative* and *agile* is product innovation. The more the latter deviates from the status quo, the more *innovative process* is instantiated—and the more agile is process change.

Software organizations need also to exploit when technologies mature by streamlining, standardizing, automating, and scaling up their processes for exploitation capability. This can be defined as the organizations' learning capability to improve and change their delivery processes over time in order to maximize process outcomes such as speed, quality, risk, or cost. Clearly, this learning mode is distinct from exploration and agility in exploitation can be viewed as lubricating a well-defined process.

Lambe and Spekman (1997) describe how exploration and exploitation are temporally organized across different phases of IT innovation (adapted for Figure 3). We later use this model to explore how each phase affects process features such as agility. Type 0 innovations can be regarded as offering general *technology push* to improve both software products and processes. Growth in the innovation base can lead to **radical** IT innovations (significant departures of existing behaviors and solutions) covering both development outcomes (new *kinds of* systems—i.e., product innovations) and development process (new *ways* of developing systems) that enable new innovative solutions and processes. Such explorations take place in short and intense periods during which hyper-competition and fast learning are valued.[3] When main features of the new product family have been fixed and become more or less standardized, organizations move to product exploitation by incrementally adding new features to the developed product platform. When such a stage is achieved (or sometimes when product explorations are being conducted), organizations move on to discover significant and radical ways to improve their product delivery processes. We call this stage *process exploration* or Type I radical innovation. Such innovations can include investments in better cross-product platforms or development of innovative process technologies (CASE tools, software libraries, collaborative tools). When the radical innovation potential in process improvements is mostly exhausted, organizations will move to what we call *process exploitation* or incremental Type I innovation.

---

[3]This is called *hyperlearning* in Lyytinen et al. (2004).

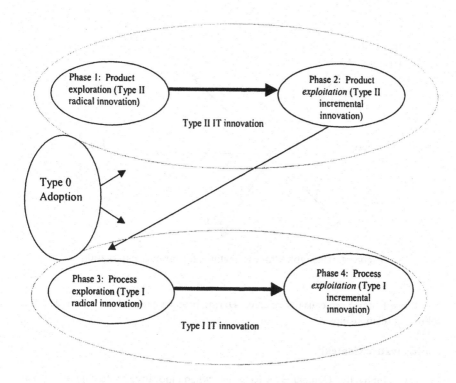

Figure 3. Organizing Logics for Exploration and Exploitation
Across Different Types of IT Innovations

2.4 A Model of Process Features During Exploration and Exploitation

Relationships between process features (innovative content, speed, cost, quality, and risk) are complex. It is impossible to optimize them all simultaneously. Relationships between them vary depending on whether new Type II innovations are discovered or incremental Type I innovations are proposed. We model process goals as directed graphs where each process goal is depicted as a separate vector and its relative size shows to what extent this process feature is being maximized.[4] An illustration of such a graph for Phase 1 is shown in Figure 4. In Phase 1, software organizations maximize innovative content, they tolerate relatively high risks, expect relatively fast product development and medium cost, but do not expect high quality. To speed up exploration, their capability to deliver any workable solution may be slowed down. Likewise, if they want to be more nimble, they may have to paradoxically sacrifice their innovativeness.

---

[4]Van Kleijnen (1980) calls these Kiwiat graphs.

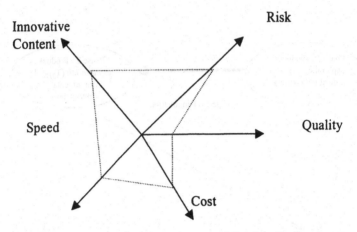

Figure 4. Desirable Process Features for Product Exploration

These features are causally related. During product exploration, we suggest the following relationships:

For **Innovative Content**[5]:

(1) + Innovative Content → + Risk (i.e., when innovative content increases risk increases)
(2) + Innovative Content → + Cost
(3) + Innovative Content → – Quality
(4) + Innovative Content → – Speed

If speed is a requirement, it must come at the expense of other outcomes, giving the following relationships:

For **Speed**:

(1) + Speed → + Risk
(2) + Speed → + Cost
(3) + Speed → – Quality
(4) + Speed → – Innovative Content

As can be seen during Phase 1, speed and innovation take precedence. However, both cannot be optimized simultaneously, and an increase in one counteracts the other.

---

[5] These causal dependencies were derived through content analysis from our interview data, which will be discussed in more detail in the next section.

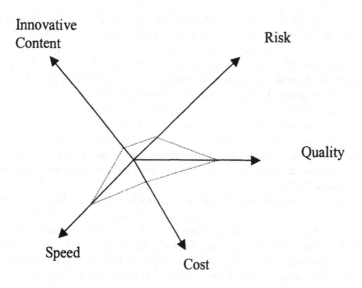

Figure 5. Process Features in Type I Incremental Innovation

In a similar fashion, we can model the process features for Phase 4[6] (Figure 5). Software delivery is faster as no effort is wasted to explore products or architectural solutions. The focus is on incremental innovations through economies of scale and scope where organizations maximize quality and speed while minimizing cost and risk by fixing product and process features. This has been assumed in the process improvement research (Humphrey 1989). The following dependencies can be observed:

(1) – Innovative Content → – Risk (i.e., when innovative content decreases risk decreases)
(2) – Innovative Content → – Cost
(3) – Innovative Content → + Quality
(4) – Innovative Content → + Speed

2.5 Some Implications for the Study of Agility

If an organization engages in radical Type II innovation, it will decrease its opportunity for incremental process innovation due to their contradicting logic. Likewise, increases in organizations' exploration will decrease their exploitation capability. Therefore, organizations that focus either on exploration or exploitation—although in

---

[6]We could similarly model the two other phases but for the brevity they are omitted here as they are not as distinct as the two extreme cases.

both modes they view agility as a desirable feature—have different mindsets about agility. During exploration, the desire to explore fast dominates, while during exploitation, the main focus is to remove friction from well-defined processes. However, the new technology (Type 0 innovation) *per se* can dramatically increase the speed by offering higher granularity (e.g., ERP parameterization), powerful abstraction mechanisms (e.g., Web services), standardized functionalities (e.g., browsers), or architectural integration mechanisms (e.g., architectural patterns). Improvements here can be dramatic and as important as radical innovations in products. When an organization shifts its focus away from radical exploration, it must increase its exploitation by fixing the product and, later, the process. It must change process measures as its focus is now on efficiency, economies of scale, and quality. This shift leads to increased trial-and-error learning (March 1991).

Software organizations need thus to innovate in a lumpy manner by balancing trade-offs between innovative content, cost, speed, quality, and risk. Over time they must exploit technologies, organize, and control in contradicting ways. Therefore, IT innovations will be appropriated through multiple innovation paths. As the contrast between early exploration and late exploitation is stark, organizations can only entertain a certain amount of transformations over a time period. They increase their innovative agility first by adopting radically new technologies (Type 0), but later shift their focus on exploitation by stabilizing product features. At the same time, they engage in other exploration–exploitation cycles, thus organizing in an ambidextrous manner (Tushman and Anderson 1986). The impacts of this stepwise transformation on process features (innovative content, quality, risk, and cost) are significant, and organizations locate themselves into alternative regions with different idea configurations of process features (see Table 1).

The first contingency presented in Table 1 is rare and can be mostly observed in bureaucratic environments. For R&D software development (pre-competitive phase),

Table 1. Contingencies for Organizational Learning in Software Development

Exploration Focus/ Exploitation Focus	Low	High
Low	Normally natural monopoly: Little impact on any process features	Pre-competitive product development: Innovative content dominates, other features tangential *Internet computing around 1993-1997*
High	Process competition in established markets: Incremental changes in speed, efficiency focus in reducing risk, quality *Internet computing 2001–*	Hypercompetition: Fluid technology and markets, speed dominates, necessary to meet minimal process/product features *Internet computing 1996–2001*

only exploration focus is high. When both exploration and exploitation are high (i.e., organizations are fast oscillating between two phases of product innovation in Figure 3), this can be regarded as hyperlearning–hypercompetition as has been observed in software development organizations between the years 1997 and 2000 (Lyytinen et al. 2004). The push toward higher exploitation comes normally from competitive demands created by the growing market size, stiffer competition, and new value propositions. The organization tilts toward process improvement and starts to compete based on process integration. Agility in software thus relates to capability to be a fast explorer or to be an effective integrator. The jump between these positions takes place when organizations recognize that the emerging technology has become mainstream and they must decide whether they will keep their focus on markets that value exploration or specialize on exploitation and start to manage process features such as quality and cost.

3 RESEARCH METHOD AND RESEARCH SITES

3.1 Research Goals and Design

We wanted to explore the following questions: Do perceptions of and need for agility change during different phases of IT innovation? How software organizations manage contradicting demands of exploration and organize their innovation for agility? Does the IT innovation model predict how agility relates to other process features? To address these questions, we conducted a 5-year longitudinal field study (Yin 1994) in Web development software companies (see Table 2). We chose multisite case study as it allowed a replication by which we could test emerging theoretical insights and triangulate both theory and data (Eisenhardt 1989). To minimize bias, we sought to maximize the variations in order to improve external validity (Yin 1994). Companies had different sizes and operated in many industries. They had experience using Web-based technologies in several domains. The geographical scope of their operations varied, as some were local while others were part of global companies. The firms also had large variation in their development experience, ranging from as few as 4 years to 40+ years.

3.2 Data Collection and Analysis

The data were gathered between June 2000 and April 2003 at three different time points (2000, 2001, 2003-2004). The exact times of data collection are shown in Table 3. For all companies, the data is not complete due to mortality (some of the companies went out of the business or were bought or sold). For some data we had problems with poor tape quality and were unable to transcribe them verbatim so only collected the main facts. We organized the data into three different temporal periods—pre-2000 (Period 1), 2000-2001 (Period 2), and 2002-2004 (Period 3)—that align with the different stages of the dot-com boom. Here pre-2000 stands for market growth and period of fast innovation, Period 2000-2001 stands for the recession and crisis, and 2002-2004 stands for the recovery.

Table 2. Firm Characteristics

FIRM	Firm 1	Firm 2	Firm 3	Firm 4	Firm 5	Firm 6	Firm 7
Division Focus	Custom e-business applications.	B2B e-Business consulting.	Spin-off. Web-based ASP for parent company's customers.	E-Business consulting in mobile computing.	Systems integrators to upgrade legacy systems with Web and mobile solutions.	E-Business solutions in mobile computing. Assembling of components and applications.	Consulting, development, product, networking and hosting services.
History	15 year old mainframe and client server shop 500 employees in 4 locations.	Part of a large, multinational consulting company.	Part of a large financial company with several thousand employees.	Multinational e-business consulting. Founded in 1995 with several thousand employees	e-Commerce development firm. Founded in 1996.	Large multi-national e-business consulting and software development firm.	Mature, large, multinational development and IT service firm.
Number of Employees in Division	Several hundred	Several hundred	70	100+	200+	700+	Several hundred
Typical work week	40 hours	50 hours	50 hours	60 hours	37.5 hours	Varies	37.5 hours
Employee turnover per year	18-30%	15-30%	<10%	3%	3%	Uncertain	Uncertain
Organizational Structure	• President • Branch manager • Field manager • Project manager	• Partner • Director • Project and technical managers	CIO, then flat	• Client manager • Project manager	Entirely flat except for salary issues.	Rigid vertical hierarchy with formalized methodologies for all aspects of business.	Company is divided into autonomous units based on market sector of client.
Project Team Characteristics	15-20 people including business analysts, architects, lead developer, other developers, QA person	Architects, analysts, expert developers, rookie developers	Informal	Flat with the following roles: project assistant, technical lead, designer, information architect	Informal	Rigid vertical hierarchy.	Broken down by customers (approximately 50/ customer) and subsequently by teams (of 10 each).

Table 3. Data Collection Summary

FIRM	Firm 1	Firm 2	Firm 3	Firm 4	Firm 5	Firm 6	Firm 7
Interview Date 1	June 2000	June 2000	June 2000	October 2000	September 2000	September 2000	November 2000
Interviewees in Time 1	Six senior employees including an executive, managers, and software architects.	A senior manager of a development group and one of his key developers.	The CIO, and five key senior technologists were responsible for the creation of the spin-off.	Five senior employees including ISD project managers, developers, and the senior technology architect.	One of the founding executives who was responsible for development of business processes.	One senior manager of IT development services.	Four senior employees including a systems architect, manager, and software engineer.
Interview Date 2	October 2001	October 2001	October 2001	August 2001	August 2001	August 2001	August 2001
Interviewees in Time 2	One software architect from first interview.	A senior manager of an IS development group and one of his key developers from first interview.	Two technologists from first interview.	Two employees from first interview.	Same interviewee from first interview.	Manager who replaced manager in first interview.	One manager from first interview.
Interview Date 3	March 2003	March 2003	No interview	No interview	March 2003	April 2003	April 2003
Interviewees in Time 3	An architect from Time 1, the replacement of executive in Time 1, and a developer not in Time 1.	Developer from Time 1.	Firm absorbed by parent company and IT employees reassigned. Interviews not available. Information gathered via e-mail with one of the original interviewees and review of online documentation of parent firm in March 2003.	Finnish office closed. Interviewees not available.	Same interviewee from first interview.	Manager who replaced manager in first interview.	One manager from first interview.

The data were obtained through semi-structured interviews with senior management and senior developers who managed the organizational knowledge bases and skills needed to execute the technology and business strategy. We also examined the archives of company documents, including systems development documentation and technology strategies and made notes. A range of one to six individuals participated from each company. A total of 19 interviews were conducted with a typical interview time of approximately 2 hours. The transcribed data currently covers about 700 pages of interviews. Specifically, we asked the firms to clarify the extent, scope, depth, and speed of change in their software development during the Web development adoption.

Data analysis was done using the inductive method (Yin 1994). The transcripts of each company for each period were subject to a within-case analysis that involved repeatedly reading the transcript and taking thorough notes about the firms' perceptions of agility, its antecedents and resulting process outcomes. After each individual case, we began cross-case comparisons that involved listing the similarities and differences among the firms in their process outcomes at each period of time. Two researchers coded the transcripts individually. Coding was compared for inter-coder reliability and differences in interpretation were identified and discussed until consensus could be found. Data codes within cases were then converted into tabular form and again analyzed by both researchers to confirm findings within and across cases and to identify any gaps or contradictions in the original models identified. Any discrepancies or contradictions were scrutinized and the original transcripts revisited for clarification. Tables were iteratively modified until both researchers were satisfied with the validity of the findings. Once the model was formally developed, a summary was written and presented for external review by participants of the study. Phone interviews were conducted with individuals from three different firms that had participated in the longitudinal study. For each of the three follow-up interviews, the models identified in the analyses were confirmed.

4 RESEARCH FINDINGS

4.1 Changes in Agility During Exploration and Exploitation

Table 1 and Figure 3 show a movement from product exploration to process exploitation. A related summary of organizational change in organizations through periods 0-3 is given in Tables 4 and 5. Overall, the tables show that the firms organized their perceptions of agility and concerns for exploration and exploitation as recommended by the model. Each firm in the early stages of Internet computing (e.g., the periods between 1995 and the first interview) were engaged in radical innovation product when compared to Period 1.

Six of the seven firms created their own product innovations and before the first interview time were regarded as radical product innovators (Phase 1). They then moved sequentially to Phase 4. One firm (Firm 6) in our data set did not conduct their own product innovation at all. Instead, it formed alliances with other radical product innovators (thus outsourcing that activity) and focused all of its time on exploitative process innovations. It sought to deploy its existing product bases quickly and thus was already

Table 4. Innovation Summary: USA Firms

FIRM	Firm 1	Firm 2	Firm 3
Time 0	**Phase 1: Product Exploration Phase**	**Phase 1: Product Exploitation Phase**	**Phase 1: Product Exploitation Phase**
Time 1	**Phase 2: Product *Exploitation* Phase.** Speed increase; risk increase; costs increase. Base technology is inherently faster. Certain amount of freezing product innovation had already begun and allowed time reduction via reuse. Projected in Time 2 that they would focus on more reuse to increase speed and decrease risk. Indication was that they planned to freeze product innovation to allow this process innovation to occur.	**Phase 2: Product *Exploitation* Phase.** No rigid methodologies. Had faster development than before but deemed to be with poor quality.	**Phase 2: Product *Exploitation* Phase.** Spun off by parent company for methodologies and process exploitation. Recognized a new environment and required radical product innovation. Quality required. Speed faster than in the parent firm, but after 24 months it was considered unacceptable in "new economy." No formal process used. Lots of experimentation with product. Product innovation was high, risks were high, quality was lower. Planning on freezing product innovation and beginning process innovation. Goal was to increase speed and quality. Did so at high cost by buying outside help (grafting). Goal was to stabilize and get speed up/quality up/risk down.
Time 2	**Phase 3 Process Exploration Phase and then Phase 4: *Circumstantial* Process *Exploitation* Phase.** Speed not a problem because project scopes were smaller as client demand for product innovation stopped. Business dropped off significantly and required elimination of many programmers. Fired all slowest programmers and kept those with understanding of effective methods (a Darwinian model). Allowed for rapid development, but not by design. Had methods as a result of market requirements and a natural selection of developers, not because they searched for methods.	**Phase 3: Process Exploration Phase.** Compared to Time 1- faster still; costs lower; quality higher. Innovation related learning stopped. Process innovation occurred in Type I as a result of stability in product and incremental innovation.	**Phase 3: Process Exploration Phase.** Product innovation frozen. Process innovation slowing down to almost frozen point. Development speed was way up. Quality was better than in Period 1. Stabilized product. Stabilized process. Goal to shore up process methods to maintain high quality and increased speed for future rollouts.
Time 3	**Phase 1: New Product Exploration Phase.** Speed for ISD still an issue but not urgent. Looking into radical new Base and product innovations. Inherent in their mission statement (a single sentence about meeting client needs with leading-edge IT innovations).	**Phase 4: Process *Exploitation* Phase.** Processes and product solutions have matured and stabilized since Time 1 and Time 2. Speed up still as a result of: new Type I innovations; stability of solutions and knowledge sets; and reuse (stable base tools and incremental innovation in base).	**Phase 4: Process *Exploitation* Phase.** Innovation frozen entirely. Quality higher, risks in ISD and costs in ISD decrease. ISD firm is swallowed up by the parent company and leadership given to marketing team. Originally spun out of parent to innovate rapidly and radically. Team disbanded in 2003 and frozen products and processes (methods) swallowed up.

Table 5. Innovation Summary: Finnish Firms

FIRM	Firm 4	Firm 5	Firm 6	Firm 7
Time 0	Phase 1: Product Exploration Phase	Phase 1: Product Exploration Phase	Phase 3: Process Exploration Phase	Phase 1: Product Exploration Phase
Time 1	Phase 2: Product Exploitation Phase then Phase 3: Process Exploration Phase. Recognized the need for speed. Believed a methodology would help. Began work on formalization of process at end of Time 1.	Phase 2: Product Exploitation Phase. Indicated there is a high risk associated with speed. Used light methods with unknowable outcomes (because of less quality testing, less needs analysis) & limited scope of product innovations.	Phase 4: Process Exploitation Phase. Limits to a fixed set of product innovations. Process innovations early. Reuse of components, affiliation with partners, and reusable methodologies. Higher quality, lower costs, and low risks because of fixed solutions.	Phase 2: Product Exploitation Phase. Speed increases; risk increases; costs increase. Technology change is inherently faster. Certain amount of freezing in product innovation had begun and allowed increased speed via reuse.
Time 2	Phase 4: Process Exploitation Phase then a new Phase 1: Product Exploration Phase. Methodologies implemented were for projects of Time 1 type. Time 2 projects were radically different and methods were inappropriate. Cost rose and speed declined as a result of product exploration.	Phase 3: Process Exploration Phase. Moved to incremental product innovation. Return of methodologies.	Phase 4: Process Exploitation Phase. Nothing different from Time 1 except even more focused on exploitation of product and process.	Phase 3: Process Exploration Phase. Moved to incremental product innovation stage. Coincides with return of methodologies.
Time 3	Closed Finnish office.	Phase 4: Process Exploitation Phase then a new Phase 1: Product Exploration Phase. Speed slower again as product innovation becomes more radical. Problem when encounter changes in Type 0 innovations. Counteracted with process innovations.	Phase 4: Process Exploitation Phase. Nothing different from Time 1 except perhaps more focused on exploitation of process.	Phase 4: Process Exploitation Phase. Focused on reuse to increase speed and decrease risk. Freezing product innovation allows process innovation.

in Phase 3 at Period 0. It achieved this at the cost of radical innovation. Not surprisingly, by Period 1, Firm 6 was already engaged in process exploitation (Phase 4).

While each firm moved eventually to Phase 4, some of them moved beyond Phase 4 (or back) to a new Phase 1, thus demonstrating ambidexterity. These organizations found that they could not be successful in engaging solely in process exploitation. In two cases (Firms 1 and 5) we observed that new product innovations made their previous process innovations less effective. These firms experienced their process agility decreasing and they needed to reevaluate tradeoffs between speed and other features. Likewise, Firm 4 found that it now incurred higher costs and slower speed. The firm found this by Period 2 and subsequently went out of business as a result of declining market demands and having the wrong capability.

4.2 Impact on Process Features and Speed

Figures 4 and 5 highlight critical interrelationships between ISD process features at different phases of innovation. Accordingly, organizations have to control interrelated and contradictory process features: speed, innovation, cost, risks, and quality. Among the data set (all 19 interviews), we found strong evidence that managers heeded these five factors (Tables 6, 7, 8, and 9).

We also found strong evidence for the types of dependencies as noted in Figures 4 and 5. Specifically, we found that organizations increased speed in innovation in Period 1, but faced a tradeoff of increased risk, increased cost, and decreased quality (Tables 6 and 7).

Likewise, Firm 7 noted, *"you have less time to think and you don't have the time to think of everything."* The dominating process feature in Period 1 was *innovation content.* We also observed that speed and innovation were inversely related. Again, in most (16 of 19) interviews, evidence was found for this inverse relationship (as can be seen in bold in Tables 8 and 9). For example, Firm 3 finished their proof of concept stage and subsequently stopped radical product innovation. As a result of moving to incremental innovation in Period 1, they were able to formalize a methodology for *"rapid software development and rapid implementations that we have to do."* Similarly, Firm 2 attributed increased speed in Period 3 to the shift to incremental innovation. Specifically, increased speed was a function of stabilization in *"methodology [PROCESS], a function of increased skill sets [BASE], and a function of using packaged product type solutions [PRODUCT]."*

In addition, the other relationships between innovation and risks, cost, and quality were observed (Tables 8 and 9). For example, in Period 1, a member of Firm 7 referred to the period before Internet development as *"the good old days"* and noted that lower risks were *"old fashioned."* Similarly, Firm 5 noted, when it began adopting radical Type 0 innovations for creating product innovations in Period 3, that development was slower, more resources were needed, and quality declined. Overall, the interrelationships of the five goals in Figures 4 and 5 were supported. With regard to phases, the primary relationships between Figures 4 and 5 were also supported when a firm is involved in product exploration (Phase 1), or in the process exploitation phase (Phase 4). As can be seen in Tables 4 and 5, during earlier phases, quality was lower and risks

Table 6. Tradeoffs between Speed versus Quality, Costs, and Risks Summary: United States Firms

FIRM	Firm 1	Firm 2	Firm 3
Time 1	Evidence of tradeoffs between speed and quality, costs, and risks	Evidence of tradeoffs between speed and quality, costs, and risks **Evidence of increases in speed and decline in quality**	Evidence of tradeoffs between speed and quality, costs, and risks
Time 2	Evidence of tradeoffs between speed and quality, costs, and risks	Evidence of tradeoffs between speed and quality, costs, and risks	Evidence of tradeoffs between speed and quality, costs, and risks
Time 3	Evidence of tradeoffs between speed and quality, costs, and risks	Evidence of tradeoffs between speed and quality, costs, and risks	

Table 7. Tradeoffs between Speed versus Quality, Costs, and Risks Summary: Finnish Firms

FIRM	Firm 4	Firm 5	Firm 6	Firm 7
Time 1	Evidence of tradeoffs between speed and quality, costs, and risks	Evidence of tradeoffs between speed and quality, costs, and risks	Evidence of tradeoffs between speed and quality, costs, and risks	Evidence of tradeoffs between speed and quality, costs, and risks
Time 2	Evidence of tradeoffs between speed and quality, costs, and risks			Evidence of tradeoffs between speed and quality, costs, and risks
Time 3		**Evidence that slowing down development reduces costs and improves quality**		Evidence of tradeoffs between speed and quality, costs, and risks

Table 8. Tradeoffs of Innovation versus Speed, Quality, Risk, or Cost Summary: United States Firms

FIRM	Firm 1	Firm 2	Firm 3
Time 1	Evidence that more radical innovation increases **risk**	Evidence that more radical innovation increases **risk**	Evidence that if you freeze innovation, speed increases Evidence that more radical innovation increases **risk**
Time 2	Evidence that if you freeze innovation, speed increases	Evidence that if you freeze innovation, speed increases	Evidence that if you freeze innovation, speed increases Evidence that if you freeze innovation, **cost decreases** Evidence that stopping radical innovation allows improved **quality** deliverables
Time 3	Evidence that if you freeze innovation, speed increases	Evidence that if you freeze innovation, speed increases Evidence that stopping radical innovation allows improved **quality** deliverables	

Table 9. Tradeoff of Innovation versus Speed, Quality, Risk, or Cost Summary: Finnish Firms

FIRM	Firm 4	Firm 5	Firm 6	Firm 7
Time 1	Evidence that if you freeze innovation, speed increases Evidence that more radical innovation increases **risk**	Evidence that if you freeze innovation, speed increases Evidence that more radical innovation increases **risk**	Evidence that if you freeze innovation, speed increases Evidence that moving to incremental innovation improves quality Evidence that incremental innovation decreases **risk**	Evidence that if you freeze innovation, speed increases Evidence that more radical innovation increases **risk**
Time 2		Evidence that if you freeze innovation, speed increases Evidence that stopping radical innovation allows improved quality deliverables	Evidence that if you freeze innovation, speed increases Evidence that moving to incremental innovation improves **quality**	Evidence that if you freeze innovation, speed increases
Time 3		Evidence that if you freeze innovation, speed increases Evidence that if you freeze innovation, **costs decrease** Evidence that moving to incremental innovation improves **quality**	Evidence that if you freeze innovation, speed increases Evidence that moving to incremental innovation improves **quality**	Evidence that if you freeze innovation, speed increases

and costs were higher. In later phases, the opposite was true, although in all phases, speed was deemed important. As such, the concern for speed did not diminish between phases, as the idea of speed was different.

The tradeoffs between innovative content and the other factors are most visible when Period 1 is considered. In Period 1, Firm 6 was already in Phase 3. They were already reaping the rewards of this and noted that their quality was higher, costs were lower, and risks were lower as they had frozen innovation and assembled *"components"* for *"a set of solutions that [they knew] how to give and [could] give them quickly."* In contrast, other firms, while moving to Phase 2, saw increased risks and costs, with decreased quality.

As each firm moved into other phases, its market matured and stabilized. Their methodologies became refined while their risk, costs, and quality moved to a new trade-off pattern (Figure 5). For example, Firm 2 entered Phase 4 during Period 3. The interviewee noted that their *"methodologies and strategies are now mature"* and that quality was improved as *"a function of better trained people, a methodology...and less innovation."*

4.3 Discussion and Conclusions

Software agility is affected by the scope and depth of innovative activity in base technologies as well as in continued process innovations in complementary assets. We explored the concept of agility in terms of the following questions: Do perceptions of and need for agility change during different phases of IT innovation? How do software organizations manage contradicting demands of exploration and organize their innovation for agility? Does the IT innovation model predict how agility relates to other process features? We observed the following: (1) concern for both exploration speed and process development speed changed significantly over the period of study, (2) software organizations tended to organize themselves differently during different innovation periods while they decide either to explore fast or deliver fast (process integrators), and (3) the variance in process features emphasized varied across phases and also between companies due to the varying focus on exploration or exploitation. Software organizations controlled their concern for agility in how good they wanted to become in managing technologies during different innovation phases. In doing so, they had to trade agility against other criteria including innovative content or risk. How these trade-offs were made depended on competencies, managerial focus, and competitive demands.

There are several avenues for future research in this fascinating area. First we need to generalize the findings here with a better and more representative sample of organizations. There is also a need to develop more careful constructs for agility and other process features. We need to explore other factors than just the organizations' learning focus to establish causal explanations of agility in organizational contexts. Finally, it needs to be seen if these findings are generalizable beyond Internet computing, and if so, when and where.

REFERENCES

Agile Alliance. "Manifesto for Agile Software," 2001 (available online at http://www. agilemanifesto.org/; accessed September 4, 2004).
Baskerville, R., Levine, L., Heje, J-P, Balasubramarian, R., and Slaughter, S. "How Internet Software Companies Negotiate Quality," *IEEE Software*, May 2001, pp. 51-57.
Carstensen, P, and Vogelsang, L. "Design of Web-Based Information Systems: New Challenges for System Development," in *Proceedings of the 9th ECIS*, Bled, Slovenia, June 27-29, 2001, pp. 536-547.
Cohen, W. M., and Levinthal, D. A. "Absorptive Capacity: A New Perspective on Learning and Innovation," *Administrative Science Quarterly* (35), 1990, pp. 128-152.
Cusumano M., and Yoffie, D. "Software development on Internet Time," *IEEE Computer* (32:10), 1999, pp. 60-69.
D'Aveni, R. A. *Hypercompetition: Managing the Dynamics of Strategic Maneuvering*, New York: The Free Press, 1994.
Eisenhardt, K. M. "Building Theories from Case Study Research," *Academy of Management Review* (14:4), 1989, pp. 532-550.
Eisenhardt, K. M., and Martin, J. A. "Dynamic Capabilities: What Are They?," *Strategic Management Journal* (21), 2000, pp. 1105-1121.
Henderson, R. M., and Clark, K. B. "Architectural Innovation: The Reconfiguration of Existing Product Technologies and the Failure of Established Firms," *Administrative Science Quarterly* (35:1), 1990, pp. 9-30.
Humphrey, W. *Managing the Software Process*. Reading, MA: Addison-Wesley, 1989.
Kessler E., and Chakrabarti, A. "Innovation Speed: A Conceptual Model of Context, Antecedents and Outcomes," *Academy of Management Review* (21:4), 1996, pp. 1143-1191.
Lambe C., and Spekman, R. "Alliances, External Technology Acquisition, and Discontinuous Technological Change," *Journal of Product Innovation Management* (14), 1997, pp. 102-116.
Levinthal, D., and March, J. "The Myopia of Learning," *Strategic Management Journal* (14), 1993, pp. 95-112.
Lyytinen, K., and Rose, G. "The Disruptive Nature of Information Technology Innovations: The Case of Internet Computing in Systems Development Organizations," *MIS Quarterly* (27:4), 2003, pp. 557-595.
Lyytinen, K., Rose, G., and Yoo, Y. "Exploring and Exploiting in High Gear: Hyper-learning in Seven Software Firms," under review, 2004.
March, J. G. "Exploration and Exploitation in Organizational Learning," *Organization Science* (2:1), 1991, pp. 71-87.
Pressman, R. "Can Internet-Based Applications Be Engineered?," *IEEE Software* (15:5), September-October 1998, pp. 104-110.
Swanson, E. B. "Information Systems Innovation Among Organizations," *Management Science* (40:9), 1994, pp. 1069-1088.
Teece, D. J., Pisano, G., and Shuen, A. "Dynamic Capabilities and Strategic Management," *Strategic Management Journal* (18:7), 1997, pp. 509-533.
Tushman, M. L., and Anderson, P. "Technological Discontinuities and Organizational Environments," *Administrative Science Quarterly* (31), 1986, pp. 439-465.
Van Kleijnen, J. *Computer and Profits: Quantifying Financial Benefits of Information Systems*, Englewood Cliffs, NJ: Prentice-Hall, 1980.
Yin, R. K. *Case Study Research: Design and Methods*, Thousand Oaks, CA: Sage, 1994.

ABOUT THE AUTHORS

Kalle Lyytinen is Iris S. Wolstein Professor at Case Western Reserve University. He currently serves on the editorial boards of several leading information systems journals including *Journal of the AIS* (Editor-in-Chief), *Journal of Strategic Information Systems, Information & Organization, Requirements Engineering Journal, Information Systems Journal, Scandinavian Journal of Information Systems,* and *Information Technology and People.* He is the former chairperson of IFIP WG 8.2 and is a member of WG 8.6. He has published over 150 scientific articles and conference papers and edited or written eight books on topics related to system design, method engineering, implementation, software risk assessment, computer-assisted cooperative work, standardization, and ubiquitous computing. He is currently involved in research projects that look at the IT-induced innovations in the software development, architecture, and construction industries, the design and use of ubiquitous applications in health care, high-level requirements models for large-scale systems, and the development and adoption of broadband wireless standards and services, where his recent studies have focused on South Korea and the United States. Kalle can be reached atkalle@po.cwru.edu.

Gregory M. Rose is an assistant professor at Washington State University. He received his Ph.D. in the CIS Department at Georgia State University, an MBA from Binghamton University, and a B.S. in business administration from the University of Vermont. Gregory has more than 20 publications including those in journals such as *MIS Quarterly, IEEE Transactions on Engineering Management, Accounting, Management and Information Technologies, Information Systems Journal, Journal of Global Information Management, Psychology and Marketing,* and *Communications of the AIS.* A 1998 ICIS Doctoral Consortium fellow, he has won multiple teaching awards, a post-doctoral fellowship from the University of Jyväskylä (Finland), and was an invited scholar at the University of Pretoria (South Africa). He is currently working on research projects involving electronic commerce, innovation theory, organizational learning, and global issues in IT. He also serves on the editorial board of *Journal of Global Information Management.* Prior to entering the doctoral program at Georgia State, he worked as a systems integrator. Greg can be reached at grose@wsu.edu.

14 IMPROVING BUSINESS AGILITY THROUGH TECHNICAL SOLUTIONS: A Case Study on Test-Driven Development in Mobile Software Development

Pekka Abrahamsson
VTT Technical Research Centre of Finland
Oulu, Finland

Antti Hanhineva
Elbit Oy
Oulu, Finland

Juho Jäälinoja
Nokia Technology Platforms
Oulu, Finland

Abstract   *This paper maintains that efficient business agility requires actions from all levels of the organization in order to strive for success in a turbulent business environment. Agility and agile software development solutions are suggested as yielding benefit in a volatile environment, which is characterized by continuously changing requirements and unstable development technologies. Test-driven development (TDD) is an agile practice where the tests are written before the actual program code. TDD is a technical enabler for increasing agility at the developer and product project levels. Existing empirical literature on TDD has demonstrated increased productivity and more robust code, among other important benefits. This paper reports results of a case study where a mobile application was developed for global markets, using the TDD approach. Our first results show that the adoption of TDD is difficult and the potential agility benefits may not be readily available. The lessons learned from the case study are presented.*

1   INTRODUCTION

This paper has its roots in the software engineering discipline where agile methods and principles have gained a significant amount of attention recently. Agile software development ideas can be traced back as early as the 1960s and even beyond (Larman and Basili 2003). Since the mid-1990s, several methods have been proposed to meet the needs of the turbulent business environment (for an overview of the existing methods, see Abrahamsson et al. 2002; Boehm and Turner 2003). Empirical evidence is scarce but quickly emerging. Abrahamsson et al. (2003) present the evolutionary path of agile software development methods and propose that the software engineering and information systems fields have, independently of each other, approached similar conclusions on the state of IS/SE development. The existing methods, to a certain extent, are idealized views, holding a strong prescriptive orientation, on how software and systems should be constructed. The agile movement seeks to provide an alternative view on software development through a set of values and principles (for details, see www.agilemanifesto.org).

The mobile telecommunications industry has shown itself to be comprised of a highly competitive, uncertain, and dynamic environment (Lal et al. 2001). Agile software development solutions can be seen as providing a good fit for the mobile environment, with its the high volatility and tough time-to-market needs. Mobile applications are generally quite small and the majority of them are developed by small software teams. Organizations operating in this type of business environment need to react rapidly to changing market needs. The efforts of organizations attempting to increase their responsiveness will fall short if agility is not pursued at all levels of the organization, including partnered or collaborative development at the interorganizational level. If organizational structures do not support rapid information sharing and short feedback cycles, agility benefits are not achieved. Indeed, a number of organizations are keenly interested in adopting some set of agile practices and principles for use. Test-driven development (TDD) is one of several agile practices. It has become popular with the introduction of the eXtreme Programming (Beck 1999) method. The aim of TDD is to offer agility benefits through an automated unit test suite and more robust code. Extensive automation is required, since agile principles promote common code ownership and expect the system to be always running. Other important benefits have also been suggested. Empirical evidence regarding the application of TDD in different environments is still thin.

This paper reports results from a case study where a mobile application was developed for global markets in a close-to-industry setting, using the controlled case study approach (Salo and Abrahamsson 2004) as the research method. The development team was very successful in achieving the business target. Yet, they applied the TDD approach with poor results. Only 7.8 percent of the code had associated unit tests. While the results remain inconclusive with regard to concrete benefits of TDD, the lessons learned from this case study bear important implications for developers and business managers. These implications are addressed.

The remainder of the paper is organized as follows. The next section introduces briefly the test-driven development approach including a review of the existing empirical body of evidence. This is followed by the description of the empirical research design. The fourth section presents the results of the empirical case, which is followed by discussion on the implications of the results and lessons learned.

2 TEST-DRIVEN DEVELOPMENT

Test-driven development is a programming technique where tests are written before the actual program code (Astels 2003). TDD is an incremental process (Figure 1). First a test is added and then the code to pass this test is written. When the test is passed the code is refactored. Refactoring is a process of making changes to existing, working code without changing its external behavior (Fowler 1999), i.e., the code is altered for the purposes of commenting, simplicity, or some other quality aspect. This cycle is repeated until all of the functionality is implemented.

The practitioner literature on TDD (e.g., Astels 2003; Beck 2003) identifies several potential benefits that can be gained by the application of the programming technique. These benefits are

- Give the developer confidence that the created code works
- Allow efficient refactoring through an extensive safety net
- Enable fast debugging through a test suite that helps to pinpoint defects

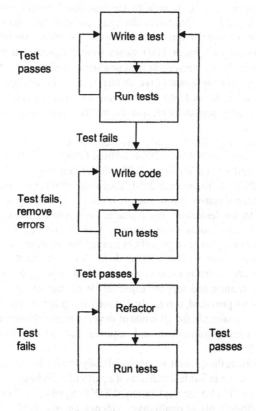

Figure 1. Steps in Test-Driven Development
(adapted from Astels 2003; Beck 2003)

- Improve software design by producing less coupled and more cohesive code
- Enable safer changes
- Create up-to-date documentation on the code
- Help developers avoid over-engineering by setting a limit on what needs to be implemented

Every time the tests pass, the developer gets a small dose of positive feedback, making the programming more fun. The unit tests in TDD have three distinct parts: setup, exercise the functionality, and check for postconditions (Astels 2003). The tests are collected into test classes to make running and maintaining the tests easier. TDD relates to refactoring in two ways: after the code is written, the refactoring is used to clean up the code, and when refactoring, the extensive test set built with TDD helps the developer gain certainty that the refactoring did not break the system.

According to quantitative data from recent studies (Edwards 2004; George and Williams 2003; Langr 2001; Maximilien and Williams 2003; Müller and Hagner 2002; Pancur et al. 2003; Williams et al. 2003; Ynchausti 2001), TDD appears to produce higher quality systems but also to increase the development time. A high test coverage is easier to achieve with TDD than with the traditional techniques. TDD forces developers to write unit tests, because the tests are such an essential part of the development that they cannot be left out. The empirical evidence found in the literature shows that the amount of tests in TDD varies from 50 percent less test code than production code to 50 % more test code than production code.

Table 1 summarizes the quantitative empirical body of evidence on test-driven development. Table 1 is divided into five columns, based on the type of finding: TDD versus traditional testing, productivity, quality, test coverage, and ratio of production code versus test code.

Qualitative data from TDD studies (Barriocanal and Urban 2002; Beck 2001; Edwards 2004; George and Williams 2004; Jeffries 1999; Langr 2001; Kaufmann and Janzen 2003; Maximilien and Williams 2003; Müller and Hagner 2002; Pancur et al. 2003; Rasmusson 2003; Williams et al. 2003; Ynchausti 2001) indicate that the test suite produced brings value a system throughout its lifetime. This is due to the fact that the changes are safer to implement in any phase of the system's life cycle. TDD also changes manual debugging to the more-structured task of writing tests. However, TDD is not easy; many developers have prejudices against the practice.

Empirical literature shows that TDD is difficult to use and that it increases the workload of developers, causing them to write less-functional code. These prejudices can be fought with training and support, especially in the beginning of the adoption of TDD. If support is not provided, it is likely that the TDD practice will not work. It also seems that TDD is not suitable for all kinds of development environments; it is highly dependent on the testing framework and requires that the developers using it be motivated and skilled.

Table 2 summarizes the qualitative empirical body of evidence on test-driven development. The first column in Table 2 indicates if a particular finding provides qualitative support (i.e., symbol "↑") for the application of TDD. Symbol "↓," on the other hand, indicates that the finding offers qualitative evidence against TDD. An empty space refers to "neither." This means that a particular finding provides a deeper understanding on a particular aspect with respect the use of TDD in certain environments.

Table 1. Quantitative Empirical Body of Evidence on Test-Driven Development

Type of Study, Reference	TDD versus Traditional Testing	Productivity	Quality	Test coverage	Ratio of Production Code versus Test Code
TDD versus traditional, (Langr 2001)	33% more in tests TDD	–	–	–	50% more tests than code
TDD versus ad hoc testing, (Maximilien and Williams 2003)	No unit tests in ad hoc testing	Minimal impact on productivity in TDD	50 % lower defect rate in TDD	–	50% less tests than code
TDD versus traditional (Edwards 2004)	–	–	45% fewer defects in TDD	–	–
TDD versus traditional (Williams et al. 2003)	52% fewer tests in TDD	Same productivity in both	40% lower defect rate in TDD	–	50% less tests than code
TDD versus iterative test last (Pancur et al. 2003)	–	–	–	92.6 % combined	–
TDD versus waterfall, (George and Williams 2003)	No unit tests in waterfall	TDD took 16 % more time	TDD passed 18% more black box tests	98% method, 92% statement 97% branch	–
TDD versus traditional (Ynchausti 2001)	No unit tests in traditional	TDD took 60 – 100% more time	38 – 267% fewer defects in TDD	–	Equal amount of test and code LOC
TDD versus traditional (Müller and Hagner 2002)	–	"Slight increase on used time in TDD"	"Slight increase on reliability in TDD"	–	–

Table 2. Qualitative Empirical and Anecdotal Body of
Evidence on Test-Driven Development

	Result	Reference
↑	The vast test set that comes with TDD helps to refactor with confidence that the code works.	George and Williams 2004; Langr 2001
↑	TDD developers are more confident in their code.	Edwards 2004; Kaufmann and Janzen 2003; Pancur et al. 2003
↑	Test set created via TDD will continue to improve the quality of the system throughout its lifetime.	Maximilien and Williams 2003; Williams et al. 2003
↑	Adding new functionality to the system built with TDD was easier than to a traditionally built system.	Langr 2001; Maximilien and Williams 2003; Williams et al. 2003
↑	TDD produces more testable code, because there is a test already written for it.	George and Williams 2003; Langr 2001
↑	In TDD, the unit testing actually happens, it cannot be left out because it is an essential part of the development.	George and Williams 2003; Maximilien and Williams 2003
↑	Most developers thought that TDD improves productivity and is effective.	George and Williams 2003
↑	The developers' time is more efficiently used writing unit tests than manual debugging.	George and Williams 2004; Williams et al. 2003; Ynchausti 2001;
↓	Resistance at first to use TDD due to inexperience and growth in the amount of work.	Maximilien and Williams 2003; Müller and Hagner 2002
↓	Developers thought that because of writing tests they had time to write less functionality.	Pancur et al. 2003
↓	Nearly half of the developers thought that TDD faces difficulty in adoption.	George and Williams 2003
	TDD training can be used to overcome negative impressions of the TDD practice.	Ynchausti 2001
	When no support for TDD was available, inexperienced developers slipped back to no unit testing development, support at least in the early stages is needed.	Jeffries 1999; Rasmusson 2003
	Given a chance, only 10 percent of students wrote unit tests.	Barriocanal and Urban 2002
↓	The TDD group produced insufficient unit tests.	Kaufmann and Janzen 2003
	If the tests are not automated, they are less likely to be run.	Maximilien and Williams 2003
↓	Graphical user interfaces are hard to build with TDD.	Beck 2001
	Writing test cases for hard-to-test code requires skill and determination from the developers.	George and Williams 2004

3 EMPIRICAL RESEARCH DESIGN

3.1 Research Method

The research approach used in this study contains elements of case study research (Yin 1994), action research (Avison et al. 1999) and experimentation (Wohlin et al. 2000). This type of specific approach has been labeled as the *controlled case study approach* (Salo and Abrahamsson 2004). The term *controlled* is used intentionally. Empirical studies include various forms of research strategies (Basili and Lanubile 1999). *Controlled* is most often associated with the experimentation approach. One central difference between the research strategies is the *level of control*. Following Wohlin et al. (2000, p. 12), "experiments sample over the variables that are being manipulated, while the case studies sample from the variables representing the typical situation." If this is accepted, the experimentation approach can be seen as "a form of empirical study where the researcher has a control over some of the conditions in which the study takes place and control over the independent variables being studied" (Basili and Lanubile 1999, p. 456). Therefore, the use of term controlled in this type of study approach implies that the researchers were in a position to design the implementation environment, i.e., the typical situation (see the next subsection on research setting), beforehand. The developers in this case study developed the product in VTT's laboratory setting close to the researchers.

3.2 Research Setting

A team of four developers was gathered to implement a mobile application for global markets. Three of the four developers were fifth or sixth year university students with industrial experience in software development. One of the developers was an experienced industrial developer. The team worked in a colocated development environment and used a tailored version (i.e., tailored to meet the needs of mobile software development) of the eXtreme Programming method. This paper focuses on one aspect of the used approach, the test-driven development technique.

The project was supported and monitored by a support team in which two of the authors participated. The supporting tasks for TDD consisted of constructing the TDD approach for mobile Java-enabled devices, providing training for the use of the approach, following the TDD process during the project, and assisting in possible problem situations. One of the authors followed the TDD on a biweekly basis and informally discussed the results with the team. On one occasion, one of the authors facilitated the team by participating in test code development, with the goal of providing the team a hands-on example on how the team's TDD practice could be improved.

3.3 Data Collection

Both quantitative and qualitative data were collected. Table 3 indicates the type of data collected, the rationale for its collection, and the interval when it was collected.

Table 3. Collected Quantitative and Qualitative Data

Collected Data	Rationale	Type	Collection Interval
Lines of code	Ratio of Test LOC/Application LOC (%)	Quantitative	After each iteration
Effort use	Test development effort used/Application development effort used (%)	Quantitative	Daily
Productivity	LOC/hour	Quantitative	Daily
Structured team interview	Team perception of the use of TDD	Qualitative	After the project
Post-iteration workshop (Salo 2004)	Team perception. Note, a process improvement mechanism (not only TDD issues)	Qualitative	After each iteration
Research notes	Research ideas, observational findings	Qualitative	Daily, during the project

The support team validated the data on a daily or weekly basis, depending on the type of data collected. The purpose of evaluating the effort used for developing tests compared with the effort used in developing the application code is to provide a metric on how much the approach is used in the project.

The qualitative data is collected from three sources: the team interview, post-iteration workshops, and the research notes. The structured interview (recorded and transcribed) was conducted after the project. One of the authors kept systematic research notes with his observations throughout the project. The purpose of collecting qualitative data is to find out if there is a correlation between qualitative and quantitative data collected in the project.

4   CASE STUDY RESULTS

4.1 Case Project Overview

The aim of the project was to produce a production monitoring application for mobile Java devices. The product is an added-value service for the existing production planning system that enables a salesperson to visually view the state of the production anywhere, anytime. The mobile Java application is based on a similar application running on the desktop environment. The project, therefore, aimed at transforming the existing product to a mobile environment with reduced functionality. The limited resources of the mobile devices, however, forced the mobile Java application to act as a browser for the existing data. The application was written in Java 2 Micro Edition, using the MIDP 2.0 profile.

Table 4. The Lines of Code for the Client, Server and the Whole Application

	Test code	Application Code	Total Code	% of Tests from Application
Client	208	2665	2873	7.8
Server	78	972	1050	8.0
Total	286	3637	3923	7.9

The project was conducted in the spring of 2004. The total duration of the project was nine weeks, which includes a system test and fixing phases. The project was divided into five iterations, starting with a 1-week iteration, which was followed by three 2-week iterations, with the project concluding in a final 1-week iteration.

4.2 Quantitative Results

This subsection presents the quantitative results of the case study. Table 4 presents overall data on the application, in terms of the total test and application lines of code for the client, the server and the whole application, including the percentage of test lines of code from the application lines of code. Table 4 highlights the fact that the level of test code is very low.

Figure 2 presents the correlation between test code and application code measured in lines of code on the client side of the application, where TDD was intended to be used. The tools used for the development of the server did not enable the use of TDD, and therefore, the server is excluded from the subsequent analysis. The data is presented by iteration and measured by lines of code.

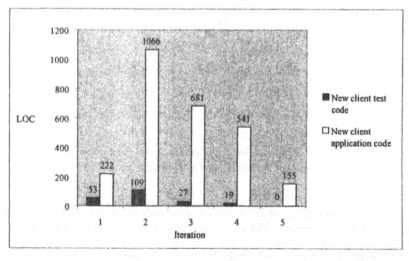

Figure 2. Correlation Between Test Code and Application Code

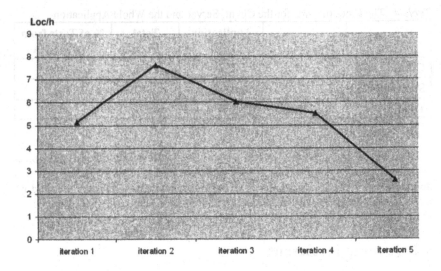

Figure 3. Total Productivity in the Case Project

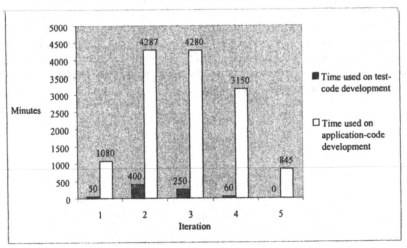

Figure 4. Correlation Between Test-Code Development Time
and Application-Code Development Time

As it can be seen in Figure 2, the amount of test code compared to the application code is significantly smaller. The total productivity (Figure 3) is lower in the short iterations (1 and 5) and higher in the longer iterations, however, it drops toward the end of the project. The test code productivity follows roughly the same pattern: in the first iteration, some test code is written, the maximum productivity is reached on iteration 2, and the amount of test code drops from there, leading to the last iteration which did not produce any test code at all.

Figure 4 presents the correlation between the test code development time and the application code development time. Contrary to the lines of code metric, the use of time metric is presented on the level of the whole application. The data is presented by iteration and measured by minutes used in the respective development modes.

Similar to Figure 2, the amount of time used on test-code development is significantly smaller than the time used in application-code development. The time used on application-code development is shorter in the first and fifth of the 1-week iterations than in the 2-week iterations. The largest amount of time was used for application-code development in the second iteration, and the time drops from there toward the end of the project. The time used on test-code development follows the same pattern as the time used in application-code development: In the beginning of the project, the most time was used for test-code development, and the time used drops from there to the last iteration, where no time was used on the test-code development. The total percentage of time used in test-code development is 5.6 percent.

4.3 Qualitative Results

During the project, the researchers perceived that the developers did not seem to see the benefit of the tests; they regarded them more as a burden. The fact that the team did not see the benefit of the tests was realized, for example, on one occasion when the team used two hours to debug the application without running the tests. Afterward, a member of the team commented that if they had run the tests, they would have caught the defect. The team's attitude toward TDD was also seen in the fact that the developers easily slipped into working in the traditional mode of developing software first and forgetting the tests until the end of the development. Comments included

> I don't think that we could have found faults [with TDD tests] that we could not have found otherwise.

> We just thought that the tests do not offer us any advantage.

The TDD practice clearly had some difficulties in adoption. The team had some negative impressions about it, but they also admitted that some of the reasons for not using TDD were their own.

> The whole TDD practice, where you write tests before the program code, is stupid....The amount of tests will grow so large there is no sense in that.

> Maybe we should have been forced to do the tests.

The limited physical resources on the client end of the application developed in the project forced the mobile application to act as a browser for the existing data. The application followed the client-server model, and because of the lack of the physical resources on the client end of the application, most of the data processing was done on the server side. So the client's main function was to act as a user interface for the server side. This creates difficulty, which also came up in the team interview.

> TDD is not easily applicable to...user interface development and that is just what we are doing. We had very few things to which it would have suited naturally.

During the project, the researchers became concerned about the low number of test code lines and tried to promote the use of TDD by making the TDD process easier for the developers. One of the authors asked the team if the approach used in the project should be made easier to use. The improvement consisted of making running the tests easier by automating the code changes needed in the main class of the application. The team did not see this as being necessary and claimed that the current way, where the changes had to be done by hand every time the team needed to change between TDD and running the application, was effective enough. The team was under delivery pressure as well.

Yet, as stated before, the team was inexperienced with TDD. They thought that they could have achieved better results if they had had more time to get acquainted with the practice and possibly had more support while developing

> This was the first time for all of us to try TDD. We probably would have been more capable of using the practice if we had used it previously to develop something [for which] it is better suited.

> Maybe if we had a bit longer time to do the training we could have been more capable of using TDD....Also if a member of the support team would have been with us while developing, it would have helped us to do TDD.

Although the team considered that TDD had difficulties when developing this kind of application, they felt that it could provide advantages in a different kind of application area

> TDD could save time at later development phases when adding functionality to application; the developer could use the tests to see if it broke the existing functionality.

> I think TDD is good for testing logic...test set could be run to verify if the application broke or not.

The qualitative findings offer interesting results. While the team observed that TDD could provide them some help, they were not very keen in utilizing the practice if not made mandatory. Even when the research team proposed a significant improvement opportunity for the TDD approach in mobile environment, the team refused to give it a try. Yet, the team conceived the TDD practice was useful with testing the logic and verifying the functionality of the software.

5   DISCUSSION

Technical agile solutions, such as TDD, are designed for the type of volatile development environment presented in this study. However, as the results show, this study is inconclusive with regard to the concrete benefits of TDD. We cannot, therefore, determine whether TDD positively or negatively affected the software development. Yet, the project was a remarkable business success, producing a fully marketable mobile application in a very short time frame. Our findings are of importance for practitioners who aim at using agile solutions in their development settings as well as for researchers who conduct case studies and experiments in the area. In the following, the results are mapped against the existing empirical body of evidence, after which the implications in terms of concrete lessons learned during the study are addressed.

5.1 Mapping the Results to Existing Empirical Body of Evidence

TDD studies have shown that TDD projects generally produce somewhere from 50 percent less to 50 percent more test code than application code (Langr 2001; Maximilien and Williams 2003; Williams et al. 2003; Ynchausti 2001). In this study, the ratio was only 7.8 percent. This could also indicate that TDD is poorly applicable for the mobile Java environment due to technical challenges. Yet, the particular approach designed for this study was pre-tested by the research team and found feasible. More importantly, the low amount of test code can be explained by observing the qualitative data, where the development team clearly indicated reluctance for adoption of TDD for actual use, due to reasons of difficulty, inexperience, and application domain. In particular, the developers expressed that TDD was not suitable the kind of application that the project involved (i.e., a browser type with a strong focus on user interfaces). TDD authors have brought this up earlier (e.g., Beck 2001). Prior experience in unit testing generally, and TDD in particular, has been found to contribute to the adoption rate. Our study is in line with these findings. The development team had not been exposed to test-first design or development prior to the project. George and Williams (2004) also propose that the adoption of the TDD practice requires determined and skilled developers.

In terms of effort used, results show that in the first iteration, the team used up to 30 percent of effort for TDD. This dropped quickly in the subsequent iterations. Qualitative evidence points out that the team found TDD provide them little or no added value, for the to reasons explicated above. It should be noted that the server side of the software was developed in the desktop environment, and the team used JUnit as the testing tool in that project. Although having a different, more sophisticated tool for TDD available, the team still did not manage to produce tests.

5.2 Lessons Learned

Half way through the case project, the research team realized that the TDD technique was not going to be systematically used within the project. Some measures (i.e., extra training and mentoring support) were used to ease the adoption of the technique but, as the results show, the situation was not improved. Therefore, it is important to understand the reasons for the reluctance to adopt the TDD technique in practice.

5.2.1 Lack of Motivation

A proper use of TDD requires that developers write about the same amount of test code as actual production code. Therefore, it requires a lot of motivation and discipline to author the extra code in a tightly scheduled project. Clearly, our developers acknowledged the extra work needed to be done, but did not see the benefits of TDD. One reason for this may have been the fact that the developers did not have to live through the maintenance phase of the product, where new features would be added without breaking the existing solution. In addition, the developers perceived the quality issues as being of less importance in such a small project.

It would have been possible to put more pressure on the team with regard to the use of TDD *per se*. Yet, the project was under business delivery pressure and the end product was their primary concern, as is the case in industry. Moreover, we find that motivation to use and acceptance of a new technology should emerge from use and actual benefits. In our case, the team did not achieve an early victory with the process innovation, which hindered effectively further application opportunities.

5.2.2 Developers' Inexperience

The development team spent a considerable amount of time in solving technical issues related to the mobile development environment and programming solutions (i.e., use of architectural patterns, threads, etc.). Only one of the team members was an expert in mobile Java programming. Moreover, the application domain was filled with domain-specific details with regard to production planning system operations. Experience with these issues would most likely have eased the adoption of the test-driven mind set. TDD is also a personal-level development practice and, therefore, may be more difficult to adopt than other agile development techniques such as rapid release cycles, agile modeling, and constant communication. The learning curve appears to be steeper in the case of TDD than in the other agile practices. While the team used a so-called green field approach (i.e., they adopted many agile techniques at once), it may well be that the project's time-frame was too tight for the most difficult practices. A more effective strategy would have been to introduce fewer new techniques on a first-of-a-kind project and recommend TDD on the following projects, when the developers would be more experienced with the other new development techniques.

5.2.3 Immature Development Environment for TDD

The TDD method relies on using an extensive set of tests that are constantly executed during development. It must be possible to run the test suite automatically without too much effort. The tools for implementing TDD in the case project's development environment were found to be immature. In addition, the development included significant user interface implementation, an area where the tools for executing TDD are only beginning to come into more general use.

5.2.4 Absence of a Mentor

A brief basic training of the concepts of TDD was provided prior to project launch. This turned out to be an overly optimistic approach for introducing a new technique in practical terms. TDD is not learned in a one-day course. We suspect that mastery of the technique requires several months of intense use. For a short project, such as the case study presented here, where developers were not familiar with the technique, a mentor within the project team is required. Constant advice and motivation from the mentor would have eased use, even in times when resistance occurred.

6 CONCLUSIONS

The mobile telecommunications industry has proved to be highly competitive, uncertain, and dynamic environment. Industries operating in such a turbulent market-place is particularly interested in trying out technical agile solutions. This study reported the results of a case study, where a development team attempted to use test-driven development in a mobile development environment with little success. Nevertheless, the project was highly successful in the business sense.

For business managers and others, this study bears important implications. In particular, this study points out that the adoption of a certain agile technique or approach is not a straightforward, silver-bullet solution. Business managers should stay alert in the midst of the hype before mandating the use of agile solutions in their organizations. Developers should keep their heads up as well. This case has demonstrated that very few if any of the technical agile solutions can be adopted and used without proper, systematic software process improvement tactics. While this study fails to provide empirical evidence either for or against test-driven development, it highlights the obstacles hindering adoption. We believe that the results of our study are applicable in other environments and agile techniques. Agile improvements at the technical level require as careful planning and follow-up as any other software engineering innovation. An interesting avenue for future research would be the use innovation theories, such as León's (1996) innovation adoption profiles, to analyze the adoption of agile solutions in practical settings. Concrete empirical evidence should still be collected, however.

This study maintains that business agility cannot be achieved without considering all organizational levels, including development teams and personnel. Software engineering research and practice has produced technical solutions, which have been the focus of this paper. Information systems research is likely to provide the needed extension to the organizational and interorganizational levels. Yet, even low-level agile changes are not easily implemented. We plan to continue the validation of agile solutions in future case studies.

REFERENCES

Abrahamsson, P., Salo, O., Ronkainen, J., and Warsta, J. *Agile Software Development Methods: Review and Analysis*, Espoo, Finland: Technical Research Centre of Finland, VTT Publications 478, 2002 (available online at http://www.vtt.fi/inf/pdf/publications/2002/P478.pdf).

Abrahamsson, P., Warsta, J., Siponen, M. T., and Ronkainen, J. "New Directions on Agile Methods: A Comparative Analysis," in *Proceedings of the 25th International Conference on Software Engineering*, Los Alamitos, CA: IEEE Computer Society Press, 2003, pp. 244-254.

Astels, D. *Test-Driven Development: A Practical Guide*, Upper Saddle River, NJ: Prentice Hall, 2003.

Avison, D., Lau, F., Myers, M., and Nielsen, P. A. "Action Research," *Communications of the ACM* (42:1), 1999, pp. 94-97.

Barriocanal, E. G., and Urban, M.-A. S. "An Experience in Integrating Automated Unit Testing Practices in an Introductory Programming Course," *ACM SIGCSE Bulletin* (34), 2002, pp. 125-128.

Basili, V. R., and Lanubile, F. "Building Knowledge through Families of Experiments," *IEEE Transactions on Software Engineering* (25), 1999, pp. 456-473.

Beck, K. "Aim, Fire," *IEEE Software* (18:5), 2001, pp. 87-89.

Beck, K. "Embracing Change with Extreme Programming," *IEEE Computer* (32:10), 1999, pp. 70-77.

Beck, K. *Test-Driven Development: By Example*, New York: Addison-Wesley, 2003.

Boehm, B., and Turner, R. *Balancing Agility and Discipline: A Guide for the Perplexed*, Boston: Addison-Wesley, 2003.

Edwards, S. H. "Using Software Testing to Move Students from Trial-and-Error to Reflection-in-Action," in *Proceedings of the 35th SIGCSE Technical Symposium on Computer Science Education*, New York: ACM Press, 2004, pp. 26-30.

Fowler, M. *Refactoring: Improving the Design of Existing Code*, Boston: Addison Wesley Longman, 1999.

George, B., and Williams, L. "An Initial Investigation of Test Driven Development in Industry," in *Proceedings of the ACM Symposium on Applied Computing*, New York: ACM Press, 2003, pp. 1135-1139.

George, B., and Williams, L. "A Structured Experiment of Test-Driven Development," *Information and Software Technology* (46:5), 2004, pp. 337-342.

Jeffries, R. E. "Extreme Testing," *Software Testing & Quality Engineering* (1:2), March/April 1999, pp. 23-26.

Kaufmann, R., and Janzen, D. "Implications of Test-Driven Development A Pilot Study," in *Proceedings of the Conference on Object-Oriented Programming Systems Languages and Applications (OOPSLA)*, New York: ACM Press, 2003, pp. 298-299.

Lal, D., Pitt, D. C., and Beloucif, A. "Restructuring in European Telecommunications: Modeling the Evolving Market," *European Business Review* (13:3), 2001, pp. 152-156.

Langr, J. "Evolution of Test and Code via Test-First Design," paper presented at the Conference on Object Oriented Programming Systems Languages and Applications (OOPSLA), Tampa Bay, FL, 2001.

Larman, C., and Basili, V. R. "Iterative and Incremental Development: A Brief History," *IEEE Software* (20), 2003, pp. 47-56.

León, G. "On the Diffusion of Software Technologies: Technological Frameworks and Adoption Profiles," in *Diffusion and Adoption of Information Technology*, K. Kautz and J. Pries-Heje (Eds.), Padstow, Cornwall, England: TJ Press Ltd., 1996, pp. 96-116.

Maximilien, E. M., and Williams, L. "Assessing Test-Driven Development at IBM," in *Proceedings of the International Conference on Software Engineering (ICSE)*, Los Alamitos, CA: IEEE Computer Society Press, 2003, pp. 564-569.

Müller, M. M., and Hagner, O. "Experiment About Test-First Programming," *IEEE Proceedings Software* (149:5), 2002, pp. 131-136..

Pancur, M., Ciglaric, M., Trampus, M., and Vidmar, T. "Towards Empirical Evaluation of Test-Driven Development in a University Environment," in *Proceedings of EUROCON 2004*, Ljubljana, Slovenia, IEEE Computer Society, 2003, pp. 83-86.

Rasmusson, J. "Introducing XP into Greenfield Projects: Lessons Learned." *IEEE Software* (20:3), 2003, pp. 21-28.

Salo, O., and Abrahamsson, P. "Empirical Evaluation of Agile Software Development: A Controlled Case Study Approach," in *Proceedings of the 6th International Conference on Product Focused Software Process Improvement*, F. Bomarius and H. Ilda (Eds.), Kansai Science City, Japan: Springer, 2004, pp. 408-423.

Williams, L., Maximilien, E. M., and Vouk, M. "Test-Driven Development as a Defect-Reduction Practice," in *Proceedings of the 14th International Symposium of Software Reliability Engineering (ISSRE'03)*, Los Alamitos, CA: IEEE Computer Society Press, 2003, pp. 34-48.

Wohlin, C., Runeson, P., Höst, M., Ohlsson, M. C., Regnell, B., and Wesslén, A. *Experimentation in Software Engineering*, Boston: Kluwer Academic Publishers, 2000.

Yin, R. K. *Case Study Research Design and Methods*, Thousand Oaks, CA: Sage Publications, 1994.

Ynchausti, R. A. "Integrating Unit Testing into a Software Development Team's Process," in *Proceedings of the XP 2001 Conference*, Caglieri, Italy, 2001, pp. 79-83.

ABOUT THE AUTHORS

Pekka Abrahamsson is a senior research scientist at VTT Technical Research Centre of Finland. He received his Ph.D. from University of Oulu, Finland, in 2002. His current responsibilities include managing the AGILE-ITEA project (http://www.agile-itea.org), which involves 22 organizations from 9 European countries. The project aims at utilizing agile innovations in the development of embedded systems. His research interests are currently focused on the development of mobile information systems, applications and services, business agility and agile software production. He has coached several agile software development projects in industry and authored more than 40 scientific publications focusing on software process and quality improvement, commitment issues, and agile software development. He is the principal author of the Mobile-D methodology for mobile application development. Pekka can be reached at Pekka.Abrahamsson@vtt.fi.

Antti Hanhineva is a software designer at Elbit Oy in Finland. He received his M.Sc. from University of Oulu, Finland, in 2004. Prior to joining Elbit, he worked at VTT Technical Research Centre of Finland. While at VTT he coached several projects on test-driven development and testing related issues in mobile development environments. He is a coauthor of the Mobile-D methodology for mobile application development. Antti can be reached at antti.hanhineva@elbit.fi.

Juho Jaalinoja is a software engineer at Nokia Technology Platforms. Prior to joining Nokia, he worked as a research scientist at VTT Technical Research Centre of Finland. His research areas include software process improvement and agile methods. He received his M.Sc. in Information Processing Science from University of Oulu, Finland, in 2004. Juho can be reached at Juho.Jaalinoja@nokia.com.

15 WEB PUBLISHING: An Extreme, Agile Experience

Mark Toleman
Fiona Darroch
Mustafa Ally
University of Southern Queensland
Toowoomba, QLD Australia

Abstract   *The proponents of agile methodologies suggest that many of the inhibitors to system development methodology adoption have largely been addressed in the underlying principles of agile methods. This paper reports the experience of a small team developing Web publishing software tools for use in building Web sites for online delivery of tertiary education study materials. These early adopters successfully used eXtreme Programming (XP) practices for this tool development exercise. Almost all XP practices were adopted, although some were adhered to more rigorously than others and some proved to be more successful than others. Continued use of XP and communication of its benefits to others has been a consequential focus for the developers.*

Keywords   Agile methodology, eXtreme Programming, experience report, Web publishing

1. INTRODUCTION

According to Fitzgerald (1998), practitioners have been reluctant to adopt software/ system development methodologies (SDMs), with more than 60 percent of them abstaining. Furthermore, he noted that nearly 80 percent of the non-adopters intended to stay that way. Fitzgerald identified a number of arguments from practitioners against the use of methodologies, and pressures preventing their adoption. It has been argued that the so-called agile methodologies may provide a solution.

Extreme programming (XP) (Beck 1999), perhaps the most well known agile methodology (Fowler and Highsmith 2001), is currently receiving much attention, particularly by practicing software developers. There are now at least two major international conferences annually[1] and there have been several special issues of journals on the topic (for example *IEEE Software*, November/December 2001, *Journal of Defense Software Engineering*, October 2002, *IEEE Computer*, June 2003, *Journal of Database Management*, April 2004). The Giga Information Group predicted that, by 2004, agile processes will be incorporated in two-thirds of corporate IT departments (Barnett 2002). Also, with software development luminaries such as Tom DeMarco (cited in Beck and Fowler 2001) making statements such as

> XP is the most important movement in our field today. I predict that it will be as essential to the present generation as the SEI and its Capability Maturity Model were to the last.

there can be little doubt this is no passing fad, but in fact a topic worthy of serious research from Information Systems academics and the software development community.

XP is centered on 12 core practices, also known now as *Xp Xtudes*, which guide the software development process.[2] These practices reflect the sentiment and intent of the 12 principles underpinning the agile manifesto.[3] Most of these practices are not new but the way they are presented as a package in XP represents to many software developers how they really develop software systems (Sleve 2002) or, in some cases, desire to develop software for clients.

XP has been successfully applied in many projects. A range of experience reports have been published which demonstrate the wide variety of situations considered suitable for trials of agile methods. These reports fall into several categories including academic teaching (Lappo 2002; Mugridge et al. 2003), tertiary student projects (Karlström 2002), small-scale industry developments (Bossi and Cirillo 2001), and large-scale industry developments (C3 Team, 1998; Elssamadisy 2001; Grenning 2001; Pedroso et al. 2002; Schuh 2001). However, there has been little attempt to grapple with the factors affecting the adoption of this new methodology. Toleman et al. (2004) contributed by examining adoption of a relatively new methodology in a specific environment. The extent to which agile methodologies might address the shortfalls in methodology uptake was examined as were the characteristics that influenced adoption of a particular methodology.

This report and the project reported here had several distinguishing features.

- The system under construction was not a typical business application, but a software infrastructure development with difficult to define, abstract requirements.

- The complexity of the system development environment required the use of multiple software products for development.

---

[1]International Conference on eXtreme Programming and Agile Processes in Software Engineering (http://www.xp2005.org) and XP Agile Universe (http://www.xpuniverse.com/home).

[2]See "Extreme Programming Core Practices" at http://c2.com/cgi/wiki?Extreme ProgrammingCorePractices.

[3]See "Manifesto for Agile Software Development" at http://www.agilemanifesto.org/.

- Much of the current debate on using agile methods centers on whether it is developers or management who resist their adoption. The situation under review was notable in that the impetus initially came from management, but the development team were also very keen to conduct a trial of the XP methodology.

- This trial was conducted without any expenditure on mentoring, training, etc.—it was all based on internal research.

- The implementation of XP was a success story.

- Most industry experience reports are quite subjective, having been authored from within the development team. In contrast, this report is an objective analysis undertaken for the purposes of furthering research on the use of agile methods and by researchers who were external to the development.

This paper provides a retrospective on the experiences of developers building Web-based publishing software tools using XP. The next section describes the approach used in this study, followed by the background to the project, the actual experience of using XP in this project, issues for discussion, and conclusions.

2   RESEARCH APPROACH

Most of the data for this experience report were gathered through interviewing members of the development team. Interviews were tape recorded and transcribed, and then edited by the interviewees. Follow-up interviews were conducted to clarify and expand on specific issues related to the project context and use of XP. Quotations or indented text italicized throughout the rest of this paper are either verbal or written statements from these primary data sources (denoted in the text as *N1*, *N2*, and *N3*).

3   SITUATION BACKGROUND

NextEd Limited is a Hong Kong based provider of Web-based software infrastructure. It services mainly tertiary education providers in the Asia-Pacific region, including the University of Southern Queensland, by providing platforms for delivery of study materials and communication services to students who study, principally, in online modes.

The project discussed in this paper required the development of a suite of tools for a scalable, flexible, and efficient continuous publishing system. The tools facilitated the generation of print and Web-based study materials provided by content experts. The target operating system was Windows NT and the languages used included Delphi, XSLT, and XML. Visual Source Safe was used for configuration management and, although not ideal, proved effective (CVS is now used throughout the organization).

The newly formed project team felt that an iterative methodology was most suited, and according to N1 it was fundamental to the project to produce *"a constant stream of outputs and engage the customer on a regular basis."* Initially made aware of XP by the organization's chief technical officer, the team took on the initiative to study this approach to software development and considered the project a suitable candidate for the use of XP. No particular development methodology for this type of project was in place in the organization. There was also recognition that management's requirements of the project were not well defined, that the project size was not expected to be large (a few thousand lines of code), and its development time was expected to be relatively short (about six months). XP provided an alternative to a traditional, heavyweight approach since there was a small team and less need to follow a process-oriented methodology. Being a small team meant members had multiple roles (project leader, proxy customer, system architect, and programmer). Management was unconcerned with the product development approach adopted for the project but was concerned with the product outcome and monitored progress accordingly. They did not put limitations on the trial of XP but noted the method required the developers to regularly deliver working software which could be given trials and tested by the customer.

4   EXPERIENCES OF THE XP CORE PRACTICES

This section reports on the information gathered during the interviews. Table 1 shows a summary of the level of adoption of the XP core practices for this project.

The discussion that follows is an analysis of the case study within the framework of the relevant XP practices.

4.1 The Planning Game

The project leader and proxy customer were in charge of functional requirements. A tool was needed to automate as much of the electronic publishing process as possible. The customers had a view of what was required. The members of the development team contributed ideas for the functionality as well. Initially, story cards were used to communicate functional requirements among the team members but this became unmanageable:

> *N1: We put all the stories on cards, a big pile of cards, and the piles get bigger—what you can see are the piles getting bigger and bigger. So we had to overcome that. Basically we have a document and in the bottom of the document we have a bundle of card...at the end of that meeting, we publish that.*

In fact, the project team used the organization's intranet to communicate progress and system development priorities:

> *N1: What we started doing was...building a weekly newsletter which detailed our problems and functionality [set] on the internet...for the organization so they could see the progress of their actual requirements...we said if you*

Table 1. XP Core Practices Experience Summary

XP Core Practices	Implementation Level	Comment
The Planning Game	Full	Worked well for both developers and client
Small Releases	Full	Successful
System Metaphor	Nil	Developers would like this
Simple Design	Full	Successful
Test Driven Development	Full	Very beneficial for development
Design Improvement (was Refactoring)	Partial	No tools and not regular
Pair Programming	Partial	Useful for developers to cross-train
Collective Code Ownership	Full	Very successful for developers—aided skill transfer
Continuous Integration	Full	Successful—infrastructure can be reused
Sustainable Pace (was 40-Hour Work Week)	Nil	Would be desirable for developers
Whole Team (was On-site Customer)	Full	At least during business hours
Coding Standards	Full	Worked well

Note: Full = full adoption; Partial = partial adoption; Nil = not adopted.

> *want anything to do with this product you must submit your requirements to us, we will manage those requirements...we handle every cycle...*

Because the customer determined the priority of software functionality, project progress was transparent and there was continuous customer involvement from the project's inception. By requiring the customer to be involved in selecting the required business functionality for implementation, the customer knew what would be provided, the project team provided it, and management could see progress being made. Communication back to the project team included specific details of the features to be included in the next software release. The project team developed a points system for features to indicate degree of difficulty and time to complete which the customers could understand and use.

> *N1: What we really want is we want you to be these five [features], and that adds up to 300 points for the two weeks.*

So the customers (and management) were able to drive the system development but through the process of setting priorities, the project team felt it had some control too.

> *N1: ...which meant that we are driving the development of it, we are forcing our company to drive....The other advantages are when you have this prioritized, your customers are going to say, "Well I really only need that, I did need it 10 minutes ago but it is not that important now."*

> *N3: Yes, it is less complex. Mainly in the area of planning. Typical planning processes for software development are pure fiction. A lot of up-front effort goes into creating charts and dependencies graphs, but I have never seen a plan like this actually followed up or kept up-to-date.*

In the case study, the customer was involved in selecting the business functionality required for implementation. The customer knew what would be provided, the project team provided it, and management could see the progress being made. Hence the customers (and management) were able to drive the system development but, through the process of setting priorities, the project team felt it had some control too.

4.2 Small Releases

After the initial build process (of about three months), releases were made available every two weeks:

> *N1: ...beside the requirements we had...levels of difficulty...okay, you have two weeks which ones do you want.*

> *N2: Incremental progress and updates ensured everyone who was interested knew where we were and why [we] completed or failed to complete certain tasks.*

> *N3: ...the key is regular releases of working software and along with that getting people using a product from as early as possible.*

> *N3: ...it is better to get the bugs out early than to release all the bugs at once.*

In the case study, after the initial build process (of about three months), the release cycle was fortnightly. This was considered advantageous because it was much easier to identify whether the project was on schedule. This is in contrast to traditional SDMs which tend to focus on delivering larger chunks of functionality much later in the development schedule.

4.3 System Metaphor

This was perhaps the least successfully implemented core practice of XP in this project. However it is not a surprising finding given that no metaphor was created at the start of system development. *N1*'s view was that "...*in hindsight that [a metaphor] would have been really helpful because we really struggled to get the idea/concept for the system out of the head of the customer.*"

In the case study, a metaphor, or common view of the project, emerged as the project developed and as the team discussed implementation of stories week-by-week. Having a clearer concept earlier would have speeded progress and facilitated communication.

4.4 Simple Design

At all times, the developers avoided unnecessary complication with respect to software architecture and coding, staying with the stories agreed with the customer each cycle. Keeping the design simple means that change, as and when it is required, is less problematic.

In this way, the team took a minimalist approach to the addition of functionality and ensured the customer received what they considered essential in the priority order they required. In traditional methodologies, design architecture is usually predefined, which does not offer the same flexible approach.

4.5 Test Driven Development

All Delphi code had tests included because a testing framework existed already. An XSL testing framework had to be developed because, at the time none was available. In fact, according to the developer, test-driven development assisted in the code development:

> *N1: If you cannot write those [test] unit specs up front, then you will fail the test runner...so writing those sort of tests helps you map out your design in the first place and you get a much better design.*

Nevertheless, writing tests prior to code was a significant change of habit for the developers, and was thus a visible difference for both them and customers who develop acceptance tests. This was a highly observable element associated with the implementation of XP where the role of the customer is extended well beyond the bounds of a traditional project.

4.6 Design Improvement (was Refactoring)

Refactoring was applied in this project but not in any automatic or systematic way using any specific tools. There is no such equivalent practice in traditional methodologies that tend to indulge in big, up-front design setting the application architecture early, and making it relatively inflexible.

In the case study, redesign and reimplementation occurred at irregular intervals, usually after normal office hours, when developers modified and improved their system designs. This was advantageous because it encouraged developers to improve their system designs. It was a manual process of noticing the need for improvements, removal of duplication, and making adjustments.

4.7 Pair Programming

Pair programming was used for certain types of problem solutions or to help another developer learn a certain procedure or gain an understanding of some part of the system. Given that the developers often worked outside normal office hours or away from the office, the continual use of pair programming was not practical for this project. The developers had no prior experience of pair programming but the team was relatively cohesive, so the concept had some acceptance.

> *N1: A lot of the time we did operate this way but there were many times when we worked alone.*

Traditional methodologies do not support this type of productive exchange and review of coding, and the nearest process is that of code walkthroughs, a form of quality assurance. Unfortunately, walkthroughs only identify problems after the code has been developed, and are typically abandoned as soon as schedules become tight. Furthermore, there is no risk management explicit in traditional methodologies to defray the exposure to the loss of key technical staff. One problem noted, however, was determination of appropriate remuneration for the efforts of the various participants in the project where this practice was used.

4.8 Collective Code Ownership

The inherent characteristics of the object-oriented (OO) software development methodology facilitates code sharing and component reuse, and as the OO paradigm becomes more pervasive the need for such mutual cooperation should become even more compelling.

In the case study, all developers were free to work on all code and were encouraged to do so. Any code may be changed provided it is done by pairs of developers, complying with coding standards and subject to a satisfactory run of all tests. This assisted in building the expertise of all involved in the project and was a particularly successful aspect of the project from the developers' perspectives.

4.9 Continuous Integration

Within the development environment of the case study, the integration of new code into the project was a natural process with system builds and all automated unit tests conducted every time code was checked into the source repository. A batch system controlled the build process, including compilation and testing, and notified the developers, by e-mail, if errors occurred.

While some initial effort was required by the development team to create an environment supportive of this XP practice, the view taken was that, once established, it would form the basis for other systems and make maintenance much simpler.

4.10 Sustainable Pace (was 40-Hour Week)

To avoid burnout so common in the IT industry, developers are restricted to about 40 hours of work per week. This also improves the accuracy of time and resource estimates for the development effort required.

The developers in the case study did not comply with this practice. The developers worked as and when they saw fit and certainly did not adhere to a 40-hour week work regime. This is not unusual in such projects.

4.11 Whole Team (was On-Site Customer)

Customer availability in an XP project gives developers continuous access, thereby lessening the need for extensive requirements documents. They can ask the customer about functionality, test cases, interfaces, etc. at any time.

> N2: ...*our close contact with most clients requires a certain degree of structured feedback and our version of XP helped us in this regard.*

An on-site customer was available in the case study project, at least during normal office hours. This represents a very visible difference to the traditional methodologies where customers tend to play a background role.

4.12 Coding Standards

A coding standard was developed during the project and is used currently within the organization. It is essentially language independent but some languages, such as XML because of its case-sensitive naming conventions, dictate certain attributes.

Since code may be worked on by any programmer at any time, coding standards are essential and must be rigorous. Coding standards have also long been incorporated into projects run under traditional methodologies although the imperative for them might seem less since code ownership is usually not collective.

5   ISSUES FOR DISCUSSION AND PROJECT INSIGHTS

The project at NextEd was a success story that applied many of the core practices (see Table 1) of XP. From both customer and developer perspectives, it delivered on the requirements, limited as they were in initial detail, to produce a publishing system for documents to the Web.

Greater customer collaboration in the experience at NextEd reflected a much improved client-developer relationship in a number of aspects and a much stronger sense of developer credibility was established. The XP planning game core practice promoted good resource planning, and placed the power of decision making on functionality in the hands of the customer. The ability to monitor progress and respond to change were highly attractive characteristics of the methodology. Test-driven development, design improvement (refactoring), and continuous integration were other core practices that delivered tangible benefits, including work practices and software tools, immediately and for future projects.

On the other hand, there were challenges associated with pair programming, the implementation of which proved to be useful but problematic. While pair programming aimed to address the problem of developers working in isolation and independently from the rest of the team, there was strong resistance to the practice from certain quarters. One difficulty arising from pair programming and collective code ownership is assessing an individual's relative worth, for example, for purposes of remuneration, promotion, etc. Also, this project, in common with many other XP trials, failed to implement the system metaphor although it was recognized that such would have been useful.

6   CONCLUSIONS

There has been much debate about the type of projects that are suitable for agile methodologies. Practitioner experience suggests that they are particularly suitable for projects where requirements are more abstract and difficult to define, as in this study. It is not surprising that organizations in this situation have either not adopted or moved away from traditional approaches.

While the opinion of NextEd upper management was not sought in relation to their perception of the success of this trial project, an appropriate product was delivered and used as a prototype for their current publishing system. Any decision relating to the further use of XP at NextEd will depend on the nature of the project and the development team structure. Appropriate characteristics suggesting the suitability of XP for particular situations are still unclear. There needs to be more research that produces empirical evidence about size and type of projects suitable for XP. However, many of the practices, such as test-driven development, pair programming, and sustainable pace, are clearly suited for implementation regardless of the project characteristics. In response to the question, Do you see the adoption of extreme programming in the industry? N1 echoed Tom DeMarco's sentiment: *"I can in my career."* Since the completion of this project, members of the development team have participated in local meetings of software developers explaining the role XP played in this and other projects on which they are engaged. A more detailed study, reported in Toleman et al. (2004), aligns diffusion theory (Rogers 1995) and adoption models (Riemenschneider et al. 2002) with an explanation of the acceptance of XP.

When examining any aspect of the software development process, anything other than actual experience is at best intelligent conjecture. Indeed, while there has been a great deal of interest and support from the developer ranks, the IS teaching and research community appears to have been a little slow to embrace this new direction in software development methodologies. Our current research includes experiments involving the use or otherwise of XP, further case studies of several groups, and projects implementing agile methods. This research is also informing our teaching curriculum and practice.

ACKNOWLEDGMENTS

We wish to thank our colleagues from NextEd who gave freely of their time in helping us understand the potential role of an agile method such as XP.

REFERENCES

Barnett, L. "IT Trends 2003: Application Development Methodologies and Processes," *IdeaByte*, September 2002 (available online at http://www.forrester.com/Cart?addDocs= 28123; accessed November 2004).

Beck, K. *Extreme Programming Explained: Embrace Change*, Boston: Addison Wesley, 1999.

Beck, K., and Fowler, M. *Planning Extreme Programming*, Boston: Addison Wesley, 2001.

Bossi, P., and Cirillo, F. "Repo Margining System: Applying XP in the Financial Industry," in *Proceedings of the 2nd International Conference on eXtreme Processing and Agile Processing Software Engineering (XP 2001)*, Villasimius, Italy, May 2001 (available online at http://www.xp2003.org/conference/papers/Chapter35-Bossi+ alii.pdf; accessed January 7, 2005).

C3 Team. "Case Study: Chrysler Goes to 'Extremes,'" *Distributed Computing*, October 1998 (available online at http://www.xprogramming.com/publications/dc9810cs.pdf; accessed January 7, 2005).

Elssamadisy, A. "XP on a Large Project—A Developer's View," in *Proceedings of the XP Universe Conference*, Raleigh, NC, July 2001 (available online at http://www. xpuniverse.com/2001/pdfs/EP202.pdf; accessed January 7, 2005).

Fitzgerald, B. "An Empirical Investigation into the Adoption of Systems Development Methodologies," *Information and Management* (34), 1998, pp. 317-328.

Fowler, M., and Highsmith, J. "The Agile Manifesto," *Software Development*, August 2001 (available online at http://www.sdmagazine.com/documents/s=844/sdm0108a/0108a.htm; accessed November 1, 2004).

Grenning, J. "Launching Extreme Programming at a Process-Intensive Company," *IEEE Software* (18:6), November/December 2001, pp. 27-33.

Karlström, D. "Introducing Extreme Programming—An Experience Report," in *Proceedings of the 3rd International Conference on eXtreme Processing and Agile Processing Software Engineering (XP02)*, Alghero, Italy, 2002 (available online at http://www.xp2003.org/ xp2002/atti/DanielKarlstrom--Introducing ExtremeProgramming. pdf; accessed January 7, 2005).

Lappo, P. "No Pain, No XP Observations on Teaching and Mentoring Extreme Programming to University Students," Agile Aliance, 2002 (available online at http://www.agilealliance.org/ articles/articles/PeterLappo--ObservationsonTeachingandMentoringXP.pdf; accessed January 7, 2005).

Mugridge, R., MacDonald, B., Roop, P., and Tempero, E. "Five Challenges in Teaching XP," in *Proceedings if the 4th International Conference on eXtreme Processing and Agile Processing Software Engineering (XP203)*, Genova, Italy, 2003, pp. 406-409 (available online at http://www.cs.auckland.ac.nz/~rick/5ChallengesTeachingXP.pdf; accessed January 7, 2005).

Pedroso Jr., M., Visoli, M. C., and Antunes, J. F. G. "Extreme Programming by Example," in *Proceedings of the 3rd International Conference on eXtreme Processing and Agile Processing Software Engineering (XP02)*, Alghero, Italy, 2002, (available online at http://www.xp2003.org/xp2002/atti/Pedroso-Marcos--ExtremeProgrammingbyExample.pdf; accessed January 7, 2005).

Riemenschneider, C., Hardgrave, B. C., and Davis, F. D. "Explaining Software Developer Acceptance of Methodologies: A Comparison of Five Theoretical Models," *IEEE Transactions on Software Engineering* (28:12), 2002, pp. 1135-1145.

Rogers, E. *Diffusion of Innovations* (4th ed.), New York: Free Press, 1995.

Schuh, P. "Recovery, Redemption, and Extreme Programming," *IEEE Software* (18:6), November/December 2001, pp. 34-41.

Sleve, G. "Agile Before Agile was Cool," *The Journal of Defense Software Engineering* (15:10), 2002, pp. 28-29.

Toleman, M., Ally, M. A., and Darroch, F. "Aligning Adoption Theory with Agile System Development Methodologies," in *Proceedings of the 8th Pacific-Asia Conference on Information Systems*, C. P. Wei (Ed.), Shanghai, China, July 2004, pp. 458-471.

ABOUT THE AUTHORS

Mark Toleman is an associate professor of Information Systems at the University of Southern Queensland where he has taught computing subjects to engineers, scientists, and business students for 18 years. He has a Ph.D. in computer science from the University of Queensland and has published more than 60 articles in books, refereed journals and refereed conference proceedings. Mark can be reached at markt@usq.edu.au.

Fiona Darroch is a lecturer in Information Systems at the University of Southern Queensland. Her computing career has been spent mainly in industry in the areas of project management, business analysis, and applications development, with a move to academia two years ago. She is currently pursuing a research Master's degree. Fiona can be reached at darroch@usq.edu.au.

Mustafa Ally is a lecturer in Information Systems at the University of Southern Queensland where he is currently teaching Java and Visual Basic .NET. His research interests are in the field of Internet Payment Systems and he has written several papers in the area of trust and security. Mustafa can be reached at allym@usq.edu.au.

16 USING THE MISSION CRITICAL MARKET DIFFERENTIATING (MCMD) MODEL TO IMPROVE BUSINESS AND INFORMATION TECHNOLOGY AGILITY

Niel Nickolaisen
Headwaters Inc.
South Jordan, Utah U.S.A.

Abstract   *The mission critical/market differentiating (MCMD) model focuses organizational resources on processes, products, and projects that will best meet and respond to market demands. Conversely, the MCMD model can help organizations reduce resource expenditures in areas that are neither mission critical nor market differentiating.*

This model was initially designed to assure information technology solutions focused on the needs of the customer and had the greatest return on invested capital. In a broader organizational application, the MCMD model helps organizations

- *identify which activities deserve their best attention and focus (i.e., pick which battles they should be fighting)*
- *simplify and streamline their operational processes*
- *limit the scope of projects and over-building of their underlying features*

1   INTRODUCTION

Over the past several years, companies have become disenchanted with technology solutions that do not deliver business value. They have outsourced key competitive processes, launched technology projects that far exceeded their planned budgets but did not deliver expected functionality, forgone investments in off-the-shelf software, and become jaded to the newest application or hardware sales pitch. Unfortunately, this has not kept us from trying to build a better technology mouse trap that creates competitive advantages in a continually changing marketplace and that captures market share by meeting the continuous escalation of customer expectations. The problem facing many companies, therefore, is to discover a way to deliver the technology they need while not over-building or over-complicating the technology and the business activities the technology supports. If companies cannot find such a balance, they risk limiting their ability to respond to market changes.

The answer, found in the mission critical/market differentiating (MCMD) model, is that internal information technology systems need to become more focused on business priorities and be more adaptable to the changing marketplace demands. However, this is difficult if our internal, operational processes are bureaucratic and get in the way of our ability to prioritize and adapt. Also, if our focus is too diffused, we might not allocate our best thinking and resources on the activities that will differentiate us in the marketplace.

2   THE MCMD MODEL

The MCMD model is a four-quadrant diagram that classifies products, processes, and projects (and their underlying features) as either high or low for two main categories: mission critical and market differentiation.

Mission critical: The degree to which our activities and processes are essential to our ability to deliver our products and services and operate as an organization.

Market differentiating: The degree to which our activities and processes help us gain market share and enter new markets.

Figure 1 is a graphical representation of this quadrant.

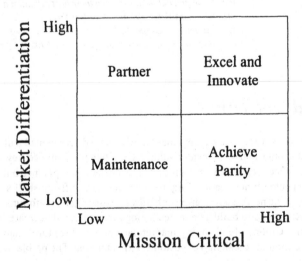

Figure 1. The MCMD Model

The quadrants are defined as

- Excel: High for both mission critical (MC) and market differentiating (MD). These are the activities that we use to gain market share, define our market value proposition, and enter new markets. Examples include product development and market and customer analysis.
- Parity: High MC, low MD. These are the bulk of our activities. We must perform these activities because they are critical to our mission or operations. If we perform these activities poorly, we do harm. Examples include customer billing and production planning.
- Partner: High MD but low MC. These are activities that do or could differentiate us in the marketplace but that we do not have to perform ourselves. Intel chips inside of Dell computers are a good example; neither would do well to try and enter the other's strategic niche, but building a partnership provides great return on investment.
- Maintenance: Low MC and low MD. These activities have no meaningful connection to our operations or our markets. Examples include office cleaning services and our user name standards. Someone may have to pay attention to these details but it is not very important to the strategic initiatives of the company.

3   THE METHODOLOGY

We start by defining the criteria we will use to segregate our activities into the four types. We then filter all of our activities through the criteria and onto the appropriate box. In some cases, activities will straddle boxes. That is all right as long as we know which activity components lay in which box. In practice, I use the model to first identify the activities that belong in the market differentiating and mission critical box. I then know that everything else falls into one of the other boxes (and most likely most fall into the mission critical but not differentiating box) and I use that information to make generalized judgments about how I will manage these activities.

After assigning our activities to their appropriate boxes, I assume that the goal or purpose of each activity is associated with its box as shown in Figure 2.

I want to ensure that I am "best-in-class" at my market differentiating and mission critical activities. These are the battles I choose to fight. I focus my best thinking, talent, and resources on these activities. I learn how to continually innovate and improve these activities and their results (I have to continually innovate and improve these activities as, over time, they move to a different box).

The goal of my mission critical but not differentiating activities is to achieve and maintain parity with the market. Doing anything more than achieving and maintaining parity with the market implies that I am over-investing in these activities (which, in addition to the poor value this provides, carries an opportunity cost: I am spending my valuable thinking, talent, and resources unnecessarily). These activities are prime candidates for simplification and standardization. In fact, I optimize my business agility the more I simplify and standardize these activities. I need to perform these activities well but I also need to ensure that they do not get in the way of my responding to the dynamics of the marketplace.

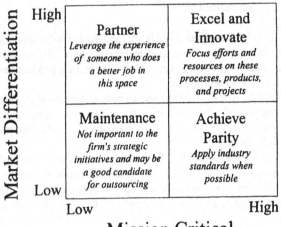

Figure 2. Aligning Activities with Goals

The differentiating but not mission critical activities give me the opportunity to partner with someone for whom these activities are differentiating and mission critical. I should exploit this opportunity as this also increases my agility.

It matters little how I handle the neither differentiating nor mission critical activities. In fact, I should invest as little thinking, talent, and resource in these activities as possible.

4   EXAMPLES AND RESULTS

4.1 Software Development

I used the MCMD model and methodology to dramatically accelerate and simplify a large software development project. The project was initially designed to build a document collaboration and management system supporting the drafting and submission of financial documents (annual reports, 10-K statements, investment memoranda, etc.). The initial technical requirements document defined over 7,000 function points, a budget of $2 million, and a development time line of 18 months. The filtering criteria were defined and the functional requirements mapped onto the MCMD. This resulted in identification of two differentiating components and 27 parity components.

A conscious choice to reuse or license existing technologies for the parity components and allocate thinking, talent, and resources on the two differentiating components was made. This resulted in a development plan of 240 function points (rather than over 7,000), a budget of $350,000 (rather than $2 million), and a time line of 4 months (rather than 18 months). Using this model not only reduced the cost and time of the project but also focused the company on the functionality that now and in the future make this a superior product.

4.2 Enterprise Software Selection and Implementation

I have also applied the MCMD model to the selection, implementation, and support of enterprise software like enterprise requirements planning systems. For most companies, ERP functionality supports mission critical but not differentiating activities (like purchasing, inventory management, financials, order management, etc.). This being the case, an ERP selection and implementation project should assume an implementation with no (i.e., zero) customizations. Customizing the business applications that support parity activities implies over-investment in these activities (as customization requires thinking, talent, and resources). In addition, customizing the business applications that support parity activities implies that these customizations will need to be revised or rebuilt in order to respond to changing market conditions.

As an example, I used the MCMD model and methodology to reduce the budget and timeline for an ERP selection and implementation project from $4.4 million and 3 years to $2.2 million and 4 months. Approaching the project this way also accelerated the company's development of its technology to support its differentiating activities. Rather than having its resources tied up for a 3-year ERP project, it was able to shift the resources much earlier to its differentiating technology.

5 USING THE MODEL AND METHODOLOGY TO IMPROVE AGILITY

I believe that in order to be adaptive to changing market conditions (many driven by advances in and the use of technology) two things must be done.

- First, fight the right battles. By this I mean allocate our thinking, talent, and resources to those activities that will improve our market position.
- Second, simplify all of our other activities. This serves us in at least two ways. First, it frees up our thinking, talent, and resources to fight the right battles. Second, it ensures that these activities will not get in the way of our ability to respond to market changes.

By using the above model and methodology, we learn how to properly allocate our thinking, talent, and resources. In addition, once we have determined that the goal of an activity is to achieve or maintain parity, we have created a context that we can use, both strategically and tactically, to simplify how we perform the activity.

As an example, I recently used this model to significantly simplify the credit-to-collections process for a wholesaler/retailer. This company had developed over 30 different types of customer accounts. We ran all of the financial management processes through the model and determined that the goal of the customer credit process was to achieve and maintain market parity. We could not find any examples where parity translated into multiple account types. Rather, because this wholesaler/retailer had two principal customer types (wholesale and retail) we collapsed the more than 30 different account types into two (one for wholesale customers and one for retail customers). Inside each of these two types of accounts, customers were either good (paid their bills and paid them on time) or bad (did not pay their bills or did not pay them on time). This simple structure allowed the wholesaler/retailer to simplify its credit department and allocate its resources to activities that could provide differentiation.

6   CAVEATS

I have used the MCMD model in multiple situations, both simple and complex. The real challenge in adopting the model is a cultural challenge. Both departments and people have a natural inclination to ensure that their business activities are classified as differentiating. Including the mission critical dimension in the model helps reduce this tendency (but does not eliminate it). Additionally, I have found that using the MCMD model to filter activities and then align resource allocation with the results of the filtering is a significant change from how resources are traditionally assigned to activities and initiatives. To pull off changes of this type and magnitude requires leadership and a solid change-management plan. The MCMD model only helps create the context for changing and simplifying activities.

7   SUMMARY

The MCMD model allows the firm to allocate its resources to products, processes, and projects in an appropriate manner. Decisions at all levels of the operation are now focused on the market and the firm's mission and the appropriate response to each level of mission criticality and market differentiating. Likewise, and perhaps even more importantly it allows a discussion within the firm about the opportunities for strategic improvements and an agile/adaptive approach to future changes.

ABOUT THE AUTHOR

Niel Nickolaisen has held technology executive (CIO) and operations executive (COO) positions in large- and medium-sized enterprises, typically in turnaround roles. He is expert in the rapid/adaptive selection, implementation, and deployment of enterprise business applications, analysis tools, and systems. He has developed a strategic and tactical alignment model that results in significantly improved returns on technology and business initiatives (by both improving the benefits and reducing the costs and risks).

Niel has in-depth knowledge of enterprise management technologies, enterprise resource planning applications, and storage management tools. He holds two patents for enterprise management tools. He is past president of the Intermountain Chapter of the Society for Information Management. He holds an M.S. in Engineering from the Massachusetts Institute of Technology and a B.S. in Physics from Utah State University. He was named IT Executive of the Year at the 2004 Gartner Research Mid-Sized Enterprise Summit.

Niel can be reached at nnickolaisen@hdwtrs.com.

Part 5

Business Agility

17 AGILITY AND INFORMATION TECHNOLOGY DIFFUSION IN THE SEMICONDUCTOR INDUSTRY

B. Donnellan
Centre for Innovation and Structural Change
National University of Ireland
Galway, Ireland

A. Kelly
Design Department
Analog Devices B.V.
Limerick, Ireland

Abstract   *New product development in the semiconductor industry is characterized by products with a high level of intellectual property content, and ever-decreasing product development cycles, designed by very scarce engineering talent. The foundation of the success of many semiconductor companies is their ability to respond quickly to turbulent market conditions. This ability is contingent on intra-organizational and interorganizational factors, which will be described in this paper. Firms are attempting to overcome these agility-related challenges by developing and deploying IT-based responses. This paper takes a practitioner perspective. The authors have a combined experience of over 35 years in the semiconductor industry.*

Keywords   Agility, IT diffusion, clockspeed, new product development, knowledge management systems

1   INTRODUCTION

The semiconductor industry is concerned with designing and manufacturing integrated circuits. Integrated circuits are the fundamental building blocks used in IT systems. Examples of integrated circuits include computer memory chips and computer processor chips. The industry has grown considerably over the last 30 years to the point where it is now constitutes over $100 billion in world-wide sales. This growth has been achieved in a very dynamic, turbulent operating environment.

To address these challenges, new product development (NPD) organizations in the semiconductor industry need to develop and maintain the ability to embrace change. Agility has become a significant factor in a firm's survival during these times of increased competition and economic uncertainty in the industry.

2   AGILITY IN THE SEMICONDUCTOR INDUSTRY

An industry's *clockspeed* is defined as a measure of the dynamic nature of that industry and depends on the nature of the products, manufacturing process turnaround times, and organization clockspeed (how quickly concepts are translated into products) (Carrilio 1999; Mendelsohn and Pillai 1999). The basis for a fast clockspeed firm's survival is the ability to move quickly from one temporary advantage to another (Fine 2000). This form of agile behavior is particularly important in the semiconductor industry, which has been characterized as having a particularly fast clockspeed (Fine 1998).

A driver of industry clockspeed in the semiconductor industry is Moore's law, an historical observation by Intel executive Gordon Moore that the market demand for functionality per chip doubles every 1.5 to 2 years. Moore's Law has been a consistent macro trend and key indicator of successful leading-edge semiconductor products and companies for the past 30 years. Given that Moore's Law drives the clockspeed of the semiconductor industry, the ability to adapt to change has become a significant factor in a firm's survival. The factors impacting such agile behavior will be described in the next section.

2.1 Agility: Interorganizational Factors

Grant (2000) and Ilvari and Linger (1999) have identified a number of interorganizational factors pervasive in knowledge-based industries such as the semiconductor industry. This section will explore the impact of these factors on a firm's agility.

2.1.1   Competing for Standards

Over the last two decades, firms have been more inclined to form collaborative projects with customers, competitors, and government agencies to achieve a standardization goal. For instance, a firm may want to work with an internationally recognized center-of-excellence in an academic institution with which it has no formal relationship. In such cases, knowledge has to be combined from participants across multiple collaborating organizations.

2.1.2   Vendor/Customer Relationships

Collaboration between semiconductor NPD vendors and their customers has increased in response to global competition and increased complexity as the semiconductor clockspeed drives technology into uncharted territory. Semiconductor companies continue to deploy technical semiconductor design expertise locally to customers throughout the world to ensure collaboration.

2.2 Agility: Intra-Organizational Factors

NPD organizations need to rapidly transfer knowledge across internal organizational boundaries, so as react quickly to either technological or commercial discontinuities. The factors at play here include virtual NPD teams and intra-organizational collaboration.

2.2.1 Virtual NPD Teams

NPD activities that span geographical boundaries have become commonplace in the semiconductor industry, as NPD has been globalized. Some of the challenges posed by distributed teams may arise from cultural differences. Culture

• shapes assumptions about which knowledge is worth managing (Sackmann 1992)

• defines relationships between individual and organizational knowledge (von Krogh and Roos 1996)

• creates the context for social interaction (Graham and Pizzo 1996)

• shapes the processes by which new knowledge is created (Hayduk 1998)

Additional challenges include differences in native language, which mitigate against the communication of technical nuances, and a scarcity of coincident working hours, caused by time-zone differences.

The response to these challenges is for the lead project personnel to spend a lot of time, upfront, documenting the project specifications and partitioning decisions. The authoring, review, and revision of such documents reduces flexibility and responsiveness, and therefore diminishes agile behavior.

2.2.2 Intra-Organizational Collaboration

Many NPD projects require cross-functional collaboration. The nature and importance of this collaboration is described by Wheelwright and Clark (1992) as follows: "Outstanding product development requires effective action from all of the major functions in the business. The firm must develop the capability to achieve integration across the functions in a timely and effective way" (p. 165).

In addition to cross-functional collaboration, semiconductor NPD organizations must collaborate between business units in order to provide responses to innovative customer needs which span traditional business unit responsibilities. This represents an agile capability to meet changing market requirements.

3   IT SUPPORT AND DIFFUSION IN THE SEMICONDUCTOR INDUSTRY

Firms have looked to IT to help develop a response to the agility challenges described in section 2. The IT response has included simulation and modeling utilities, support for knowledge sharing and peer reviews.

3.1 IT Support of Agility in Semiconductor NPD Processes

3.1.1 Modeling and Simulation

From the financial modeling made possible by spreadsheet applications to the use of yield management applications in the hotel, car-rental, and airline industries, the adoption of modeling and simulation applications in NPD has transformed industries (Schrage 1999). In the semiconductor context, modeling and simulation are core activities of the circuit design process and support agility in respect of customer interactions, communication, and collaboration. Modeling and simulation fulfills a number of functions.

- They provide the ability to verify whether the design task is successful in comparison to the desired specification. This is the role of functional simulation and verification.

- The ability to iterate quickly on the outcome of a simulation facilitates design changes in an agile market, as targets change during NPD.

- The role of rapid iteration is also an enabler of innovation, as the engineer reflects upon the outcome of a simulation, leading to insights regarding the operation of a design.

- Communication of complex ideas (e.g., the consequences of various design decisions) is enabled via third party interaction with the model.

- Peer reviews are facilitated by enabling a critique of modeling methods and simulation outcomes and a review of design specifics.

The ability of the simulation model to act as an archetype facilitates communication and collaboration, acting as a frame of reference around which differences in understanding and context can be highlighted and explored. This brings the following benefits:

- Within a global team, the challenges of virtual NPD teamwork outlined in section 2.2, such as differences in context and understanding, may be managed.

- The interorganizational factors affecting semiconductor NPD vendors and their customers, as outlined in section 2.1, are reduced as they share a common understanding of the design as it progresses during the design process.

3.1.2 High-Level Design Abstraction

A significant development in support of agility has been the move since the early 1990s, toward high-level design abstraction for digital designs. This high-level design abstraction allows designs to be described in text form, rather like software design. Akin to the "agile manifesto" in software development, continuous delivery of working designs is facilitated by a high level of automation brought to the design process by IT. Such a process allows a near-final design to be produced regularly, incorporating the latest design changes, which may then be evaluated with respect to the requirements. It is not unusual to see a new design every day in order to check consistency as the design progresses.

3.1.3 eCatalogs

Learning is a key activity in the development of a firm's ability to adapt and change. "Conventional explanations view learning as a process by which a learner internalizes the knowledge, whether 'discovered,' 'transmitted' from others, or 'experienced in interaction' with others" (Lave and Wenger 1991, p. 47). The knowledge being sought is, in fact, knowledge about knowledge or *meta-knowledge* (Kehal 2002; Swanstrom 1999). The focus of much attention in agility-related IT initiatives in the semiconductor industry is on meta-knowledge.

An eCatalog, in this context, is an application that generates a list of previously designed products in the NPD community. Such eCatalogs enable NPD staff to quickly find out if previously designed products are similar to those currently under development. Problems identified in the NPD process that are addressed by eCatalogs include

- a lack of awareness of what previously designed circuit blocks had been created and might be available for reuse in future projects

- the need to provide a mechanism by which NPD staff can easily make their products more easily "discovered" by members of the NPD organization outside of their own organization unit

The meta-knowledge embedded in eCatalogs allows the global NPD organization to leverage its knowledge assets, allowing the flexibility in product design beyond that which could be achieved by one design team. As such, eCatalogs provide a response to the intra-organizational challenge of cross-business unit collaboration.

3.1.4 NPD Design Repositories

A repository, in this context, provides a store of previously designed products that could be reused. Each of the repository's elements has an extensive support kit associated with it (i.e., contextual information about previous usage, data formats compatible with existing NPD systems, validation data, interface information, etc.). The goal of such repositories is to provide a library of robust and supported reusable circuit designs available for download, obtained from both internal and external sources. They contain previously designed products packaged in a format suitable for delivery as intellectual property to either internal groups or external groups (or both). Their purpose corresponds, generally, to what Hansen et al. (1999) termed a *codification* strategy where the value of the repository lies in connecting people with reusable codified knowledge or to what Swan et al. (1999) termed a *cognitive* strategy where the primary function of the repository is to codify and capture knowledge so that the knowledge can be recycled.

Like eCatalogs, design repositories facilitate the leverage of information processing (IP) across the organization, providing a response to collaborative challenges. However, in contrast to eCatalogs, design repositories require a significant up-front investment in preparation of the support kit associated with each piece of IP.

3.1.5 Peer Reviews

Peer reviews are an integral part of an NPD process, and have been characterized as a justification activity following the creation of an archetype (Nonaka and Takeuchi 1995). In this context, an archetype may be thought of as a prototype, which may be in the form of a model. The peer review activity facilitates the justification of design decisions and the design and verification activity (Bergquist et al. 2001). In this way, the knowledge of a group of designers may be brought to bear on the design.

The medium for the peer review is the model and associated simulation results. During the peer review process, the model and the simulations may be scrutinized for validity and applicability to the design context. The peer review supports agility by enabling the designer to externalize and illustrate the design outcomes, allowing collective experience to be brought to bear in validating the design. A successful peer review process will reduce or eliminate unplanned design iterations which cost lost time-to-market and associated opportunities.

3.2 Diffusion of IT Support of Agility in the Semiconductor NPD Process

This section examines the extent to which the systems described previously have been diffused throughout the industry.

3.1.1 Modeling, Simulation, and High-Level Design Abstraction

Throughout the last two decades, the leading firms in this industry have been pioneers in the development of modeling, simulation, and high-level design tools for in-house use by their own design teams. There is little doubt that the availability of advanced technology in this area has been an advantage to these companies. Today the complexity of the design tasks needed for consumer applications, such as mobile devices and gaming technology at an affordable price, has reduced the ability of even the largest companies to develop their own IT for simulation, modeling, and high-level design.

With over 100 significant IT product offerings in this space, and annual revenues of the top two software vendors in this area of $2.4 billion in fiscal year 2003, there is extensive diffusion of these tools throughout the semiconductor industry.

3.2.2 eCatalogs and Design Repositories

As a response to the agility challenges of turbulent markets and product complexity, eCatalogs and design repositories have seeded a flurry of IT development activity in semiconductor design companies over the past decade. Based upon the objectives of intellectual property packaging and distribution on the one hand, and enabling collaboration between experts on the other, the aim is to increase agility in the NPD process.

Design repositories require engineering staff whose role is to make the design IP flexible and applicable to a variety of situations. This involves parameterization of the design and implementation of standard interfaces. For example, certain processor cores have achieved a high degree of standardization, fueled by their application in mobile products. The interfaces and programming language of these cores have become accepted industry wide and, as such, the up-front preparatory work of the design repository engineering staff can be leveraged into new projects. Therefore, repositories have been successful in regard to this "digital IP." They have been less successful for "analog IP," which tends to be less standardized.

eCatalogs support the communication and collaboration required for all IP types, but have been more applicable to analog IP because of the difficulty in standardizing. No matter how well packaged the IP is, however, the experience is that some communication between the IP user and the original developer is always required, which goes against the intention of the design repository as a source of reusable codified knowledge.

It takes time and effort to document the IP for cataloging and to prepare designs for a repository; issues such as motivation, reward, and group culture have mitigated against the wholesale diffusion of these applications.

4 CONCLUSIONS

This paper has given practitioners' perspectives on agility and IT diffusion in the semiconductor industry. Forces impacting agility in the industry were described. Inter-organizational factors include vendor/customer collaboration, management, and standardization efforts. Intra-organizational factors include globally distributed teams and intra-organizational collaboration. IT-based approaches to supporting agility were described, including modeling, simulation, and high level design utilities, eCatalogs, and design repositories. Observations were made on the extent to which these systems have successfully diffused throughout the industry. Modeling, simulation and high-level design utilities were seen to be central to the semiconductor NPD process, and therefore widely diffused, supporting agility by providing the capability to continuously integrate design changes. Additionally, models were seen to act as an archetype, which provides a response to the agility challenges described. The successful diffusion of eCatalogs and design repositories were seen to be mixed. Design repositories were successfully diffused for digital IP, which suits standardization and can be leveraged over time. The difficulty in standardizing analog IP made it less applicable to repositories and more applicable to eCatalogs, which provide meta-knowledge regarding the design and its developer.

REFERENCES

Bergquist, M., Ljungberg, J., and Lundh-Snis, U. "Practicing Peer Review in Organizations: A Qualifier for Knowledge Dissemination and Legitimization," *Journal of Information Technology* (16), 2001, pp. 99-112.

Carrilio, J. "Industry Clockspeed and Dynamics: Appropriate Pacing of New Product Development," Working Paper, Washington University, St. Louis, MO, 1999.

Fine, C. *Clockspeed: Winning Industry Control in the Age of Temporary Advantage*, Reading, MA: Perseus Books, 1998.

Fine, C. "Clockspeed-Based Strategies for Supply Chain Design," *International Journal of Operations Management* (9:3), 2000, pp. 312-221.

Graham, A. B., and Pizzo, V. G. "A Question of Balance: Case Studies in Strategic Knowledge Management," *European Management Journal* (14:4), 1996, pp. 338-346.

Grant, R. "Shifts in the World Economy: The Drivers of Knowledge Management," in *Knowledge Horizons: The Present and the Promise of Knowledge Management*, C. Despres and D. Chauvel (Eds.), Boston: Butterworth-Heinemann, 2000, pp. 27-55.

Hansen, M., Nohria, N., and Tieney, T. "What's Your Strategy for Managing Knowledge?," *Harvard Business Review*, March-April 1999, pp. 106-116.

Hayduk, H. "Organizational Culture Barriers to Knowledge Management," in *Proceedings of the Fourth Americas Conference on Information Systems*, E. D. Hoadley and I. Benbasat (Eds.), Baltimore, MD, 1998, pp. 591-593.

Iivari, J., and Linger, H. "Knowledge Work as Collaborative Work: A Situated Activity Theory View," in *Proceedings of the 32nd Hawaii International Conference on System Sciences*, Los Alamitos, CA: IEEE Computer Society Press, 1999.

Kehal, M. "Searching for an Effective Knowledge Management Framework," *Journal of Knowledge Management Practice*, February 2000.

Lave, J., and Wenger, E. *Situated Learning: Legitimate Peripheral Participation*, Cambridge, England: Cambridge University Press, 1991..

Mendelsohn, H., and Pillai, R. R. "Industry Clockspeed: Measurement and Operational Implications," *Manufacturing & Service Operations Management* (1:1), 1999, pp. 1-20.

Nonaka, I., and Takeuchi, H. *The Knowledge-Creating Company*, Oxford: Oxford University Press, 1995.

Sackmann, S. A. "Cultures and Subcultures: An Analysis of Organizational Knowledge," *Administrative Science Quarterly* (37:1), 1992, pp. 140-161.

Schrage, M. *Serious Play: How the World's Best Companies Simulate to Innovate*, Boston: Harvard Business School, 1999.

Swan, J., Newell, S., Scarborough, H., and Hislop, D. "Knowledge Management and Innovation: Networks and Networking," *Journal of Knowledge Management* (3:3), 1999, pp. 262-275.

Swanstrom, E. "MetaKnowledge and MetaKnowledgebases," in *The Knowledge Management Handbook*, J. Liebowitz (Ed.), London: CRC Press, 1999.

Von Krogh, G. , and Roos, J. (Eds.). *Managing Knowledge: Perspectives on Cooperation and Competition*, London: Sage Publications, 1996.

Wheelwright, S., and Clark, K. *Revolutionizing Product Development*, New York: Simon and Schuster Inc., 1992.

ABOUT THE AUTHORS

Brian Donnellan is a lecturer in Information Systems at the National University of Ireland, Galway, Ireland. He was formerly employed in the Design Department at Analog Devices B.V., Limerick, Ireland. Brian can be reached at brian.donnellan@nuigalway.ie.

Anthony Kelly is an integrated circuit design engineer, with 15 years experience in various design engineering and management roles. He holds an MBA and B.Eng. from the University of Limerick, Ireland, and is currently undertaking a Ph.D. by research. Anthony can be reached at anthony-L.kelly@analog.com.

18 ASSESSING BUSINESS AGILITY: A Multi-Industry Study in The Netherlands

Marcel van Oosterhout
Eric Waarts
Jos van Hillegersberg
RSM Erasmus University
The Netherlands

Abstract   *This study reports on a cross-industry analysis of the current drivers for agility and agility gaps, which companies are facing in four industry sectors in the Netherlands. A framework was constructed to measure the gaps between the current level of business agility and the required level of business agility. The questionnaire and in-depth interviews reveal that today's businesses lack the agility required to quickly respond to largely unanticipated changes. The paper presents rankings of generic and sector-specific agility gaps. These show that although some generic drivers exist, key drivers are very different across industry sectors.*

1 INTRODUCTION

1.1 Background

It has been stated (Preiss et al. 1996) that the current highly dynamic business environment increasingly requires businesses to adjust and act swiftly, in other word to be *agile*. As a result, the concept of *agility* receives growing attention. Numerous books and articles have appeared that attempt to define business agility. Academic literature and the professional press have discussed the topic by reporting on recent unexpected threats to businesses such as terrorism, unanticipated regulations, or sudden market changes, and how agility can help to overcome these. Several consultancies and ICT vendors have made helping organizations to achieve agility their key business strategy (e.g., IBM's "On-Demand" strategy and HP's "Adaptive Enterprise" strategy). They provide a variety of organizational and technical solutions that should help to achieve the proper level of agility to handle unexpected waves of change.

However, as was clearly shown in a panel discussion on the agile enterprise at the recent CIO Summit at Massachusetts Institute of Technology (Schrage 2004), there is by far no consensus as to what exactly agility is, nor on how one could achieve agility. Very few studies have attempted to empirically study the need for agility. What are factors that drive the need and what is the relative importance of these factors? Moreover, research that assesses the current level of agility is scarce. The few studies we have identified with this aim are usually limited in their sector focus (usually manufacturing) and research method (usually only a questionnaire or single case study). This paper aims to resolve the current confusion about business agility, to develop a framework for analyzing agility, and to apply and test the framework in four important business sectors (mobile telecom, finance, utilities and logistics) by using a comprehensive multiple method approach for data collection (multiple surveys and in-depth interviews).

1.2 Research Questions and Approach

The overall research question of this paper is: *What are the key internal and external drivers where business lacks the necessary level of agility?*

To address this question, we will subsequently investigate the following sub-questions:

- *What is agility and how is it different from the traditional concept of flexibility?*
- *What are the internal and external drivers that may require agility?*
- *For which drivers does today's business lack the required agility?*
- *What are the enablers that can provide agility?*

Our approach is to first develop a definition of business agility (section 2). Based on the literature, we develop a conceptual model on drivers, enablers, and gaps for business agility (section 3). We selected a combination of quantitative (survey) and qualitative (interview) research methods to analyze the constructs in the framework (section 4). Based on this data, the key drivers for business agility and the main agility gaps are determined (section 5). Next, using qualitative data collected in interviews, we explore the enablers, disablers, and best practices for creating agility in the organization and business network (section 6). Finally we explore main conclusions, limitations and future research directions (section 7).

2   WHAT IS AGILITY?

2.1 Definition of Agility

Even though much has been said and written on the subject, a consensus on a definition of agility has not yet emerged. First, the key commonalities and differences in concepts and definitions will be discussed; subsequently a definition for this study will be formulated. The Agility Forum distinguishes four strategic dimensions: enriching customers, cooperating to compete, leveraging resources, and mastering change for defining business agility. These terms often reappear in definitions proposed by others. It is seen as the way to cope with the competition, business practices, and corporate structures of the 21st century. Companies must be proactive and must view change as normal and as an opportunity.

Definitions of Business Agility

The ability of an organization to thrive in a continuously changing, unpredictable business environment (Dove 2001)

The ability of an enterprise to develop and exploit its inter- and intra-organizational capabilities (Hooper et al. 2001)

Agility is primarily concerned with the ability of enterprises to cope with unexpected changes, to survive unprecedented threats from the business environment, and to take advantage of changes as opportunities (Sharifi and Zhang 2000)

Agility is considered as being able to deal with changes that are, to a large extent, unpredictable, while the response is more innovative (Whadhwa and Roa 2003)

Agility is the successful exploration of competitive bases (speed, flexibility, innovation pro-activity, quality, and profitability) through the integration of reconfigurable resources, and best practices in a knowledge-rich environment to provide customer-driven products and services in a fast changing market environment (Ramasesh et al. 2001)

Agility is the ability to thrive in a competitive environment of continuous and unanticipated change and to respond quickly to rapidly changing, fragmenting global markets that are served by networked competitors with routine access to a worldwide production system and are driven by demand for high-quality, high-performance, low-cost, customer-configured products and services (Goldman et al. 1995)

From the definitions in the box, some general aspects do come forward. Agility is a way to cope with (to a large extent) unforeseen changes. Furthermore, how a company can deal with changes is important: is it able to respond in a timely manner and with ease? Response is innovative rather than pre-engineered. Moreover, it is important to note that agility is relevant on two different levels: the enterprise level and the business network level. These two levels naturally interact. When the network around a company is agile, it will require the company to be agile too. Second, when the network is agile,

Part 5: Business Agility

it will facilitate the enterprise to be agile. In a situation where the enterprise is the only agile link in the network, this will often inhibit the company from reacting appropriately.

2.2 Flexibility Versus Agility

Dealing with change has always been an important issue in organizations. In areas where change is predictable and the response required can be largely predetermined, organizations need to be flexible. To a large degree, flexibility can be engineered into the organization's processes and IT systems. Changing the parameters in a traditional ERP-package to accommodate for the occurrence of a predictable change is a good example of this. In other cases, changes can arise unexpectedly and the required response is more difficult to predetermine. In such cases, flexibility cannot easily be engineered into the organizational processes and systems. Being able to react quickly to such changes requires a new level of flexibility, which we refer to as *agility*. This is in line with common definitions of agility.

Taking all of these considerations into account, we define *agility* in this study as follows:

Business agility is being able to swiftly and easily change businesses and business processes outside the normal level of flexibility to effectively deal with highly unpredictable external and internal changes

If businesses find it difficult to cope with major changes, which go beyond their normal level of flexibility, they are faced with an *agility gap*. The two terms and the way we analyze them in this study are presented in Figure 1.

3   CONCEPTUAL FRAMEWORK

In this section, the conceptual framework and underlying elements are explained.

3.1 Framework Introduction

Building on the work by Sharifi and Zhang (1999), we constructed a framework to analyze business agility in detail (see Figure 2). Factors that are taken into account are the general external environment factors (politics, economics, society, and technology) and the four key agility dimensions (Goldman et al. 1991): cooperating to enhance competitiveness, enriching the customer, mastering change and uncertainty, and leveraging the impact of people and information. In addition, in line with Mason-Jones and Towill (1999), Van Hoek et al. (2001), and Yusuf et al. (2004), we explicitly regard companies not as isolated entities but as part of a business network that affects the level of agility of the individual company. A business network-wide strategy to cope with turbulence in the business environment is considered eminent for all parties in the network. Therefore, we have added the business network dimension to the original model of Sharifi and Zhang (1999).

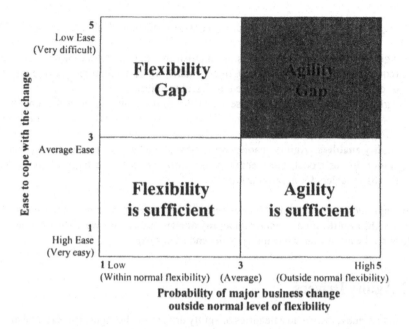

Figure 1. Flexibility Versus Agility

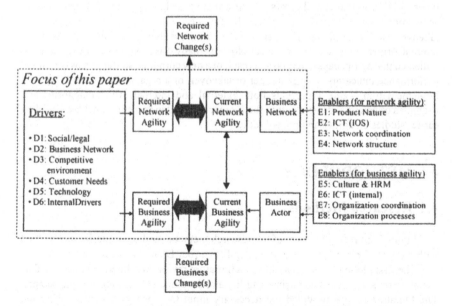

Figure 2. Research Model for Studying Business and Network Agility

Figure 2 shows our research model. It consists of three interrelated elements.

- **Agility drivers**: Agility drivers are internal or external factors influencing the required level of business agility. In our model, we have identified six categories of drivers. Agility drivers require businesses to adjust.
- **Agility gaps**: Agility gaps arise when the firm has difficulty in meeting the required level of agility for changing from one state to another in a timely and cost effective manner.
- **Agility enablers**: Agility enablers are a means for a business to enhance business agility. In our model, these enablers are presented in four categories. We also identify enablers for *network agility*.

Although our empirical study encompasses all three elements, in this paper we will focus on the identification of important **agility drivers** and **agility gaps**. We will briefly reflect on the means to enable agility at the end of this paper.

3.2 Agility Drivers

In this study, two broad categories of agility drivers are distinguished, external and internal agility drivers. External agility drivers are grouped in the following domains of external change: social or legal, business network, the competitive environment, changes in customer needs, and technology. The internal agility drivers consist of three types: (1) performance indicators, (2) information technology, and (3) mergers and acquisitions. Internal drivers are internally initiated changes (e.g., a new strategy, a takeover, etc.) that require the organization to adapt. Although initially unpredictable internal drivers may sound like a paradox, in many cases large corporations have indicated that agility gaps emerged as a result of a new corporate strategy, newly defined performance indicators, a large merger or takeover, or a organization-wide IT system implementation. Table 1 presents both external and internal driver categories and examples of potential drivers within the categories, used in this study. All are based on earlier studies on agility and related topics.

4   METHODOLOGY

4.1 Research Methods

Figure 3 gives an overview of the research methods (and their interrelations) used within our research project on business agility in four Dutch business sectors.

The first phase in this research was a literature review and Internet research. This literature review focused on business agility and developments in four selected sectors. The literature review provided the necessary input to construct a survey. We used feedback from experts and two workshops to test and improve the survey.

Table 1. Overview of Potential External and Internal Agility Drivers

Driver Category	Examples of drivers	Related literature references
D1 Social/legal	• Deregulation • Legal/political pressures • Social contract changes • Environmental changes and emergencies/disasters	D'Aveni 1999 Gartner Research 2003 Sharifi and Zhang 1999 Kaptein and Wempe 2002
D2 Business Network	• Mergers • Takeovers • Consolidations • Partnerships	Best 2001 Porter 1980 Van Weele 2001
D3 Competitive Environment	• Increasing pressure on cost • Responsiveness of competitors to changes • Increasing rate of change in product models and product lifetime shrinkage • Threat of entry of new players	Goldman et al. 1995 Porter 1980 Sharifi and Zhang 1999 Swafford 2003 Volberda 1999
D4 Customer Needs	• Demand for customized products and services • Need for quicker delivery time and time to market • Increasing expectation of quality • Sudden changes in order quantity and specification • Shifts in customer tastes	Da Silveira et al. 2001 Goldman et al. 1995 Maskell 2001 Robben and Overstraeten 1999 Sharifi and Zhang 1999 Swafford 2003
D5 Technology	• Introduction of wireless connectivity • Emerging technologies to easily connect to partners' information systems (applications integration/middleware/messaging) • Increasing number of viruses	Gartner Research 2003 Swafford 2003 Vervest and Dunn 2000
D6 Internal	• Changes in customer loyalty and other performance indicators • Information technology implementation • Mergers and acquisitions	Gartner Research 2003

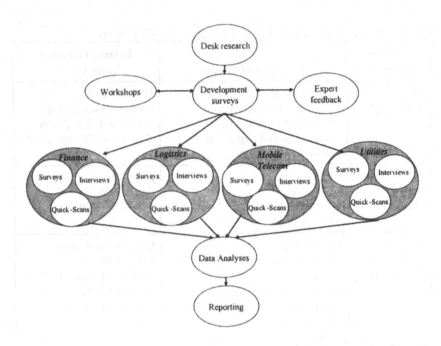

Figure 3. Research Setup

We focused on four sectors for collecting empirical data (see section 4.3). We have chosen different methods of data gathering in order to provide a rich picture on the topic. We have gathered quantitative data via online surveys. This was complemented with in-depth qualitative data, gathered via interviews with executives and via workshops. The results were validated by interviews with sector experts and a (shorter) quick-scan survey among managers.

4.2 Questionnaire

We constructed a questionnaire containing 99 items in four parts covering the various elements of our research framework. A copy of the full questionnaire can be obtained from the researchers. The survey was hosted on a Web site in order to get a quick response. The digital output of the surveys was directly read into a database. Parts B (65 items over five subparts) and C (34 items over three subparts) of the survey were built up dynamically. In part B, various agility drivers were presented to the respondent. To establish whether a driver demands a company to change in the near future, each suggested driver in the survey had to be scored on a five-point Likert scale. If the "probability of major business change outside the normal level of flexibility" due to a certain driver was high (score 4 or 5), a second question was posed regarding the "ease to cope with the required business change" in the business network (also on a five-point

Likert scale). If this question was answered with "very difficult" (score 4 or 5), this driver creates an agility gap (see Figure 1). In the final part of the questionnaire, part D, for the top 10 agility gaps, open questions were generated. For each agility gap, the respondent was asked to elaborate on the bottleneck(s) and measures taken with regard to the agility gap. In this way, the questionnaire generated both quantitative data on the agility gaps as well as qualitative data on agility bottlenecks and enablers.

4.3 Selection of the Sectors Analyzed

We have chosen not to perform a broad random survey among businesses in all kinds of sectors, but to focus on a limited set of business sectors. With this approach, we can get deeper insight into the factors determining change and the difficulties firms have coping with these changes. In particular, we have analyzed four sectors in the Dutch business community, each of which can be considered to be changing rapidly:

* Logistics (logistics service providers)
* Finance (retail banking)
* Utilities (distribution and sales of energy)
* Mobile telecom (mobile telecom operators)

We have chosen these four highly dynamic business sectors because they constitute an important segment of the total Dutch business community and they are confronted with a wide variety of internal and external drivers of change.

4.4 Data Gathering and Research Sample

For the interviews with executives within each sector, a sample of companies was selected. Criteria to select companies were their position in the market (top market share players, considerable size) and a number of new players were interviewed. Within each company, at least two executives were asked to fill out the survey as a basis for the in-depth interviews, which were held with at least two executives. One interview was held to cover the marketing perspective of business agility (mainly with CEOs and Marketing executives) and one to cover the operations and ICT perspective (mainly with COOs, CIOs, and CTOs). The average duration of the interview was 90 to 120 minutes. The basis for the interviews was the agility gaps found in the survey and the main agility issues found in the sector research. From each interview, minutes were taken and checked for accuracy with the interviewee. Table 2 provides an overview of the research sample for the case studies.

As a validation of the results found in the surveys and interviews and to gather data from more respondents within the four sectors, a shorter, quick-scan version of the survey was sent to a random sample of company contacts in different market segments (see Table 3).

We have used SPSS to analyze the quantitative data and we have organized expert sessions to extrapolate overall findings.

Table 2. Research Sample Case Studies

Sectors	Finance	Mobile Telecom	Logistic Service Providers	Utilities (Energy)	Total
Number of companies participated in interviews	7	4	6	4	21
Number of respondents filling out full surveys	10	11	8	8	37
Number of interviews with executives	13	8	9	6	36
Expert interviews	3	3	3	2	11

Table 3. Research Sample Quick-Scan Surveys

Sectors	Quick-Scan Respondents
Finance	67
Mobile Telecom	17
Logistic Service Providers	12
Utilities (energy)	6
Other: Industry	12
Government	25
Consumer Packaged Goods	6
ICT	12
Various	24
Total	**181**

4.5 Analyzing the Urgency of Agility Gaps: The Agility Gap Ratio

In order to analyze the urgency of the various agility drivers, an agility gap ratio was calculated from the survey results. Drivers that have a high probability of change (score 4 or 5) and a low ease of coping (score 4 or 5) create an agility gap. In order to analyze the urgency of the various gaps, we calculated an agility gap ratio by using the following formula:

$$AgilityGap\ Ratio_{\,i} = \left[4 * \left\{ \frac{\displaystyle\sum_{j=1}^{m} \left(\frac{\displaystyle\sum_{k=1}^{l} p_{ijk}}{l} \right)}{m} \right\} \cdot \left\{ \frac{\displaystyle\sum_{q=1}^{l} \left(\frac{\displaystyle\sum_{r=1}^{s} e_{iqr}}{s} \right)}{t} \right\} \right] \%$$

with the following meanings:

p_{ijk} The probability of business change, as indicated by respondent k , from company j, referring to driver i (only non-blank answers have been taken into consideration)

e_{iqr} The degree of ease to achieve business change, as indicated by respondent r, from company q, referring to driver i (only non-blank answers have been taken into consideration)

i   The agility driver concerned

j   The company of the respondent who responded to the survey

k   The individual respondent from company j

l   The number of respondents from company j

m   The number of responding companies

q   The company of the respondent who responded to the survey with one or more individual respondent scoring p_{ijk} (the probability of business change on driver i) with a high score of 4 or 5 (only if the probability of business change scored 4 or 5 a question was posed to the respondent about the ease to cope with this business change)

r   The individual respondent from company q scoring p_{ijk} (the probability of business change on driver i) with a high score of 4 or 5

s   The number of respondents from company q scoring p_{ijk} (the probability of business change on driver i) with a high score of 4 or 5

t   The number of responding companies with an individual respondent scoring p_{ijk} (the probability of business change on driver i) with a high score of 4 or 5 (only if the probability of business change scored 4 or 5 a question was posed to the respondent about the ease to cope with this business change) (in case of a high agility gap ratio m = s)

The agility gap ratio has been scaled to a number between 0 percent (no gap at all) and 100 percent (largest gap possible). The higher the percentage, the more urgent the agility gap.

5   FINDINGS

We will focus our findings on the assessment of the drivers and gaps. The results of the study reveal a number of drivers that generate *generic* agility gaps, present in all sectors under study, and a number of *sector* specific gaps.

5.1 Generic Agility Drivers and Gaps

We have identified agility gaps that are generic (i.e. gaps that are present in all four sectors). The top 15 generic agility gaps (with their respective driver category number) based on their average agility gap ratio are shown in Figure 4. The values represent the average gap ratio per change driver over the four sectors analyzed.

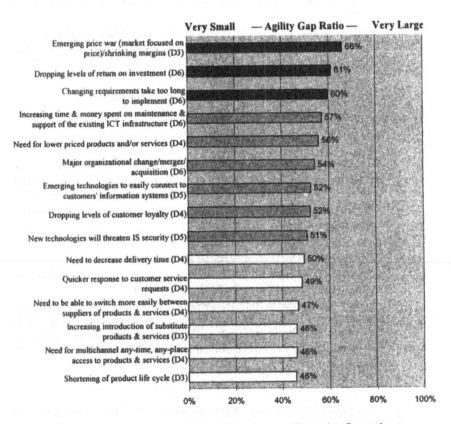

Figure 4. Overall Agility Gap Top 15 (Source: Executive Survey)

The emerging price war and the need for lower-price products and services are influencing all sectors analyzed. Companies have a number of difficulties coping with the required changes. Lowering the price requires another way of working and influences the way companies are structured and operate. The top 15 generic agility gaps also indicate that most problems are found in the implementation of the (resulting) changing requirements in the respondent's own organization and in the business network. To a large degree, this can be explained by the existing legacy infrastructures (where increasingly more time and money are spent for maintenance and support). Figure 4 also indicates that the need for agility is not just created by unpredictable changes in the outside world. A lot of internal changes (such as mergers and acquisitions and changes in systems and procedures) require organizations to become more agile as well (four out of six drivers in the top six are internal drivers, category D6).

5.2 Sector-Specific Agility Drivers and Gaps

When we look at the individual sectors, we see a lot of differences and variety.

The first observation in the finance sector (Figure 5) is the fact that the price war is not the most dominant agility driver in this sector. The financial sector has to deal urgently with several high-impact regulations. Another gap occurs in meeting the need for multichannel access. These gaps seem very much related to other gaps in the upper zones. The new regulatory and multichannel demands put pressure on the huge legacy systems base. Attempts to handle these requirements increase costs. The apparent solution to outsource resources and personnel is complex and creates more gaps in dealing with this radical change in the organization.

The logistics sector (Figure 6) is confronted with a high number of high-urgency agility gaps. Due to fierce competition in the commodity services, prices are under pressure. The consolidation trend has resulted in a large number of mergers and acquisitions. Economies of scale have been achieved, but it is often a patchwork of IT and orga-

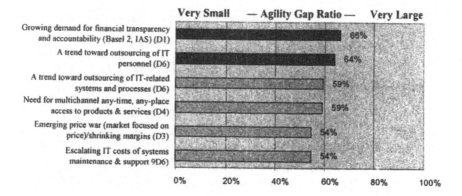

Figure 5. Overview of Most Urgent Agility Gaps for Finance Sector

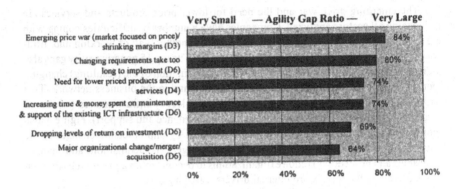

Figure 6. Overview of Most-Urgent Agility Gaps for Logistics Sector

nizational architectures. As a result of the outsourcing trend, logistics service providers have often inherited customers' logistics systems, or have to integrate tightly to those systems. Finally, the need for chain-wide tracking and tracing also requires integration to partners' information systems. Jointly, these developments have resulted in complex and heterogeneous IT architectures that need to be maintained and changed. As a result, new products, services, and regulations require substantial resources in order to be implemented. Note that the gaps related to price pressure and systems integration and adaptation are severe (> 70%).

The main gaps for the mobile telecom sector (Figure 7) seem to originate from the intensified competition. New services have resulted in customized products and services that need to be put on the market in ever-shorter time. The core systems to handle this variety of products cannot be adjusted quickly enough to implement the new requirements. Note that the gaps are not very severe (< 70%) and that potentially disruptive innovations such as wireless (WIFI) and IP telephony are only causing moderate gaps. It seems that the mobile telecom sector has, over time, developed best practices to cope with the rapid technological change.

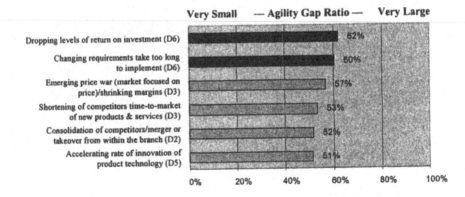

Figure 7. Overview of Most-Urgent Agility Gaps for Mobile Telecom Sector

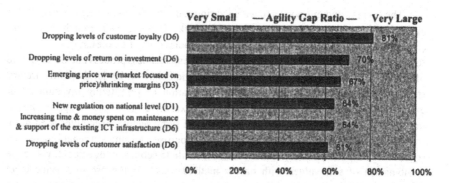

Figure 8. Overview of Most-Urgent Agility Gaps for Utilities (Energy) Sector

The utilities sector (Figure 8) is confronted with a high number of high-urgency agility gaps. These are a result of the new regulations that enforced the open market. Although this did not come as a surprise, still the impact may have been underestimated. The new phenomenon of having to worry about dropping levels of customer loyalty and customer satisfaction and a potential price war did create large gaps. IT infrastructures were never designed for processes needed in an open market. Organizational culture was more directed toward product quality than customer service.

6   QUALITATIVE FINDINGS ON ENABLERS OF AGILITY

Although the main focus of this paper is on the analyses of drivers and gaps for agility in four business sectors in the Netherlands, we briefly want to discuss some preliminary results of our analyses of enablers of business agility. This analysis is based on the interviews we did with executives and remarks given by respondents to the questionnaire.

What are the best practices within the four sectors in creating agility in their organization and business network? Since perceived agility needs are substantially different across the sectors, a sector-specific approach is needed in order to achieve the necessary level of business agility within sector companies. There will not be a single solution for companies to become more agile.

There are various methods to make changes in the way organizations and networks are organized. In the 1990s, the concept of business process redesign (Hammer and Champy 1993) gained popularity among managers as an approach for IT-enabled organizational change. In practice, BPR has had conflicting results. Many BPR projects failed due to poor change management, the focus on short-term gains, and the lack of attention for individuals (Attaran 2004). BPR can be used as one of the methods to make companies more agile, but other enablers, such as culture and attention to human resources management, should also be taken into account.

The surveys and interviews revealed various best practices and enablers in creating agility in the organization and business network. These ranged from ICT, culture (change-oriented, customer-oriented), human resources (i.e., flexible employability, job rotation, cross-functional teams, new competencies), business process outsourcing, and off-shoring. Current costing systems assume static behavior. Under dynamic circumstances, they can give a very erroneous indication of prioritizing investments or expenses, which can hinder the level of agility. Executives used various approaches to improve the level of business network agility. In some sectors, executives used more soft values (such as mutual trust, shared values, expertise, and ethics) as enabling factors (e.g., in finance and utilities). Other sectors (mobile telecom and logistics) favored the combination of soft values with harder methods, such as the use of service level agreements, grading tools to audit partners, management cockpits to monitor the partner performances, etc.

Overall, executives identified culture and HRM as the key enablers for agility. Agility can be stimulated by changing reward systems, giving people room for innovation and out-of-the box thinking, and the ongoing focus on innovation and renewal. However, executives also indicated legacy problems in the area of culture and HRM which needed to be overcome (such as inherited values and ways of doing things, resistance to change, control structures, reward mechanisms).

Companies state that an agile ICT infrastructure is an important basis for business agility. With agile, one should not think of complete freedom to decentralized departments and business units to build or buy whatever system they need, nor of a rigid centralized system and inflexible IT-department. Rather, agile ICT architectures are designed for controlled change by using modern service architecture technologies and agile development processes. An agile ICT architecture is a centrally orchestrated structure based on simplification of processes and components, standardization and interoperability, scalable architectures, reusability of components, shared service centers, and flexible reconfigurable architectures. New (start-up) players in the sectors researched demonstrate the opportunities of such new ICT paradigms. Currently, due to the existence of legacy systems and a lack of standards, ICT is still felt to be a main disabler for business agility in larger organizations. Escalating IT costs of systems maintenance and support and the fact that changing requirements take too long to implement cause many companies to worry about their current ICT infrastructure. This supports the analyses of Attaran (2004, p. 595) on a number of BPR cases where "IT was the biggest barrier to rapid and radical change, because radical change required IS redesign." As stated in our definitions on flexibility versus agility, creating an agile ICT infrastructure goes beyond the engineering of flexibility by changing some parameters in an ERP package. The ICT infrastructure should be based on real-time systems with exception triggers to respond to rapid changes in customer demand and other agility drivers. Some attributes of an agile ICT infrastructure mentioned by Kruse (2002) are integrated enterprise applications using enterprise application integration, sophisticated supply chain planning and execution systems, collaborative processes and systems, seamless process automation, a fluid network of suppliers and partners, and ICT capacity sharing (e.g., on the basis of grid computing).

7 CONCLUSIONS AND RECOMMENDATIONS

7.1 Methodological Conclusions and Reflection

The overall research objective of this paper was to come up with a framework to analyze drivers for business agility and to measure the gaps between the current level of business agility and the level of business agility needed.

We found no established measurement framework for business agility available in the literature. Therefore, we have chosen to develop a new theoretical framework based on a broad review of the literature, and to take a multimethod approach while making use of structured questionnaires and interviews to cover all important aspects. In our questionnaire, we used two questions ("probability of major business change" and "ease to cope with the change") for respondents to express their most-urgent agility gaps. We used an agility gap ratio to assess the urgency of the various gaps. In our methodology, we measured the perception of the respondents with regard to gaps; we did not objectively measure gaps on the basis of objective metrics. Future research could focus on the development of a set of such metrics and actually measuring these metrics.

We analyzed enablers and disablers for business agility via interviews and qualitative free-text remarks of respondents to the questionnaires. This provided interesting qualitative insight into the enablers and barriers for achieving agility. However, we did not construct a set of measures to objectively measure whether certain items were (perceived to be) disablers or enablers for business agility.

As stated by Whadhwa and Roa (2003), the boundaries between flexibility and agility are blurred. We have made a first attempt to develop a questionnaire to indicate the importance of agility drivers. Respondents were asked about the predictability of each category of change drivers. One could argue that a stricter difference should be made between change drivers that require more flexibility versus change drivers that require more agility. On the other hand, although the probability of a change driver might be high, the predictability of necessary changes in the business in most cases is quite low. For instance, the probability of expected changes due to government regulation in the utilities sector was high, but the predictability of necessary changes in the business and organization systems and processes was rather low. Therefore, this change driver caused a high need for agility. Given the difficulty of coping with the change, this driver posed an agility gap.

7.2 Substantive Conclusions with Regard to Drivers and Gaps

What are the (main) gaps between the current level of business agility and the level of business agility needed in the four sectors? Based on the survey and interviews with executives, we have come up with the top 15 agility gaps per sector analyzed. The results show a number of gaps to be present in all four sectors. Furthermore, we found a number of variations between the four sectors analyzed. The emerging price war and the need for lower-price products and services combined with fast changing customer requests is dramatically influencing all sectors analyzed. Companies feel severe difficulties in coping with the required changes. In many cases a totally different way of organizing the company and its business network is required. Companies are very worried about the pace at which solutions can be implemented. To a large degree, this can be explained by the existing organizational structures, cultures, and legacy infrastructures. Executives in all sectors researched feel the unpredictability of government regulation and government measures forcing them to make their processes and systems more agile. Examples of such regulations are demands for more financial *transparency* and *accountability* (e.g., Basel 2, International Financial Reporting Standards, and International Accounting Standards), deregulation measures in the utilities sector, and European Union food law regulations, containing clear requirements for traceability. Especially, the lack of implementation details and timing makes it necessary to implement the required changes in a short time frame. The results also indicate that the need for agility is not just created by unpredictable changes in the outside world; often internal changes (such as mergers and acquisitions and changes in systems and procedures) cause organizations to become more agile as well. This is reflected in the relatively large number of drivers in category D6, which scores relatively high as an agility gap.

7.3 Further Research

This research was conducted in the period January 2004 to August 2004. The research focused on four business sectors in the Netherlands. In order to gain more insight into the dynamics of business agility, we have two recommendations for further research. First, we recommend extending the assessment instrument with objective measurable metrics. This would be the basis for an *agility barometer*. This instrument would indicate, on the basis of objective measurable metrics, the level of business agility within a specific company or business network. Furthermore, such a barometer would make comparisons of companies on their agility score more feasible. Besides measuring the drivers for agility, this barometer should include measures for enablers of business agility as well. A further refinement of the instrument would be a stricter distinction between the change drivers requiring more flexibility and change drivers requiring more agility based on the level of predictability of necessary changes in the business per individual change driver.

Second, we recommend broadening the scope of the current research project to other countries. We expect that cultural and geographic differences influence the need for agility and level of business agility. An international benchmark would make it possible to compare the level of business agility and the competitive position of the Dutch business community with business communities in other countries.

ACKNOWLEDGMENTS

The authors gratefully acknowledge the financial support of Hewlett Packard for funding this research. Furthermore, we thank Professors Peter Vervest and Kenneth Preiss for their comments and feedback, all of the companies for their participation, and our research assistants—Rinske

Verwaal, Roelof Valkenier, Barbara Hertogs, and Stijn van den Bout—for their support in the field research.

REFERENCES

Attaran, M. "exploring the Relationship Between Information Technology and Business Process Reengineering," *Information and Management* (41), 2004, pp. 585-596.

Best, R. J. *Market-Based Management: Strategies for Growing Customer Value and Profitability* (3rd ed.), Upper Saddle River, NJ: Prentice Hall, 2001.

D'Aveni, R. "Strategic Supremacy through Disruption and Dominance," *Sloan Management Review* (40:3), 1999, pp. 127-135.

Da Silveira, G., Borenstein, D., and Fogliatto, F. S. "Mass Customization: Literature Review and Research Directions," *International Journal of Production Economics* (72:1), 2001, pp. 1-13.

Dove, , R. *Response Ability: The Language, Structure and Culture of the Agile Enterprise*, New York: John Wiley and Sons, 2001.

Gartner Research. *Drive Enterprise Effectiveness: The 2003 CIO Agenda*, Boston: Gartner Group, 2003.

Goldman, S., Nagel, R., and Preiss, K . *Agile Competitors and Virtual Organizations*, New York: Van Nostrand Reinhold, 1995.

Goldman, S., Preiss, K., Nagel, R., and Dove, R. *21st Century Manufacturing Enterprise Strategy*, Iacocca Institute, Lehigh University, Bethlehem, PA, 1991.

Hammer, M., and Champy, J. *Reengineering the Corporation*, New York: Harper Collins, 1993.

Hooper, M. J., Steeple, D., and Winters, C. N. "Costing Customer Value: An Approach for the Agile Enterprise," International Journal of Operations and Production Management (21:5-6), 2001, pp. 630-644.

Kaptein, M., and Wempe, J. *The Balanced Company*, Oxford, England: Oxford University Press, 2002.

Knechel, W. R. *Auditing Assurance and Risk* (2nd ed.), Mason, OH: Southern Western, 2001.

Kruse, G. "IT-Enabled Lean Agility," *Control*, November 2002, pp. 19-22

Maskell, B. "The Age of Agile Manufacturing," *Supply Chain Management: An International Journal* (6:1), 2001, pp. 5-11.

Mason-Jones, R.,and Towill, D. R. "Total Cycle Time Compression and the Agile Supply Chain," *International Journal of Production Economics* (62), 1999, pp. 61-73.

Porter, M. E. *Competitive Strategy: Techniques for Analyzing Industries and Competitors*, New York: Free Press, 1980.

Preiss, K., Goldman, S. L., and Nagel, R. N. *Cooperate to Compete: Building Agile Business Relationships*, New York: Van Nostrand Reinhold, 1996.

Ramasesh, R., Kulkarni, S., and Jayakumar, M. "Agility in Manufacturing Systems: An Exploratory Modeling Framework and Simulation," *Integrated Manufacturing Systems* (12:6-7), 2001, pp. 534-548.

Robben, H., and Overstraeten, P. *Competing in Changing Markets, International Survey*, Universiteit Nyenrode, Breukelen, The Netherlands, 1999.

Schrage, M. "The Struggle to Define Agility," *CIO Magazine*, August 15, 2004 (available online at http://www.cio.com/archive/081504/schrage.html).

Sharifi, H., and Zhang, Z. "A Methodology for Achieving Agility in Manufacturing Organizations," *International Journal of Operations and Production Management* (20:4), 1999, pp. 496-513.

Sharifi, H., and Zhang, Z. "A Methodology for Achieving Agility in Manufacturing Organizations: An Introduction," *International Journal of Production Economics* (62), 1999, pp. 7-22.

Swafford, P. *Theoretical Development and Empirical Investigation of Supply Chain Agility*, Unpublished Ph.D. Dissertation, Georgia Institute of Technology, Atlanta, GA, April, 2003.

Van Hoek, R. I., Harrison, A., and Christopher, M. "Measuring Agile Capabilities in the Supply Chain," *International Journal of Operations and Production Management* (21:1-2), 2001, pp. 126-147.

Van Weele, A. J. *Purchasing and Supply Chain Management: Analysis, Planning and Practice* (3rd ed.), London: Thompson International, 2001.

Vervest, P., and Dunn, A. *How to Win Customers in the Digital World: Total Action or Fatal Inaction*, Berlin-Heidelberg: Springer-Verlag, 2000.

Volberda, H. W. *Building the Flexible Firm: How to Remain Competitive*, Oxford, England: Oxford University Press, 1999.

Wadhwa, S., and Rao, K. S. "Flexibility and Agility for Enterprise Synchronization: Knowledge and Innovation Management Towards Flexagility," *Studies in Informatics and Control* (12:2), 2003, pp. 111-128.

Yusuf, Y. Y., Gunasekaran, A., Adeleye, E. O., and Sivayoganathan, K. "Agile Supply Chain Capabilities: Determinants of Competitive Objectives," *European Journal of Operational Research* (159:2), December 2004, pp. 379-392.

ABOUT THE AUTHORS

Marcel van Oosterhout is a scientific researcher at the RSM Erasmus University. He has participated in many (inter)national research and consulting projects. His research interests include smart business networks, electronic business, and e-logistics. Marcel can be reached at moosterhout@rsm.nl.

Eric Waarts is Professor of Marketing at the RSM Erasmus University. His interests are concentrated on marketing, competitive behavior, innovation, and international marketing strategy. He has published a wide range of books and articles on these topics. Eric can be reached at ewaarts@rsm.nl.

Jos van Hillegersberg is an associate professor at the RSM Erasmus University. His research interests include (global) software development for e-business, ICT support for coordination of global teams, and ICT architectures. He has worked on many research and consulting projects. Jos can be reached at jhillegersberg@rsm.nl.

19 A FRAMEWORK FOR ENTERPRISE AGILITY AND THE ENABLING ROLE OF DIGITAL OPTIONS

Eric Overby
Emory University
Atlanta, Georgia U.S.A.

Anandhi Bharadwaj
Emory University
Atlanta, Georgia U.S.A.

V. Sambamurthy
Michigan State University
East Lansing, Michigan U.S.A.

Abstract   *In turbulent environments, enterprise agility (i.e., the ability for firms to sense environmental change and respond appropriately) is an important determinant of firm success. We present a framework for enterprise agility, identify the underlying capabilities that support enterprise agility, and explicate the enabling role of information technology and digital options.*

Keywords   Agility, enterprise agility, strategic agility, business agility, digital options, information technology

1 INTRODUCTION

As strategic and operating conditions become increasingly turbulent due to factors such as hyper-competition, increasing demands from customers, regulatory changes, and technological advancements, the ability to sense relevant change and respond appropriately becomes an important determinant of firm success. The term *agile* is commonly used to describe firms that are able to thrive in rapidly changing environments (Dove 2001; Sambamurthy et al. 2003; Weill et al. 2002). Agility builds upon other concepts in management theory that pertain to firm success in turbulent environments, including dynamic capabilities (Teece et al. 1997), strategic flexibility (Ansoff 1980; Hitt et al. 1998), and market orientation (Kohli and Jaworski 1990; Narver and Slater 1990).

Enterprise agility is commonly broken down into two components: sensing and response. We develop a framework for the different combinations of sensing and response capabilities that firms may have, exploring the underlying capabilities (and deficiencies) that affect enterprise agility. The paper provides a conceptual schema and suggests normative insight for firms seeking to improve their enterprise agility. We also discuss how firm investments in information technology enable enterprise agility. Drawing on prior work in digital options (Sambamurthy et al. 2003), we explain how IT enables both the sensing and response components of agility by extending the reach and richness of firm knowledge and processes.

2   BACKGROUND

We define *enterprise agility*[1] as the ability of firms to sense environmental change and respond appropriately. The components of sense and respond are reflected in the various definitions of agility published in the academic literature, although some of the terminology differs. For example, Dove (2001) referred to the response component as "response ability," which he defined as the physical ability to act, and to the sensing component as "knowledge management," which he defined as the intellectual ability to find appropriate things to act on. Other terms in the definition also vary. For example, "environmental change" has been referred to as "market opportunities" (Sambamurthy et al. 2003), "continuous and unpredictable change" (Ward 1994), and "opportunities and threats" (Bessant et al. 2001). For purposes of breadth, we consider environmental change to encompass changes precipitated by competitors' actions, consumer preference changes, regulatory or legal changes, economic shifts, technological advancements, etc. Figure 1 illustrates how our definition corresponds to other published definitions.

In our context, an *appropriate* response is one that is supportive of a firm goal, such as to increase market share, capture new customers, or fend off competition. This adds in the element of strategy between sensing and response. The following quotes from a focus group comprised of six business school academics and two industry practitioners on the topic of enterprise agility illustrate this point:

> You must have metrics associated with sensing and response. I.e., what are we sensing, why, and what decisions does it drive? Objectives will differ; you might want to shorten days of inventory, cycle time, or time to market. So it's not just sense and respond, but sense and *appropriately* respond. To judge appropriateness, the response must be measured against some goal.

---

[1]References to agility in this paper will relate to agility at the enterprise level. We consider enterprise agility, business agility, and organizational agility to be synonymous for purposes of this paper.

Definition of Enterprise Agility	Components of Other Definitions
Sense	Detect (1); Anticipate (7); Sense (8)
Environmental Change	Competitive market opportunities (1); Continuous and unpredictable change (2); Appropriate things to act on (4); Continuous and often unanticipated change (6); Evolving conditions (7); Environmental change (8)
and	
Respond Appropriately.	Seize ... with speed and surprise (1); thrive (2); intelligently, rapidly and proactively seizing opportunities and reacting to threats (3); readily implement (5); fast response to ... seize the day (7); respond efficiently and effectively (8)

Citation in which agility is defined:

1. Sambamurthy et al. 2003
2. Ward, 1994
3. Bessant et al. 2001
4. Dove 2001

5. Weill et al. 2002
6. Sarkis 2001
7. Prewitt 2004
8. Ambrose and Morello 2004

Figure 1. Relationship of the Definition of Enterprise Agility
to Other Definitions of Agility

An analogy is the squirrel in the road. The pending environmental change that the squirrel senses is that there's a car coming down the road. The squirrel responds by running back and forth, but its response is not appropriate because it gets run over.

Relative cost and quality also factor into the appropriateness of a response. For example, a response that is prohibitively expensive would not be appropriate; neither would a response of inadequate quality (Dove 2001). Another dimension of appropriateness is speed, which should be evaluated relative to the environmental change and will depend on such factors as whether the change was due to a competitor's move, a new technology, a regulatory change, etc. It will also vary by industry. For example, a quick response in one industry (e.g., aircraft manufacturing) may not be a quick response in another industry (e.g., mobile telephone manufacturing.) Consider the following quote from the focus group:

Agility will vary by industry. Consider the example of an elephant. Elephants are pretty agile for their environment. So speed is relative: responses might take years but still be agile.

Several aspects of the concept of enterprise agility are closely related to other concepts in management theory, many of which have informed our theorizing. We discuss three of these concepts: dynamic capabilities (Teece et al. 1997), market orientation (Kohli and Jaworski 1990; Narver and Slater 1990), and strategic flexibility (Aaker and Mascarenhas 1984; Ansoff 1980; Grewal and Tansuhaj 2001) and describe how they inform, yet are distinct from, enterprise agility.

Dynamic capabilities are a firm's ability to integrate, build, and reconfigure internal and external competencies to address rapidly changing environments (Teece et al. 1997). A basic tenet is that firms must continuously adapt their capabilities in order to maintain competitiveness (and perhaps competitive advantage.) Although the concept of dynamic capabilities shares many of the same concepts with enterprise agility—particularly its relevance to rapidly changing environments—dynamic capabilities is a much broader concept. Dynamic capabilities is relevant to all types of firm processes, whereas enterprise agility includes only those processes relevant for sensing environmental change and responding appropriately. In a sense, enterprise agility can be thought of as being enabled by a specific subset of dynamic capabilities.

The market orientation of a firm is reflected in the organization-wide generation of market intelligence pertaining to current and future customer needs, dissemination of the intelligence across departments, and organization-wide responsiveness to it (Jaworski and Kohli 1993; Kohli and Jaworski 1990). Market intelligence includes information about customers, competitors, and other factors such as technology and regulatory developments. As such, the market orientation concept includes all of the drivers of *environmental change* encompassed in the definition of enterprise agility. Similarly, both concepts explicitly include responsiveness to market intelligence and environmental change. However, there are slight differences between the two concepts. First, market orientation is an over-arching management philosophy or orientation. Enterprise agility, on the other hand, is better conceptualized as a set of capabilities and does not rise to the level of an overall orientation. Second, market orientation is heavily rooted in information processing: information is gathered, disseminated across departments, and acted upon. Conversely, enterprise agility is not necessarily as reliant on information processing. For example, it is possible for firms to act with agility without disseminating information across departments. In fact, disseminating information across departments may actually delay response and make firms less agile. Last, market oriented firms are largely focused on customer needs,[2] and excessive focus on the customer can cause a firm to miss environmental change caused by other factors, such as that created by new technologies (Christensen and Bower 1996). Because enterprise agility is not as tightly coupled with customer needs analysis, agile firms may be less likely to fall into this customer focus trap.

Definitions of strategic flexibility include "the capability of a firm to proact or respond quickly to changing competitive conditions and thereby develop and/or maintain competitive advantage" (Hitt et al. 1998) and "the organizational ability to manage economic and political risks by promptly responding in a proactive or reactive manner to market threats and opportunities" (Grewal and Tansuhaj 2001). Firms possessing strategic flexibility tend to have flexible resource pools and diverse portfolios of strategic options, which allows them to practice effective "surprise management"

---

[2]Narver and Slater's (1990) definition of market orientation explicitly includes customer orientation.

(Ansoff 1980). A review of the definitions reveals that strategic flexibility and enterprise agility are quite similar, although there is one major distinction. By construction, strategic flexibility refers to strategic issues, i.e., those that affect the businesses that a firm is in and how it creates competitive advantage in those businesses (Porter 1987). Strategic issues are distinct from operational or tactical issues (Porter 1996). Enterprise agility applies to both strategic and operational issues. For example, firms may need to be agile to handle strategic issues such as those created by competitor moves or changing customer preferences. In addition, firms may also need to be agile to handle operational issues such as those created by new regulations. For example, consider a new federal law that increases firm liability for worker's compensation claims. Agile firms must be able to sense how this change affects their operations and implement any needed safety improvements in a timely manner. Thus, because firms can be agile in both strategic and operational issues, enterprise agility envelops and extends strategic flexibility.

In addition to applying to both strategic and operational moves, enterprise agility can also apply to both proactive and reactive moves (Dove 2001). Proactive moves are innovative and place firms in a leadership position, whereas reactive moves are necessary to retain viability and competitiveness. To illustrate, consider two competing firms, A and B. Assume that firm A has sensed a pending technological and/or regulatory change such as the FDA's approval of sucralose sweetener (marketed as Splenda) and launched a new line of low-calorie foods. Firm B, which does not track regulatory and technological developments as closely as does Firm A, senses the change in market demand created by firm A and quickly responds to launch its own line of low-calorie foods made with sucralose. Note that both firms have sensed and responded to environmental change: firm A has behaved proactively in the face of regulatory and technological change, while firm B has behaved reactively due to a competitor's move. Thus, both moves might be considered agile, depending on whether they meet the criterion of appropriate response.[3]

3 FRAMEWORK FOR ENTERPRISE AGILITY

We present a framework for the different combinations of sensing and response capabilities that firms may have. Our framework consists of a 2 × 2 matrix with sensing on the x-axis and response on the y-axis and is shown in Figure 2. Agile firms are positioned in the upper-right quadrant (quadrant I), as they possess strong sensing and response capabilities. Firms with weak sensing and response capabilities are positioned in the lower-left quadrant (quadrant IV). Firms that are strong in either sensing or response, but not both, are positioned in the lower-right quadrant (quadrant II) and upper-left quadrant (quadrant III), respectively.

---

[3]Using the terminology commonly used in the strategy literature, firm A could be considered a "first-mover" and firm B a "fast follower" (Kerin et al. 1992; Lieberman and Montgomery 1988; Makadok 1998). We suggest that order of market entry is not necessarily associated with agility, as both first movers and fast followers can be agile.

3.1 Quadrant I (High Sensing, High Response): Agile

In order to explicate the characteristics of firms in quadrant I, we further decomposed our definition of agility to examine (1) the types of environmental change that firms must be able to sense and (2) the types of responses that firms can implement. A summary of this decomposition appears as Table 1. From this we are able to construct a profile of an agile firm.

Recall that relevant forces of environmental change include competitors' actions, consumer preference changes, economic shifts, regulatory and legal changes, and technological advancements. Different firm capabilities may be required to sense each of these types of change. For example, a firm may need a strong *market intelligence* capability to track competitors' actions and consumer preference changes. This may involve monitoring competitors' new product offerings, pricing and promotion strategies, and distribution strategies, as well as researching consumer needs and wants. Market intelligence may also help a firm sense changes due to economic shifts such as a downturn in the overall economy or rising commodity prices. Similarly, a strong *government relations* and/or *legal* department may be required to sense impending regulatory and legal changes of relevance to a firm. For example, telecommunications firms must be able to sense regulatory changes that impact their ability to offer different services (local and long-distance, landline and mobile telephone service, Internet service, cable television service, etc.) and the prices they can charge in different markets. Last, strong *research and development* and *information technology* capabilities may be needed to sense technological advancements and the ways in which a firm might leverage them to gain advantage.[4]

The relative importance of each of these forces of change (and the corresponding firm capabilities needed to detect them) will vary across industries and across time. For example, technological advancements may be very important early in the life cycle of products in industries such as consumer electronics. However, as technology stabilizes, competitors' actions in the form of price reductions or product bundling may become the more salient driver of environmental change. Despite fluctuation in their relative importance, most (if not all) of these forces are likely to be relevant to contemporary firms. Thus, most firms will require some degree of expertise in each of the corresponding underlying capabilities (market intelligence, R&D, IT, etc.).

After sensing environmental change, there are multiple responses that a firm can make: (1) embark on a new venture (complex move), (2) adjust an existing venture (simple move), and (3) take no action (Ferrier et al. 1999). In other words, the scope of responses can differ (Dove 2001). The first response classification, embark on a new venture, encompasses such responses as launching a new product, creating a new distribution channel, or targeting a new customer segment. For example, Apple's launch

---

[4]It is worth noting that some of these capabilities (legal, research and development, IT. market intelligence gathering, etc.) might be shared between a firm and its partners, or outsourced altogether. An exploration of how outsourcing of selected capabilities might impact firms' overall sensing capability is beyond the scope of our research but may represent a fruitful area for future research.

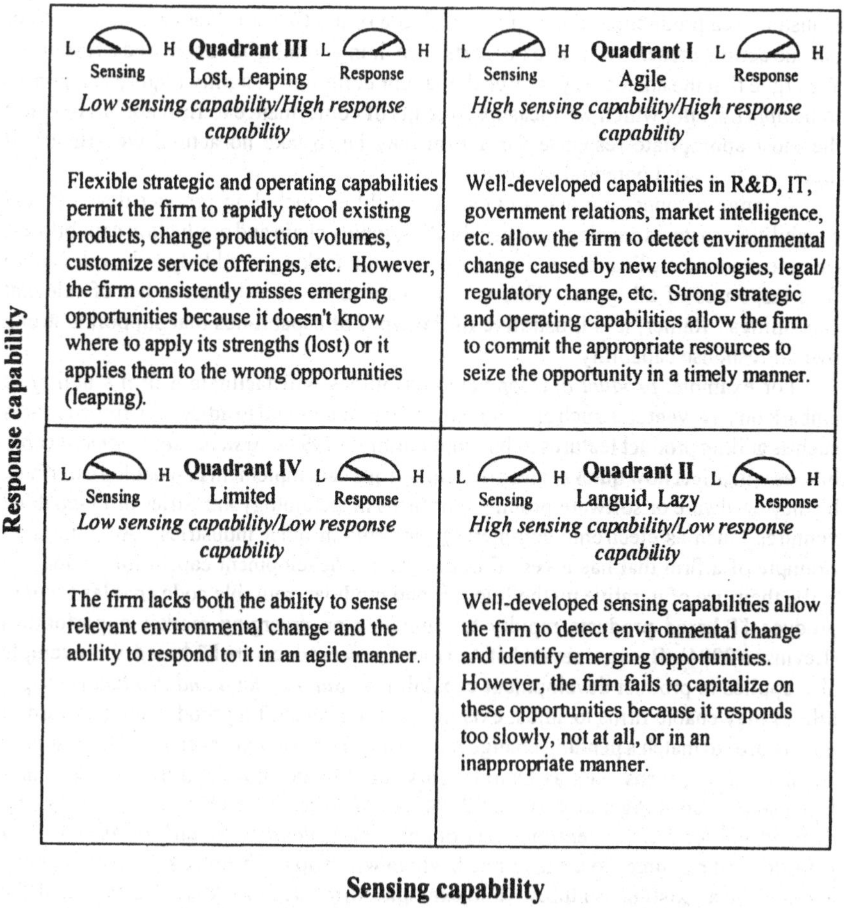
L H Quadrant III L H
Sensing
Lost, Leaping
Response
Low sensing capability/High response capability
Flexible strategic and operating capabilities permit the firm to rapidly retool existing products, change production volumes, customize service offerings, etc. However, the firm consistently misses emerging opportunities because it doesn't know where to apply its strengths (lost) or it applies them to the wrong opportunities (leaping).
L H Quadrant I L H
Sensing
Agile
Response
High sensing capability/High response capability
Well-developed capabilities in R&D, IT, government relations, market intelligence, etc. allow the firm to detect environmental change caused by new technologies, legal/regulatory change, etc. Strong strategic and operating capabilities allow the firm to commit the appropriate resources to seize the opportunity in a timely manner.
L H Quadrant IV L H
Sensing
Limited
Response
Low sensing capability/Low response capability
The firm lacks both the ability to sense relevant environmental change and the ability to respond to it in an agile manner.
L H Quadrant II L H
Sensing
Languid, Lazy
Response
High sensing capability/Low response capability
Well-developed sensing capabilities allow the firm to detect environmental change and identify emerging opportunities. However, the firm fails to capitalize on these opportunities because it responds too slowly, not at all, or in an inappropriate manner.
Response capability
Sensing capability

Figure 2. Framework of Different Combinations of Sensing and Response Capabilities

of the iTunes music store in 2003 is an example of a firm responding to environmental change (technological advancements in music distribution) by embarking on a new venture (Apple Computer 2003). The second classification, adjust an existing venture, encompasses such responses as making a price change, increasing or decreasing production of an existing product, or adjusting product features. Responses in the second group can be thought of as incremental compared to responses in the first classification. For example, consider The New York Times Company's production of hundreds of thousands of extra copies of *The Boston Globe* (which it publishes) to sell to New England Patriots fans in Houston, TX, during the 2004 Super Bowl (Prewitt 2004). This is an example of a firm responding to a market opportunity (thousands of additional *Globe* readers in Houston, TX, for a few days) by adjusting an existing venture (the

Houston-area production, distribution, and sale of the *Globe*.) The last classification, take no action, presents a paradox of sorts: can doing nothing be considered a response? We argue that the answer is yes. Recall that our definition of agility requires responses to be *appropriate*, which we measure in terms of conformance to firm goals. Because the most appropriate response for a firm may be to take no action, we argue that inactivity is a valid potential response.[5]

A range of operating and strategic capabilities, including product development capabilities, systems development capabilities, supply chain and production capabilities, flexible resource utilization, and strategic decision making, are likely to be relevant to firm responses of all types. This is not meant to be an exhaustive list of relevant capabilities. Rather, it is illustrative of the types of capabilities that support a strong overall response capability.

For example, *product development* capabilities will facilitate a firm's ability to embark on new ventures such as launching new products and to adjust existing ventures such as adding product features (Clark and Fujimoto 1991). *Systems development* capabilities will affect how quickly and efficiently firms can implement IT-enabled offerings, be they hardware or software products for firms in technology industries or IT-enabled ventures (such as electronic commerce) for firms in other industries. Acxiom is an example of a firm that has invested in its systems development capabilities. Specifically, their use of iterative methodologies and modular, reusable code enables them to produce IT-based products rapidly to capitalize on emerging market opportunities (Levinson 2004). Because several of Acxiom's new products are IT-based, this example also applies to product development capabilities. *Supply-chain and production* capabilities may enable firms to adjust existing ventures by shifting production (upward or downward) to match a pending change in demand. For example, because of high supply chain visibility, firms such as DaimlerChrysler (Mayor 2004) and the United States Defense Logistics Agency (Overby 2004) are able to sense changes in supply and demand and scale their operations accordingly. *Flexible resource utilization* can allow firms to shift resources to areas of need, which will help them embark on new ventures and/or adjust existing ventures. For example, firms such as Merrill Lynch and the Guardian Life Insurance Company of America (Prewitt 2004) have flexible budgeting and staffing systems that permit them to reallocate resources to where they are most needed. A fifth item we include is *strategic decision making* capability. Not only must firms have enabling capabilities related to product development, supply chain, etc., but they must also have the ability to determine if a given response (be it complex, simple, or standing pat) is supportive of their strategic goals. In addition, they must be able to make this decision quickly to capitalize fully on the opportunity.

---

[5]This relates to the distinction between a firm being agile and actually *displaying* its agility. For example, consider two competing firms in the telecommunications industry, firms A and B, both of which have strong sensing and response capabilities. Further assume that a regulatory change permits both firms A and B to offer cable television service in certain markets. Although both firms sense the opportunity and have the available resources to seize it, only firm B decides to do so. Firm A declines the opportunity because its strategy is to focus on its core competency of telephone service. Note that only firm B acts in an agile manner, although firm A could have. Thus, firm A is an agile firm, but it does not display its agility in this case.

Table 1. Decomposition of Sensing and Response Capabilities

	Relevant Types	**Selecting Enabling Capabilities**
Sensing Environmental Change	• Competitors's actions • Consumer preference changes • Economic shifts • Regulatory/legal changes • Technological advancements	• Market intelligence • Government relations • Legal • Research and development • Information technology
Appropriate Response	• Embark on new venture (complex) • Adjust existing venture (simple) • No action	• Product development • Systems development • Supply chain • Production • Flexible resource utilization • Strategic decision-making

Returning to the framework, we can infer that firms in quadrant I have several characteristics, including strong sensing capabilities supported by R&D, market intelligence, IT, legal, and government relations activities as well as strong response capabilities supported by strategic decision-making, product development, systems development, supply chain, and resource utilization skills.

An example of an agile firm is Wal-Mart. During a recent hurricane season in Florida, Wal-Mart was able to leverage its strong IT and data analysis capabilities to sense which disaster-related products were in the greatest demand, which included both predictable items such as flashlights and batteries and less predictable items such as beer and strawberry Pop-Tarts. Using its supply chain and distribution capabilities, Wal-Mart was able to deliver additional disaster-related inventory to stores in affected areas to respond to this unusual spike in demand (Hays 2004).

3.2 Quadrant II (High Sensing, Low Response): Languid, Lazy

Firms in quadrant II (high sensing, low response) lack the response capabilities needed to seize emerging opportunities, although they are able to sense them. We characterize these firms as *languid* or *lazy*. Others have characterized such as firms as *catatonic* (Dove 2001). There are multiple potential reasons why firms might be able to sense environmental change relevant to their business but still fail to response to it in an agile manner, including those related to deficiencies in response-enabling capabilities such as product development, supply chain, or strategic decision-making. These deficiencies might be created by such factors as unnecessary bureaucracy, risk aversion, resource rigidity, poorly integrated processes, and/or agency problems. For example, unnecessary bureaucracy could slow down the strategic decision-making process, causing firms to miss emerging opportunities. This is related to the notion of "analysis paralysis," a condition in which a firm fails to make a timely decision because it is weighing too many possible options. Another possible reason, risk aversion, could cause firms to pass on an opportunity even when responding to it would be beneficial. Resource rigidity could prevent firms from being able to reallocate resources such as personnel, budget funds, or technology to areas of need. Poorly integrated processes may slow down product development and systems development, causing firms to miss opportunities. Last, agency problems may create incentives for managers to fail to act on opportunities that would be beneficial to the firm as a whole.

An example of a quadrant II firm was Xerox's Palo Alto Research Center (PARC) in the 1970s. Xerox engineers sensed impending changes in the computing industry and developed multiple innovations such as the graphical user interface, the mouse, and Ethernet. However, due to multiple issues, including conflicting strategies and issues with the U.S. Justice Department, Xerox did not market these innovations. Thus, although Xerox was able to sense changes in customer demand, it was unable to respond to it in a profitable manner (Alexander and Smith 1988).

3.3 Quadrant III (Low Sensing, High Response): Lost, Leaping

Firms in quadrant III (low sensing, high response) have strong response capabilities but are unable to sense the correct opportunities to pursue. We characterize these firms as *lost* or *leaping*. Others have characterized such as firms as *spastic* (Dove 2001). This lack of a sensing capability may be due to several factors, including skill deficiencies in such areas as market intelligence, R&D, IT, legal, and government relations. These deficiencies might be created by such factors as over-reliance on outsourced providers, lack of integration, and competitive complacency. For example, lack of integration may hinder information flows within a firm, harming its overall sensing capability. Over-reliance on outsourced providers may cause firm expertise in the outsourced area (be it IT, legal, R&D, government relations, or market intelligence) to atrophy, making it difficult for firms to sense relevant environmental change. This is consistent with the theory of absorptive capacity (Cohen and Levinthal 1990), which suggests that firms must have a base of prior knowledge in an area in order to make sense of new developments in that area. Last, competitive complacency (Ferrier et al. 1999) may cause firms to become comfortable in their current strategic positions, causing them to ignore signals of change.

An example of a quadrant III firm is Cisco Systems circa 2001. Cisco has frequently received accolades for its supply chain capabilities which allow it to respond quickly to customer demand (McCormack et al. 2003; Poirier and Bauer 2001). However, Cisco failed to sense the downturn in the market for networking equipment in 2001, leading to a $2.2 billion inventory write-off in the third quarter of 2001. Some commentators contend that Cisco's flexible response capabilities may have even exacerbated the situation by streamlining Cisco's ability to acquire inventory in order to respond to demand that never materialized (Berinato 2001).

3.4 Quadrant IV (Low Sensing, Low Response): Limited

We characterize firms in quadrant IV (low sensing, low response) as *limited*. Not only do these firms lack the ability to sense environmental change, but they also lack response capabilities. The deficiencies presented for firms in quadrants II and III apply to firms in quadrant IV.

4 INFORMATION TECHNOLOGY, DIGITAL OPTIONS AND AGILITY

Information technology plays an important role in enabling the sense and response capabilities of firms (Bradley and Nolan 1998; Sambamurthy et al. 2003; Weill and Broadbent 1998). To the extent that environmental change is caused by advances in information technology or that appropriate responses depend on firms' IT competence, IT is directly related to enterprise agility. First, as discussed in the previous section, firms must have an adequate level of IT competence to be able to sense IT-based change relevant to their business. Consider that firms that sensed the opportunities created by emerging information technologies such as interactive HTML pages and the secure sockets layer (SSL) protocol were able to implement electronic commerce strategies before many of their competitors (Kalakota and Robinson 2001). Second, systems development capability is an important enabler of appropriate responses for firms in information technology-driven industries such as financial services, retailing, telecommunications, and hardware/software (Sambamurthy et al. 2003). Systems development capability is also important for firms in other industries. For example, many firms rely on information technology to support customer and supplier channels. The changing dynamics of customer and supplier relationships often require frequent modification and enhancement to supporting information systems (Lyytinen and Rose 2003). Third, IT may be indispensable for agility in contemporary environments (Haeckel 1999). This is because the volume of information that firms must process to sense relevant change has outstripped human capacity to process it. IT is required to augment human information processing so that managers can make sense out of what would otherwise overwhelm them. Similarly, responses in contemporary environments are often too complex for timely implementation without such IT support as communication infrastructure and automation. Haeckel and Nolan (1993) referred to managing in conditions so turbulent that sensemaking and action are impossible without IT as "managing by wire."

While the direct relationship between information technology and agility is important, the indirect relationship may be even more pronounced. Much of the business value of IT stems from its complementarities with business processes (Barua et al. 1995). Under this theory, IT contributes to performance in business processes such as product development, manufacturing, and supply chain, which in turn contribute to firm performance. Thus, other firm processes mediate the effect of IT on performance, although IT may also have direct effects on performance in certain circumstances. We submit that this is also the case for enterprise agility.

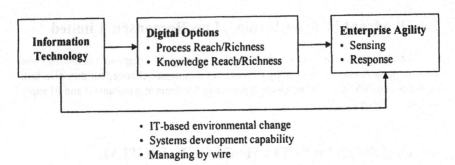

- IT-based environmental change
- Systems development capability
- Managing by wire

Figure 3. Relationship Between IT, Digital Options, and Enterprise Agility

Theory suggests that IT indirectly supports agility by providing firms with digital options, which are defined as a set of IT-enabled capabilities in the form of digitized work processes and knowledge systems (Sambamurthy et al. 2003). A basic premise of this theory is that IT enhances the reach and richness of a firm's knowledge and processes. Enhancements in the breadth of resources (reach) and quality of information (richness) available to a firm provide the firm with digital options. Digital options create a platform for enterprise agility by improving a firm's sensing capability and providing it with the knowledge and flexibility it needs to respond to opportunities created through environmental change. They are options in the sense that a firm may exercise them to apply to emerging opportunities, or they may remain unused, depending on a firm's environment and strategy (Fichman 2004; Trigeorgis 1996). The graphic in Figure 3 illustrates how IT provides firms with digital options and how these digital options enhance enterprise agility. Figure 3 also displays the direct relationship between IT and enterprise agility described above.

Digital options are created through enhancements to the reach and richness of firm knowledge and processes. *Knowledge reach* refers to the comprehensiveness and accessibility of codified knowledge that is available to a firm. Such knowledge may reside in internal databases, partner databases, or public databases. Well-architected IT systems can assist firms in accessing, synthesizing, and exploiting knowledge from a wide range of sources. Not only can IT extend knowledge reach, but it also enhances *knowledge richness* by providing firms with high-quality information that is timely, accurate, descriptive, and customized to the recipient.[6] Information technologies such as decision support systems, data warehouses, and OLAP tools can help firms develop rich knowledge through real-time data monitoring, pattern recognition, and strategic scenario modeling (Wixom and Watson 2001). Knowledge reach and richness enhance firms' sensing capabilities by providing managers with high quality information about the state of the business, which helps them identify emerging opportunities and/or threats. For example, rich knowledge related to customer purchase behavior can help

---

[6] We based some of these elements on Evans and Wurster's (2000) conceptualization of richness.

managers sense profitable new customer segments (Glazer 1991). Rich knowledge related to internal processes can help managers identify deficiencies such as fulfillment problems that are likely to be exposed as the competitive environment evolves. Also, the searching and filtering functionality of IT allows firms to monitor a wide range of data sources, providing firms with great reach to monitor developments related to new regulations, laws, technologies, and economic conditions. Knowledge reach and richness also support response capability by providing managers with the information they need to make strategic decisions in a timely manner. In addition, they support firms' response capabilities by providing managers with visibility to the resources (employees, equipment, budget, etc.) available to pursue emerging opportunities.

Similarly, IT creates digital options by extending *process reach* so that firms are better integrated internally and with external customers, suppliers, and partners. Infrastructural information technologies such as e-mail, voice mail, databases, intranets/extranets, and groupware extend process reach, both within and external to a firm. Other information technologies such as supply chain systems, procurement systems, portals, transactional Web sites, and collaborative systems represent more specialized investments that extend process reach to external stakeholders. While process reach facilitates greater process participation among relevant internal and external stakeholders, *process richness* improves the quality of information available to process participants by making it more timely, accurate, relevant, and customized. Process reach and richness support firms' response capabilities by improving coordination internal and external to the firm, which enhances response-enabling capabilities such as product development, systems development, supply chain, production, and strategic decision-making. By supporting high-quality information exchange among numerous stakeholders, process reach and richness also enrich firms' opportunities to sense relevant environmental change.

Although individual information technologies can improve both a firm's knowledge and its processes, we submit that some technologies are more knowledge-oriented and others are more process-oriented. Further, we submit that knowledge-oriented IT is more directly supportive of a firm's sensing capability and that process-oriented IT is more directly supportive of a firm's response ability. To illustrate, data warehouses, data mining, OLAP, and other reporting tools are examples of knowledge-oriented information technologies, as these technologies help firms identify patterns within and extract knowledge from data. Because these technologies can help firms make sense out of apparent noise (Haeckel 1999), they directly support firms' sensing capability. Process-oriented IT systems are designed to help firms conduct business processes such as procurement, production, distribution, and billing. Examples of such systems include enterprise resource planning systems and supply chain systems. These technologies support firms' response capabilities by facilitating process integration and visibility, which in turn enables processes to be adjusted quickly in order to meet changing environmental conditions. Process-oriented systems often provide the raw data to knowledge-oriented systems such as data warehouses, although knowledge-oriented functionality such as reporting is often built directly into the process-oriented IT (e.g., a reporting module in an ERP system).

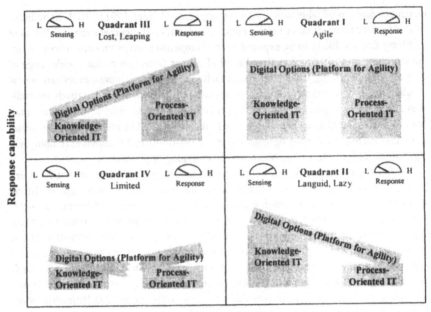

Figure 4. Relationship Between Digital Options and
the Enterprise Agility Framework

In terms of the framework, firms in quadrant III (low sensing, high response) may have sophisticated process-oriented IT but suboptimal knowledge-oriented IT. This is because strong process-oriented IT provides quadrant III firms with response capabilities, but deficiencies in knowledge-oriented IT may be one of the reasons why these firms fail to sense relevant environmental change. Similarly, firms in quadrant II (high sensing, low response) may have strong knowledge-oriented IT but poor process-oriented IT. These firms may leverage knowledge-oriented IT to help them sense environmental change, but their lack of process-oriented IT hinders their ability to develop and implement responses, perhaps because they cannot reach the relevant stakeholders or communicate with them in a sufficiently rich manner. Deficiencies in either knowledge-oriented or process-oriented IT create an imbalance in the digital options *platform*, making it an unstable base from which to launch agile moves. On the other hand, knowledge-oriented and process-oriented IT may be a key reason why firms in quadrant I (high sensing, high response) have the sensing and response capabilities to be highly agile. They combine to provide firms with a stock of digital options that creates a solid platform from which to launch agile moves. Conversely, because firms in quadrant IV (low sensing, low response) lack both knowledge-oriented and process-oriented IT, they are unable to accumulate a stock of digital options, hindering their overall agility. Figure 4 maps firms' knowledge-oriented and process-oriented IT capabilities to the enterprise agility framework and illustrates the concept of instability in the digital options platform.

4.1 How IT Might Hinder Enterprise Agility

Depending on how it is deployed and managed, IT may actually hinder enterprise agility in certain circumstances. For example, monolithic IT architectures may hinder agility by limiting the range of strategic responses available to a firm. Such architectures may make it difficult for the firm to adjust processes to changing conditions, creating high costs when the firm seeks to pursue new strategies. Other systems may limit information visibility by storing data in ways that make it difficult to retrieve and/or interpret. Also, some systems may limit process reach by being incompatible with systems adopted by customers and suppliers. These issues, however, are not endemic to information technology in general, although some may be either reflective of early generations of information technology (e.g., monolithic, incompatible.) Rather, these issues stem from inappropriate investment in and/or management of information technology, just as issues may stem from inappropriate investment in and/or management of other firm resources such as human resources or manufacturing equipment. This calls attention to the importance of firm-level IT planning, implementation, and maintenance (Bharadwaj 2000; Weill and Broadbent 1998).

5 CONCLUSION

By juxtaposing firm sensing and response capabilities, our framework illustrates the enabling characteristics that support enterprise agility. We focused on the role of information technology, drawing upon digital options theory to show how IT supports agility by extending the reach and richness of firm knowledge and processes.

The framework helps to illustrate that both the sensing and response components must be present for a firm to be agile. For example, a firm that is highly effective at sensing environmental change but that is slow to act or acts inappropriately will not be agile. Similarly, a firm that is well positioned to respond appropriately will not be agile if it is unable to sense the correct opportunities to pursue. Thus, each of the components is a necessary, but not sufficient, condition for enterprise agility. However, the components are related, and they are likely to operate in a virtuous cycle. For example, a firm's ability to sense environmental change can greatly increase its likelihood of being able to develop appropriate responses by giving it a head start on its competitors. In turn, a strong response capability can provide incentives for a firm to look for emerging opportunities, thereby improving its sensing capability. Effective use of information technology is one method for firms to kick off and sustain this virtuous cycle, as IT enhances both sensing and response capabilities.

REFERENCES

Aaker, D. A., and Mascarenhas, B. "The Need for Strategic Flexibility," *Journal of Business Strategy* (5:2), 1984, pp. 74-82.
Alexander, R. C., and Smith, D. K. *Fumbling the Future: How Xerox Invented, Then Ignored, the First Personal Computer*, New York: W. Morrow, 1988.

Ambrose, C., and Morello, D. I. "Designing the Agile Organization: Design Principles and Practices," Gartner, Inc., 2004, pp. 1-25.

Ansoff, H. I. "Strategic Issue Management," *Strategic Management Journal* (1:2), 1980, pp. 132-148.

Apple Computer. "Apple Launches the iTunes Music Store," 2003 (available online at http://www.apple.com/pr/library/2003/apr/28musicstore.html; accessed current October 13, 2004).

Barua, A., Kriebel, C. H., and Mukhopadhyay, T. "Information Technologies and Business Value: An Analytic and Empirical Investigation," *Information Systems Research* (6:1), 1995, pp. 3-23.

Berinato, S. "What Went Wrong at Cisco," *CIO Magazine*, August 1, 2001, pp. 52-62.

Bessant, J., Francis, D., Meredith, S., Kaplinsky, R., and Brown, S. "Developing Manufacturing Agility in SMEs," *International Journal of Technology Management* (22:1/2/3), 2001, pp. 28-54.

Bharadwaj, A. S. "A Resource-Based Perspective on Information Technology Capability and Firm Performance: An Empirical Investigation," *MIS Quarterly* (24:1), 2000, pp. 169-196.

Bradley, S. P., and Nolan, R. L. *Sense & Respond: Capturing Value in the Network Era*, Boston: Harvard Business School Press, 1998.

Christensen, C. M., and Bower, J. L. "Customer Power, Strategic Investment, and the Failure of Leading Firms," *Strategic Management Journal* (17:3), 1996,, pp. 197-218.

Clark, K., and Fujimoto, T. *Product Development Performance: Strategy, Organization, and Management in the World Auto Industry*, Boston: Harvard Business School Press, 1991.

Cohen, W. M., and Levinthal, D. A. "Absorptive Capacity: A New Perspective on Learning and Innovation," *Administrative Science Quarterly* (35), 1990, pp. 128-152.

Dove, R. *Response Ability: The Language, Structure, and Culture of the Agile Enterprise*, New York: John Wiley & Sons, Inc., 2001.

Evans, P., and Wurster, T. S. *Blown to Bits: How the New Economics of Information Transforms Strategy*, Boston: Harvard Business School Press, 2000.

Ferrier, W. J., Smith, K. G., and Grimm, C. "The Role of Competitive Action in Market Share Erosion and Industry Dethronement: A Study of Industry Leaders and Challengers," *Academy of Management Journal* (42:4), 1999, pp. 372-388.

Fichman, R. G. "Real Options and IT Platform Adoption: Implications for Theory and Practice," *Information Systems Research* (15:2), 2004, pp. 132-154.

Glazer, R. "Marketing in an Information-Intensive Environment: Strategic Implications of Knowledge as an Asset," *Journal of Marketing* (55:4), 1991, pp. 1-19.

Grewal, R., and Tansuhaj, P. "Building Organizational Capabilities for Managing Economic Crisis: The Role of Market Orientation and Strategic Flexibility," *Journal of Marketing* (65:2), 2001, pp. 67-80.

Haeckel, S. H. *Adaptive Enterprise: Creating and Leading Sense-and-Respond Organizations*, Boston: Harvard Business School Press, 1999.

Haeckel, S. H., and Nolan, R. L. "Managing by Wire," *Harvard Business Review* (71:5), 1993, pp. 122-132.

Hays, C. L. "What They Know About You," *The New York Times*, November 14, 2004, Section 3, p. 1.

Hitt, M. A., Keats, B. W., and DeMarie, S. M. "Navigating in the New Competitive Landscape: Building Strategic Flexibility and Competitive Advantage in the 21st Century," *Academy of Management Executive* (12:4), 1998, pp. 22-42.

Jaworski, B. J., and Kohli, A. K. "Market Orientation: Antecedents and Consequences," *Journal of Marketing* (57:3), 1993, pp. 53-70.

Kalakota, R., and Robinson, M. *E-Business 2.0: Roadmap for Success*, Boston: Addison-Wesley, 2001.

Kerin, R. A., Varadarajan, P. R., and Peterson, R. A. "First-Mover Advantage: A Synthesis, Conceptual Framework, and Research Propositions," *Journal of Marketing* (56:4), 1992, pp. 33-52.

Kohli, A. K., and Jaworski, B. J. "Market Orientation: The Construct, Research, Propositions, and Managerial Implications," *Journal of Marketing* (54:2), 1990, pp. 1-18.

Levinson, M. "How to Build an Agile IT Department," *CIO Magazine* (17:21), August 15, 2004, pp. 58-63.

Lieberman, M. B., and Montgomery, D. B. "First-Mover Advantages," *Strategic Management Journal* (9:Summer), Special Issue, 1998, pp. 41-58.

Lyytinen, K., and Rose, "The Disruptive Nature of Information Technology Innovations: The Case of Internet Computing in Systems Development Organizations," *MIS Quarterly* (27:4), 2003, pp. 557-595.

Makadok, R. "Can First-Mover and Early-Mover Advantages Be Sustained in an Industry with Low Barriers to Entry/Imitation?," *Strategic Management Journal* (19:7), 1998, pp. 683-696.

Mayor, T. "The Supple Supply Chain," *CIO Magazine* (17:21), August 15, 2004, pp. 66-70.

McCormack, K. P., Johnson, W. C., and Walker, W. T. *Supply Chain Networks and Business Process Orientation: Advanced Strategies and Best Practices*, Boca Raton, FL: CRC Press, 2003.

Narver, J. C., and Slater, S. F. Slater "The Effect of a Market Orientation on Business Profitability," *Journal of Marketing* (54:4), 1990, pp. 20-35.

Overby, S. "Inside an Agile Transformation," *CIO Magazine* (17:21), August 15, 2004, pp. 48-54.

Poirier, C. C., and Bauer, M. J. *E-Supply Chain: Using the Internet to Revolutionize Your Business*, San Francisco: Berrett-Koehler Publishers, Inc., 2001.

Porter, M. E. "From Competitive Advantage to Corporate Strategy," *Harvard Business Review* (65:3), 1987, pp. 43-59.

Porter, M. E. "What Is Strategy?," *Harvard Business Review* (74:6), 1996, pp. 61-78.

Prewitt, E. "The Agile 100," *CIO Magazine* (17:21), August 15, 2004, pp. 44-47.

Sambamurthy, V., Bharadwaj. A., and Grover, V. "Shaping Agility Through Digital Options: Reconceptualizing the Role of Information Technology in Contemporary Firms," *MIS Quarterly* (27:2), 2003, pp. 237-263.

Sarkis, J. "Benchmarking for Agility," *Benchmarking* (8:2), 2001, pp. 88-107.

Teece, D., Pisano. G., and Shuen, A. "Dynamic Capabilities and Strategic Management," *Strategic Management Journal* (18:7), 1997, pp. 509-533.

Trigeorgis, L. *Real Options: Managerial Flexibility and Strategy in Resource Allocation*, Cambridge, MA: MIT Press, 1996.

Ward, C. "What Is Agility?," *Industrial Engineering* (26:11), 1994, pp. 14-16.

Weill, P., and Broadbent, M. *Leveraging the New Infrastructure: How Market Leaders Capitalize on Information Technology*, Boston: Harvard Business School Press, 1998.

Weill, P., Subramani, M., and Broadbent, M. "Building IT Infrastructure for Strategic Agility," *Sloan Management Review* (44:1), 2002, pp. 57-65.

Wixom, B. H., and Watson, H. J. "An Empirical Investigation of the Factors Affecting Data Warehousing Success," *MIS Quarterly* (25:1), 2001, pp. 17-41.

ABOUT THE AUTHORS

Eric Overby is a doctoral student at the Goizueta Business School at Emory University. His area of specialization is information systems. Prior to pursuing an academic career, Eric was a senior manager in the consulting practices of BearingPoint, Inc. and Arthur Andersen LLP. He has worked with multiple Fortune 500 companies including The Coca-Cola Company, BellSouth, DuPont, Colgate-Palmolive, the Southern Company, and Georgia-Pacific, providing guidance in such areas as product development, legal and risk consulting, and IT and electronic commerce strategy, development, and implementation. His research explores patterns of activity in electronic markets and other virtual environments, and he is also interested in the business value of information technology. Eric can be reached at eric_overby@bus.emory.edu.

Anandhi Bharadwaj is an associate professor of Information Systems in the Goizueta Business School at Emory University. She received her Ph.D. from Texas A&M University. Her research focuses on strategic and organizational issues related to information technologies and capabilities. Anandhi's research has been published in journals such as *Management Science*, *MIS Quarterly*, *IEEE Transactions in Engineering Management*, and *Annals of Operations Research*. She has served as an associate editor for *MIS Quarterly* and currently serves as an associate editor for *Information Systems Research* and on the editorial board of *Journal of the AIS*. Anandhi can be reached at ab@bus.emory.edu.

V. Sambamurthy (Ph.D., University of Minnesota, 1989) is the Eli Broad Professor of Information Technology at the Eli Broad Graduate School of Management at Michigan State University. He is also the Executive Director of the Center for Leadership of the Digital Enterprise, a new research center devoted to examining issues related to the interactions between business strategy, business process management, governance, and information technology management. He has expertise in how firms successfully leverage information technologies in their business strategies, products, services, and organizational processes. Most of his work has been funded by the Financial Executives Research Foundation, the Advanced Practices Council (APC), and the National Science Foundation. His work has been published in journals such as *MIS Quarterly*, *Information Systems Research*, *Management Science*, *Organization Science*, *Decision Sciences*, and *IEEE Transactions on Engineering Management*. He has served on the editorial boards of a variety of journals, including *MIS Quarterly*, *Management Science*, *Information Systems Research*, *Management Science*, *IEEE Transactions on Engineering Management*, and *Journal of Strategic Information Systems*. Currently, he is the Editor-in-Chief of *Information Systems Research*. He can be reached at smurthy@msu.edu.

20 AGILE ENTERPRISE CORNERSTONES: Knowledge, Values, and Response Ability

Rick Dove
Paradigm Shift International
Questa, NM U.S.A.

Abstract   *The concept of the agile enterprise emerged in the early 2990s from a Department of Defense/National Science Foundation-sponsored industry-collaborative study at Lehigh University. The intent was to forecast the competitive environment of 2005 and beyond. The accuracy of that work is evident in today's emerging business strategies, practices, and technology-infrastructure support. In general, however, agility is creeping into the business environment with compelling spot applications, such as outsourcing and business process management initiatives. This paper examines new risk-management value-understandings, the nature of reality confronted by agile enterprise, and updates previously published agile-enterprise system-engineering concepts. The purpose of this paper is to illuminate requirements for those who would design and build the necessarily agile IT infrastructure support.*

Keywords   Agility, agile enterprise, response ability, knowledge management, value propositioning, reality factors, business process management (BPM), enterprise risk management (ERM)

1   PERSONAL EXPERIENCES

My purpose is to advance the state of knowledge of agile-enterprise *fundamentals* with this paper. Not much has been said in the literature of fundamentals and principles. Generally the focus has been on specific business practices, response-enabling and responsive infrastructure modalities, and much on agile programming. Fundamentals in specific areas have been addressed by Stephen Haeckel (1995, 1999) for sense-and-respond enterprise concepts: the KBSI TEAMWORK project (Benjamin et al. 1999) for adaptive-process analysis and modeling tools; "Manifesto for Agile Software Development" (Beck et al. 2001) for positioning extreme programming on principles, and spawning a community of practice; Anna Börjesson and Lars Mathiassen (2003) for case analysis of software improvement practices aligned to agile enterprise needs; IBM, Microsoft, and Hewlett-Packard for infrastructure development and support tools; and Gartner and Meta Group for the important cultural-change vanguard-role they spearhead.

As there is little focus in the literature, or in practice, for fundamentals and principles of agile systems and agile enterprise, I will review the formation of my perspectives and subsequent research.

My interest in agile systems began in the 1980s, when I led a software company that introduced a CAD-like tool and object-oriented methodologies to the design of a factory-wide control system. This had a profound impact on my appreciation for the role that architecture and design principles play in the integration of complex systems that must undergo continuous change.

In the early 1990s, I was co-investigator of a project at Lehigh University that identified agility as the competitive frontier (Nagel and Dove 1991), and subsequently set-up and led The Agility Forum's research agenda (Dove 1998). Choosing an industry-collaborative workshop approach, we analyzed existing flexible systems and the breadth of change they accommodated (Dove 1996). Purposely, we involved people who were wrestling with real problems in need of agile solutions, laboring under real constraints imposed by business and cultural reality. The collaboration involved over a thousand people in a few hundred organizations, over the course of approximately four years, and produced, among many other things, an Agile Enterprise Reference Model (Dove et al. 1996). That work by the Agility Forum succeeded in influencing world-wide appreciation and attention is evident in current technology focus, business strategies, and academic pursuits.

In the late 1990s, I continued with collaborative research to refine and verify agile design principles for business systems of all types, including business processes and corporate strategies as systems. I thought I was closing a life-chapter with the publication of these results in *Response Ability—The Language, Structure, and Culture of the Agile Enterprise* (Dove 2001b).

Along came a visionary CEO, starting up a major semiconductor foundry business in Malaysia, with a green field opportunity to build a radically different enterprise strategy—one that wouldn't shackle pursuit of new opportunity in markets, business strategy, and business process. In my role as CIO, he wanted an enterprise IT infra-structure that would enable agile-ERP (enterprise resource planning) without penalty, and painless rapid interconnect to customers and suppliers with disparate systems. He also wanted real-time transparency with Web-enabled access to all operational status, financial status, and project and production work-in-process. Many lessons were learned, but the most poignant was the need for a new agile-security strategy (Dove 2004b) demanded by the new potential for serious corporate damage—an inevitable consequence of agile enterprise.

This was followed by an interim division-presidential position at a company with metal rapid prototyping technology. The challenge was to transform an embedded research and development organization and culture into a semi-standalone enterprise, with some shared and many new business processes, and with a culture compatible with its agile technology and market opportunity.

Learning from these confrontations with business-change reality, my focus turned to agile business process management, agile cyber security, organizational and human behavioral reality, and decision-making behavioral factors (Dove 2005b). My earlier characterizations of agility needed a third dimension added to the two of *response ability* and knowledge management—that of value propositioning, as this is what determines decisions for action.

This paper addresses response ability, knowledge management, and value propositioning—as cornerstones of agile anything. Before looking at the cornerstones, context will be set by first looking at the basic value proposition for being agile, and then the reality factors of the business environment that must be addressed for effective agility.

2 THE VALUE PROPOSITION

Plain and simple, the value proposition for enterprise agility is rooted firmly in risk management—more specifically, *enterprise risk management* (ERM). The purpose of agility is to maintain both reactive and proactive response options in the face of uncertainty. Current ERM extends standard risk management strategies to a larger set of business risks, notably those of operations and project decisions, but is generally focused on risk analysis as it affects available choices. Half the story. The other half of risk *management* is to proactively increase the choice options with lower risk alternatives. Precisely the purpose of agility.

CIO Magazine's Scott Berinato, writing on ERM and its relationship to IT, says, "The reason these risks are suddenly being accounted for is because the systems are becoming ever more critical. Today, one bad IT decision can severely hamper—or even take down—a company" (2004, p. 52). Decisions about IT infrastructure and business-process support affect the entire organization, with major operational impact—especially if they fail to perform as and when expected.

Rockwell Collins, an aerospace company, is cited in that same article as an early adopter of ERM decision-making procedures. They lost 20 percent of their revenue generation capabilities as a result of 9/11, yet

> The company has turned a profit every single quarter after 9/11. And in January 2004, *Forbes* called Rockwell Collins the best-managed aerospace firm in America...."We're able to react [to that complex environment] because of our risk mind-set," says [CIO John-Paul] Besong. "With what happened to us, our *agility* was called to task. And we had the risk methodology in place to handle it" (Berinato 2004, p. 48).

They have clearly made the connection between agility and risk management.

Agility expands the options for response when unpredictable events occur—by reducing the cost of response, the time of response, the predictability of response, and the range of response. It does this principally through infrastructure, systems, and business processes that are structured for *response ability*. And, as will be shown, it is not necessary to reengineer massively or disruptively to gain benefits—because the very nature of agile structuring supports graceful, incremental migration. Agility is, after all, about effective change management.

3   REALITY AND RISK

The *enterprise risk management–integrated framework* (COSO 2004, p. 5) from the Committee of Sponsoring Organizations of the Treadway Commission contains the following caveat:

> While enterprise risk management provides important benefits, limitations exist....limitations result from the realities that human judgment in decision making can be faulty, decisions on responding to risk and establishing controls need to consider the relative costs and benefits, breakdowns can occur because of human failures such as simple errors or mistakes, controls can be circumvented by collusion of two or more people, and management has the ability to override enterprise risk management decisions. These limitations preclude a board and management from having absolute assurance as to achievement of the entity's objectives.

These reality factors hurt precisely because they are insufficiently recognized when would-be-agile system and process requirements are established. If they are understood for what they are, and addressed with respect, they can be greatly mitigated and often precluded.

Seven areas of uncontrollable business-environment behavior were first identified by the Agile Security Forum (Dove 2004a). They were subsequently generalized as a framework of reality factors for employment, along with other frameworks, in agile systems requirements development (Dove 2005a).

Reality factors stem from human behaviors and organizational behaviors, which can be whimsical, willful, vengeful, criminal, forgetful, distracted, expedient, unknowing, and otherwise act outside of what we wish they *ought* to do. According to Ashby's law of requisite variety, a system must be at least as agile as the environment with which it is expected to deal.

Although the reality-factors framework remains constant, the issues within are enterprise-situation dependent. We will look at them as they were identified for electric utility companies concerned with agile cyber-security strategies. The generalizations to any company with any agile-strategy concern should be transparent.

Increasing pace of new technology. Upgrading and replacing the IT infrastructure and applications is necessary for acceptable-practice parity, and increasingly demanded by regulatory bodies for cost containment and improved customer service. Yet we see new vulnerabilities in legacy systems still being discovered and exploited. Newer technology brings new and different vulnerabilities—that's what new technology does. Decreasing technology life cycles and increasing technology variety amplifies the situation. The historical record is undeniable—and demands appreciation and mitigation.

Increasing complexity of systems. The march is on for better integration of systems that support operations. Likewise for more network reach: network node count is growing and networks are interconnecting on larger scales with more sophistication. The complexity of software systems alone has long passed our abilities for analytical predictability. Networked business operations overlaid with a networked global community have added new combinations and complexity. We cannot predict with any assurance at all the results of a system change, no matter how small. Companies merge and race to interconnect; they upgrade, replace, and add new technology continuously; competition and opportunity drives evolving customer and supplier interfaces; and business operations are fragmenting and distributing business processes globally. The law of unintended consequences irrefutably expresses itself naturally in complex systems under change—and demands appreciation and mitigation.

Creeping agile-business practices. Whether an enterprise (an electric utility, for example) considers itself agile or not, it cannot avoid outsourcing imperatives for IT, billing, call centers, and other business processes; nor for electronic response-enhancing interconnects with energy suppliers, energy brokers, cogenerators, demand-response customers, AMR (automated meter reading), SCADA (supervisory control and data acquisition) field assets, and wireless-linked field personnel. These alone don't constitute an agile enterprise strategy, but they are, nevertheless, part of today's business strategy, driven by needs for better spot-responsiveness. Inescapable, yet each move brings new and greater security vulnerability—demanding appreciation and mitigation.

Increasing globalization. It is not a regional game anymore. Enterprises (an electric utility, for example) are outsourcing business processes off-shore, buying energy off-shore, and merging multinationally. Globalization brings more interconnected business operations—and with it, different ethics, different values, different perceptions of risk, different interconnected technology, and different nation-state interests. This means more sources of vulnerability, at the least. But economics and growth-pursuits will not be denied—and demand appreciation and mitigation.

Natural human behavior. Security impacts individual productivity and goal priorities. In so doing, it is often ignored or circumvented in actual daily decision making and practice. We humans are wired the way we are. We make decisions every day, all day long—as IT system administrators, as policy makers, as procedure followers, as users in all departments at all levels, and even as disgruntled employees. Our perceptions of what is right or expedient are biased by hopes and expectations, as well as the latest alligator that influences our immediate priorities and values. We are the source of human error. On top of all of this, we are whimsical. Rules are made to be broken, and they are, in any event, made for others who are less wise than we. Murphy's law is not a joke. And all of this just deals with people who are trying to do the right thing. But the perverse also exist. Optimal by-the-book actions and decisions do not and will not prevail anywhere—demanding appreciation and mitigation.

Natural organization behavior. Organizations are aggregates of natural human behaviors. On top of that, collective behavior is different than individual behavior. Security impacts organizational productivity and goal priorities. In so doing, strategy is typically designed and deployed inadequately. Among decision makers, there are inherent conflicts which remain unresolved, power politics and positions that exert biased influence, and competition for limited resources. Research shows (Cyert 1992; Simon 1997) that decision makers are ruled first by individual rather than group objectives, mitigate conflict by compromising greater values to achieve consensus, seek solutions that are acceptable rather than optimal, and vary risk-seeking and risk-averse behavior with economic conditions. Neither local optimality (within company or department) nor global valuation (for community or company) are standard characteristics of organizational decision making and behavior. It won't be changed. It is the nature of the beast—demanding appreciation and mitigation.

Agile threat sources. Ashby's law of requisite variety demands that a response system be at least as agile as the environment that creates the need for response. Scourge technology has advanced to the point where we now refer to zero-hour attacks for the time it takes from release to massive Internet presence. Meanwhile, the increasing sophistication of attack development and tool technologies has already reduced the time between vulnerability discovery and exploitation to mere days. Infected machines and public distribution of attack tools mobilizes massive resources quickly. Large-scale grass-roots retaliation occurs when independent personal reactions weigh-in patriotically on national disputes or indignantly target companies on the wrong side of a thought community. Amateur and professional alike benefit from this loosely connected global collaboration of independent resources. These developments are less than three years old—more are on their way. As more value is made more available for theft and damage, the targets of opportunity become irresistible—demanding appreciation and mitigation.

4   AGILITY CORNERSTONES

Enterprise agility has three core enabling elements.

- Accurate timely awareness that a change should be made, enabled by focused *knowledge management* processes

- Effective prioritization and choice-making among competing response-alternatives, enabled by *value-propositioning skills*

- A facilitated ability to change business processes and to customize operational responses in real time, which we call *response ability*

4.1 Knowledge Management

Knowledge management is an overused term with broad interpretation, but with real meaning for the agile enterprise, as discussed in Dove (1999). Knowledge about external and internal events and status that call for attentive response is the fuel of agility. "We should have known" is an off-hand observation of hindsight; but when the ability to respond exists, it becomes a glaring pain. Maybe it's inaccurate information-network knowledge that inhibits timely service restoration. Perhaps it's mismatched supply-demand realities that impact production capability. Possibly it's lack of operational or corporate transparency that runs afoul of Sarbanes-Oxley. Maybe it's lack of knowledge about new security threats and vulnerabilities, or a lack of knowledge about who needs newly available information or who needs obsolete knowledge cor-

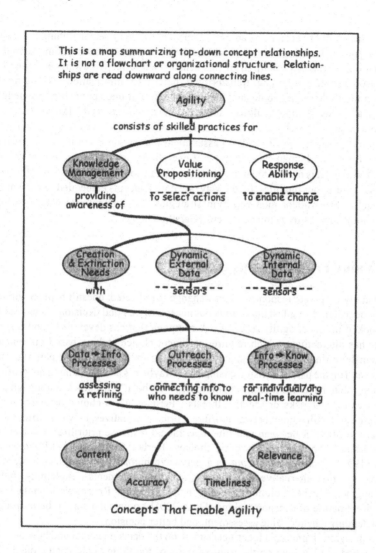

This is a map summarizing top-down concept relationships. It is not a flowchart or organizational structure. Relationships are read downward along connecting lines.

Figure 1. Knowledge Management for Agility

rected. In all cases, not knowing things that should be known is frustrating to managers, and met with decreasing tolerance by both stakeholders and law.

Figure 1 is a concept map of knowledge management aspects that support the agile enterprise.

When knowledge management focuses on awareness, it deals with distinctions between data, information, and knowledge. Monitoring external and internal events and status produces data, and lots of it. That data becomes information when it is filtered for relevancy, timeliness, accuracy, and content. But no action takes place on that information until it becomes meaningful knowledge, a very personal thing that resides in heads, not in databases. Good awareness demands good sensors in both external and internal environments. With all of this sensor data, effective awareness must have processes for selecting and transforming data into information, providing that information to the right people, and helping them turn it into actionable knowledge.

Data has four distinct qualities. *Accuracy* and *timeliness* can be facilitated, or even accomplished, with technologies and outside services. *Relevancy* requires thoughtful human intervention—for it needs an assessment that action is required. *Content* is a blend—for only a human can determine if everything needed for intelligent action is present, and what is needed to augment sensor data to complete the data-to-information process. These four qualities, by the way, are core concepts embedded in current U.S. Defense of Department modernization strategies for warfighting—where real-time information superiority is the new focus (Garstka 2000).

4.2 Value Propositioning Skills

Timely corporate response, when a change is indicated, doesn't happen without a timely decision. But a fast decision is not necessarily a good decision—a crucial area overlooked in earlier agility research. A company that has developed good *response ability* has alternatives, which require intelligent choice-making based on insightful problem definitions and sound value propositioning skills—both on the part of decision makers and on the part of decision champions. Maybe it's a choice among new software solutions that have conflicting champions. Maybe it's a choice among alternate responses to new risks or security threats. Perhaps it's a choice between what to outsource and with whom, between different pricing initiatives, between different new services to offer, or between real-time operational response priorities. Decisions are much easier when there are few or no choices. Herbert Simon's Nobel Prize winning work (1997) identified *satisficing* as a pervasive human psychological force which accepts the first alternative that satisfies stated requirements—explaining, but not excusing, why the best solutions are often not considered. Recent work on the human behavioral nature of decision making (Dove 2005b) points the way to better problem understandings, better value assessment, and better decisions.

A decision champion's focus needs to be on the decision maker and how decisions are reached, rather than on the righteousness of the thing being championed. This understanding is especially lacking when technology is being championed, as both champion and decision maker are variously seduced, overwhelmed, impressed, confused, skeptical, and even repulsed when technology is the issue. Where technology projects or products are concerned, too often there is no acceptance of responsibility for crafting effective value propositions. There seems instead a belief that technology stands naked for all to see and evaluate, needing only a guided tour of features and obvious benefits, and that an inappropriate evaluation is a fault of the evaluator and not of the champion. I have shown elsewhere (Dove 2005b) that an effective value proposition is not about the solution, but rather about the problem and value perceptions of the people who will choose a solution.

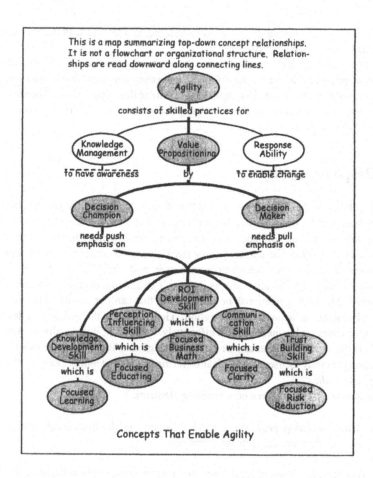

This is a map summarizing top-down concept relationships. It is not a flowchart or organizational structure. Relationships are read downward along connecting lines.

Figure 2. Value Propositioning for Agility

Figure 2 is a concept map of value propositioning aspects that support agile enterprise.

The thing a decision champion must accomplish is to win approval from those who control corporate priorities and strategy, those who commit funds and resources. This may mean an engineering project manager winning approval for an internal development project, an account manager seeking selection as an external supplier of products or services, or a business manager seeking budget, capital, or strategy approval. In all cases, the process is fundamentally the same. In this respect, we see that some key responsibilities and skills of technically focused people, business-focused people, and sales-focused people are identical (we pause while all parties shudder at this repulsive thought). They are all successful only to the extent that they can be effective champions of the projects and products they want decision makers to value and select. When they play the role of the champion effectively, they are indistinguishable. All face the same decision makers employing the same decision logic, and all win with the same skills, perspective, and argument strategy.

On the surface, a decision champion is the person seeking to show better value than all other alternatives. It is tempting to think that the champion therefore has more to lose if value is not perceived in its best light. But of course this is not true—all parties have a lot to lose. Both parties need the same basic skills, one with a communications-push emphasis and the other with a communications-pull emphasis.

4.3 Response Ability

The ability to change effectively, or rather its lack, tends to be the pain felt initially that creates a call for more agility. Maybe it is a project that overruns cost, takes much to long, fails to meet performance expectations, or simply wasn't approved because it can't be integrated into the current legacy environment. Perhaps it is an unexpected operational situation that overwhelms resources and capabilities. Possibly it is regulatory or compliance requirements that can't be accommodated quick enough or affordably. Maybe it is rising risk or vulnerability that can't be mitigated responsibly, or an ugly merger or acquisition integration. Generally it is the inability to develop, support, or change a business process effectively. Whatever, it is usually the sense of failure in the face of a necessary or desired change that illuminates the need. This realization generally focuses an organization on the factors that inhibit change—the lack of *response ability*.

Response ability has three core enabling elements.

• A *culture of change proficiency*, molded by language for discussing and debating types of change and competency at change

• A *system response architecture*, structured as reconfigurable systems of reusable modules in a scalable framework (RRS)

• A *process for change management*, with designated responsibilities for strategic business engineering and tactical change implementation

Change proficiency is a competency facilitated or impeded by an organization's culture. Change proficiency is fostered, nurtured, and developed in organizations by people who recognize it as a worthwhile pursuit. It is practiced, refined, talked about, debated, valued, and taught; and it seeps into the culture through this frequent exercise of language. The metric and change-domain frameworks shown in Figure 3 form a common language for change proficiency.

Naive discussion often confuses change proficiency with time and cost of change—when in fact quality, and scope of change are equally important. *Quality* demands a predictable and robust result, accomplished on time, on budget, and on spec. *Scope* is the principal difference between flexibility and *response ability*—measuring a capability for accommodating unanticipated change, rather than a fixed set of predefined options.

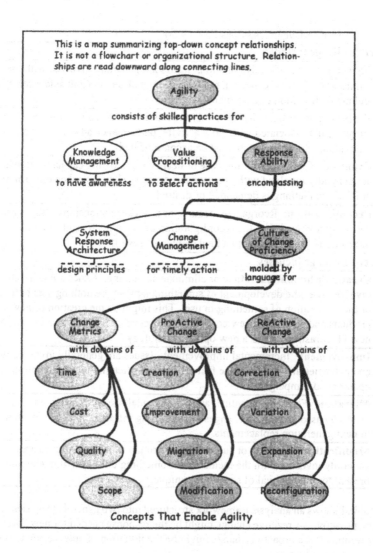

This is a map summarizing top-down concept relationships. It is not a flowchart or organizational structure. Relationships are read downward along connecting lines.

Agility

consists of skilled practices for

Knowledge Management — Value Propositioning — Response Ability

to have awareness — to select actions — encompassing

System Response Architecture — Change Management — Culture of Change Proficiency

design principles — for timely action — molded by language for

Change Metrics — ProActive Change — ReActive Change

with domains of — with domains of — with domains of

Time — Creation — Correction

Cost — Improvement — Variation

Quality — Migration — Expansion

Scope — Modification — Reconfiguration

Concepts That Enable Agility

Figure 3. Language of Change-Proficiency Culture

Understanding a problem space effectively requires an understanding of the dynamics that will constantly change its nature. A problem stated in today's immediate and static terms is a fleeting characterization, as the environment that causes and defines the problem will continue to change. An analysis framed to consider different types of changes forces problems to be understood in terms of their dynamics—whether the problem be a new market opportunity that needs to be developed, a merger opportunity that requires integration, a business process that might be outsourced, or simply an intolerable integration mess that needs to be fixed.

Table 1. Response-Dynamics Issues Framework

Reactive change includes
Correction: Rectify a dysfunction. Issues are generally involved with the failure to perform as expected, recovery from malfunction and side effects, and the rectification of a problem.
Variation: Real-time change within the mission of the solution space. Issues are generally associated with daily activity, performance adjustments, and interaction variances which must be accommodated.
Expansion/Contraction: Increase or decrease of existing capacity. Issues are generally involved with quantity and capacity changes, when either more or less of something is demanded or desired.
Reconfiguration: Reorganize resource or process relationships. Issues are generally involved with the reconfiguration of existing elements and their interactions, sometimes with added elements as well.
Proactive change includes
Creation/Elimination: Make or eliminate something. Issues are generally involved with the development of something new where nothing was before, or the elimination of something in use. This might be the creation of new products and services, a new corporate culture, new knowledge and skills, a new IT infrastructure, or a new operating strategy.
Improvement: Incremental improvement. Issues are generally involved with competencies and performance factors, and are often the focus of continual, open-ended campaigns.
Migration: Foreseen, eventual, and fundamental change. Issues are generally associated with changes to supporting infrastructure, or transitions to next generation replacements.
Modification: Addition or subtraction of unique capability. Issues are generally involved with the inclusion of something unlike anything already present, or the removal of something unique.

Table 1 shows an analysis framework structured into two general categories: reactive and proactive. A reactive change might be the response needed for new Sarbanes-Oxley compliance; a proactive change might be the initiation of outsourcing to reduce costs or provide new services.

System Response Architecture. A system is any organization of common-purpose interacting components: a team of people, a network of controllers, an IT ERP suite, a chain of suppliers, or an interrelated set of business processes. Definitions of key terms as they used here follow:

* System: A group of modules sharing a common interaction framework and serving a common purpose.
* Framework: A set of standards constraining and enabling the interactions of compatible system nodules.
* Module: A separable system subunit with a self contained capability-purpose-identity, and capable of interaction with other modules.

Hundreds of various systems exhibiting good *response ability* in business environments were analyzed by working groups at the Agility Forum in the 1990s. Common design principles enabling good response were identified and subsequently refined (Dove 2001b). The conclusion was that response-able systems are reconfigurable systems of reusable modules in a scalable framework, employing principles shown in Figure 4. Key is attention to parsimony in framework design, and attention to requisite variety in module population—two prime principles of good systems engineering.

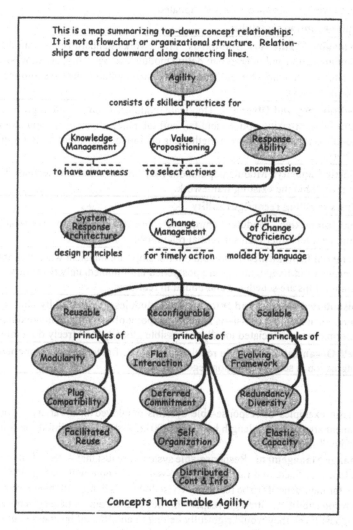

Figure 4. Agile-Design Principles Framework

Table 2. Agile-Design Principles Framework

Principles enabling reusability
Self-Contained Modules. Modules are distinct, separable, self-sufficient units cooperating toward a shared common purpose.
Plug Compatibility. Modules share defined interaction and interface standards; they are easily inserted or removed.
Facilitated Reuse. Modules are reusable/replicable; responsibilities for ready reuse/replication and for management, maintenance, and upgrade of component inventory are specifically designated.
Principles enabling scalability
Evolvable Framework Standards. Frameworks standardize inter-module communication and interaction; define module compatibility; are monitored/updated to accommodate old, current, and new modules; they are minimized (parsimonious).
Redundancy and Diversity. Duplicate modules are employed to provide capacity right-sizing options and fail-soft tolerance; diversity among similar modules employing different methods is exploited, with attention to requisite variety.
Elastic Capacity. Module populations may be increased and decreased widely within the existing framework.
Principles enabling reconfigurability
Flat Interaction. Modules communicate directly on a peer-to-peer relationship; parallel rather than sequential relationships are favored.
Deferred Commitment. Module relationships are transient when possible; decisions and fixed bindings are postponed until immediately necessary; relationships are scheduled and bound in real-time.
Distributed Control and Information. Modules are directed by objective rather than method; decisions are made at point of maximum knowledge; information is associated locally, accessible globally, and freely disseminated.
Self-Organization. Module relationships are self-determined; component interaction is self-adjusting or negotiated.

Classic examples of response-able systems employed in a variety of business environment are covered at length by Dove (2001a, 2001b), and exhibit the principles expanded in Table 2.

Change Management. Response-able systems are just that—*able*. But they must be developed, utilized, and maintained purposely by people with designated responsibilities for their benefits to be realized. These functions come with both strategic and tactical responsibilities. Strategic responsibilities plan for and initiate systems change; at the highest level, they would rightfully belong to an office of business engineering. Tactical responsibilities affect systems change, through management and implementation of the change process, which I will call change engineering.

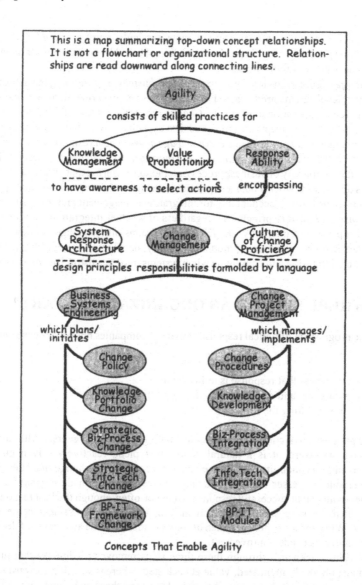

This is a map summarizing top-down concept relationships. It is not a flowchart or organizational structure. Relationships are read downward along connecting lines.

Concepts That Enable Agility

Figure 5. Change Management Framework

On the *business engineering* side, *change policy* establishes and maintains the proactive risk management options, and demands that a culture of change proficiency be implemented. *Knowledge portfolio change* ensures that an organization has the knowledge it needs, when and where it needs it, and requires that someone manage the organizational knowledge portfolio. *Strategic business process change* recognizes responsibility for monitoring and determining when a new or different process would be advantageous. *Strategic IT change* is responsibility for corporate standards and policy—and especially infrastructure frameworks and security. *BP-IT framework change* is responsibility for the prudent evolution of both IT-infrastructure frameworks and business process frameworks.

Change engineering elements mirror those in *business engineering*, but at the tactical project level. Some are triggered by the business engineering elements, and some are triggered by operational practices. *Change procedures* responsibility ensures that change proficiency concepts are employed, lest expediency or unfamiliar change situation encourages an *ad hoc* procedure. *Knowledge development* responsibility facilitates exposure, collaboration, and learning. *Business process integration* responsibility respects the complexity of business process interaction, ensuring that unintended consequences do not arise when a business process is changed. *Information technology integration* responsibility is accountable for integration management and the maintenance of *response architecture* principles—regardless of whether integration activity is outsourced or performed internally. *BP-IT modules* responsibility manages module change in all frameworks—maintaining module inventory, developing or acquiring new modules, and configuring and employing when systems must be customized or assembled.

4   WHERE SHOULD AN ORGANIZATION START?

The progression of typical response activity at companies not yet agile is generally from

(1) awareness that response is indicated to
(2) evaluating and deciding upon the best action to take to
(3) implementing the response

Yet the progression of competency development is generally the reverse. Although this may seem backward, it is a natural course in typical, reactively driven business environments. An inability to affect a management-demanded change first stubs its toe on intractable processes and infrastructure. Once these are made *response able*, it becomes evident that successful responses were not-often-enough the best responses to make—then the processes of decision making and value assessment come under scrutiny. When these are honed, it then becomes evident that the awareness of decision-triggering events needs improvement.

Working backwards through these three steps removes roadblocks that provide immediate, although attenuated, value at each step. whereas working forward cannot provide value until all three are in balance. However, these statements are only true when looking at total-enterprise agility. When a specific department or process is the focus, it may well be that the lack of timely information is the roadblock, rather than effective decisiveness or response implementation. There is ample evidence that incremental successes in process reengineering, working one area at a time, is a much surer way to corporate-wide success. For one, the incremental process provides proof of values and methods to other areas with high resistance and inertia. For another, it can attack high-payoff, fast-result, low-cost areas to build momentum and convert skeptics. Importantly, it narrows the focus to a few variables rather than the complexity and variability of corporate-wide infrastructures and processes.

5 CONCLUSION

Agility is a strategic objective that must coexist in harmony and synergy with other objectives, priorities, and capabilities, whether at the enterprise or departmental level. It is enabled by infrastructure, business processes, and strategic policy; but in the end, it is limited by the visceral knowledge and values of change proficiency held by all involved. Agility can't be bought in a box—it must be actively practiced as a mind set. And to be effective, it must be fit to the specifics of the organizational needs and realities.

The need for enterprise agility is rooted in enterprise risk management. The effectiveness of enterprise agility is rooted in reality-factors mitigation. The enablement of enterprise agility is rooted in infrastructure *response ability*—because reality rules, and a necessary path of graceful, incremental migration is that reality.

Graceful, incremental migration is necessary because few companies can take a time-out for massive reorganization. Graceful, because awkward attempts will derail the appetite for transformation. Incremental, because it reduces perceived risk. Developing the *response ability* aspect of agility first demonstrates a compelling capability asset that demands to be leveraged. Its presence creates pressure for better knowledge management and better value propositioning, instigating the transformation to agile enterprise

Against the Gods—The Remarkable Story of Risk (Bernstein 1996, p. 1) suggests that "the revolutionary idea that defines the boundary between modern times and the past is the mastery of risk: the notion that the future is more than a whim of the gods and that men and women are not passive before nature" ...or passive before the reality of the enterprise environment. Agility converts the future from an enemy into an opportunity.

Football has response statistics down to a science: 3.9 seconds for the quarterback to put the ball in play, or likely failure. We don't yet have similar relevant performance metrics, or response-timing awareness, for enterprise agility, or for IT agility. Clearly there is much yet to do on fundamental understandings for agile enterprise.

REFERENCES

Beck, K., Beedle, M., van Bennekum, A., Cockburn, A., Cunningham, W., Fowler, M., Grenning, J., Highsmith, J., Hunt, A., Jeffries, R., Kern, J., Marick, B., Martin, R., Mellor, S., Schwaber, K., Sutherland, J., and Thomas, D. "Manifesto for Agile Software Development," 2001 (available online at www.AgileManifesto.org).

Benjamin, P., Erraguntla. M., Mayer, R, and Marshall, C. "Toolkit for Enabling Analysis and Modeling of Adaptive Workflow (TEAMWORK)," *ACM SIGGROUP Bulletin* (20:3), December 1999, p. 9.

Berinato, S. "Risk's Rewards," *CIO Magazine*, November 1, 2004, pp. 46-58.

Bernstein, P. *Against the Gods—The Remarkable Story of Risk*, New York: Wiley, 1996.

Börjesson, A., and Mathiassen, L "Organizational Dynamics in Software Process Improvement: The Agility Challenge," in *IT Innovation for Adaptablity and Competitiveness*, B. Fitzgerald and E. Wynn (Eds.), Boston: Kluwer Academic Publishers, 2004, pp. 135-156.

COSO. "Enterprise Risk Management—Integrated Framework," Committee of Sponsoring Organizations of the Treadway Commission, 2004 (available online at www.coso.org/publications.htm).

Cyert, R, and March, J. *A Behavioral Theory of the Firm*, Oxford: Blackwell Publishing, 1992.

Dove, R. *Design Principles for Highly Adaptable Business Systems with Tangible Manufacturing Examples, Maynard's Industrial Handbook*, New York: McGraw-Hill, 2001a.

Dove R. "A Framework Driven Procedure for Developing Agile-System Requirements—With an Agile-Security Strategy Example," unpublished paper, 2005.

Dove, R. "Frameworks for Analyzing and Developing Agile Security Strategies," Santa Fe, NM: The Agile Security Forum, 2004a (available online at www.AgileSecurityForum.com/docs/AsfPaperSixFrameworks.pdf).

Dove, R. "Knowledge Management, Response Ability, and the Agile Enterprise," *Journal of Knowledge Management*, March 1999, pp. 18-35 (available online at www.parshift.com/Files/PsiDocs/Rkd9Art1.pdf).

Dove, R., "Realsearch: A Framework for Knowledge Management and Continuing Education," in *Proceedings IEEE Aerospace Conference*, Vale, CO, March 1998 (available online at www.parshift.com/Files/PsiDocs/RealSrch1.zip).

Dove, R. "Rectifying the Security Gap," Santa Fe, NM: The Agile Security Forum, 2004b (available online at www.AgileSecurityForum.com/docs/AsfPaperConceptCall.pdf).

Dove, R. *Response Ability: The Language, Structure, and Culture of the Agile Enterprise*, New York: Wiley, 2001b.

Dove, R. "Tools for Analyzing and Constructing Agile Capabilities," Bethlehem, PA: Agility Forum, January 1996 (available online at www.parshift.com/Files/PsiDocs/Rkd4Art4.pdf).

Dove, R. *Value Propositioning—Perception and Misperception in Decision Making*, Tucson, AZ: Iceni Books, 2005b.

Dove, R., Hartman, S., and Benson, S. "An Agile Enterprise Reference Model, with a Case Study of Remmele Engineering," Bethlehem, PA: Agility Forum, 1996.

Garstka, J. "Network Centric Warfare: An Overview of Emerging Theory," Alexandria, VA: Phalanx, Military Operations Research Society, December 2000 (available online at www.mors.org/publications/phalanx/dec00/feature.htm).

Haeckel, S. H. *Adaptive Enterprise: Creating and Leading Sense-and-Respond Organizations*, Boston: Harvard Business School Press, 1999.

Haeckel, S. H. "Adaptive Enterprise Design: The Sense-and-Respond Model," *Planning Review* (23:3), 1995, pp. 6-42.

Nagel, R., and Dove, R. *21st Century Manufacturing Strategy: An Industry-Led View*, Collingdale, PA: DIANE Publishing Company, 1991.

Simon, H. *Administrative Behavior* (4th ed.), New York: Simon & Schuster 1997.

ABOUT THE AUTHOR

Rick Dove is CEO of Paradigm Shift International and chairman of the Agile Security Forum. He has a BSEE from Carnegie-Mellon University and did graduate work at the University of California, Berkeley, in Computer Science. He has run companies producing software products, manufacturing machinery and services, and strategic planning and management services. He was co-principle investigator for the program at Lehigh University that initiated interest in agility, and led the subsequent Agility Forum research and industry involvement activity. He is author of *Response Ability: The Language, Structure, and Culture of the Agile Enterprise* and *Value Propositioning: Perception and Misperception in Decision Making*. Rick can be reached at dove@parshift.com.

Part 6

Challenges Ahead

21 HOW TO MAKE GOVERNMENT AGILE TO COPE WITH ORGANIZATIONAL CHANGE

Yvonne Dittrich
Jan Pries-Heje
Kristian Hjort-Madsen
IT University of Copenhagen
Copenhagen, Denmark

Abstract   *In Denmark, the largest organizational change project with information technology ever is being shaped. By January 2007, all counties and municipalities will be reorganized. More than 1 million employees will be affected, and all public IT systems will have to change. To make this huge change project a success, agility is needed.*

In 2003, a kind of pilot study for the coming change project was undertaken. Five municipalities on the Island of Bornholm merged. In this paper, we report on the merging process—especially the IT diffusion—through an in-depth interview study.

Our analysis of the interview data leads us to suggest five means in order to make the Danish government agile enough to cope with the upcoming major reorganization. First, the organizational change should be integrated and aligned with the IT change. Second we recommend an early start. Third, an IT vision is needed. Fourth, we recommend a rethinking of the existing public service provision. Finally, we see a need for new tools and techniques. Together we believe these five means, if implemented throughout the Danish government, will create the agility that is needed to cope with the major organizational change by 2007.

Keywords: Agility, design in use, eGovernment, mergers, organizational change, user empowerment

1 INTRODUCTION

A bill has recently been passed in parliament that will result in a total reorganization of the county and local levels of government in Denmark. The idea is to decentralize more government responsibility which requires that local units have the size to take on the added responsibility. By January 1, 2007, it is expected that the existing 271 municipalities will be merged into 100 and the current 14 counties will be amalgamated into five regions. Furthermore, it is suggested that all of the new municipalities should have one entry point for the citizens, for example, in the form of a one-stop citizen service. The Danish government is, therefore, forced to develop a strategy for the convergence of all of the affected IT systems that is agile and ready to adapt quickly to changes while also sensitive to the diffusion of new IT. Thus we believe that the balance between agility and diffusion of information technology will become a key issue for the Danish government when it undertakes the largest structural reform in 30 years.

A kind of pilot project for the structural reform was undertaken in 2003 on the Danish island of Bornholm with the merging of five municipalities and one county into the Regional Municipality of Bornholm. With regard to the structural reform in Denmark, we believe that a lot can be learned about agility, organizational change, and IT-diffusion from the process that Bornholm went through. Bornholm started out with no prior experiences for a benchmark and the process was expensive and very stressful for the employees.

In this paper, we report first results from an interview-based case-study focusing on change management and the development of work practices. We emphasize learning that can be used in the reorganization of the Danish municipalities mandated for 2007. We relate our findings and measures to the literature on agility, organizational change, work practice, and technology.

The remainder of this paper is laid out as follows. Section 2 of this paper discusses relevant theory on agility, change, and design in use. Section 3 introduces the Bornholm case. Section 4 lays out our research method. Sections 5 and 6 details our findings from analyzing our findings on organizational change and on design in use, and section 7 discusses the case findings in relation to agility. Finally, in section 8, we identify the challenges faced by the Danish government and the 100 upcoming amalgamated municipalities, and discuss how they can become agile enough to cope with the changes they are facing.

2   AGILITY, CHANGE, AND DESIGN IN USE

The discussion on agile organizations and agility in development relates management of organizational change and the development of practices that help implement the changes as part of day-to-day work. For analyzing the merger on Bornholm, we have developed an analytical framework combining the existing literature on agility with a top-down organizational change perspective and a bottom-up work practice perspective.

The joining of municipalities can be seen top-down as an *organizational change* process. When we go inside the organization and come closer to the individual adoption of the organizational change and IT, we can take a bottom-up point of view and look at it as *work practice* and *design in use*.

2.1 Agility

The discussion of agility is, on the one hand, addressing organizational change and management issues, while, on the other hand, emphasizing the importance of practices and technical support that help the people in an organization to handle change.

In this section, we will identify characteristics of agility with the purpose of developing a framework that can be used to analyze our case.

According to the Oxford Advanced Learners Dictionary Web site (http://www.oup.com/elt/oald/), lean means thin and fit or containing little or no fat. However, it can also mean "strong and efficient." According to the same dictionary, agile means that you are able to move quickly and easily or that you are able to think quickly and in an intelligent way.

Lean manufacturing is a term that grew out Japanese production methods where the focus is the absolute elimination of waste. This is implemented by just-in-time production where a process withdraws only the number of parts needed when they are needed. Recently agile manufacturing (Newman et al. 2000) has become widely accepted. Agile manufacturing regards an ability to conflate flexible manufacturing and component reuse. Flexible manufacturing is an ability to reconfigure a manufacturing system quickly and cheaply to assemble a varying part mix. Agility invokes a design philosophy that includes reuse and enables rapid redesign for entirely new applications. Thus the first characteristic of agility that we will use in our analysis is *rapid redesign*.

Dove (2001) defines agility as something more than rapid redesign and flexibility. He defines agility as both a physical ability to act, called response ability, and the intellectual ability to find appropriate things to act on, which he calls knowledge management. The first part of this definition is cognate to what we have called rapid redesign and flexibility. He just calls it change proficiency and "reusable/reconfigurable/ scalable" structural relationships that enable change. The second part, however, is new. Dove divides the knowledge management part into knowledge portfolio management and collaborative learning facilitation. We will use this part of Dove's definition of agility as our third characteristic: *knowledge management and learning*.

What types of knowledge are we then talking about when discussing changes in an organization heavily dependent on IT? A few years ago Kensing and Munk-Madsen (1993) build a model of user-developer communication. The model covers communication related to analysis and design of IT. It claims that the main domains of discourses in design are (1) users' present work, (2) technological options, and (3) the new system. The hypothesis is that *knowledge* of these three domains must be developed and integrated in order for the design process to be a success. Thus when we analyze our Bornholm case for agility, understood as knowledge management and learning, we will use the three discourses to do so.

The third characteristic we will use is *flexibility*, meaning that one is able to change to suit new conditions or situations. The importance of flexibility in developing software for rapidly changing business environments is well recognized in software development especially for Internet applications (Aoyama 1998; Baskerville et al. 2001). Agility in software development refers to the ability to not only quickly deliver the products, but also the ability to quickly adapt to changing requirements (Aoyama 1998). What we can learn from the discussion on agile development is the emphasis on concrete, everyday work practices that support the flexibility of an organization as well as well-developed and maintained infrastructures and tools that support those practices

The discussion on knowledge implicitly points to the role of the people involved in the change. In relation to software engineering, the term agility was introduced in 2001 when a group of people involved in finding, testing, and defining new methods meeting at a skiing resort in North America came up with an agile manifesto (Agile Manifesto 2001):

> We are uncovering better ways of developing software by doing it and helping others do it. Through this work we have come to value: (1) Individuals and interactions over processes and tools. (2) Working software over comprehensive documentation. (3) Customer collaboration over contract negotiation. (4) Responding to change over following a plan.

Following this line of thought, the fourth and final characteristic that we will call agility is whether *individuals are prioritized* over processes and standards.

2.2 Organizational Change

Agility of an organization has to do with change and the management of change. Organizational change in relation to IT is still attracting considerable attention. Dunphy (1996) studied organizational change in corporate settings and found that any theory of change should incorporate at least a metaphor of the nature of the organization, an analytic framework, an ideal model of an effectively functioning organization, an intervention theory, and a definition of the role of change agents.

Three different schools of organizational thought have provided metaphors of the nature of the organization. The oldest approach to organizational design and change builds on the belief that you can identify the one best way of carrying out any job. The organization is perceived as a production system where it is possible to optimize the system's efficiency and effectiveness. In the 1930s and 1940s, the classical view of organizations was challenged and a new people-oriented perspective, rather than a mechanical one, emerged, where organizations are seen as cooperative social systems that allow people to meet their emotional needs. So the metaphor for an organization is a (large) group of people with a culture among them and visible communication and interaction processes between them. The third school of thought has been called the political-emergent perspective (Borum 1995; Burnes 1996). It is characterized by the belief that organizations and change are shaped by the interests and power struggles between special-interest groups or coalitions.

It is possible to combine tools and techniques from the three different perspectives. Kotter (1996), for example, recommends eight stages in leading a change process: (1) establish a sense of urgency, (2) build support, (3) develop a change vision, (4) communicate the change vision, (5) empower and enable action, (6) generate short-term wins, (7) consolidate and revitalize change, and finally (8) anchor new approach in culture. The first, third, and fourth of these stages are close to the view of an organization as a production system, whereas the second, sixth and eighth stages clearly show the organization as a social system. The second and fifth stages are take power and special interests into account (see Kotter and Cohen 2002).

Organizational change processes can rarely be considered a linear function (Weinberg 1997), and often the best change strategy is to keep as much stability around the change as possible simply to allow enough energy and attention for the people changing behavior.

2.3 Design in Use

The third analytical perspective we apply allows us to focus on the concrete work practices. This perspective tries to understand the interaction and mutual dependencies between the actual work practices and the structures, procedures, and technologies that are implemented and used by it. Organizational structure and technology are not seen as something stable and fixed, determining what actually goes on, but something that is subject to ongoing interpretation, negotiation, and adaptation.

Suchman (1983) describes office procedures as results of practical action. Analyzing the handling of a past-due invoice, she shows that what on the surface can be regarded as an orderly procedure is in fact constructed through the work practice of the administrators involved. Likewise Gerson and Star (1986) show that organizational processes are never fixed. In fact the continuous maintenance of processes and structures used as basis for decisions requires articulation of developments, constraints, interests and consequences. In the health insurance company analyzed by Gerson and Star, this "due process" is placed with a committee specifically designed for this task. Computer systems both mirror the result of due processes and provide constraints for ongoing negotiation and redesign.

Although many have the impression that governmental decision making is guided by rules, Lenk et al. (2002) use a case of a single parent asking for social benefit to show that, in practice, the application of rules does not explain reality. Dittrich et al. (2003) studied the introduction of new technical support for municipal service provision and found that the development of service provision practices results in adaptation and changes of the technology used. Such practices of "design in use" indicate that at least the less-formalized aspects of service provision (Lenk et al. 2002) are subject to due process and articulation work as are similar processes in office work in private companies. Additionally the legal base for decision making changes quite frequently. To understand better how the specific organization—or reorganization—of service provision and the design and use of the technology interacts, close-up studies and analysis of the role that technology plays in the service provision is needed.

3 CASE: BORNHOLM

Bornholm is a smaller Danish island with 45,000 inhabitants situated in the Baltic Sea. In January 2001, the mayors from the five municipalities on Bornholm met. The result of their meeting was a suggestion for a local election about the amalgamation of the five existing municipalities on the island.

The background for this suggestion was a local debate that had been going on for some time. It was often claimed that having five very small municipalities in such a limited geographical area led to both economic and democratic ineffectiveness.

The five city councils supported the election with great majority and a local election was held in May 2001. A total of 74 percent of the island's population voted yes to an amalgamation of the five municipalities. It was decided that a new regional municipality of Bornholm should be effective from January 2003.

4   RESEARCH METHOD

A little more than a year after the amalgamation, or merger as we will call it in the remainder of this paper, we conducted an in-depth interview study focusing on the outcome of the Bornholm merger. The purpose of the study was to reconstruct and understand the complex merging process in order to identify lessons to be learned.

We decided to interview users and IT professionals from Bornholm as well as developers from KMD, the semi-public provider of IT. To capture both management and shop floor perspectives, we interviewed representatives from all three groups. We interviewed 12 people. Eight of them were from Bornholm, of which half were IT people and the remainder IT users primarily from the "one-stop shops," single points of access to the citizen services that were introduced and placed at the former town halls as part of the change process. One-stop shops deal with more or less any issue a citizen may bring.

Of the remaining four people interviewed were three from KMD and one from the Danish Federation of Municipalities. Table 1 gives an overview of our interviewees. For the purpose of anonymity, we have changed everyone's name and used city names from the island of Bornholm as pseudonyms.

We asked the interviewees to reflect on their experiences with the merger. We supplemented the interviews by examining artifacts—documents, presentations, and newspaper clippings—from before and after the merger.

Typically all three authors conducted the interviews. One of us concentrated on having a good dialogue and making sure that all the issues in our semi-structured interview guide were covered, while the other two took notes. Furthermore, all of the interviews were taped, and central parts from each interview were transcribed and summarized for detailed data analysis. Formally, our research method can be described as an in-depth case study relying on data triangulation (Yin 1994).

The interview notes including the transcribed parts were then analyzed in an iterative hermeneutic process. This revealed six interesting lessons, three on the change process itself, and three on the design process. In the two next sections we will lay out our findings.

5   LEARNING FROM THE CHANGE PROCESS

This section takes the top-down perspective looking at the organizational change process that took place at Bornholm.

Table 1. An Overview of Our Interviewees

Name (Pseudonym)	Organization and Role
Anne Arnager	Employed since 2000. Works in the one-stop citizen service in Rønne, the largest city on Bornholm. Gaya Gudhjem is her superior.
Berit Balka	Employed since 1988. Works in the one-stop citizen service in Nexø, the second largest city on Bornholm.
Diana Dueodde	Employed with KMD, the semi-public supplier of IT. Responsible for development support. Headed the steering committee on behalf of KMD
Gaya Gudhjem	Employed since 1989. Chairman of the group that looked at debtor IT systems for collecting money.
Heidi Hasle	Employed since 1976. Worked with property tax collection in Rønne.
Nils Nylars	Responsible for all IT development in the new regional municipality.
Mikael Myreby	CIO for all IT in the new regional municipality.
Ole Olsker	Senior consultant from the Danish Federation of Municipalities. Visited Bornholm many times throughout the merging process.
Ron Rutsker and Soren Sandvig	Both employed with KMD. Responsible for some of the specific development of estate and taxing systems.
Teo Tejn	Works with debtor systems and tax collection in Rønne.
Viggo Vang	Employed in the IT department. Reports to Mikael Myreby.

Because the politicians on Bornholm prioritized a rather long period for political discussions about the organizational setup of the new regional municipality, the execution phase for the IT part of the merger was very short. During the planning phase after the election in May 2001, 22 working groups were formed, one of them focusing on IT. But the working groups were only supposed to map out, describe, and identify problem areas. They were told not to make any major decisions with regard to the future organization of the IT organization in the new regional municipality of Bornholm because this was seen as a political decision. *"Up to the election of a new regional council on May 29, 2002, everybody was told not to do anything,"* said Mikael Myreby. To people from the outside, this was experienced as decision avoidance. Ron Rutsker and Soren Sandvig, from KMD, experienced this as a lack of decision power. They said, *"We experienced a kind of decisional vacuum. Nobody knew who was to answer what."*

Another related problem was ignorance of how much a change process actually implies. For example, it requires a lot of extra time, but that time wasn't allocated. Gaya Gudhjem said, *"No time was set aside specifically for the development work. Thus we didn't have time to really advance as we should have. There were things that just hobbled along."*

By January 1, 2003, the amalgamation was done and only one regional municipality existed on Bornholm. But in fact a lot happened right after that New Year. For example in the local tax administration, property tax bills were sent out twice. We were told that some people actually paid twice. A lot of work to redo the property tax collection manually was required. Anna Arnager gave us about another example where a person called in very mystified that he shouldn't pay tax:

> *We had a case where a person called because he hadn't paid property tax. We checked it in the system, but his tax was actually paid. Then we looked more deeply into it and found that the tax was paid through an Internet bank. The man declined that he had paid via Internet and when we checked we found that a total stranger had paid the tax for this man using his old debtor number. From that we learned never to reuse debtor numbers.*

5.1 Non-Flexible Empowered Employees

The election for the new Bornholm city council took place in May 2002, but the new council did not make any decisions before the summer holiday. After summer, the contract between Bornholm and KMD was finally signed and the work in the 22 working groups restarted—it had been stalled for a long period due to the request to not make decisions. However, many of the people participating in the working groups were still hesitant to make decisions because they didn't know their own role in the future. Viggo Vang said, *"The users were not involved in the whole merging process. The reason being that it was not decided where each individual would be [geographically and job wise] after the merger."*

The only thing the employees knew at this point was that everything would change: the organization, their job, and probably their geographical location (to another town most likely). This caused a lot of uncertainty and a lack of willingness to make important decisions. Nils Nylars said,

> *At this time we did not know our future organization; neither did we know what goals to pursue. That is the reason why most of the work came down to discussing the conversion of data. We didn't know who was going to work with the systems. And we didn't know anything about the interfaces [between people and systems]. For example we did not know whether there would be a one-stop citizen service in the new regional municipality.*

However, in a few places it was actually known very early who was to have which job after the merger. For example, this happened in the unit responsible for tax collection. *"Everybody knew who was going to be director of that company [municipal unit]. Therefore they were in charge,"* Mikael Myreby said.

Users were expected to take responsibility for the restructuring, but in reality KMD took over the design of the new systems because the working groups were not able to make decisions.

The workers in the different working groups had been empowered to map out the existing processes. Berit Balka, who had a job in the information desk before the merger, said,

> *Before the merger we met every 3 months and tried to unify and standardize our work processes. So we meet and we told what pictures [referring to screens] we needed. These meetings continued until Christmas at which point we were told which job we were going to have.*

So the first result of our analysis of the interview data is that the IT system users were expected to take responsibility for the restructuring, but in reality KMD was setting the agenda. So the "empowered users" lacked flexibility to imagine something for others than themselves.

5.2 Too Much Change at the Same Time

As we said above, the working groups were not able to make actual IT decisions before the end of 2002. In fact, the initiation of the new amalgamated IT function happened in October 2002, but the first couple of months they turned inward and concentrated on defining an IT strategy. *"We used all of October and November to write the IT strategy,"* said Viggo Vang.

Mikael Myreby emphasized that the late establishment of the new IT organization created huge problems: *"The reason being that everything from IT systems to the intranet was new."* Thus it seems that the lack of time for the execution phase dramatically increased the cost of the merger.

Another problem identified in our analysis was that it was expected that savings from the merger would materialize more or less immediately. Unfortunately that was not the case. Diana Dueodde said, *"Bornholm did not harvest any savings in the beginning. You don't do that from day 1."*

The official figure for the costs associated with the Bornholm merger was more than eight million U.S. dollars (using a 6-to-1 currency exchange rate). We received access to the data behind this figure and found that it only included money for IT investments and some of the working time before and after the merger took effect on January 1, 2003. We present the main figures in Table 2.

However, our interviews clearly told us that considerable time was invested in the change process *after* the merger (i.e., to define and agree on how to work in the new organization). Formally this wasn't accounted for as extra time but in fact it was time that was not used to service the people on Bornholm. Even when we visited 18 months after the merger, there were still new processes related to the merger that were being discussed. Our best estimate is that the merger may have had costs up to 50 percent more than are shown in the official figures (Table 2).

It was not that people were not trying to cope with the many changes. The head of IT development, Nils Nylars, told us: *"You have to prioritize the changes. You only have limited energy. We reached a point here where the employees said NO, now we cannot take any more change. We need a project stop."*

Table 2. Costs in Relation to the Merger on Bornholm
(All figures are converted to U.S. dollars)

		2002	**2003**
Merging committee		1,364,901	
Integrating IT systems			2,308,272
Converting KMD systems	1,818,792		
Dental Care system	21,313		
Ramboel Care	468,167		
IT investments		613303	833,732
Establishing a common telephone system			265,396
Moving costs			356,367
Extra income to politicians			246,333
Total		**1,978,204**	**4,010,100**

We believe that the real problem was that too much was happening in the same very short time period. Gaya Gudhjem told how she experienced the merging process: "*It was not the merging of the systems that was worst. It was the merging of cultures. And it was whether I got the table [here referring to whom was getting which job after the merger].*" And she continued, "*The biggest change from before to now is the culture. And the people that worked alone before had the worst experience. Suddenly they needed to cooperate.*"

So our second result from analyzing the data is that too much uncoordinated change at the same time dramatically increased the cost of the merger.

5.3 No Clear IT Vision

Although a clear vision of how to organize the new regional municipality so every organizational unit became an independent company existed, IT was discussed surprisingly late in the merging process. Even though the merger was agreed upon almost two years in advance, the IT part of the merger was only seriously considered half a year before the actual merger and executed in the last couple of months in 2002.

After the clear public support in the ballot for the merger, the legal foundation for the new regional municipality was negotiated with the central government, and later accepted by the Danish national parliament with the introduction of a new law on the merger. The local preparations for the merger started mid-2001. But neither in the central negotiations between the Ministry of the Interior and Bornholm nor in the local preparation work on Bornholm were the IT challenges seriously discussed before the middle of 2002. IT was simply not considered an important, nor problematic, part of the merger.

After the merger, one of the largest problems on Bornholm was that the IT changes were perceived as a simple data convergence task. Maybe because all of the five existing municipalities were primarily using an IT system provided by KMD they did not perceive the IT integration challenges to be very large. Furthermore, IT challenges were considered a problem for the IT provider and consequentially not a large issue in the merger. Mikael Myreby said,

All the five municipalities on Bornholm were KMD customers, and from the beginning there was a belief that everybody could just use the systems from Rønne [the largest of the five municipalities]. However, it turned out that all the municipalities have had different organizational structures and as a result of that; used the KMD-systems differently.

And Ron Rutsker and Soren Sandvig, from the IT supplier KMD, said,

In the user tests, we clearly experienced that there were different ways of doing things [in the five municipalities]. Especially the BGS system [used to identify a specific estate in a building file] was used differently. Some used a three-digit number [for referring to a building] while others just referred to a name such as Meadow Farm.

One problem that came out very clearly in our analysis was that the carefully described processes didn't work out. The head of IT development in the new organization, Nils Nylars, said,

At the point in time where we created the workflow descriptions people perceived things as they were in the old system. As of today [August 2004] we haven't had time to envision a unified way to work. The first year after the merger was just pure survival.

Another problem was that energy was used for the wrong things in the new organization. Nils Nylars said,

As a manager you have to remember that the employees are used to collecting money. They know how to do that. They just do it different ways [in different municipalities]. So we have learned that we should have focused much earlier on the new way of doing things—the vision for how to cooperate in the future. That lesson surprised us, but it is very clear for us today.

According to Kotter (1996), a vision is needed in a change process to motivate, to show direction, and to help in coordinating and integrating action. Thus the third result of our analysis is that a clear and communicated vision of how to integrate the differing work procedures and the deployment of IT was lacking in the Bornholm merger.

6   INTRODUCTION OF ONE-STOP SHOPS: REDESIGNING SERVICE PROVISION

This section takes the bottom-up perspective looking at the Bornholm case from a work practice and design in use perspective. We start in the one-stop shops as they provide an example of the necessity to redesign municipal service provision when merging different municipalities. Four of old city halls were closed. Instead, one-stop shops have been introduced to provide the municipal services for the citizens.

The one-stop shop in Rønne is situated in a large, open-plan office that before the merger had already welcomed the visitors of the city hall. Visitors still meet the information desk and the cash counter when entering the city hall. For specific advice, they turn to the one-stop shop personnel whose desks are turned to meet visitors. The back office units situated in the same building also still man front office desks in the open area. The specialists working there take care of requests regarding their specific area. As Rønne is the biggest of the former independent city halls, it hosts quite a few of these units. The employees have the possibility to occupy separate offices in case the request and support is of a more private character. Most of the one-stop shop employees in Rønne also work with other tasks, mainly debt-collecting business, as this part of the municipal services belongs to the same unit.

Although working with similar tasks, the one-stop shop in Nexø is organized differently. A counter in the reception areas provides space for two employees. Behind the counter, a number individual desks are placed, providing space for more concentrated work at the computer and for longer consultations with the citizens. A small office is provided in a corner, to allow for privacy and to provide a workplace for specialists from other units who visit Nexø for appointed meetings with citizens. Nexø was one of the smaller municipalities that earlier had been dominated by the fishing and fish-processing industry. Today it hosts an internationally reputed design school. The Nexø one-stop shop, therefore, handles more issues concerning foreigners, visas, and permits of residence than any of the other of the one-stop shops on the island.

When we performed the interviews the different lay-out, culture and character of the 2 one-stop shops became visible. Internal organizational specificities, local and demographic differences, and previous experiences of the personnel staffing the one-stop shops influence the distribution of tasks, the development of expertise, and, with that, the organization of service provision and requirements regarding computer support. So it would be interesting to visit the municipalities in another two years and see how the situation developed further.

Our analysis revealed three aspects that seem especially relevant.

6.1 Poor Integration of Organization and IT Infrastructure Development

Among the municipal workers, the one-stop shop employees probably were the worst prepared for the change awaiting them. As no one-stop shop existed previously, no experience with such an organization was provided. The majority of the employees we interviewed did not choose the one-stop shops as their new work place, as nobody understood the requirements for this kind of work.

Only three weeks before switching to the new organization, the employees received the information about their new work place. The necessary training took place parallel to starting up the one-stop shops and was still going on when we performed the interviews (in August 2004). There was no time or place to think about necessary IT support beforehand, as the working groups preparing the data integration and the implementation of the software configurations were organized according to the traditional sectors of municipal service provision. There was no time or place for the preparing "articulation work" (Gerson and Star 1986).

The introduction of the one-stop shops is an example for our fourth finding, that the development of the organization and the development of the supporting infrastructure were not well integrated. In other sectors, this contributed to a lack of willingness of the employees to take decisions on behalf of others. In respect to the one stop shop, it led to a lack of IT support as discussed in the next section.

6.2 No Appropriate IT Support for One-Stop Shops

One-stop shops are meant to provide access to all municipal citizen services. Their introduction clashes with the traditional organization of computer support for public service provision. The computer systems supporting municipal administration in Denmark are provided centrally by KMD. The data is accessed via rather traditional mainframe terminal interfaces using commands consisting of character-number combinations for navigation. Taking over the front office tasks and consulting with the citizen on a wide variety of issues implies that the employees are using many of the different systems that are designed to support the service provision in the different units. One of the difficulties for one-stop shop workers is to navigate between and within the different systems that are optimized for personnel working only with the respective area. The largest difficulty in the beginning, therefore, has been to remember all the codes, as several of our interviewees emphasized, to learn the commands to access the data the different systems provide.

Although the sector-specific procedures and information access are documented in a set of folders, this information does not help much in everyday work. For example, Berit Balka said, *"If there is a woman coming in who has decided to divorce from her husband, and needs a flat and has to sell a house and needs social benefit, you just cannot take a folder and read up on what to do."* Therefore, they developed a customized work folder where they collect the most important short cuts and other necessary information. One-stop shop work relies heavily on a set of practices: *"When somebody comes with need for support I always first do an A1850 on the person to get the basic data and see whether they have been in contact with the municipality before"* (Berit Balka).

The new organization of the service provision on Bornholm is not supported by the organization and architecture of the software systems. Also the sector-specific documentation of procedures does not fit. Making things work with IT that does not fit or no IT support has been one of the stress factors in the merger. The introduction of one-stop shops requires a rethinking of service provision, but also a rethinking of the IT support for municipalities.

This, however, is not a straightforward task. The way computer support for municipal service provision has developed in the past implements a sector-specific organization of the service provision. Although the data is integrated behind the scenes leading to a net of dependencies on the server side, the access to these mainframe systems—which even the IT department of Bornholm perceives as black boxes—is organized sector-wise. Client-side integration with other local systems is possible but often results in partial duplication of the data and delayed update of the mainframe data. For example, local administrative systems for the organization of home care updates the central state register which is then used to update the mainframe side of the above-mentioned municipal software provider. *"It can take up to two days before this data is accessible for other units of the municipal administration,"* as Viggo Vang explained.

So our fifth finding from our analysis is that the traditional IT support does not fit with the one-stop shops cutting across traditional sectors of municipal service provision.

6.3 No Means for Discussing and Designing the IT Infrastructure

Designing the IT infrastructure is an issue that is not just relevant for the mainframe systems, which are described as black boxes or as screens that are accessed through codes. Besides those, the one-stop personnel rely heavily on the central server providing online forms and instructions on how to fill them out, and the municipal telephone exchange that contains information about all employees, their tasks, and a individual calendar system that shows whether and when each employee is available. To forward case-specific questions that cannot be solved by accessing the data in the respective application or for getting advice regarding a more complicated case, they rely heavily on being able to contact the respective case worker or expert responsible. One of the major hazards, especially for the one-stop shop personnel, was that this new telephone system did not work in the beginning. Besides this main support, a set of other systems is used: the cashier system, as citizens can pay different fees and even taxes in Sweden directly to the city hall, the e-mail system for communication, and the extra- and intranet are just a few examples.

To consciously plan the reorganization of services together with the reorganization of the necessary design of information systems, one would need some way of describing the presently used technology and planing how to organize future IT support. Such design artifacts and methods would not only be necessary for major reorganizations, but might provide support for the ongoing negotiation and continuous design of the service provision in the two one-stop shops, for the due process (Gerson and Star 1986) of municipal service provision.

Neither the software as it is designed today, nor the development processes support the design in use that takes place when information technology is used not only as a data repository but as support for service provision. To support a more flexible and agile organization of service provision that, on one hand, becomes possible with today's network and Internet technology and that, on the other hand, is required when merging municipalities, the traditional software support has to become itself more flexible and adaptable.

So our sixth and final finding is that one of the reasons why users during the Bornholm merger did not involve themselves in any discussion of IT infrastructure was that they simply had no means to discuss changes in the infrastructure.

7 DISCUSSION

The analysis sections 5 and 6 resulted in complementing but in some cases also contradicting causes for what many of the participants perceived as a problematic change process. From a change management point of view, we found that empowered employees nevertheless were non-flexible. We found that too much (uncoordinated) change at the same time dramatically increased the cost of the merger. And we found a lack of a clear and communicated IT vision.

The bottom-up focus on the introduction of and the developing work practices in the one-stop shops led to the conclusion that there was a lack of coordination between the organizational change and the development of IT infrastructure. We found that the traditional IT support didn't fit with the one-stop shops cutting across traditional sectors. And we found missing means to discuss changes in the IT infrastructure.

7.1 Remedies to Cope

As the problem analysis differs, the remedies that can be identified differ as well: The increase in cost and time because of too much change at the same time can be countered by careful planning, allowing enough room for one change at a time (Weinberg 1997).

The way to cope with non-flexible but empowered employees would be to build an environment for the individuals that leads them to take responsibility for defining and discussing tasks, and work flows that they themselves will not have responsibility for after the change.

The lack of a clear and communicated IT vision leads, of course, to the need to define and communicate a vision and make expectations clear from day one (Kotter 1996).

The lack of coordination between the organizational change and the development of the IT infrastructure can be met with active integration of both dimensions of change. This would probably address the problem of too much uncoordinated change as well. If changes can be perceived as meaningful complements, the tolerance for change might be higher. Also an early decision regarding the placement of employees could clarify their mandate regarding decisions on the future IT support. Such coordination would be supported by a vision of how to use IT in the future organization, but the concrete development would probably change the initial vision as things evolve.

One-stop shops cutting across traditional sectors are one way to implement the single point of access to municipal services that the new law requires. However, they question the traditional sector-specific organization of municipal service provision, and require a different kind of support. To develop support that better fits, it should also be adjustable to local specializations as they becomes visible. When comparing the two one-stop shops we visited, one would need a means to not only discuss single applications but also their interaction. Space and time for articulation work has to be provided (Gerson and Star 1986).

7.2 Discussing Agility

In section 3, we defined an agility framework with the following characteristics: (1) the ability of making rapid redesign, (2) flexibility, understood as being able to change to suit new conditions or situations, (3) knowledge management in relation to users' present work, technological options, and the new system, and (4) whether individuals are prioritized over processes. If we now take a look at our suggested measures to cope with the problems identified in the case we can ask: How are our suggestions related to agility? In Table 3, we have given an answer simply by comparing each of the six Bornholm lessons and their remedies against each of the four characteristics of agility.

The proposed remedies from an organizational change perspective in themselves do not comply well with our four characteristics of agility. However, when we combine the measures proposed with a work practice-oriented analysis, then the picture changes. For example, measure 4 can also be seen as a remedy for too much uncoordinated change. Here the work practice perspective allows for a different interpretation of the same phenomenon leading to a recommendation supporting the agility of an organization. Understanding measure 3 as a support for the coordination of organizational change with the development of the IT infrastructure allows us to see the contribution of a seemingly top-down and inflexible instrument to the flexibility of an organization. The frustration of the one-stop shop workers over the failure of the technological infrastructure to work indicates that one way to strengthen individuals in coping with change is to provide suitable support.

Interpreted that way, the measures we suggest are in good accordance with the four characteristics of agility. So it is fair to say that we recommend that the changes in of government about to take place in Denmark need a *transformation to agile*.

8   CONCLUSION

From a scientific perspective, the conclusions in this paper are that it is necessary to relate government agility to an analytical perspective that focuses on the deployment of technology in the concrete work practices in addition to one on organizational change processes. The paper has demonstrated the importance of taking on a proactive approach to the major integration challenge that awaits in 2007. Only by becoming agile can the largest public change project ever undertaken in Denmark succeed.

The interesting thing about the Bornholm case is that it is a kind of pilot for the hundreds of similar projects about to take place starting on January 1, 2007. So a highly first relevant question is: What can be done to avoid the problems we identified at Bornholm? Based on our analysis, we propose the following:

- Actively integrate the reorganization of the municipality with the design and development of the infrastructure.

- Start early to have time for these activities and to be able to decide on changes with enough time.

Table 3. Comparing Our Six Suggested Measures with Characteristics of Agility

Results of Analysis	Requirements to the Agile Organization and IT Infrastructure in the 100 New Municipalities	Rapid Redesign	Flexibility	Knowledge	Individuals Over Processes
1. Non-flexible empowered workers	Create an environment for the individual to take responsibility (requires leadership). Create benevolence.	No difference	Yes	Yes	Yes
2. Too much uncoordinated change	Enough room for one change at a time. An alternative approach would be the active integration of different change dimension (see # 4)	No	No	No	Yes
3. No clear IT vision	Define and communicate an IT vision and clarify expectations.	No	Yes, indirectly	No	No
4. The organizational change and the IT infrastructure development were not well coordinated	Active integration of organizational change and IT infrastructure development.	Yes	Yes	Yes	No
5. The traditional IT support does not fit with the one-stop shops that cut across traditional sectors	A more modular understanding of municipal service provision and respective design of IT support.	Yes	Yes	Yes	No
6. Users had no means to discuss changes in the infrastructure	Tools, techniques to design IT infrastructure.	Yes	Yes	Yes	Yes

- Develop an IT vision in order to coordinate the development work in different sectors.
- Be prepared to rethink municipal service provision. The introduction of one-stop shops means more than the placing the interfaces to municipal administration and systems on the same desktop.
- New tools and techniques are needed to design (and develop) not only single applications but also a whole infrastructure consisting of such diverse applications as telephone exchange and access to mainframe applications.

The central politicians in Denmark have publicly declared that they expect a leap forward—the Minister of the Interior even called it a "tiger leap"—in the use of IT in government as a result of the Danish structural reform. One of our interviewees, Diana Dueodde, commented, *"There may be a tiger leap waiting in the future, but it will not come at the same time as the structural reform."* Our analysis seems to propose that the merging of several municipalities will force both the municipal organizations and the IT support to develop more agility. So the leap forward might be the ability to actively design the IT infrastructure together with the municipal service provision in reaction to policy changes and evolving citizen needs.

The analysis presented in this paper suggests that the design and development of IT infrastructures beyond the single piece of software or hardware is an important area for future research. As outlined by Bleek (2004) and Hjort-Madsen and Gøtze (2004), IT infrastructures rarely involve the development of new systems from scratch. Interoperability between IT systems and business processes is the key to creating one-stop shops and we, therefore, need a better understanding of the management of these infrastructures.

REFERENCES

Agile Manifesto. "Manifesto for Agile Software Development," 2001 (available online at http://agilemanifesto.org; accessed October 12, 2004).

Aoyama, M. "Web-Based Agile Software Development," *IEEE Software* (15:6), November/ December 1998, pp. 56-65.

Baskerville, R., Levine, L., Pries-Heje, J., Ramesh, B., and Slaughter, S. "How Internet Software Companies Negotiate Quality," *IEEE Computer* (34:5), 2001, pp. 51-57.

Bleek, W.-G. *Software-Infrastruktur—Von analytischer Perspektive zu konstruktiver Orientierung,* Hamburg: Hamburg University Press, 2004.

Borum, F. *Strategier for organisationsændring,* Copenhagen: Handelshøjskolens Forlag, 1995.

Burnes, B. *Managing Change* (2nd ed.), London: Pitman Publishing, 1996.

Dittrich, Y., Eriksén, S., Ekelin, A., Elovaara, P., and Hansson, C. "Making E-Government Happen Everyday: Codevelopment of Services, Citizenship and Technology," in *Proceedings of the 36th Hawaii International Conference on System Sciences,* Los Alamitos, CA: IEEE Computer Society Press, 2003.

Dittrich, Y., Eriksén, S., and Hansson, C. "PD in the Wild: Evolving Practices of Design in Use," in *Proceedings of the Participatory Design Conference,* T. Binder, J. Gregory, and I. Wagner (Eds.), Malmö, Sweden: Computer Professionals for Social Responsibility, June 2002, pp. 124-134.

Dove, R. *Response Ability: The Language, Structure, and Culture of the Agile Enterprise,* New York: Wiley, 2001.

Dunphy, D. "Organizational Change in Corporate Settings," *Human Relations* (49), 1996, pp. 541-552.

Gerson E. M. , and Star, S. L. "Analyzing Due Process in the Workplace," *ACM Transactions on Office Information Systems* (4:3), July 1986, pp. 257-270.

Hjort-Madsen, K., and Gøtze, J. "Enterprise Architecture in Government: Towards a Multi-Level Framework for Managing IT in Government," in *Proceedings of 4th European Conference on e-Government,* Dublin, Ireland, June 2004, pp. 365-374.

Kensing, F., and Munk-Madsen, A. "PD: Structure in the Toolbox," *Communications of the ACM* (36:6), June 1993, pp. 78-85.

Kotter, J. P. *Leading Change,* Boston: Harvard Business School Press, 1996.

Kotter, J. P. And Cohen, D. S. *The Heart of Change: Real-Life Stories of How People Change Their Organizations,* Boston: Harvard Business School Press, 2002.

Lenk, K., Traunmüller, R., and Wimmer, M. "The Significance of Law and Knowledge for Electronic Government," in *Electronic Government: Design, Applications and Management,* Ake Grönlund (Ed.), Hershey PA: Idea Group Publishing, 2002, pp. 61-77.

Newman, W., Podgurski, A., Quinn, R., Merat, F., Branicky, M., Barendt, N., Causey, G., Haaser, E., Kim, Y., Swaminathan, J., and Velasco, V. "Design Lessons for Building Agile Manufacturing Systems," *IEEE Transactions on Robotics and Automation* (16:3), 2000, pp. 228-238.

Paulk, M. "Extreme Programming from a CMM Perspective," *IEEE Software* (18:6), 2001, pp. 19-26.

Suchman, L. A. "Office Procedure as Practical Action: Models of Work and System Design," *ACM Transactions on Office Information Systems* (1:4), October 1983, pp. 320-328.

Weinberg, G. M. *Quality Software Management, Volume 4: Anticipating Change,* New York: Dorset House, 1997.

Yin, R. K. *Case Study Research. Design and Methods* (2nd ed.), London: Sage Publications, 1994.

ABOUT THE AUTHORS

Yvonne Dittrich is an associate professor from Hamburg University. Her research interests are use-oriented design and development of software, codevelopment of work practice and software, end-user development, and eGovernment. Yvonne can be reached at ydi@itu.dk.

Jan Pries-Heje is an associate professor at the IT University of Copenhagen, Denmark. Jan holds M.Sc. and Ph.D. degrees from Copenhagen Business School. He is a certified ISO 9000 auditor and Bootstrap assessor, and has been project manager for a number of multi-media and IT-related change projects. From 1997 through 2000, he worked as a consultant in IT quality and software process improvement. He is chairman of the Information Systems Research in Scandinavia (IRIS) Steering Committee, serves as the Danish National Representative to IFIP TC8 (since 1999), and is currently an associate editor for *MIS Quarterly, Information Systems Journal,* and *European Journal of Information Systems.* His research interests include information systems development, software engineering, and software process improvement. He focuses on organizational and managerial issues. Jan has published more than 100 papers in these areas in journals and conferences. He can be reached at jpr@itu.dk.

Kristian Hjort-Madsen is employed in the Danish Ministry of Science, Technology and Innovation. He is currently writing his Ph.D. on the management of IT infrastructures in the public sector in a public-private partnership program with IBM Denmark, KMD Denmark, and the IT University of Copenhagen. His research specializes in information systems management and the use of enterprise architectures in public institutions. Kristian can be reached at khm@itu.dk.

22 REFLECTIONS ON SOFTWARE AGILITY AND AGILE METHODS: Challenges, Dilemmas, and the Way Ahead

Linda Levine
Software Engineering Institute
Carnegie Mellon University
Pittsburgh, PA U.S.A.

Abstract   *What are the drivers for the burgeoning interest in agile methods? Have these drivers stimulated a similar rethinking on other fronts? What have we discovered? In this paper, I take a reflective stance in order to look at these larger issues and patterns. This stepping back is informed primarily by involvement in a multi-year research project on Quality Software Development @ Internet Speed and ongoing research on diffusion theory and the practices of technology adoption. I suggest the shift toward agile models and methods signals a larger transformation in the workplace toward the organization of the 21ˢᵗ century. This transition state is "between paradigms" and turbulent, marked by relentless change and volatility. The transition is a work in progress and by no means complete.*

Keywords   Agile, agile methods, organizational dynamics

1   INTRODUCTION

Agility and agile methods have been popularized through the proponents of the Agile Alliance, their Agile Manifesto, and related writings (Agile Manifesto 2001). The concept of agility also has a longer history in manufacturing. More recently, Grover and Malhotra (1999) studied the interface between operations and Information Systems and Kathuria et al. (1999) linked information systems choices to manufacturing operations in order to understand how information systems support manufacturing operations and competitive strategy. Dove (2001) claims that agility requires an "ability to manage and apply knowledge effectively, so that an organization has the potential to thrive in a continuously changing and unpredictable business environment"(p. 9). Initially, he characterized agility as having two key elements: response ability and knowledge management. Subsequently, Dove (2005) added a third dimension of value propositioning.

For agile approaches to be fully understood—to mature and to gain ground—we would be wise to consider what agility means as part of a larger landscape, and what kind of shift it marks in technology development and in organizational behavior and change. This is the concern of this paper: to reflect upon the current preoccupation with agility, describe some of what we have learned about Internet-speed software development, and characterize challenges for the future.

What are the drivers for the burgeoning interest in agile methods? What have we discovered? In this paper, I take a reflective stance to look at such larger issues and patterns. Primarily, my stepping back is informed by two efforts: (1) involvement in a multi-year research project on Quality Software Development @ Internet Speed and (2) ongoing research on diffusion theory and the practices of technology adoption.

Agility in software development has implications for organizational agility. I will suggest that the shift to agile methods and models signals a larger transformation in the workplace toward the organization of the 21st century. This transition state is turbulent, marked by continuous change and volatility. Experimentation in this time of turbulence has attempted to break down and speed up old models, disrupting traditional approaches and turning conventional concepts and methods on their heads. No clear or easy solutions have resulted. The transformation is a work in progress, one that is by no means complete. To be realized, it will require a melding of inquiry across a wide range of disciplines and initiatives, including organizational development, diffusion of innovations, process improvement, knowledge management, complex adaptive systems, chaos theory, systems thinking, software engineering, and information systems.

We begin by looking briefly at definitions of agility, considering connotations and metaphors for agile behavior. Then, I discuss the current state of agility and Internet-speed software development, as informed by our research findings. Finally, I speculate on a desired state—and on challenges that the future holds for a next generation of agile approaches. Discussion of the future also involves consideration of conundrums and dilemmas.

2   DEFINING AGILE

What do we mean by agile? Is it simply fast? Are agile and fast one and the same? Agility implies speed, although something that is fast is not necessarily agile. Developers and customers alike appreciate speed, through being "first to market" and in terms of responsiveness. We know that developers are invested in how the use of agile methods emphasizes discovery, improvisation, and patterns.

Members of the Agile Alliance have expressed the following preferences and values (Agile Manifesto 2001):

- Individuals and interactions over processes and tools
- Working software over comprehensive documentation
- Customer collaboration over contract negotiation
- Responding to change over following a plan

Do customers support agile methods? Perhaps, but not in precisely the same way that developers do—rather, they care as the use of such methods translates into the results, benefits, and profits that they seek. Thus, customer interest is indirect. This trend is evident even in large Department of Defense acquisitions, which are notoriously late and over budget, and where acquisition program managers are expressing interest in whether agile methods can better satisfy their goals and result in the delivery of quality systems in a more timely fashion. Some are actively advocating for agile methods. Unfortunately, these same customers are often at a loss when it comes to identifying an appropriate means for governance—for oversight and monitoring agile development efforts. Development efforts that embrace the left-side values presented above do not lend themselves well or easily to program monitoring. We will discuss this further under the topic of challenges.

Agility, by definition, exists in relief against a norm or opposite. In this regard, agility is relative; we know that a behavior is agile because we can compare it, if only in our own heads, with a visible or invisible state that is slower, clumsy, brittle, or inflexible. Who, we might ask, displays agility? Acrobats, ballerinas, and racing car drivers may all be agile. Gazelles, deer, and big cats may be agile. Elephants and hippopotami are not agile, or so we believe.

Merriam Webster (2004) defines agile from the Middle French and from the Latin *agilis,* from *agere* to drive, act as "**1:** marked by ready ability to move with quick easy grace [and] **2:** having a quick resourceful and adaptable character <an *agile* mind>." Agility is defined as "the quality or state of being agile: **NIMBLENESS, DEXTERITY** <played with increasing *agility*>."

Agility, then, for purposes of our discussion is made up of several attributes. We can liken it to a table which stands on four legs:

- *speed*: quick, fast.
- *nimble*: able to improvise, and use patterns creatively to construct new solutions on the fly, flexible.
- *adaptable*: responsive (sense and respond), dynamic and interactive in response to a customer, or to changing circumstances.
- *resourceful*: thoughtful or exhibiting some discipline. This, however, is not the same as a traditional "command and control" approach with defined, formal procedures.

This definition will be useful, especially in later discussion, where we discuss controversies between process-based and agile approaches. This has special implications for the role of discipline in agility.

3   WHAT WE HAVE LEARNED SO FAR: THE CURRENT STATE

In this section, I will briefly summarize key research findings from a multi-year study (2000–2003) on Quality Software Development @ Internet Speed. Detailed findings are available elsewhere. This is not a survey; rather, this is intended to serve as a catalyst for discussing a future state and the challenges ahead. Passing references are made to related research on agility and fast-paced development to a limited extent.

Our three-part study on Internet-speed software development used a mixed-methods research design involving the collection of multiple kinds of data (Tashakkori and Teddlie 1998). Case studies of Internet-speed software development in Phase 1 were complemented with a Discovery Colloquium held in Phase 2. Phase 3 continued the original case studies.

3.1 Phase 1: Case Studies of Internet Software Development

During the first phase, in Fall 2000, we conducted detailed case studies of Internet software development at 10 companies in two major metropolitan areas. The firms ranged in size from 10 employees to more than 300,000 employees, in different industries in the private and public sectors including financial services, insurance, business and consulting services, courier services, travel, media, utilities, and government services. Some of the firms were new Internet application start-up companies while others were brick-and-mortar companies with new Internet application development units.

Our objective was to understand how and why Internet-speed software development differs from traditional software development. We collected data through open-ended interviews and analyzed it using grounded theory (Strauss and Corbin 1990). With this methodology, we were able to develop a theory for a problem under investigation without prior hypotheses. The analysis identified core categories and their inter-relationships, explaining how and why Internet-speed software development differs from traditional approaches. In essence, we uncovered three major causal factors.

- A desperate rush-to-market
- A new and unique software market environment
- A lack of experience developing software under the conditions this environment imposed

As a result, a new development process that depends on new software development cultures evolved. In this process, software product quality becomes negotiable. Eight identifiable practices (see Figure 1) characterizing the Internet-speed software development process emerged from Phase 1 (Baskerville et al. 2001).

3.2 Phase 2: Discovery Colloquium

Our Phase 2 objectives were to synthesize knowledge on best practices for quality and agility in Internet-speed software development. We held a one-day Discovery Colloquium on Innovative Practices for Speed and Agility in Internet Software Development using innovative open-forum search techniques to enable what has been called *creative abrasion* (Leonard 1999).

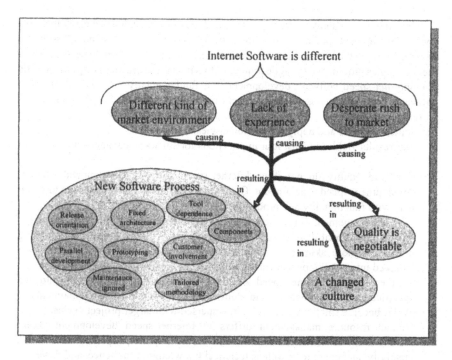

Figure 1. Results from Phase 1
(Figure 1 from B. Ramesh, J. Pries-Heje, and R. Baskerville, "Internet Software Engineering: A Different Class of Processes," *Annals of Software Engineering* (14), December 2002; © Kluwer Academic Publishers; with kind permission of Springer Science and Business Media.)

The colloquium benefited from the Phase 1 findings and included participants from Phase 1 companies as well as selected experts. Software practitioners from entrepreneurial small companies and large brick-and-mortar companies, Internet business strategists, and leading software development experts also participated.

Participants joined one of several breakout groups dedicated to exploring a core issue. The groups first identified observations relating to their core issue, and then developed hypotheses about possible associated factors. The groups tested the hypotheses, identifying linkages, contradictions, and interdependencies among them. They identified principles, promising practices, and other dynamics (Levine et al. 2002). Although the findings from the colloquium distinguished Internet speed as a set of practices, it denoted the underlying principles as principles of agility.

Subsequently, also as part of Phase 2, we set about to compare and analyze differences between seemingly *traditional* and *agile* principles and related practices. We adopted a set of principles, rigorously developed in a workshop on software development standards held in Montreal using a multistage Delphi study involving well-respected researchers and practitioners (Bourque et al. 2002). It exemplifies the best attempt to date to define general metaprinciples for traditional software development.

Based upon our analysis (Baskerville et al. 2003) we concluded that many Internet-speed development practices look deceptively similar to long-standing software development practices. However, a close examination of how Internet-speed development practices unfold, and the agile principles to which these practices respond, reveals that Internet-speed software development is a fundamentally new way to develop software. Each Internet-speed development practice can also be found in traditional software development. What distinguishes the practices is how Internet-speed developers combine and apply them—sometimes to extreme.

Our results yielded at least four implications for software management:

- Cost and quality do not drive Internet-speed software development. Rather, development speed is paramount. Quality becomes negotiable, a moving target in play with functionality and product availability.
- Project management in Internet-speed development differs from project management in traditional development. Projects do not begin or end, but are ongoing operations more akin to operations management. Development problems are chunked into small jobs that can be rolled out as small, tailor-made products.
- Maintenance in Internet-speed development is sometimes merged into the specification–build–release cycle along with new functionality, or maintenance cycles become small project cycles interspersed with larger project cycles.
- Human resource management differs in Internet-speed development. Team members are less interchangeable, and teams require people with initiative, creativity, and courage as well as technical knowledge, experience, and drive.

3.3 Phase 3: Case Study Continues

In 2002, we returned to study our original 10 companies which were developing application software for the Internet. At the time of the interviews, only five of the original nine companies remained in business or were available to participate in the study. Only one of the small Internet software houses had survived. To maintain the representative nature of the selection of companies, we added an additional company—a small innovative Internet software house. In all, six companies participated in Phase 3.

In 2002 (as in 2000), we used semi-structured interviews as a forum for collecting data, following the same study guide. Again, the data were analyzed using grounded theory techniques to develop a central story line or core category.

We traced trends and changes and observed new circumstances. A comparison of the 2000 and 2002 data shows how major factors, such as market environment and lack of experience, emerged to change the software process and the attitude toward quality. The interrelationship between the core factors of speed and quality, together with the other major factors, unfolded in a decision process wrought with trade-offs and balancing decisions at multiple levels in the software organization. These trade-offs and balancing decisions—a high-speed balancing game—were taking place at three different levels: the market, the portfolio, and the project.

Two major changes had taken place from 2000 to 2002. First, quality was no longer being treated as a disadvantaged stepchild. Speed and quality must be balanced for companies to survive in the newer market. Second, related monetary factors have been reversed: the unending supply of money characteristic of the boom has dried up; and good people are no longer scarce resources.

At the market level, during the two time periods, we saw values shift from a fever-pitched struggle for first-mover advantage to a slower, less intense consolidation of best practices. Notably, the changing market and IT economy slowed the interest in IT products, while at the same time easing the intense competition for human resources necessary for wide-scale software development. In 2002, with the market focused on a narrowed scope of Internet applications, competition remained intense but concentrated.

At the portfolio level, from 2000 to 2002, we detected a shift from a resource-rich, build-everything blast to a resource-constrained, tightly managed, and well-organized stable of ideal jobs. As a result of the changing market, the companies began to make major adjustments to their project portfolios. The *business case* became the primary vehicle for apportioning resources and selecting projects for inclusion or continuation within the portfolio. With falling resources, managers began to "cherry pick" the most ideal projects to meet their customers' needs.

At the project level, from 2000 to 2002, project values moved from speed-at-all-costs to an economized scope. Denied the resources to build products without a clear economic justification, project managers began to consolidate the product development to embrace construction of fewer products. The major Internet speed development values persisted, such as parallel development, limited maintenance and documentation, frequent releases, etc. These factors are still necessary to maintain customer satisfaction and compete in the (more focused) marketplace. The factors are also noted for enabling quick, economical products.

The study suggests that the nature of the balancing game has evolved with the shifting of the market and organizational environments over recent years. The peak of the dot-com boom was characterized by few constraints on financial resources, but severe constraints on availability of qualified personnel and very tight deadlines. At this peak, the balancing game was focused more toward achieving speed, often at increased project costs and lower levels of quality. This situation later evolved into market conditions that expect higher levels of product quality and lower costs while still demanding product development agility. As a result of market changes, the balancing games at the organizational and portfolio levels have grown in importance compared to the dominance achieved by the project balancing game in 2000.

4   WHERE ARE WE GOING: THE FUTURE STATE

Use of agile methods and agility is consistently associated with software development techniques. But more recently, we have seen fledgling signs of expansion. Ironically, the contracting of the market and the tightening of resources has contributed to an enlarged scope and increased complexity in enacting the balancing games at the portfolio and organization levels. This may spur further growth for agile approaches in atypical areas.

That said, the current state for agile methods is still isolated and limited. We have a partial understanding of what agility means for software development activities. For example, we know that agile methods work well with small teams (especially those that are colocated), where requirements are emergent, and in a turbulent environment of constant change. Agile methods are not recommended in the development of life critical systems; and its use in developing embedded software remains unclear (Ambler 2004). We have little understanding of the consequences of agile approaches for technology adoption and implementation activities. Within the development and adoption arenas, we have yet to fully grapple with the implications of agility for people, process, and new technology.

Our best insights into agility are still achieved through discrete activities—through projects which exist like islands in our organizations. From the development perspective, we have information on different agile methods, where they apply, particular emphases, and some acknowledged limitations. From an adoption perspective, we can speculate that an agile approach would favor pilots, trials, and demonstration projects; and from a knowledge transfer perspective, an agile approach would favor high customer involvement through face-to-face interaction or "body contact."

The challenge for the future is two-part. First, we must optimize the current state with vertical coupling to loosely integrate and propagate agile approaches for development, deployment, and knowledge transfer. This lightweight alignment would allow us to leverage what we know, and to reinforce these otherwise discrete areas of success. Second, and more radically, we must tackle the issue of scaling to investigate options for agile approaches and opportunities that can span organizations. On its face, this might seem contradictory since use of agile methods favors small teams with high contact. But to realize the potential for agile, we must ask how such methods adapt and scale. Perhaps they will do so in entirely new ways.

Austin and Devin (2003) speculate that old production models for software development are no longer useful. Rather, agile software development has the potential to be artful making. They write:

> Artful making (which includes agile software development, theater rehearsal, some business strategy creation, and much of other knowledge work) is a process for creating form out of disorganized materials. Collaborating artists, using the human brain as their principal technology and ideas as their principal material, work with a very low cost of iteration. They try something and then try it again a different way, constantly reconceiving ambiguous circumstances and variable materials into coherent and valuable outputs (pp. xxv-xxvi).

Whereas industrial making places a premium on detailed planning, closely specified objectives, processes, and products, artful making is different, fusing iteration and experimentation.

Austin and Devin point out that, "if you think and talk about iteration as experimentation, low cost of iteration seems to make business more like science. Its broader effect, though, is to make business more like art" (p. xxv). The authors go on to build an artful framework employing the analogies of theatrical production, extending beyond surface collaboration to the on-cue innovation that theater companies routinely achieve. In a similar vein, Stefan Thomke (2003) investigates experimentation in innovation, as it "encompasses success and failure; it is an iterative process of understanding what doesn't work and what does" (p. 2). He reminds us that both results are equally important for learning.

Finally, on a related topic, Dee Hock (1999) has characterized the organization of the 21st century organization as a *chaord*. The term chaord was formed out of combining the first three letters of the word chaos, with the first three letters from the word order. Hock and other leading scientists believe that the primary science of the next century will be the study of complex, self-organizing, nonlinear, adaptive systems, often referred to as complexity theory or chaos theory (De Geus 1997; Wheatley 2001). They assert that living systems arise and thrive on the edge of chaos with just enough order to give them pattern, but not so much to slow their adaptation and learning. This is not unlike the challenge for agility. We ask: Does this represent the larger paradigm shift of which agile methods are a part?

5   CHALLENGES, DILEMMAS, AND CONUNDRUMS

Achieving the future state is a challenge in itself—enhancing, adapting, applying, and scaling agile approaches is no easy feat. In addition, several dilemmas or conundrums have become evident. I will single out three to discuss briefly relating to process, discipline, and oversight.

The first controversy surrounds the role of process in agile methods. Typical views pit agility against process, and agile methods against process-intensive or *monumental* models like the software Capability Maturity Model (SW-CMM®) (Highsmith 2000). Paulk (2001) takes a closer look at how such approaches are not entirely at odds and illustrates how a development group following extreme programming might simultaneously embrace CMM, at least up until level 3. At level 3, the approaches diverge. Boehm (2002) and Boehm and Turner (2003) argue that agile and plan-driven methods each have a "home ground." They emphasize balance and attempt to make a case for hybrid strategies. Nevertheless, this split between process and agility has become a lightning rod, reinforcing entrenched positions and a strict drawing of lines.

For example, Steven Rakitin (2001) offers the following pointed and skeptical view in response to the values of agile developers. He argues that the values on the right (below) are essential, while those on the left serve as easy excuses for hackers to keep on irresponsibly, throwing code together with no regard for engineering discipline. He provides "hacker interpretations" that turn agile value statements such as "responding to change over following a plan" into chaos generators. Rakitin's hacker interpretation of "responding to change over following a plan" is roughly "Great! Now I have a reason to avoid planning and to just code up whatever comes next." He offers the following translations:

- **Individuals and interactions over processes and tools**
  Translation: Talking to people gives us the flexibility to do whatever we want in whatever way we want to do it. Of course, it's understood that we know what you want—even if you don't.

- **Working software over comprehensive documentation**
  Translation: We want to spend all our time coding. Real programmers don't write documentation.

- **Customer collaboration over contract negotiation**
  Translation: Let's not spend time haggling over the details, it only interferes with our ability to spend all our time coding. We'll work out the kinks once we deliver something.

- **Responding to change over following a plan**
  Translation: Following a plan implies we would have to spend time thinking about the problem and how we might actually solve it. Why would we want to do that when we could be coding?

While we might find reassuring appeal in the "sensible middle ground" (DeMarco and Boehm 2002), I suggest we closely examine our assumptions and first principles for agility and stability—to ensure that we do not fall into an easy trap of compromise. DeMarco and Boehm reassure us that "the leaders in both the agile and plan-driven camps occupy various places in the responsible middle. It's only the overenthusiastic followers who over interpret discipline and agility to unhealthy degrees" (p. 90). Alas, the challenges of agility and agile methods are only beginning to emerge; and innovation rarely comes from the responsible middle.

A second controversy is related to process issues and it concerns the role of discipline. Agile proponents tend to see CMM as engendering bureaucratic, prescriptive processes, fostering a command and control environment. Process and discipline are viewed as of whole cloth in this reductive manner. Unfortunately, more subtle definitions of discipline (for example, self organizing, nonlinear, or adaptive modes) have not yet been brought to bear in this argument.

Where does discipline fit in the context of agility? Under the auspices of agility, there must be some structure, order, and organization. We know that, in actuality, it takes time to speed up, unless you are simply cutting things out (Smith and Reinertsen 1998). By extension, it takes discipline to be agile. What kind of discipline, albeit adaptive and self organizing, is at play in the agile environment? Here, new approaches to experimentation (Thomke 2003) and frameworks such as artful making (Austin and Devin 2003)—where the emphasis is on a method of control that accepts wide variation within known parameters—will help us arrive at new understanding. If we are to embrace agile methods and move forward, we must begin such inquiry.

The final dilemma concerns the matter of governance. At present, we are faced with two conflicting models—one for development which can be agile, but no equivalent for project management, for oversight and monitoring. As I have indicated already, acquisition program managers have expressed interest in their development teams using agile methods. However, they are entirely at a loss to identify appropriate mechanisms that could be employed for monitoring and oversight of systems development. It is naïve to assume that oversight is antithetical to agile approaches, and thus once again we are challenged to reach beyond comfortable and convenient walls to explore new territory.

6   CONCLUSION

For agile approaches to be fully understood—to mature and to gain ground—we must consider what agility means as part of a larger landscape, and what type of shift it marks in technology development and in organizational behavior and change. What are the drivers for the burgeoning interest in agile methods? What have we discovered?

In this paper, I step back to consider these questions, as informed by my involvement in a multi-year research project on Quality Software Development @ Internet Speed and ongoing research on diffusion theory.

I begin with a brief look at definitions of agility, and conclude that agility is more than speed, extending beyond to encompass nimbleness, adaptability, and resourcefulness. Then I discuss the current state of agility and Internet-speed software development, using case study findings from 2000 and 2002.

Our case study suggests that a balancing game has evolved with the shifting of the market and organizational environments over recent years. In 2000, the peak of the dotcom boom was characterized by free flow of financial resources, severe constraints on availability of qualified personnel, and very tight deadlines. Project activities formed the focus for the balancing game and speed was to be achieved almost at all costs. A new development process that depended on new software development cultures emerged. We were also able to identify eight distinct practices characterizing an Internet-speed software development process.

In 2002, we detected a shift from this build-everything gold rush to a resource-constrained, carefully managed stable of jobs. As a result of the changing market, the companies were making major adjustments to their project portfolios. The business case became the primary vehicle for selecting projects for inclusion or continuation within the portfolio. Managers were cherry picking the best projects to meet their customers' needs. Denied the resources to build products without a clear economic justification, project managers were consolidating product development to embrace construction of fewer products. The major Internet speed development values persisted, such as parallel development, limited maintenance and documentation, frequent releases, etc. These factors were, and still remain, necessary to maintain customer satisfaction and compete in the more focused marketplace.

The future holds key challenges for a next generation of agile approaches. Of particular note are the need to (1) loosely integrate and propagate agile approaches for development, deployment, and knowledge transfer, and (2) tackle the issue of scaling to investigate options for agile approaches and opportunities that can span organizations.

Finally, I conclude with a short discussion of conundrums and dilemmas. The first of these controversies surrounds the role of process in agile methods. Typical views pit agility against process, and agile methods against process-intensive or monumental models. These are views that we must get past, at the same time as we resist the trap of too-easy compromise.

The second controversy also relates to process issues and concerns the role of discipline. Agile proponents tend to see CMM as engendering bureaucratic, prescriptive processes, fostering a command and control environment. Process and discipline are viewed as cut from whole cloth in this limited manner. Unfortunately, more subtle definitions of discipline (for example, self organizing, nonlinear, or adaptive modes) have not yet been brought to bear in this dialogue. Where does discipline fit in the context of agility? If we are to embrace agile methods and move forward, we must begin this inquiry.

The third and final controversy relates to governance. We must investigate appropriate and meaningful mechanisms that can be employed for monitoring and oversight of projects using agile methods. If we do not do so, agile methods will never come of age in large programs.

Agility in software development has implications for organizational agility—and the shift to agile methods and models signals a larger transformation in the workplace and the organization of the 21st century. As we have noted, this transition state is turbulent, marked by continuous change. No clear or easy solutions have resulted. The transformation is a work in progress, one that is by no means complete. To be realized, it invites investigation across a range of disciplines and initiatives, including organizational development, diffusion of innovations, process improvement, knowledge management, complex adaptive systems, chaos theory, systems thinking, software engineering, and information systems.

REFERENCES

Agile Manifesto. "Manifesto for Agile Software Development," 2001 (available online at http://agilemanifesto.org/).

Ambler, S. W. *The Object Primer* (3rd ed.), Cambridge, England: Cambridge University Press, 2004.

Austin, R., and Devin, L. *Artful Making: What Managers Need to Know about How Artists Work*, Upper Saddle River, NJ: Pearson Education Inc. Publishing as Financial Times Prentice Hall, 2003.

Baskerville, R., Levine, L., Pries-Heje, J., Ramesh, B., and Slaughter, S. "How Internet Software Companies Negotiate Quality," *Computer* (34:5), May 2001, pp. 51-57.

Baskerville, R., Levine, L., Pries-Heje, J., Ramesh, B., and Slaughter, S. "Is Internet-Speed Software Development Different?," *IEEE Software* (20:6), November-December 2003, pp. 70-77.

Boehm, B. "Get Ready for Agile Methods, with Care," *IEEE Computer* (35:1), January 2002, pp. 64-69.

Boehm, B., and Turner, R. *Balancing Agility and Discipline: A Guide for the Perplexed*. Reading, MA, Addison-Wesley, 2003.

Bourque, P., Dupuis, R., Abran, A., Moore, J. W., Tripp, L., and Wolff, S. "Fundamental Principles of Software Engineering: A Journey," *Journal of Systems and Software* (62:1), May 2002, pp. 59-70.

De Geus, A. *The Living Company*, Boston, MA: Harvard Business School Press, 1997

DeMarco, T., and Boehm, B. "The Agile Methods Fray," *Computer* (35:6), June 2002, pp. 90-93. .

Dove, R. *Response Ability—The Language, Structure, and Culture of the Agile Enterprise*, New York: Wiley, 2001.

Dove, R. *Value Propositioning—Perception and Misperception in Decision Making*, Tuscon, AZ: Inceni Books, 2005.

Grover, V., and Malhotra, M. "A Framework for Examining the Interface Between Operations and Information Systems: Implications for Research in the New Millennium," *Decision Sciences* (30:4), Fall 1999, pp. 901-920.

Highsmith, J. *Adaptive Software Development: A Collaborative Approach to Managing Complex Systems*, New York: Dorset House Publishing, 2000.

Hock, D. *Birth of the Chaordic Age*, San Francisco: Berrett-Koehler Publishers, 1999.

Kathuria, R., Anandarajan, M., and Igbaria, M. "Linking IT Applications with Manufacturing Strategy," *Decision Sciences* (30:4), 1999, pp. 959-991.

Leonard, D. *When Sparks Fly: Igniting Creativity in Groups*, Boston: Harvard Business School Press, 1999.

Levine, L., Baskerville, R., Loveland Link, J. L., Pries-Heje, J., Ramesh, B., and Slaughter, S. "Discovery Colloquium: Quality Software Development @ Internet Speed," SEI Technical Report CMU/SEI-2002-TR-020, Pittsburgh, PA: Software Engineering Institute, 2002.

Merriam-Webster Incorporated. *Merriam-Webster Online Dictionary*, 2004 (available at http://www.m-w.com/).

Paulk, M. C. "Extreme Programming from a CMM Perspective," *IEEE Software* (18:6), November-December 2001, pp. 19-26.

Paulk, M. C., Weber, C. V., Curtis, B., and and Crissis, M. B. *The Capability Maturity Model: Guidelines for Improving the Software Process*. Reading, MA: Addison-Wesley, 2001.

Rakitin, S. "Manifesto Elicits Cynicism," Computer (4:12), December 2001, p. 4.

Ramesh, B., Pries-Heje, J., and Baskerville, R. "Internet Software Engineering: A Different Class of Processes," *Annals of Software Engineering* (14), December 2002, pp. 169-195.

Smith, P. G., and Reinertsen, D. *Developing Products in Half the Time*, New York: John Wiley & Sons, 1998.

Strauss, A., and Corbin, J. *Basics of Qualitative Research: Grounded Theory Procedures and Techniques*, Newbury Park, CA: Sage Publications, 1990.

Tashakkori, A., and Teddlie, C. *Mixed Methodology: Combining Qualitative and Quantitative Approaches*, Thousand Oaks, CA: Sage Publications, 1998.

Thomke, S. *Experimentation Matters: Unlocking the Potential on New Technologies for Innovation*, Boston: Harvard Business School Press, 2003.

Wheatley, M. J. *Leadership and the New Science: Discovering Order in a Chaotic World* (revised ed.), San Francisco: Berrett-Koehler Publishers, 2001.

ABOUT THE AUTHOR

Linda Levine is a senior member of the technical staff at Carnegie Mellon University's Software Engineering Institute. Her research focuses on acquisition of software intensive systems, agile software development, systems interoperability, diffusion of innovations, and knowledge integration and transfer. She holds a Ph.D. from Carnegie Mellon University. She is a member of IEEE Computer Society, Association for Information Systems, National Communication Association, and cofounder and vice chair of IFIP Working Group 8.6 on Diffusion, Transfer, and Implementation of Information Technology. Contact Linda at ll@sei.cmul.edu.

Part 7

Panels

23 LOOKING BACK AND LOOKING FORWARD: Diffusion and Adoption of Information Technology Research in IFIP WG 8.6—Achievements and Future Challenges

Karlheinz Kautz
Copenhagen Business School
Copenhagen, Denmark

Robert W. Zmud
University of Oklahoma
Norman, OK U.S.A.

Gonzalo Leon Serrano
Technical University of Madrid
Madrid, Spain

Eleanor H. Wynn
Intel Corporation
Hillsboro, OR U.S.A.

Tor J. Larsen
Norwegian School of Management
Sandvika, Norway

E. Burton Swanson
University and California, Los Angeles
Los Angeles, CA U.S.A.

Working Group 8.6 has existed for more than 10 years now. During this period, members have continuously challenged the work of the group. Recently, researchers at the Copenhagen Business School conducted an interim review of the group's work in the form of a literature analysis of all WG 8.6 conference contributions. That review concludes that WG 8.6 works toward and within its own aim and scope declaration, but that there are a number of challenges. One is that WG 8.6 has no joint terminology and no shared theoretical basis. One recommendation from the review team, therefore, was that beyond researching new technologies like mobile information system and management fashions and fads such as business agility, WG 8.6 should stay with its roots and do work to explicitly contribute to IT diffusion theory and terminology. On the basis of this interim review, a group of founding, regular, less-regular, and more-recent members of WG 8.6 take a brief look back and a more extended look forward to discuss the achievements and the future challenges of WG 8.6.

The participants of the panel will provide their positions in 10-15 minutes statements.

Robert W. Zmud, Michael F. Price College of Business, University of Oklahoma, is a founding member of WG 8.6 and has contributed to the group's work in various ways. His position comprises a request to broaden the field of diffusion and adoption research to include the adoption, diffusion, and transfer of entities (information, knowledge, business practices, best practices, etc.) that are associated with IT and to place more emphasis on end-stage outcomes (e.g., de-adoption, infusion, institutionalization).

Gonzalo Leon Serrano, Department of Telematic Systems Engineering, Technical University of Madrid, is a founding member of WG 8.6, but has not been an active participant in the group's work for several years. From his recent experience as an adviser for the Spanish government, he discusses the way that governments and the European Commission are addressing the technology transfer and diffusion issue and its consequences. His request is to integrate these issues into the group's work.

Eleanor H. Wynn, IT Innovation at Intel Corporation, recently jointed WG 8.6 and organized one of its conferences. She sees a future challenge in extending the concept of diffusion and adoption into the area of complex systems and social network dynamics. Based on her work on adaptive systems modeling of distributed servers and distributed engineers in an IT service organization, she discusses the challenge of embedding innovation diffusion in a socio-technical network of software engineers into the group's work.

Tor J. Larsen, Department of Leadership and Organizational Management, Norwegian School of Management, is a founding member of WG 8.6 and has organized two of the group's conferences, as well as participating in nearly all others. He is occupied with the fundamental issue of terms employed by the group and what they might mean. Thus, he brings forward the demand to work harder on answering the question of what *diffusion* actually means. In this context, he argues for comparing the group's concepts with others such as advertising, marketing, and consultancy.

E. Burton Swanson, Anderson School of Management, UCLA, is a founding member of WG 8.6 and has participated in a number of its conferences. His starting point arises directly from the interim review, literally taking the challenges presented and providing ideas of how WG 8.6 can overcome its apparent shortcomings.

Karlheinz Kautz, Department of Informatics, Copenhagen Business School, is a founding member of WG 8.6 and has participated in all of the group's conferences. As one of the authors of the interim review of the group's work, which is included in this volume, he will briefly introduce that document and otherwise act as facilitator.

24 AGILE SOFTWARE DEVELOPMENT METHODS: When and Why Do They Work?

Balasubramaniam Ramesh
Georgia State University
Atlanta, GA U.S.A.

Pekka Abrahamsson
VTT Electronics
Oulu, Finland

Alistair Cockburn
Humans and Technology
Salt Late City, UT U.S.A.

Kalle Lyytinen
Case Western Reserve University
Cleveland, OH U.S.A.

Laurie Williams
North Carolina State University
Raleigh, NC U.S.A.

Agile software development challenges traditional software development methods. Rapidly changing environments, evolving requirements, and tight schedule constraints require software developers to take a fast cycle approach to the process of software development. Agile software development occurs in a dynamic and learning environment rather than in a mature and standardized software market (Cockburn 2001). Agile methods support shorter project lifecycles in order to respond to complex, fast-moving, and competitive marketplaces. The features of the system emerge throughout the development process, while heavily relying on feedback from the customer.

The rise of software development on Internet time has created tremendous interest among practitioners in agile development. Organizational agility, the ability to react quickly and flexibly to environmental or market changes, is an intended outcome of the use of agile methods (Goldman et al. 1995; Newman et al. 2000). Best known agile methods include eXtreme Programming (Beck et al. 1999), SCRUM (Schwaber and Beedle 2002), feature-driven development (Palmer and Felsing 2002), dynamic systems development method (Stapleton 1997), Crystal family (Cockburn 2001), and agile modeling (Ambler 2002). Variations of accelerated software development techniques have been presented as Internet time development (Cusumano and Yoffie 1999), Internet speed development (Baskerville et al. 2001), short cycle time development (Baskerville and Pries-Heje 2004), agile development (Aoyama 1998), Web development (Vidgen 2002), high speed development (Baserkerville et al. 2003), etc.

Although there is strong interest among researchers and practitioners on the use of agile methods, current knowledge on their applicability and effectiveness is fragmented and limited to the specific aspects of agile development. The applicability of the agile approach is constrained by several factors such as project size and type, experience level of project personnel, and committed customers. Beyond a few case studies and surveys (e.g., Grenning 2001; Rumpe and Schrder 2002), the effectiveness and applicability of agile methods have been the subject of debate (Boehm 2002). Organizations are reluctant to adopt agile methods unless they are convinced by the benefits of taking this new approach (Lindvall et al. 2002).

The panel will address the ongoing debate in the software development community on the applicability and effectiveness of agile methods by addressing the topic: "Agile Software Development Methods: When and Why Do They Work?" The panel will explore the characteristics of the organizational and project environment as well as the variety of practices that make agile methods successful.

Balasubramaniam Ramesh will introduce the panel and briefly explain the ongoing debate on the applicability of agile methods.

Pekka Abrahamsson will briefly compare the characteristics of popular agile methods and identify the common features of these methods and how they contribute to successful projects.

Alistair Cockburn will describe how specific agile practices have been successfully employed in industrial practice and provide insights into the nature of the project environments in which agile methods are appropriate.

Kalle Lyytinnen will discuss how discuss how agile methods may provide dynamic capabilities and foster hyper-learning to achieve agility.

Laurie Williams will discuss how specific practices such as pair programming lead to desired project outcomes such as fewer code defects, shorter cycle time, and higher job satisfaction.

Each of the panelists will also identify the project environments in which agile methods are unlikely to be successful and suggest the characteristics of environments where they are appropriate.

REFERENCES

Ambler, S. W. *Agile Modeling*, New York: John Wiley and Sons, 2002.

Aoyama, M. "Web-Based Agile Software Development," *IEEE Software* (15:6), 1998, pp. 55-65.

Baskerville, R., Levine, L., Pries-Heje, J., Ramesh, B., and Slaughter, S. "How Internet Software Companies Negotiate Quality," *IEEE Computer* (34:5), 2001, pp. 51-57.

Baskerville, R., and Pries-Heje, J. "Short Cycle Time Systems Development," *Information Systems Journal* (14:2), 2004, pp. 237-264.

Beck, K., Hannula, J., Hendrickson, C., Wells, D., and Mee, R. "Embracing Change with Extreme Programming," *IEEE Computer* (32:10), October 1999, pp. 70-77.

Boehm, B. "Get Ready for Agile methods, with Care," *IEEE Computer* (35:1), 2002, pp. 64-69.

Cockburn, A. "Agile Software Development," in *The Agile Software Development Series*, A. Cockburn and J. Highsmith (Eds.), Boston: Addison Wesley Longman, 2001.

Cusumano, M., and Yoffie, D. "Software Development on Internet Time," *Computer* (32:10), 1999, pp. 60-69.

Goldman, S., Nagel, R., and Preiss, K. *Agile Competitors and Virtual Organizations*, New York: Van Nostrand Reinhold, 1995.

Grenning, J. "Launching XP at a Process-Intensive Company," *IEEE Software* (18:6), 2001, pp 3-9.

Lindvall, M., Basili, V., Boehm, B., Costa, P., Dangle, K., Shull, F., Tesoriero, R., Williams, L., and Zelkowitz, M. "Empirical Findings in Agile Methods," in *Proceedings of the XP/Agile University 2002: Second XP Universe and First Agile Universe Conference*, Chicago: Springer-Verlag GmbH., 2002, pp. 197-207.

Newman, W., Podgurski, A., Quinn, R., Merat, F., Branicky, M., Barendt, N., Causey, G., Haaser, E., Kim, Y., Swaminathan, J., and Velasco, V. "Design Lessons for Building Agile Manufacturing Systems," *IEEE Transactions on Robotics and Automation* (16:3), 2000, pp. 228-238.

Palmer, S. R., and Felsing, J. M. *A Practical Guide to Feature-Driven Development*, Upper Saddle River, NJ: Prentice-Hall, 2002

Rumpe, B., and Schrder, A. "Quantitative Survey on Extreme Programming Project," in *Proceedings of the Third International Conference on eXtreme Programming and Agile Processes in Software Engineering*, Alghero, Italy, 2002, pp. 95-100 (available online at http://www.xp2003.org/xp2002/atti/Rumpe-Schroder--QuantitativeSurveyonExtremeProgrammingProjects.pdf; accessed February 18, 2005).

Schwaber, K., and Beedle, M. *Agile Software Development with SCRUM*, Upper Saddle River, NJ: Prentice-Hall, 2002.

Stapleton, J. *DSDM: The Method in Practice*, Reading, MA: Addison Wesley, 1997.

Vidgen, R. "Constructing a Web Information Systems Development Methodology," *Information Systems Journal* (12:3), 2002, pp. 247-261.

25 ENABLING BUSINESS AGILITY THROUGH INFORMATION TECHNOLOGY MANAGEMENT

V. Sambamurthy
Michigan State University
East Lansing, MI U.S.A.

Robert W. Zmud
University of Oklahoma
Norman, OK U.S.A.

Arun Rai
Georgia State University
Atlanta, GA U.S.A.

Robert Fichman
Boston College
Boston, MA U.S.A.

1 OVERVIEW

Agility is the organizational ability of a firm to continually sense promising competitive opportunities and respond through innovative moves in the form of new product introductions, new process improvements, new alliances, or other similar competitive actions. Given the intensifying nature of competition, globalization, and the high velocity of economic cycles, agility has become a prominent issue of interest to business and Information Systems professionals. Research attention to the connections between information technology management and business agility has begun to grow.

The goal of this panel is to offer alternative conceptualizations and perspectives on the enabling role of information technology management to develop agility as an organizational capability. The panelists develop conceptualizations that are anchored in different boundary disciplines for information technology management: strategic management, supply chain management, complex adaptive systems, and real options. Three questions are examined by each panel member.

1.   What is a significant challenge in promoting organizational attention to agility?

2.   What conceptual frameworks will guide a better understanding about how to overcome these challenges in organizations?

3.   What are the emerging implications for positioning information technology management as an enabler of agility?

2   POSITIONING IT MANAGEMENT AS A DIGITAL OPTIONS GENERATOR FOR AGILITY

V. Sambamurthy, Eli Broad Graduate School of Management,
Michigan State University

Existing conceptualizations of agility define it as the organizational ability to sense opportunities and threats in the business environment and respond through the appropriate assets and capabilities to seize those fleeting windows of competitive opportunities.   Agility is regarded as an important organizational capability for contemporary firms. Studies have found that agile firms outperform other firms because of their ability to continually launch competitive moves. However, the role of agility in formulating corporate strategy is not fully resolved. Agility tends to be equated more with the exploration activities of firms. Therefore, an excessive focus on agility could lead to a lopsided investment in exploration capabilities to the detriment of exploitation and harvesting of current competitive position and capabilities. Therefore, there is a need to understand how firms balance attention to agility as another strategic behavior rather than an end in itself. This presentation will develop a portfolio perspective about strategic behaviors in corporate strategy that includes agility as one desirable behavior and capability.

Further, this presentation argues that information technology assets and capabilities provide firms with digital options to enable their portfolio of strategic behaviors. Based on ongoing field research, the presentation will outline the different ways in which information technology management could enable the portfolio of strategic behaviors and capabilities. The presentation will offer some implications for research and practice on the role of IT management in enabling business agility.

3   THE ROLE OF AGILITY IN ENABLING MARKET POSITION: IMPLICATIONS FOR INVESTMENTS IN IT ASSETS AND CAPABILITIES

Robert W. Zmud, Michael Price College of Business, University of Oklahoma

Crafting business strategies that produce, relative to competitors, above average returns has never been easy. Essentially, the aim is to position the firm within a product-market space such that the firm is able to provide a unique value proposition within the product-market space. If a firm is alone in a viable product-market space, the firm clearly holds a unique value proposition. Such a state, if it ever exists, does not last long as competitors will quickly enter product-market niches that are seen as generating above average returns. What is crucial, then, is both establishing a profitable strategic position and then being able to sustain the position over time.

Scholars studying how firms evolve their strategic positions have observed that two very different types of strategic actions are necessary: exploitative and exploratory. Exploitative strategic actions refer to systematic efforts directed to constantly improve the competencies associated with an existing strategic position. Exploratory strategic actions, on the other hand, refer to extemporaneous efforts directed at discovering new strategic positions or new competencies that might be instrumental in creating new strategic positions. Exploratory strategic actions create new product-markets. Once a new product-market is created, firms with favorable strategic positions in the product-market strive to exploit their position in order to sustain the position. Other (known and unknown) competitors, however, engage in exploratory strategic actions in efforts to supplant this product-market through its radical transformation or through the creation of substitute product-markets. Inattention by an exploiting firm to the behaviors of the exploring firms carry the threat of locking a firm out of these emerging and attractive product-market spaces.

Strategic agility, of varying forms, as well as IT investments, of varying forms, are both required in enabling firms to undertake exploitative and exploratory strategic actions. Conceptual models are presented that suggest, given differing market environments and the nature of the strategic agility required within these market environments, appropriate levels of investment in both IT assets and IT capabilities. It is anticipated that these conceptual models will prove useful to executives desiring to appropriately align their levels of IT investment to specific strategic positions.

4 A BUSINESS NETWORK PERSPECTIVE ON DIGITALLY-ENABLED AGILITY

Arun Rai, Center for Process Innovation and Department of Computer Information Systems, Robinson College of Business, Georgia State University

The architecture of an interfirm business network has a profound impact on its agility and that of its member firms. It shapes the capability of business networks to dynamically balance emergent and predictable behavior. Complex adaptive systems, coupled with related theories on networks and allocation of decision rights, offer powerful theoretical perspectives to identify specific architectural considerations for business network agility. These considerations are (1) the *relative distribution* of hub and niche nodes and their networking ties, (2) the *probabilistic distribution* of the set of nodes and their interconnections, (3) the *degree of aggregation and dimensionality* of information and decision rules, and (4) the *degree of homogeneity* of interpretive and behavioral schema. The implications of these architectural considerations for digital-enablement of business network agility will be evaluated and illustrated using best practice exemplars.

5   THE RELATIONSHIP BETWEEN REAL OPTIONS THINKING AND ORGANIZATIONAL AGILITY

Robert Fichman, College of Business, Boston College

Flexible information technology platform technologies are widely seen as key enablers of organizational agility. Yet, the uncertainty that attends IT platform investments renders traditional valuation approaches (e.g., based on NPV or ROI) wholly inadequate. Such approaches ignore the value of two forms of flexibility: (1) the value that flows from flexibility in how an investment project is managed, and (2) the value that results from flexibility in what the project produces, i.e., the degree of flexibility infused in the delivered platform itself. In response, a growing stream of research has advocated the application of *options thinking* to the valuation of uncertain IT investments. Early work focused on the application of real options pricing models to quantify investment value. However, these models are just the tip of the options thinking iceberg. No value will come from real options unless an organization has adopted a compatible management philosophy. In this presentation, Fichman I will present *real options infusion* as a construct to capture the extent to which a firm has assimilated a management philosophy based on options thinking. He will argue that real options infusion has three dimensions: the extent of options-oriented valuation tools; the extent of options-oriented project management processes; and extent of options-oriented organizational culture or norms. He will then explore the relationship between real options infusion and two types of agility. In particular, Fichman will argue that options infusion can be viewed as a *complement* to agile software development methods, and as an *antecedent* to business agility.

Index of Contributors